SYSTEMATIC THEOLOGY

A Modern Protestant Approach

KENNETH CAUTHEN

Toronto Studies in Theology
Volume 25

The Edwin Mellen Press
Lewiston/Queenston

Systematic Theology: A Modern Protestant Approach
by Kenneth Cauthen

This is volume 25 in the continuing series
Toronto Studies in Theology
Volume 25 ISBN 0-88946-769-2
TST Series ISBN 0-88946-975-X

The Edwin Mellen Press
Box 450
Lewiston, New York
USA 14092

The Edwin Mellen Press
Box 67
Queenston, Ontario
CANADA L0S 1L0

Printed in the United States of America

I believe in God the Father Almighty,
Maker of heaven and earth:

And in Jesus Christ his only Son our Lord:
Who was conceived by the Holy Ghost,
Born of the Virgin Mary:
Suffered under Pontius Pilate,
Was crucified, dead, and buried:
He descended into hell;
The third day he rose again from the dead:
He ascended into heaven,
And sitteth on the right hand of God the Father Almighty:
From thence he shall come to judge the quick and the dead.

I believe in the Holy Ghost:
The holy Catholic Church;
The Communion of Saints:
The Forgiveness of sins:
The Resurrection of the body:
And the Life everlasting.
Amen

TABLE OF CONTENTS

PREFACE

A preface provides the opportunity to address a
personal word to the reader about the intent of what
follows. I have been a teacher of systematic theology
and related subjects in a liberal Protestant seminary
for a quarter of a century. This book represents an
attempt to write the textbook that I always wanted but
never found. In particular, there is need for an
introductory presentation of Christian thought that will
not set forth as the primary intention the point of view
of the author. Rather the ideal text will introduce
students to the issues, the options, and the major
perspectives that two thousand years of effort have
produced. It will let the student in on many points of
view in order to illustrate the variety as well as the
unity that characterizes the intellectual work of the
Christian community. It will offer some interpretive
schemes by which contrasting and conflicting standpoints
can be understood. It will get at cultural influences
and the deep unquestioned presuppositions which shape
thinking as well as simply laying out what this person
or that school of thought had to say. In short, I
wanted a textbook that would introduce students to the
whole range of Christian thought from a modern
Protestant perspective, not a statement of what a given
individual believes. The works of Paul Tillich, Karl
Barth, Emil Brunner, John Macquarrie, Gordon Kaufman,
and others are important for what they are, but I wanted
to introduce the student to many people like them, plus
the history out of which they have come.

The nearest thing I ever found to my ideal was
Walter Marshall Horton's CHRISTIAN THEOLOGY: AN
ECUMENICAL APPROACH, but that book is long out of date.
A whole generation has passed, bringing forth

developments in process theology and the rise of
liberation theologies, black theologies, feminist
theologies, theologies of hope, and so on that Horton
knew not of three decades ago. So I have tried to write
my own text for use in the mid-80's. My effort has been
to put between two covers the basic information that a
beginning student needs to know about the Bible, the
history of Christian thought, and the challenge of the
modern world, as well as the major theological responses
to it. Enough has been said about contemporary points
of view to form the basis for further study. I have
tried, for the most part, to keep my own opinions out of
it and to give an objective interpretation of the issues
and options in the past and present. At times, I have
drawn conclusions and suggested what the truth might be,
but the reader should be able to discern easily enough
when I am speaking for myself and when I am presenting
the views of others.

Christian theology is far too vast a subject to be
covered by one book. Hence, selectivity that inevitably
becomes arbitrariness enters into every attempt to
introduce it. Moreover, every presentation of Christian
thinking proceeds from a point of view. The material in
this book has been selected from an orientation which
can be defined as the non-conservative academic tradition in modern American Protestant theology. Every word
in that description eliminates theologians, topics,
contexts, influences, and evaluations that other
perspectives might include. Even with that framework
the choice of persons, points of view, and interpretive
patterns reflects the outlook, knowledge, and aims of
the author. Any beginning text would suffer from a
similar arbitrariness in the choice of persons and
points to be included and to be left out. All efforts

would, of course, refer to the Biblical motifs which shape every doctrine. Certain developments in the first five centuries, e.g., the Trinitarian and Christological controversies, are crucial for all subsequent Christian thinking. After 451 AD the problem of choice becomes more evident. Augustine is more important for the West than for the East. Roman Catholic authors would pay more attention to the medieval period than this Protestant review did.

The Protestant Reformers loom large in these pages. A major presupposition of this analysis is that the challenge of the modern world to traditional Christian thought is fundamental. Hence, every chapter has devoted a large section to delineating what elements in the modern mentality have required that Christian doctrines be reformulated. Primary attention has been given to those theologians and schools of thought that have attempted to come to terms with the modern world and yet retain the essentials of the historic faith. Conservative Protestant thinking in the 19th and 20th centuries receives scant attention. Liberalism, neo-orthodoxy, and subsequent developments in those centers of theological thought that moved away from orthodoxy during the last century have been the focus of attention.

Following this particular strand of history was a deliberate, if arbitrary, choice. The result is offered as one way of introducing Christian thought. Those who stand within the path that has been traced will find it more helpful than others perhaps in letting them see where they have come from intellectually and in getting acquainted with the issues, options, controversies, and claims that have shaped the past that has shaped them.

I have sometimes with a smile identified the stance
I am taking in this book -- the non-conservative
academic tradition in modern American Protestantism --
by saying that it is what they teach at "YalenUnion,"
two representative and sometimes rival (if here somewhat
forcibly merged) schools who stand in the line of the
historical development that is the subject matter of
this text. Complete honesty would require it be said
that the content of this volume represents what the
author thinks to be important and what he knows about as
one particular American Protestant who wants, in the
words of Harry Emerson Fosdick, to be both "an
intelligent modern and a serious Christian."

Kenneth Cauthen
June 19, 1986

NOTE

This introduction can best be used by consulting
other resources to follow up on concepts, topics,
persons, and schools of thought which are mentioned in
the text but not treated extensively. The following are
recommended:

I. The Bible
INTERPRETER'S DICTIONARY OF THE BIBLE. 4 vols.
Nashville: Abingdon Press, 1962. Supplementary volume,
1976.

II. Topics and Concepts
Cohen, Arthur, and Halverson, Marvin (eds.). A
HANDBOOK OF CHRISTIAN THEOLOGY. Nashville: Abingdon
Press, 1980.

Harvey, Van. A HANDBOOK OF THEOLOGICAL TERMS. New
York: The Macmillan Co., 1964.

Richardson, Alan, and Bowden, John. THE WESTMINSTER
DICTIONARY OF THEOLOGY. Philadelphia: Westminster
Press, 1983.

III. History of Doctrine
Gonzáles, Justo. HISTORY OF CHRISTIAN THOUGHT. 3
vols. Nashville: Abingdon Press, 1970-1975.

Kelly, J.N.D. EARLY CHRISTIAN DOCTRINES. New
York: Harper and Row, 1978.

Pelikan, Jaroslav. THE CHRISTIAN TRADITION: A
HISTORY OF THE DEVELOPMENT OF DOCTRINE. 5 vols.
Chicago: University of Chicago Press, 1971 ----. By

1985 the first four volumes had been published covering
the period up to 1700.

Placher, William C. A HISTORY OF CHRISTIAN
THEOLOGY. Westminster Press, 1983.

IV. Modern Thought

Cauthen, Kenneth. THE IMPACT OF AMERICAN RELIGIOUS
LIBERALISM. Washington: University Press of America,
1983.

Heron, Alasdair. A CENTURY OF PROTESTANT THOUGHT.
Philadelphia: Westminster Press, 1980.

Marty, Martin, and Peerman, Dean (eds.). A
HANDBOOK OF CHRISTIAN THEOLOGIANS. Nashville: Abingdon
Press, 1984.

Finally, the Endnotes which follow each chapter contain
references which may be used to follow up ideas,
persons, and points of view mentioned in the text.

SYSTEMATIC THEOLOGIES

Along with this introductory text you should read
one or more contemporary systematic theologies in order
to see the unity and wholeness of a comprehensive point
of view. The following are recommended:

Aulén, Gustaf. THE FAITH OF THE CHRISTIAN CHURCH.
Philadelphia: The Muhlenberg Press, 1948. (Swedish
Lutheran Neo-orthodox)

Barth, Karl. DOGMATICS IN OUTLINE. New York:
Philosophical Library, 1949. (Continental Neo-Orthodox)

_____. CHURCH DOGMATICS: A SELECTION.
New York: Harper Torchbook, 1962. Brief selections

from his *magnum opus*.

Brunner, Emil. DOGMATICS. 3 vols. Philadelphia: Westminster Press, 1950, 1952, 1962. (Continental Neo-orthodox)

Cobb, John, and Griffin, David. PROCESS THEOLOGY: AN INTRODUCTORY EXPOSITION. Philadelphia: Westminster Press, 1976, (Process Theology)

Cone, James. A BLACK THEOLOGY OF LIBERATION. Philadelphia: J.B. Lippincott, 1970. (Black Theology)

DeWolf, Harold. A THEOLOGY OF THE LIVING CHURCH. New York: Harper & Brothers, 1953. (Liberal, Personalist)

Henry, Carl (ed.). BASIC CHRISTIAN DOCTRINES. New York: Holt, Rinehart and Winston, 1962. (Evangelical, Conservative)

Gilkey, Langdon. MESSAGE AND EXISTENCE. New York: Seabury Press, 1979. (Revisionist)

Kaufman, Gordon. SYSTEMATIC THEOLOGY: A HISTORICIST APPROACH. New York: Charles Scribner's Sons, 1968. (Late Neo-orthodox)

Macquarrie, John. PRINCIPLES OF CHRISTIAN THEOLOGY. New York: Charles Scribner's Sons, 1977. (Existentialist, Modern)

Ruether, Rosemary R. SEXISM AND GOD-TALK. Boston: Beacon Press, 1983. (Feminist, Liberation)

Suchocki, Marjorie H. GOD, CHRIST, CHURCH. New York: Crossroad Publishing Co., 1982. (Feminist, Process)

Tillich, Paul. SYSTEMATIC THEOLOGY. 3 vols. Chicago: University of Chicago Press, 1951, 1957, 1963. (Liberal, Neo-orthodox)

Wainwright, Geoffrey. DOXOLOGY: A SYSTEMATIC THEOLOGY. New York: Oxford University Press, 1980. (British, Methodist, Liturgical) Explores the link between worship and doctrine.

See pp. 15-27 of the text for brief descriptions of the classifications listed in the parentheses above to indicate the point of view of the author.

Analytical Table of Contents
(pages xvi-xxv, following)

CHAPTER I
THE TASK AND METHOD OF CHRISTIAN THEOLOGY

CHAPTER II

GOD, CREATION AND PROVIDENCE

I. The God-Problem: Reasons for Speaking of God

    A. Philosophical-Metaphysical

    B. Religious-Existential

II. Belief in God in the Modern World

III. Language about God

IV. The Reality of God in the Bible and in Christian History

    A. The Bible

    B. Classical Theology

    C. Modern Theology

V. The Nature of God

    A. Basic Affirmations

        1. God as the Holy One

        2. The Nature of the Holy One

            a. God as Ultimate in Being: Sovereignty

            b. God as Personal in Nature: Personhood

            c. God as Perfect in Character: Goodness

    B. Tensions Within the Being and Nature of God

        1. Tensions Between Basic Characteristics

            a. Ultimacy and Absoluteness versus Personhood and Relatedness

            b. Ultimacy versus Goodness (The Problem of Evil)

CHAPTER III

HUMANITY, SIN AND SALVATION

I.   Humanity as a Problem

II. Humanity as Created

    A. Biblical and Classical Conceptions of Humanity

    B. Conceptions of Humanity in Modern Theology

III. Humanity as Fallen

    A. Biblical and Classical Views of Human Fallenness

    B. Modern Reinterpretations of Sin

IV. Humanity as Redeemed

    A. Biblical and Classical Conceptions

    B. Salvation in Modern Theologies

V.   Summary of Continuing Issues

    A. Universality and Inevitability versus Freedom and Responsibility

    B. God's Initiative and Human Response in Salvation

    C. Growth in Grace Despite Persistence of Sin

    D. Augustinian versus Irenaean Perspectives

CHAPTER IV

THE PERSON AND WORK OF CHRIST

CHAPTER V

THE SPIRIT AND THE CHURCH

CHAPTER VI

HISTORY, HOPE AND THE KINGDOM OF GOD

CHAPTER VII
THE PRESENT AND FUTURE OF THEOLOGY

I.   The recent Past and Present

Secular Theology

Dionysian Theology

Ecological Theology

Black Theology

Feminist Theology

Revisionist Theology

Process Theology

Fundamentalist Theology

Main-Line Evangelical Theology

The New Evangelical Theology

Eschatological Theology

Liberation Theology

II. The Present and Near Future

   A. Trends and Concerns

      1. Liberation Theology

      2. Christianity and Other Religions

      3. Theology in a Planetary Society

   B. Reflections and Conjectures

      1. The Old Dilemma: Message and Situation

      2. New Theologies of the 21st Century

      3. Uniting Particular Aims with Universal
         Global/Ecumenical/Ecological Conscious-
         ness

CHAPTER I
THE TASK AND METHOD OF CHRISTIAN THEOLOGY

I. What is Christian Theology?

Theology is the activity in which Christians reflect upon and express what they have experienced or believe. It is also the effort to say how they arrived at these convictions and why they affirm them.

A. REFLECT UPON AND EXPRESS. The word theology comes from the Greek language and literally means reasoning about God (theos -- God: logos -- reason). This definition is appropriate since regardless of the topic under consideration -- whether sin, salvation, or the church, etc. -- it is always examined in relationship to the reality of God as understood through the Biblical witness to Jesus Christ. (1) In so far as it is reflection, theology is a second order activity which depends on the experience of God or on the response of faith to God's self-initiated revelation as the primary datum of the religious life. Theology is the effort to articulate, analyze, clarify, organize, systematize, relate, and otherwise order what is given to faith or experience in encounter with God. (2) As such it is an activity of reason, and it makes use of rationally created principles, categories, standards, and rules of thought -- including logic. (3) Finally, theology is a critical and normative enterprise. It does not simply describe or analyze; it also makes judgments about what is authentic, valid, and appropriate as expressions of Christian belief.

Throughout Christian history groups of Christians have produced creeds to give expression to their distinctive or approved convictions.[1] Often such confessions are an attempt to state right belief (orthodoxy) and to identify wrong ideas (heresy). Many of the early creeds such as the one formulated at Nicea (325 AD) or at Chalcedon (451 AD) had that function. But whether we speak of the internal dialogue going on in the heart and head of an individual Christian, or whether we have in mind the standard works on the subject in the past and present, or whether we refer to the creeds of various Christian groups, theology rises when Christians think about what they believe and articulate it in some way. Theology, of course, is expressed not only in formal creeds and books but also in hymns, liturgies, prayers, sermons, and in every aspect of the life of the church.

B. HOW AND WHY. So far the focus has been on the WHAT -- the content of Christian belief. Attention must now be turned to the HOW and the WHY -- the method of Christian thought. Method and content are interrelated, of course, in that reflections about the HOW and the WHY of belief are part of the WHAT. Nevertheless, it is useful to distinguish between them. Theology as a part of its task specifies how one arrives at a set of convictions, and it indicates why certain beliefs are accepted as authentic. Christians do not always become self-conscious or formal about the basis of their faith. But when they do, method involves a statement of the sources and norms of the Christian Gospel. Where does Christian truth come from? How are the various sources -- such as the Bible, tradition, reason, and experience

-- related to each other? How does one go about combining the truth from various sources into a coherent body of doctrine? What are the criteria by which the truth and adequacy of claims made by Christians to be judged? If there are conflicts among the sources, what takes priority? Theological method deals with questions of authority and with the standards by which affirmations are to be assessed. Where is Christian truth to be found, and how do we test claims that are made so as to distinguish truth from error?

SYSTEMATIC THEOLOGY refers to a more or less comprehensive and complete statement of the content and the method of Christian thought.

Theology, then, involves reasoning, thinking, and constructive imagination. It searches and interprets the givens from the past (the Bible, the creeds, and the classical texts of the great theologians) and attempts to state the essentials of the Christian message for here and now in the light of contemporary experience, thought forms, and needs. Or it may begin with the situation of human beings in the world today and then turn to the Bible and tradition and seek to find Christian insight that is credible and relevant. Methods vary. But however they go about it, Christians do theology when they reflect upon and express what they believe and say why they believe it.

The description of the nature, task, and method of theology is itself the product of theological work. Hence, definitions of theology reflect the variety and conflict that are also in evidence when dealing with particular topics such as God, humanity, Christ, or the church. The definition of what theology is and does is expressive of the particular outlook of the writer or speaker. The general description given so far would be more or less accepted by most theologians as a beginning. However, any spelling out of the specifics regarding the sources, norms, and purposes of theology would begin to exhibit the variety of theological perspectives.

II. Theology as Inevitable and Necessary

In the broad sense every Christian is a theologian or does theology. Everyone reasons about faith to some extent. Every sermon, every prayer, every hymn, every sacramental observance of the Lord's Supper and Baptism involves assumptions and has implications beyond the actual words used. Preachers just don't read the Bible and stop. They add their own words. Even if believers only read the Bible, their interpretation brings into play presuppositions not immediately derivable from the text. The question, then, is not whether we engage in theological reflection but at what level, with what degree of systematic thoroughness and comprehensive consistency. In that sense, theology is inevitable.

But is theology necessary? It would be difficult to argue that systematic theology of a comprehensive sort is absolutely necessary, since, according to Emil Brunner, the Bible itself reflects nothing of that process which the church has called "dogmatics." Israel existed for a thousand years without anything like a formal creed. However, Brunner goes on to argue that if dogmatics does not belong to the essence of the church,

it is an important part of its well being. He proceeds
to show that church history gives a three-fold basis for
the relative necessity of theology.[2] 1. The first
source of systematic theology was the struggle against
false doctrine. When conflicting versions of the Gospel
began to appear, it became necessary to distinguish
between right belief and false teaching. This requires
theological reflection, analysis, and constructive
theorizing. 2. Another impetus to dogmatics was the
need to instruct new converts in preparation for
baptism. They must be taught something, and their
questions must be answered. 3. A final root of reflec-
tive thinking was engagement in Biblical exegesis. The
interpretation of one passage leads to questions about
its relationship to other passages and to the Scriptures
in their entirety. Interpreting the deeper and central
teachings of the Bible leads toward systematic summaries
of God's Word to humanity.

Beyond this, however, is the relative necessity of
theology which arises out of the present task of
Christian witness in the world. What is the meaning of
the Gospel in today's language and applied to our
questions about the meaning of existence before God?
What is the heart, the essence, the core of the Good
News as it appears in a variety of New Testament books,
which do not always speak in one voice with identical
content? Moreover, given our consciousness of the
relativity of all thought forms and the distance between
the world-view of the Bible and ours, how are we to know
what the abiding, universal truth of the Gospel is? To
answer that question requires theological reflection.
It involves relating the teachings of the Bible to
science, to philosophy, sociology, and psychology, to

contemporary moral problems, and to all of the various
truth claims and value perspectives that vie for the
loyalty of people. Doing all of that is what we mean by
theology. Hence, if we are to understand for ourselves
what the Gospel is and to interpret it to others in
credible and applicable ways, then we must become
theologians. In this sense, theology today, as in all
of church history, is relatively necessary.

In summary, there is a deeper reason arising from
the very nature of the Bible that makes theology important. The Bible is not a book of systematic theology.
It is a library of many kinds of material produced over
hundreds of years. The work of theological reflection
is necessary to discover in the totality of Scripture,
particularly the New Testament, the content of the
Gospel that is to be the heart of preaching and the
guide to Christian practice in the world today.
Theology is required to discover the unity and wholeness
of Christian truth and to insure clarity of witness in
the world.

III. Knowledge of God

Theology presupposes knowledge of God sufficient
for its purposes. But how does the reality of God
become known to the church and to believers? Before
proceeding with an interpretation of the nature, task,
and method of theology as it is understood in
contemporary thought -- the central focus of this
chapter -- it may be useful to look briefly at the
background out of which present understandings have
emerged.

A. THE BIBLE. The Bible assumes throughout that
the reality of God has been made known by the divine
presence and activity among humankind. The existence of
God is never in question. Only the fool says that there
is no God (Ps. 14:1). God has become known in a wide
variety of ways: through personal appearances (Gen.
7:16, 18:9, 32:22-30; Ex. 3-4, 14:25-30; Ex. 24, 33; Is.
6:1-13), dreams (Gen. 20:3, 28:12, 41:1-36; Matt. 1:18-
25, 2:1-15), angels (Gen. 16:9, 22:11; Ps. 103:20; I
Kings 22:19), and by disclosure of the divine name (Ex.
3:13-15). In addition to these special appearances to
individuals, knowledge of God is also provided in ways
that are in principle open to all people by observation,
reason, and experience. God is disclosed in nature (Ps.
19:1; Is. 40:26; Ps. 104: Roms. 1:18-21), in mighty acts
in history visible to all (Ex. 7:5; Is. 26:9, 52:10;
Jer. 33:9), and in the reason and conscience (Roms.
2:14-16; I Cor. 11:13-16; and perhaps John 1:9). The
insight about life offered in the Wisdom literature
(Ecclesiastes, Job, and Proverbs) would appear to be
based as much on human reflection as on direct revelation from God. Revelation occurs especially in the Word
that God speaks for the sake of disclosing the divine
will for humanity (Ex. 4:11-16, 20, 24). The prophets
are recipients and proclaimers of the Word of God that
comes to them (I Kings 17:2, 8; Is. 5:9; Jer. 1:9; Ezek.
3:15). It is truly the case, then, that God has been
revealed in "many and various ways" (Heb. 1:1 RSV).

The central mode of divine disclosure according to
the Bible is in certain events in history. God has made
a series of covenants with humankind and in them has
made known the divine requirements and the way of

salvation. Covenants were made with Noah (Gen. 6:18, 9:1-17), with Abraham, Isaac, and Jacob (Gen. 12; Ex. 2:24), and with Moses (Ex. 3, 19:1-6). A covenant is an agreement with promises and responsibilities on both sides. The law of God is given to define Israel's duties. The Old Testament prophets constantly called the people to task for violating the covenant, pronounced God's judgment as punishment, and spoke of a new age in which the promises of God would be consummated in an era of peace, righteousness, and prosperity. The covenant with Israel at Sinai is the framework within which the relationships between God and Israel are given their normative definition. Through this arrangement the divine will is most clearly and definitively disclosed. For Christians, of course, the supreme revelation is given in the person and work of Jesus of Nazareth, in and through whom the new covenant was made. This point is so central that here it need only be stated generally, since the whole Christian theology has as its fundamental task the interpretation of the meaning, the presuppositions, and the implications of the final and normative self-disclosure of God in that series of events constituted by the person, the life, the deeds, the teachings, the example, and the death and resurrection of Jesus as the Christ. The entire New Testament is devoted to this exposition. In Christ the Word of God through whom the world was created was made flesh (John 1:1, 14).

The disclosures of God to humanity occurred first in the inner life of individuals or in the experience of groups who witnessed certain events. For the most part the revelatory occurrences were expressed orally and passed on by word of mouth to contemporaries and to later generations. Gradually, however, portions of the oral tradition were written down and in time themselves became authoritative as Scripture. Beginning with the reform of King Josiah in 621 BC and continuing over a period of about a thousand years, the collection of books that was to become our present Bible was put together as the written Word of God. The Protestant Reformers accepted the list of books approved by the council of Jewish rabbis at Jamnia in 90 AD -- the Hebrew Bible -- as their Old Testament. Roman Catholics accept a larger body of writings which appeared in the Septuagint -- a Greek translation of Jewish writings made in Alexandria in the 3rd century BC. In the early days of the church Scripture meant the Old Testament. Only gradually did the Gospels and other writings acquire authority as written documents. Beginning about the middle of the 2nd century lists of approved books began to appear, culminating in the 4th and 5th centuries with the 27 books which now make up the New Testament canon. The first official listing of the present collection that makes up the New Testament can be found in the Easter Letter of Athanasius for the year 367.[3]

B. CLASSICAL THEOLOGY. As the canonical Scriptures came into being and were granted special or normative authority, a number of problems arose. How are insights and truth claims from non-Biblical sources to be regarded? In particular, what weight is to be assigned to post-Biblical traditions that grew up in various church communities? Again, how are the views of the philosophers -- especially the Greek masters -- to be treated in relation to Biblical truth? The problem of Scripture in relation to tradition and of divine revelation in relation to human reason and experience has been treated in various ways over the centuries. Most of that history will have to remain untold on these pages.

Generally speaking, the main line of theology from the earliest days onward down to modern times (classical theology) regarded the Bible as an infallible source of moral and religious truth when properly interpreted. The Spirit worked in and through the personality and literary styles of the various human authors to preserve them from error. Several modes of interpretation were resorted to in order to deal with moral difficulties or seeming contradictions. Different levels of meaning could be found, making it possible to preserve the internal harmony of the Bible or to avoid other difficulties that a simple or merely literal understanding would present. Typological exegesis could show that Christ was prefigured or anticipated (in "types" of Christ) in various personages or events of the Old Testament. Allegorical exegesis found symbolic meanings beneath the surface of the literal or historical sense of the text. Often every detail in a passage was thought to stand for spiritual truths. These approaches led to the truest or deepest meaning of the Scriptures. It was common in the medieval period for exegetes to find four levels of interpretation in every passage (the literal, the allegorical, the moral, and the anagogical or eschatological). In the patristic period, however, the School of Antioch argued for the literal or historical meaning against the allegorical tendencies of the School of Alexandria. In the medieval period Thomas Aquinas was close to the Antiochene point of view, although he did not reject allegorical interpretation.

While reason on its own might discern many truths about God, the world, and human existence, nothing clearly taught in the Scriptures could be called into question. The early church theologians and the scholastics of the Middle Ages readily used the categories and methods of reasoning they took over from the Greek philosophers. Moreover, the findings of reason might provide a foundation or supplement to church doctrine. Augustine, Anselm, and Aquinas used various rational proofs to demonstrate the existence and perfection of God. Aquinas worked out a systematic structure with two levels. At the level of nature, reason could provide a substructure of religious truth, while at the level of grace, revelation added a superstructure of supernaturally revealed propositions related to incarnation, the atonement, the trinity, and the way of salvation through Christ. However, for all the classical thinkers no philosophical truth could knowingly be allowed to supplant or contradict what the Bible as God's own self-attested Word truly intended to teach.

Regardless of how absolute the objective authority of the Bible might be, it still had to be interpreted. Even an infallible Book requires a dependable interpreter if truth is to be maintained. Moreover, in the very earliest period the New Testament as a recognized canon or norm alongside the Old Testament was only beginning to come into being. Hence, the real standard in practice soon became the tradition of the Apostles as it was taught by the bishops functioning as the preservers and interpreters of the truth. This tradition (the rule of faith or the canon of truth) was handed down by Christ to the Apostles and through them to the continuing life of the church itself. No sharp distinction was made between the authority of Scripture and of tradition. The Gospel is Christ, the Word of God in person. The Apostles are the authentic witnesses to and interpreters of the Gospel. The Apostles handed down the Gospel to the church. The church preserves and passes on the true doctrines of the Apostolic faith. Thus, church tradition is nothing other than Scriptural truth itself correctly articulated for the faithful. As time passed the official decisions of the church in settling disputes became a part of the authoritative tradition. Along with this the writings of the early theologians themselves were revered. All of this is summed up by the Second Council of Constantinople in 553 which pledged allegiance to "the things which we have received from the Holy Scriptures and from the teachings of the holy fathers and from the definitions of one and the same faith by the four sacred councils." The Councils in question were Nicea in 325, Constantinople in 381, Ephesus in 431, and Chalcedon in 451. The ideal rule had been stated by Vincent of Lerins in 434 in the dictum that the standard was what had been believed "everywhere, always, by all."

The Protestant Reformation marked a turn toward a more exclusive form of Biblical authority. Martin Luther, John Calvin, and their successors asserted the strict priority of Scripture over tradition. The Bible alone contains all that is necessary for salvation and instruction. It is to be the final norm in all matters of faith and practice. Anything in tradition that has no Biblical basis is to be rejected, both in matters of doctrinal truth and church worship. Moreover, the Bible does not derive its authority from the church. Rather the church is to be subject to Scripture as its foundation and norm. The Holy Spirit works in the heart of the believer as an internal witness to the authority of the Scriptures and as a guide to its true meaning for life and faith. The objective truth of the Bible (the Word) has to be appropriated and confirmed subjectively in experience (the Spirit). Luther said, "God must tell you in your own heart that this is God's Word." The allegorical method of interpretation was rejected in favor of the plain, literal, grammatical, and historical meaning of the text.

While both Luther and Calvin regarded the Gospel witness to Christ as the theological center of the Bible -- its essential heart and core -- the former went much further with this than the latter. Luther regarded the whole Bible as the cradle in which Christ is laid. Everything in the Bible is to be measured and judged by the extent to which it witnesses to the good news of salvation in the Word made flesh. In this sense this Bible contains or witnesses to the Word rather than being the Word of God itself, although he often taught that every word in the Bible came directly from God. In the light of his more fundamental Christocentric principle he could be quite free in his evaluation of certain books and passages. He regarded James as clearly inferior to Romans, calling the former "an epistle of straw." He acknowledged that some of the specific predictions of the Old Testament prophets turned out to be wrong. The Book of Esther and the Book of Revelation do not belong in the Bible. Luther could even say that anyone living now who had the gift of the

Spirit as fully as the prophets and apostles could produce another set of ten commandments or another Testament.

Calvin was not so bold and was much closer to a doctrine of verbal inspiration. The Bible is an absolute rule or law of truth. Calvin insisted on the fundamental unity of the Bible and found binding truth nearly everywhere. Consequently, he sometimes had to work hard to reconcile apparent contradictions. Although Christ is the heart of the Bible, God speaks on every page. The Bible was composed by the dictation of the Holy Spirit. Yet even his views did not go as far in the direction of total inspiration of every word as the rigid and uncompromising theories which developed in Protestant orthodoxy in the next two centuries.

Compared to the medieval period, especially to thinkers like Anselm and Aquinas, Luther and Calvin gave relatively little place to the contribution of philosophy. God is indeed revealed in the whole creation, so that there is a two-fold source of the knowledge of God. Calvin thought that humanity had a natural and universal awareness of deity. Luther taught that there is a general perception of God possessed by all. Reason and conscience, they held, do put us in touch with the reality of a Supreme Power and Judge. But because we are finite and because we are sinners, the knowledge of God and of the meaning of life are so fragmented, distorted, and inadequate that it cannot lead us to salvation. Only the Bible which speaks of God's special revelation in Christ can lead us to the Gospel that can save us from the ruin and ignorance of our fallen, finite state. Reason can serve us well in matters of the secular life relating to science, art, medicine, technology, and the governance of society. But it cannot lead us to true and authentic knowledge of God which brings forgiveness, reconciliation, and eternal life.

Philosophy was reintroduced in an Aristotelian form in the Protestant orthodoxy that followed, beginning with Philip Melanchthon. Frequently, the two-level structure of reason and revelation that Aquinas had erected was reintroduced. Reason provides a substructure of truth. Revelation, specifically the Bible, provides the superstructure. Johan Gerhard distinguished between articles of belief which are pure (based on revelation alone) and those which are mixed (rationally known and revealed). He agreed with Aquinas that reason can offer valid proof for the existence of God, but only revelation provides certainty to faith. The Bible, for all Protestant thought, is the objective authority as the authentic witness to Christ. The Holy Spirit provides an internal witness or subjective confirmation by which the believer is assured that the Bible is indeed the written Word of God which points to the Word made flesh.[4]

IV. Types of Modern Theology

Currents of thought arose in the modern world which profoundly challenged all forms of classical theology.[5] Empirical science showed the cosmology of the Bible and the accounts of the origin of the world and of humanity it contained to be literally untrue. This raised the possibilty that the Scriptures might be wrong in matters of faith as well as in matters of fact. The use of historical methods to study the Bible undermined the theory of verbal inspiration and showed that the thought forms of the Bible were historically conditioned. Hence, it could not be used as an infallible source of pure doctrinal truth once and for all given in an absolute manner. New philosophies replaced older ways of thinking. These developments generated fresh approaches to Biblical truth and to the knowledge of God. Every chapter will add detail to the ways in which Christian theology has been reconstructed in order to meet the challenge of the modern world. The remainder of this chapter will deal with new ways of thinking about the authority of Scripture in relation to secular knowledge, as well as other questions relating to the nature, task, and method of Christian theology. It will be helpful at this point to identify several types of theology that have appeared in the 19th and 20th centuries. Each has its own distinctive way of coming to terms with the intellectual and practical challenges raised for Christian thought in the modern world. The first type to be mentioned -- orthodoxy -- makes an effort to continue the older ways of thinking with minimal adaptations to modernity. In the extreme form of fundamentalism the reigning conclusions of science and historical criticism are rejected in so far as they challenge the notion of an infallible Bible. All the other types recognize the necessity of reconstructing classical orthodoxies of all forms in order to prevent Christianity from becoming obsolete.

A. PROTESTANT ORTHODOXY (Conservativism and Fundamentalism): The mark of all orthodoxy is that truth has been given somewhere in the past. The present task is to discover and restate that right belief for today. For Protestant orthodoxy Christian truth is found supremely in the Bible, which is the norm by which everything is to be measured. Theology, then, is primarily the exposition of the basic doctrinal teaching of the Bible. The Bible is a compendium of Christian truth without error or need for correction, when it is rightly understood and interpreted.

A variety of emphases are to be found at this end of the spectrum. At the far extreme are to be found those who insist on the verbal inspiration of the Scripture. The Bible in its original manuscripts contains no error of any sort -- scientific, historical, factual, or doctrinal. Theologians of this stripe would insist that the accounts of creation in Genesis are to be taken literally, so that Darwinian theories of evolution must be rejected. Ranging across a continuum are other points of view which recognize a variety of culturally conditioned factors. But what is central is the idea that the Bible rightly understood and interpreted is God-given truth that is not to be questioned or qualified. The authority of the Bible is absolute not relative, not just the highest on a continuum. Its authority is objective, not subjective. It does not simply contain the Word of God. It does not just become the Word of God on some occasions when God speaks through it to people. It is the Word of God written down containing infallibly the truth essential for salvation given once and for all. Reason and experience may independently yield many truths about God and human life, but every religious assertion is to be subjected to the authority of the Scriptures. They are preserved from doctrinal error by divine inspiration and will provide us with reliable truth when read and interpreted under the guidance of the Holy Spirit. The Spirit confirms in the believer's heart that the Bible is indeed God's own Word.[6]

B. LIBERALISM. Liberal theology arose in the 19th century in order to reconstruct orthodoxy in the light of modern knowledge, especially science and new historical studies of the Bible. Liberals believed that the essentials of the ancient Gospel were in harmony with the best that human reason and experience can discover. Historical studies had shown (1) the vast gap between the thought world of the Bible and that of the present day and (2) that all statements of theology are historically relative and culturally conditioned, including those found in the Bible. Hence, it is necessary to distinguish between the propositional teachings of the Bible and the categories of the creeds and the classical texts, on the one hand, and the abiding, universal truth of the Gospel, on the other hand. It was in this context that religious experience became the ground and norm of religious truth.

For liberalism theology is the conceptual expression of the normative religious experience of the Christian community. Behind the words and ideas of the Bible itself lies the experience of Israel and the early Christians. Historical study showed that the Bible contains a developing body of beliefs. Scholars traced the evolution of Hebrew religion from the polytheism of the Patriarchs to the monotheism of II Isaiah (Is. 40-66). This progression of thought reached its height and perfection in the life, example, teachings, and ministry of Jesus of Nazareth. In him we find the norm of religious truth. The task of theology today is to find language that expresses for our age the universal truth of the Gospel found in Jesus. Harry Emerson Fosdick spoke of the contrast between "abiding experiences and changing categories." Theology is the attempt to find credible and applicable ways of speaking that capture the heart of those abiding experiences of faith, hope, and love to which the Bible witnesses. In this way it will be possible, again in the words of Fosdick, to be "a serious Christian and an intelligent modern." Without this reinterpretation Christianity will become the slave of outdated dogma and lose its appeal to thinking modern people.[7]

    C. NEO-ORTHODOXY. Neo-orthodox theology came into prominence after World War I. Its aim was to rediscover the truth of classical theology that liberalism had obscured in its effort to be up to date. The social catastrophes of the 20th century shattered the optimism of the liberals and sent the neo-orthodox thinkers back to the Bible, Augustine, Luther, and Calvin to discover a Word from Beyond. Such a Word was needed in a civilization whose foundations were being shaken by wars, totalitarianism (Hitler, for example) and the threat of the Bomb. Neo-orthodoxy (or neo-Reformation theology as it was also called) reaffirmed the transcendence of God, the radical sinfulness of humanity, salvation by grace through faith, the need for a divine Savior, the moral ambiguity of history, and the importance of a Kingdom beyond this world--themes important in historic orthodoxy, especially in the Protestant Reformation.

For neo-orthodoxy theology is the interpretation in today's language of that cluster of normative revelatory events to which the Bible give authoritative witness. In the Old Testament the Exodus and the making of the Covenant are central, while in the New Testament the focus is on the life, death, and resurrection of Jesus the Christ. The Bible is given special authority in this perspective. However, the neo-orthodox as well as the liberals make a distinction between the actual texts of Scripture and something which lies behind the words and thought forms. For the liberals it was the religious experience of individuals and the community which were expressed in the Biblical writings. For the neo-orthodox it was certain crucial events that manifested God's revealing and saving activity to humankind. The Bible recites these mighty acts of God and gives us the normative authoritative interpretation of their meaning. The task of theology is to state in contemporary language what these events mean for our understanding of God, the nature and destiny of humanity, and the saving work of Jesus as the Christ.

These thinkers were called neo-ORTHODOX because they restated basic orthodox motifs. But they were NEO-orthodox because like the liberals they recognized the historical relativity of all theologies from the past and the need to speak intelligently to modern people. Hence, they accepted science and the historical criticism of the Bible. Generally speaking, they regarded the creation stories, the virgin birth, the bodily resurrection, the second coming of Christ, etc. as "myths" to be taken "seriously but not literally" (Reinhold Niebuhr). They contain important religious and existential meanings expressed in anachronistic patterns of thought. Hence, theologies must change from age to age in order both to preserve the essential motifs of Biblical faith and to speak intelligently to particular historical situations.[8]

D.   PROCESS THEOLOGY.   This is an increasingly influential point of view in the present-day.   Its approach illustrates the method of a theology that makes an alliance with a philosophical perspective.   Process theologians share with the liberals and the neo-orthodox the desire to be modern and Christian.   Their way of doing this is to use the philosophical vision of Alfred North Whitehead as a thought form in which to state the ancient Gospel.   Whitehead thought that the world was made up not of individual substances (discrete things) with attributes but of processes with patterns. Experiences organically related to each other in pursuit of aims which yield satisfaction when they are being actualized -- that is the clue to reality.   This view stands in opposition to an older scientific outlook which saw nature as composed of tiny bits of dead matter interacting mechanically, which produced the concept of the world as a machine, void of life, freedom, and value.   God, according to Whitehead, strives to lure the world forward into those comprehensive, complex, and intense organic harmonies which maximize the divine enjoyment as well as that of all experiencing subjects.

Against this background theology is the attempt to state the essentials of Biblical religion within the framework of the vision of reality found in process philosophy.   Process theologians may be called liberal in that they believe in the ultimate harmony of Biblical revelation and human experience.   Process philosophy and

Christian theology provide the most compelling elucidation of experience. Together they provide a way of
understanding the world and of seeking fulfillment which
is true both to the Gospel and to our search for a
coherent and convincing rational outlook. Process
theology sees the Biblical God in terms of Creative-
Responsive Love, a Caring Companion who feels our
sorrows, while interacting persuasively with us in a
never ceasing aim to lure us forward toward just,
harmonious, and satisfying fulfillment. Jesus perfectly
embodies and clarifies the divine aim and purpose and
thus is the Christ -- the incarnation of the divine
Logos (John 1:1). Some see the Logos as the principle
and process of "creative transformation" (John Cobb)
which is at work everywhere and at all times to persuade
all life onward toward an increase of truth, goodness,
and beauty.[9]

E. LIBERATION THEOLOGY. Liberation is probably
the single most important theme on a world-wide basis in
theology today. This theology comes in many versions --
black, feminist, third-world, native American, etc. It
arises as a theology "from below" as a quest of some
oppressed group for liberation. Liberation theologians
interpret freedom from bondage as including not only
redemption from guilt, sin, and death in religious terms
but also release from every economic, political, social,
and psychological enslavement which is imposed on the
poor and the weak. Its intellectual alliances are not
so much with philosophy as with the social and
behavioral sciences which analyze the oppressive
structures that demean human life. Latin American
theologians, in particular, have made use of Marxist
social philosophy. The aim of liberation theology is

not so much to make Christianity credible to the modern age as to proclaim a Gospel that arises from and speaks to those in bondage and urges them to become the subjects of their own emancipation. Liberation theologians call attention to the socio-economic conditioning of the dominant theologies -- whether conservative or liberal -- and castigate them as ideologies of the ruling classes which have corrupted the Biblical Word which was originally addressed to the oppressed.

In this setting theology is critical reflection on praxis, practice, action. It arises out of a consciousness of oppression and is finally for the sake of liberation. What Hegel said about philosophy can be said about theology: it arises at sundown, after the day's work is over. Theology is the "second act" (Gustavo Gutierrez). The first act is liberating action in behalf of the downtrodden. Or, to paraphrase Karl Marx, the purpose of theology is not so much to understand the world as to change it. Theology is not an arm-chair exercise. It emerges out of the life and struggle of real people to be free. The Good News is that God is at work in the world setting captives loose, healing the sick, and putting down the oppressors from their mighty seats (Luke 4:16-21).

Moreover, theology is contextual, situational, experiential. It comes into being out of some particular real life situation at some time and place. Truth is concrete. It is arrived at inductively, moving from the particular to the universal. It asks what the Gospel means here and now in and for the experience of some oppressed group in their unique life history.

Especially in its feminist form liberation theology is
adventuresome, experimental, suspicious of fixed norms
and established boundaries. It has a revolutionary
tendency in all of its varieties by its very nature.
Liberation theologians sometimes have to decide whether
the quest for liberation can be carried on within
oppressive religious and social systems or whether they
must become exiles and strangers in quest of a new order
in which the prevailing values are turned upside down.[10]

F. REVISIONISM. Revisionist theology is,
according to David Tracy, a strong and emerging form of
thought found in both contemporary Catholic and
Protestant thought. It incorporates a wide variety of
outlooks but shows a broad agreement on methodological
questions. Process theology is but one of many examples
of this orientation to the task and method of Christian
theology. Revisionist theologians are committed to the
confrontation, mutual illumination, and possible reconciliation of the meanings found in common human
experience and in the historic Christian tradition.
Theology, then, investigates these two sources of
religious truth and correlates the results into a
systematic whole, which is to be tested for adequacy by
appropriate rational criteria provided by philosophical
modes of analysis.

The revisionists are thoroughly modern in
consciousness and are fully committed to the values and
beliefs of a contemporary secular outlook. As such they
regard this life here and now as the locus of
human meaningfulness, and they reject the supernaturalistic elements of anachronistic orthodoxy. They accept
the methods and conclusions of science within its own

proper sphere but deny that the empirical sciences tell us all there is to know about reality, meaning, and value. At the same time revisionists are committed to the heart of Christian tradition embodied in its normative sources, Scripture in particular but including the classical texts produced over the centuries. They are like the liberals in wanting to be both "intelligent moderns and serious Christians." But they live in the last half of the 20th century and have learned from Marx and Freud, as well as from the neo-orthodox theologians. In this regard, they have no optimistic illusions about the human future. In short, they are dedicated to a revision of both modern secularity and classical orthodoxy in the light of their mutual illumination.[11]

THEOLOGIANS REPRESENTING VARIOUS SCHOOLS OF THOUGHT

Conservative	Liberal
CarlHenry	Friedrich Schleiermacher
Edward J. Carnell	Albrecht Ritschl
Bernard Ramm	Adolf Von Harnack
Francis Schaeffer	William Adams Brown
G.C. Berkouwer	Harry Emerson Fosdick
Louis Berkhof	Walter Rauschenbusch
A.H. Strong	A.C. Knudson
Hal Lindsey	Shailer Mathews
	D.C. Macintosh
	Henry Nelson Wieman

Neo-orthodox

Karl Barth
Emil Brunner
Anders Nygren
Gustaf Aulén
Reinhold Niebuhr
H. Richard Niebuhr
Paul Tillich*
Rudolf Bultmann*

Process

John Cobb
Schubert Ogden
David Griffin
Marjorie Suchocki
Norman Pittenger
Daniel Day Williams

Liberation

Latin American
  Gustavo Gutiérrez
  Juan Luis Segundo
  Hugo Assmann

Black
  James Cone
  Deotis Roberts
  Gayraud Wilmore

Revisionist

David Tracy
Langdon Gilkey
Gordon Kaufman
Gregory Baum
Leslie Dewart

Feminist
  Rosemary Ruether
  Carter Heyward
  Letty Russell

*Classifications such as this are of limited usefulness.

Bultmann and Tillich, for example, might better be placed somewhere between liberalism and neo-orthodoxy. Designations are more accurate in some cases than in others. Many thinkers combine emphases from different orientations. Many process theologians are also revisionists and could be called neo-liberal as well. Tillich, Bultmann, H. Richard Niebuhr, as well as John Macquarrie (not listed above), could be called existentialist theologians. Wolfhart Pannenberg and Jürgen Moltmann are both influential in this country but fit neither of the above schools of thought well. They represent a kind of post-neo-orthodox eschatological theology. William Temple and other British and American thinkers combine liberal, neo-orthodox, and Anglican perspectives into a kind of liberal and quite modern orthodoxy. Many other names could, of course, be added to the above listings. Finally, each theologian must be taken individually and not forced into pre-formed categories, although the classifications do indicate shared convictions that can be abstracted from their total thought.

V. MODERN VIEWS OF REVELATION, EXPERIENCE AND REASON

The question of how God is known is raised and answered in distinctive ways in modern theology. Revelation, reason, tradition, the Bible, and experience have already been introduced as sources of Christian truth. The interpretation of these categories in 19th and 20th century Christian thinking shows both continuity and discontinuity with the ways they were thought of in classical thought. It should already be apparent that these terms are not completely independent of each other. Frequently the meaning of one can be completed only by connecting it with others. Both the relative autonomy and the interdependence of these factors will become evident in the ensuing discussion.

A. REVELATION. Theology does not begin from zero. Christians have been almost unanimous in claiming that God has taken the initiative to become known to humanity. This unveiling of God in history and in experience is what is meant by revelation. More specifically, revelation is God's self-initiated self-disclosure in certain special events in Israel's history and supremely in the person of Jesus Christ as witnessed by Scripture. Several things may be noted.

1. God becomes known primarily in a community -- the people of Israel and the church. Revelation occurs in the history of a people struggling with the meaning of existence and searching for salvation.

2. Christian knowledge of God is centered in a particular person who appears in the history of Israel in the fullness of time as the culmination of a long series of divine disclosures. Jesus Christ is the primary manifestation and embodiment of the Word of God to humankind.

3. The normative interpretation of the meaning and content of divine revelation in Israel's history and in Jesus Christ is given in the Old and the New Testaments. In this secondary sense the Bible may be said to be the Word of God. More precisely, most modern Protestants are more likely to say that the Bible contains the Word of God. This means that a distinction needs to be made between the words of the Bible and the Word of God. The

Word is known to us through the words of Scripture. This distinction enables modern theologians to distinguish between the language and thought forms of the Biblical writers which are culturally relative and the revelation of God in Christ which is universal and normative for Christian thinking. We have the Word only in the words of Scripture. The task of theology is to discover the Word in the words and to state it in a form that is credible and relevant to a particular situation.

Another way of putting this is to say that revelation is found in the combination of event and interpretation. God is known to us through certain crucial happenings (the Exodus and the making of the Covenant at Sinai, the life, death, and resurrection of Jesus) as interpreted by the Bible. Event and interpretation are united in the witness of Scripture, but much modern theology rests on the premise that we can distinguish between the revelatory essence of the original event and the historically relative words of the Bible on which we are absolutely dependent for the nugget of truth which they contain.[12]

The problem of history and faith -- the relationship of the original unity of the revelatory event and its interpretation in Scripture to subsequent interpretations -- has been central to 19th and 20th century theology. The issue can be elucidated by noting four typical ways it has been dealt with.[13] (1) One might identify the essence of Christianity with its original formulation, as for example in the teachings of Jesus (Adolf Harnack) or (2) locate it in the total Gestalt of its development through a long sequence of varying external forms (Alfred Loisy). (3) Another possibility is to deny that there is any immanent essence to be located anywhere and to identify Christianity with the history of all its expressions (the history of religions school). (4) A final option is to note that the original unity of event and interpretation can be known and appropriated in the present by two modes of knowing: the disinterested, descriptive study of the "event side" by the methods of secular history and the personal, evaluative appropriation of the "interpretive" side by a subjective judgment or decision (faith). This duality yielded the distinction between the Jesus of history as known by critical historians and the Christ of faith known in the church by faith. In this Kantian fashion Albrecht Ritschl distinguished between judgments of fact and judgments of value. Jesus is divine because he has the value of God for us. In a similar way, Richard Niebuhr distinguished between external history and internal history, while Rudolf Bultmann made the same point by differentiating between <u>Historie</u> and <u>Geschichte</u> -- the latter category in both cases signifying the location and meaning of revelation. All three of these latter thinkers illustrate the widespread conviction that God can be known only from the point of view of subjective involvement, i.e., personal experience or faith.

4. A prominent theme in much Protestant thought in the 19th and 20th centuries is that it is God as such who is known in the revelatory events or experiences contained in the Bible. This means that knowledge of God refers not primarily to propositions of doctrine about God but to a personal meeting, encountering, or experiencing of God as God. Revelation is not primarily the communication of supernatural knowledge but the

disclosure of a Subject to subjects. What is revealed
is God, not ideas or beliefs. Doctrines are needed to
interpret and communicate this personal meeting of God
in experience, but the primary focus is that God reveals
God, not truths about God.

This distinction between revelation and truths of
revelation is related to the contrast between event and
interpretation and between the Word of God and the words
of the Bible made in the previous section. All of them
arise out of the rejection by modern theologians of the
view that the Bible contains one pure system of doctrine
from cover to cover -- an assumption more or less held
in Protestant orthodoxy. Some way had to be found by
liberal, neo-orthodox, and contemporary thinkers to
preserve the idea that the Bible contains the norm of
theology without being bound to the older notion of the
infallibility of the Bible as a repository of true
doctrines once and for all given.

At this point it is necessary to introduce the
concept of tradition. Tradition refers to teachings and
practices -- ways of believing and doing things -- which
grew up in the churches outside and after the process
which produced the Biblical canon. It is the medium
through which the truth of faith is handed down from
generation to generation. Believing communities are the
carriers and embodiments of vital religious belief.
Tradition is the form and substance of living faith in
the extended life of churches over the years. It is
expressed in creeds, confessions, and official documents
as well as in more informal ways. We may refer to the
Protestant tradition or more narrowly to the Methodist
tradition or Baptist tradition and so on. Many tradi-

tions flourish in which the faith has been transmitted. Traditions both preserve the truths originally given and develop them further, or at least give distinctive and approved expression to them.

In previous centuries a great debate ensued over the authority that was to be granted to tradition. Protestants insisted that the standard was Scripture alone. Catholics claimed that authoritative interpretations were to be found in Scripture and tradition. For example, the Immaculate Conception of Mary, the Bodily Assumption of Mary, and the Infallibility of the Pope are dogmas which have official sanction and which the faithful are obliged to accept. None is found on the Bible, though the Catholic Church sees them as legitimate developments that build upon the foundation of Scripture. The Church is authorized to be the preserver, transmitter, and developer of the truth of faith in ways that guarantee the authenticity of its official teachings. Protestants give a secondary role to tradition, insisting that all doctrines must be measured by what is authorized by the Bible alone. Creeds and confessions of faith may have a useful value in summarizing and systematizing the approved faith of a given group, but they are not to have a place alongside and equal to Scripture in authority. However, the old debates no longer are as sharp as they once were. Protestants, for example, generally acknowledge that the particular traditions in which they stand do shape their faith and practice, their thought and life. No church just leaps over the centuries to model itself after the New Testament vision. But still the question remains concerning the authority of post-Biblical developments and expressions of faith and practice.

The self-disclosure of God in Jesus Christ norma-
tively interpreted by the Bible and carried through
history in various church traditions -- these elements
can be called "the givens." Revelation, Scripture, and
tradition come down to us from the past. But believers
and their communities live in the present in a particular culture with its own world-view, its convictions
about reality, and its system of values. Hence, we must
introduce some additional elements that enter into the
making of theological perspectives. They can be
conveniently subsumed under the headings of experience
and reason.

B. EXPERIENCE. Experience is a slippery word
which we all use but which is hard to define. Let us
mean by it for the moment what happens to us and in us.
It refers to what we ourselves have decided, done, felt,
seen, touched, and known for ourselves. Or it may refer
to what has happened to and within the community of
faith in its own first-hand encounter with realities
temporal and eternal. Experience is what we perceive,
feel, choose, intuit, grasp, and otherwise come to know
on the basis of particular occasions of being in touch
with the real and the ideal, with being, goodness, and
beauty, with the world and God. In this sense a lively
experience of God first-hand is an essential part of the
Biblical story of individuals and of Israel and the
early church. Likewise, Christian history is filled
with personal testimony of the saints and not so saintly
who have known and chosen God in their own lives,
hearts, and struggles.

It may be helpful to examine in more detail the role of experience in the theologies of recent centuries. Philosophical skepticism and the impact of scientific thought form an important part of the background. In the 18th century David Hume and Immanuel Kant dismantled traditional natural theology (knowledge of God gained by reason apart from revelation). They refuted the traditional arguments for the existence of God. Kant left reason incompetent to deal with divine reality on a theoretical or cognitive basis. Moreover, modern science beginning in the 17th century was developing a cosmology in which the world was a self-contained, closed system of causes and effects in which every event could be explained without recourse to the hypothesis of God. No transcendent Ground or Purpose seemed essential to account for the operation of nature viewed as a giant machine, except as it might suggest an original Creator who set things in motion but now leaves them to operate automatically in accordance with natural law. Moreover, science seemed to imply a world best described in deterministic, mechanistic, and materialistic terms. This is the view of "scientific materialism," which, according to Alfred North Whitehead, was virtually unchallenged from about 1650 to around 1900. Such a world -- if that be the total story -- had no place for freedom, value, meaning, and purpose.

Yet alongside the material things being described with mathematical exactitude in Newtonian physics were human beings. Persons are conscious minds who think, feel, and will. The effort to relate the world of mind and soul, of consciousness and will, to the world of physical things, of matter in motion, was a basic problem of modern philosophy. The logical possibilities are relatively few, and the major options have all been tried. All is God and the appearance of God in material and mental forms (Spinoza). There are material things and conscious minds plus God (the dualism of Descartes). The real is mind or some form of consciousness, and the material world is the phenomenal product of mental reality (Berkeley and the idealists of various sorts). The real is matter, and mind is an epiphenomenon of material activity (Hobbes and the materialists).

It can scarcely be doubted that the conflict between the cosmology apparently implied by modern science and the world view of the Bible and classical theology has been the main source of the fundamental epistemological and metaphysical problems theologians have had to face in the centuries following Luther and Calvin.[14] If we indeed live in a non-teleological world consisting of a network of mechanical causation, then the only place for purpose to arise, if at all, is in the human subject. This inward focus is part of a major shift in philosophical thinking in the modern world which is generally referred to as the turn to the subject -- centering on consciousness and its activities as the clue to reality, meaning, and purpose. This many-sided story cannot be told here, but this turn is illustrated in a long sequence of thinkers from Descartes on to Kant, Hegel, **Kierkegaard**, Heidegger, and Whitehead. Experience as the **activity of** a subject or as constituting a subject (**mind, consciousness**, spirit, will, etc.) is a clue to much **modern thought** both in philosophy and theology.

Summarizing a complicated intellectual history and running the risk of oversimplification, it may be said that this turn to the subject provided four related ways to come to turns with the threat of "Scientific materialism" and philosophical skepticism regarding a theoretical knowledge of God.[15]

(1) The critical idealism of Kant provided one approach. Kant distinguished between the realms with which science and religion (and morality) deal. Science is based on sensory experience, that is, reality as it appears to us (phenomena). Theoretical reason cannot transcend this limitation to gain knowledge of things as they are in themselves (noumena). Neither can there be cognitive or theoretical knowledge of God, since God is not an object of sense perception. Moreover, the traditional arguments for the existence of God (cosmological, teleological, and ontological) are fatally flawed. But in addition to theoretical reason, which makes judgments of true and false (science), there is the practical reason, which deals with judgments about right and wrong, with moral values and with religion. In this connection, Kant spoke of a free, moral self, somehow transcendent to the phenomenal realm of nature described by the sciences. The inner self is conscious of a sense of moral oughtness (the categorical imperative) -- the reality of which requires the postulation of freedom, God, and immortality. Hence, by restricting scientific knowledge, Kant made room for religious faith erected on the basis of moral obligation, which is a universal feature of human selfhood. By this maneuver he provided an autonomous basis for morality and religion free from the need of supernatural revelation, on the one hand, and from the destructive attacks of philosophical skepticism (Hume) and "scientific materialism," on the other hand.

Much 19th and 20th century Protestant thought is dependent in one way or another on this "Copernican revolution" in thought. Generally speaking, this influence is seen in the emphasis on religious experience in liberalism (moral intuition or mystical awareness of God, e.g.) and on the emphasis on personal encounter with God (the I-Thou meeting divinely initiated) in neo-orthodoxy and in the sharp distinction made between detached, theoretical thinking and involved, committed thought and action (faith and obedience) made by existentialist theologians. The common thread is that moral and religious truth is not discovered primarily by examining the objective processes of nature or by speculative thought. Instead, God is known by a unique, special kind of non-theoretical, non-cognitive apprehension or in personal value judgments, decision, and faith. In all these perspectives, especially those that continue the Kantian anti-metaphysical bias, religious knowledge tends to be mediated to persons through some faculty of the self which in one way or another resembles Kant's idea of the practical reason.

(2) The post-Kantian metaphysical idealists provided a second approach. They, like Kant, reduced the material world to the status of phenomena (appearance) and grounded nature in the activity of Mind or Consciousness or Spirit. Prior to and underlying the distinction of subject and object, self and nature, is a universal Consciousness in which both are grounded. For the absolute idealists (Hegel, Josiah Royce, etc.) the world of nature described by science is a manifestation or expression of an all-embracing Mind or Spirit (the Absolute). The personalists (Borden P. Bowne and the

Boston school, e.g.) viewed nature as the product or creation of a Cosmic Person. The idealists provided a rational and theoretical knowledge of God which established the primacy of mind, purpose, freedom, and meaning in the universe. At the same time knowledge of God was, for some at least, an immediate intuitive (self-evident) awareness of some Unconditioned Ground of both finite spirit and observable nature. Paul Tillich represents a continuation of this idealistic tradition, especially as it was mediated to him through Schelling.

(3) Still another post-Kantian development was the appeal to a religious a priori in humanity. This refers to a formal capacity in the self for religious experience. The content is provided in history by particular experiences of God which result in various world religions and communities of faith. Rudolf Otto, Ernst Troeltsch, and the Lundensian school of Swedish Lutheranism (e.g. Anders Nygren) represent this appeal to religious experience.

(4) A number of thinkers following Kant embodied idealist and romanticist motifs, separately and in combination. What they have in common is a distinction between the outer world of physical things and the inner world of the spirit. Whatever science may say about the world of nature and matter, there is a sure foundation for morality and religious faith in the human consciousness, feeling, and intuition. Note the distinctions made by the following diverse group between understanding and reason (Coleridge), the natural and the supernatural (Bushnell), the sensuous consciousness and the higher religious consciousness (Schleiermacher), and nature and moral personality (Ritschl). The latter

realm in every case is the arena and basis for moral values and religious experience, that is, for the knowledge of God.

Schleiermacher is of particular importance here, since he has been called the father of modern Protestant theology. Coming out of a tradition of romanticism and pietism, he argued that religion is not primarily a matter of cognitive knowledge of God or of ethics or of action but a matter of feeling. In particular, God is immediately known or apprehended in the "feeling of absolute dependence."[16] Feeling here is not first of all emotion but an awareness of being in relation to God. From Schleiermacher through Ritschl and down to D.C. Macintosh and H. Richard Niebuhr, we may trace a stream of empirical theology. The common thread running through this diverse tradition, full of conflicts among its members, is the claim that God can be known only from the point of view of faith, i.e., some immediate, personal relationship to God.[17] Liberals tended to talk more of experiencing God and saw continuity between religious faith and the rest of life and thought. Existentialists like H. Richard Niebuhr and Bultmann speak of personally deciding for God and tended, like other neo-orthodox thinkers, to see discontinuity between faith and reason (science and disinterested theoretical speculation). D.C. Macintosh wanted to make theology an empirical science in which religious experience would provide the data for analysis, as sense experience is the basis of the sciences of nature.[18]

Neo-orthodox theologians, especially Karl Barth, rejected a century of liberal thought because of its anthropocentrism. In this connection that means locating the source of knowledge of God in humanity in some universal, given fact or relationship in which everybody is in possession of God (actually or potentially) by virtue of being a person. Saving, reliable, authentic knowledge of God is God-given, said Barth, proceeding from the freely chosen act of a transcendent Lord who by grace comes to us in Christ. In Barth's case this means that by divine condescension we are given a real creaturely participation in the Reality of God.[19] In all of its forms neo-orthodoxy shifted the emphasis from general experience to specific divine revelation. Theology is to be based on a particular self-disclosure of God and not on human experience in general which yields a true apprehension of God which somehow harmonized with Christian faith.

In the post-neo-orthodox decades American Protestant theology has witnessed a shift of emphasis from revelation to experience and reason. The revisionists seek a correlation of meaning derived from classical Christian sources (Scripture and tradition) and meanings derived from an analysis of common human experience. The claim is that a phenomenological investigation of common human experience will disclose dimensions of ultimacy and transcendence. This religious depth is a universal feature of human life and will inevitably appear in an appropriate and adequate analysis. Langdon Gilkey argues that this investigation will not provide a complete doctrine of God but does require the postulation of an Ultimate Source or Ground of Being and Meaning.[20] Particular revelatory experiences of communities and individuals must be called upon to provide material content to fill out this apprehension of transcendence. This special experience in the history of a community is what is meant by revelation. Christians find the clue to the Ground of Being and Meaning in the Biblical witness to Jesus as the Christ.

Process theologians follow Whitehead in the view that the sole justification for thought is "the elucidation of immediate experience." An authentic elucidation will yield the process vision of reality. Christian experience will complete and fulfill the philosophical scheme and add up to a harmonious synthesis of revelation, reason, and experience.[21] Feminist theologians have made experience the starting point and justifying reference of theological claims. In particular their awareness of the oppressive weight of dominating patriarchal values and their yearning for equality, justice, and fulfillment are norms by which the claims of Biblical truth must be measured. Yet the equalitarian ideal has rootage also in some parts of the Bible.[22] Black theologians have made black suffering the starting point of their reflections, while black liberation is a situational norm that is united to the universal norm of salvation through Christ.[23]

C. REASON. Reason refers to the human capacity for discovering and creating patterns of meaning useful for understanding and coping with reality. All cultures produce conceptions of God, the world, humanity, good and evil, right and wrong, history, and the human prospect on earth -- all of which are important to Christian thinking. But how much can be known that is valid and true in relationship to what is presented to us in "the givens" which the church acknowledges? In particular, can reason discern anything about the reality and nature of God? The relationship between "the givens" of faith and the discoveries of the human mind constitute the traditional problem of "revelation and reason." The answers to the question vary from those who say that reason can contribute nothing of substance alongside or in addition to revelation (Karl Barth, though reason can be the servant of faith) to those who think that reason can know essentially everything that really matters apart from the special revelation of God in Christ and Scripture (the deists and the modernistic liberals). More typical are those who see reason as having something to contribute but needing revelation to complete, transform, or measure the deliverance of rational inquiry.

For centuries, as John Baillie has pointed out, the problem of revelation and reason was thought to have a simple solution, at least in terms of the definition of the issues.[24] A distinction was made between revealed knowledge and natural or rational knowledge. Revealed knowledge (or revelation) is the communication of supernatural truths from God to humanity through Christ, the Bible, and tradition. Natural knowledge is the truth about God and life than can be discovered by people by their own unaided rational powers (i.e., reason). In the last two centuries this consensus has broken up, partly for reasons already stated. They have to do with changed conceptions of both revelation and reason.

Typically, today revelation is not thought of primarily as the communication of supernatural truths about God, humanity, and the world. Rather it is often seen as the self-disclosure of God as Subject to human beings as subject. More generally, knowledge of God is not seen basically as propositions of doctrine about God.

Something is prior to cognitive understanding expressed in beliefs. There is a kind of non-theoretical, non-cognitive apprehension of divine reality which can be expressed in appropriate intellectual categories and symbolic imagery.

If revelation is not first of all the communication of supernatural truth, then it appears to take its character in some form of experience and/or personal (existential) relationship. Two questions then arise. (1) What is the nature of this togetherness of God and humanity in which divine self-disclosure takes place, and on what is it based? The answers are many, and they converge and diverge in complex ways. Liberals tended to affirm a universal or potential knowledge of God which is qualified or perfected through participation in the church and/or under the influence of Jesus. It might be a kind of awareness or perception (Schleiermacher's "feeling of absolute dependence") or some sort of intuition of the Cosmic Ground of moral values (some American liberals like William Adams Brown). This might be supplemented by a rational knowledge of God (idealists like the Boston Personalists). In this framework revelation, reason, and experience were more or less harmonious and mutually supporting.[25]

Neo-orthodox thinkers typically spoke of the "divine-human encounter" (Brunner as a gift of grace initiated from God's side). Knowing God requires a response to God's graceful presence (Barth and Brunner), sometimes interpreted as a leap of faith or a subjective decision in the presence of objective (rational) uncertainty (Kierkegaard). The existentialist theologians (Richard Niebuhr and Bultmannm, e.g.) spoke of

Christian faith arising in a kind of personal decision or commitment of the will which is radically different from detached, theoretical, cognitive knowing (a matter of practical reason and not theoretical reason in Kant's sense). In neo-orthodoxy reason and experience are sharply contrasted with revelation.[26] For Tillich there is an immediate awareness of an Unconditioned Reality (Being-itself) which is the source of everything finite. In taking this position he continues a tradition of German idealism which speaks of an Infinite Ground of spirit and nature (self and world, subject and object), an identity in the depth of things in which all temporal contrasts are transcended and united.

(2) How is the here and now in which God is known related to the self-disclosure of God then and there in the experience of Israel and the early church to which the Bible gives witness? As indicated, liberals tended to say that the universal or general apprehension of God given to all in reason and experience is modified or qualified or perfected in particular communities of faith (the church) through which the impact of Jesus is mediated through history. Some contemporary revision-ists like Langdon Gilkey, echoing the liberal viewpoint, maintain that revelation gives particular content to the general sense of a transcendent Ground of Being and Meaning which is disclosed to an analysis of the partic-ulars of certain forms of common human experience.[27] Toward the neo-orthodox end of the spectrum revelation simply comes to us then and now from Beyond as a miracle of grace in specific acts of divine self-communication. For Barth God's becoming available to us in Christ connects on to nothing general or universal in us. The Bible becomes the Word of God as God speaks to us

through its words in witness to Jesus Christ who is the Word in Person.[28] For Brunner the divine self-communication links onto a "point of contact" in the sense of responsibility which all have through the general revelation of God in creation but which has been obscured by our sinfulness.[29] For those in the broad middle revelation involves a transformation or clarification or completion of what Richard Niebuhr calls our "natural religion."[30] While modern theologians usually do not speak of some pure immediacy which remains incommunicable, they do distinguish between the personal meeting (encounter, experience, awareness, etc.) of God in the revelatory occasion and its interpretation in human words, categories, and symbols. And they do debate endlessly the question of the proper sources, norms, and forms of authentic articulation.

Likewise, changes occurred in the understanding of reason. In particular, one aspect of this transformation is important to note. The development of historical consciousness resulted in the widespread acceptance of the relativity of reason. Reason is historical reason. It is somebody's reason operating at a particular time and place in history. Reason is not universal, the spectator of all time and existence, but perspectival. Everybody has a point of view, and rational demonstration of one's own conclusions is impossible. We can prove our point of view only on the basis of assumptions peculiar to our own outlook. Hence, reason is culturally conditioned and historically relative.

Can reason prove the existence of God? Thomas Aquinas says yes; Immanuel Kant and David Hume say no. The logical positivists earlier in this century claimed

that the word God is non-sense, since there is no possible empirical referent by which we might test any
claims made about a supersensible reality. The atheistic existentialists thought that belief in God was
absurd in the face of the chaos and suffering in the
world. Modern theologians have allied themselves with
all these and a variety of other estimates of the powers
and conclusions of reason. Hence, the problem of revelation and reason has been resolved in all sorts of ways
since the 18th century. Some of them connect with
previous patterns in Christian thinking, while others
have distinctly modern accents.

Two generalizations, however, may be hazarded. (1)
The main directions of Christian theology in the 19th
and 20th centuries have reflected some of the dominant
characteristics of the "mentality" (reasoning) of the
age in which it functioned. The liberals shared with
the century of Hegel and Darwin an optimism about
history and human possibilities. It seemed reasonable
to believe that there was a basic order, harmony, and
progressive tendency in the cosmos. This led them to
develop theologies based on the intimate presence of God
in nature, history, and human life. An Immanent Spirit
was gradually infusing its own qualities into the world.
Evolution and progress were key ingredients in the cultural reason which dominated the age.

Post-World War I theologians reflected the cultural
loss of confidence in progress and the decline of faith
in an ultimate ground of coherence and purpose undergirding nature and history. Neo-orthodox thinkers
shared the 20th century sense of the depths of radical
evil in humanity and the pervasive presence of chaos,

absurdity, and injustice in world history. Reason seemed to dictate this revised estimate of things. Hence, neo-orthodoxy turned from culture toward revelation in quest of a Word from Beyond that could save humanity from the folly and pride which had led to the present debacle symbolized by Hitler's Holocaust and the mushroom cloud over Hiroshima.[31]

In summary, theologians could be found allied with every influential epistemological position held by philosophers. Some affirmed with Hume and Kant the metaphysical impotence of reason. Others appropriated the confident rationalism of Hegel and other like-minded idealists. A few could be found in the 20th century in agreement with logical positivists and so on. Yet despite the variety of technically held positions regarding the powers of reason, Protestant thinkers of the last two centuries have tended to share some of the larger ideological assumptions of cultural reason: the affirmation of an underlying rationality and harmony in the nature of things in the 19th century and the denial of same in the 20th century.

(2) Modern theologians have accepted the Enlightenment demand that religion be reasonable. Hence, the powerful currents of science and secularization in recent centuries have affected the operating assumptions of theologians as they have sought to make Christianity relevant to the modern mind.[32] Miracles, supernatural interventions into the causal order of nature, and the three-storied universe of the Bible have been rejected in obedience to the compelling rationality of scientific modes of thought. The assured results of the natural sciences have been appropriated as the framework within

which the Gospel must be preached to a civilization come of age, although the atheistic and mechanistic implications drawn by some from scientific methods and cosmologies were resisted. In these ways, too, theologians have accepted the cultural reason of modernity and have done their work under the constraints of a whole set of assumptions that distinguish their operating world view from 1700 years of Christian thought prior to Newton and Darwin.

More recently process theologians have made use of the grand philosophical vision of Alfred North Whitehead in an effort to reach the scientifically-oriented modern mind, while defying the powerful bias against all metaphysics current in the same world. Liberation theologians have employed various resources of social philosophy, history, and the behavioral sciences. Their aim has not been so much to make the Gospel credible as to analyze and document the oppressive structures which enslave the masses of the third world, women in nearly every society, and blacks under white domination. In every age and setting theologians must decide in what respects they will accept or reject the reigning cultural mentality and how they will relate the insights of reason, as they understand it, to the claims of revelation, Scripture, and tradition.

This brief sketch illustrates some of the ways in which theological reflection has dealt with the question of Christian knowledge in the modern world. While it is incomplete as a historical survey, it may serve to pose the methodological question of how revelation, reason, and experience are to be conceived, defined, and related to each other as sources and norms of Christian truth.

Where does Christian truth come from (sources)? How is it to be tested (norms)? What authority is to be assigned to revelation, reason, and experience in rela- tion to each other? What has the priority? Do they mutually support each other, or are they in conflict? These are basic questions that any theological methodol- ogy must answer.

VI. The Task and Norms of Theology

Widespread agreement can be found today that theology has a two-fold task: (1) to state the content of the Christian Gospel and (2) to relate it to the needs of today. Paul Tillich is typical and representa- tive rather than unique in suggesting that theology moves between the poles of "message" and "situation."[33] Defining the task of theology as two-fold reflects a self-consciousness about historical relativity which is characteristic of 19th and 20th century theologians. Hence, distinguishing explicity between setting forth the Gospel and making it relevant to a particular time and place is a mark of modern thought and not of the classical theologies produced before the rise of histor- ical consciousness.

Given the assumption that there are two tasks of theology, there must be a standard to measure whether each is being successfully carried out. Correlated with the work of setting forth the message is what can be called the universal norm. Meeting this criterion means conforming to the historic givens which constitute the heart of the Christian belief system. Theologians will define this criterion differently depending on their

backgrounds and points of view. Generally speaking, it
will center around what is thought to be given,
required, and implied by the revelation of God in Jesus
as the Christ as proclaimed in the New Testament.

Protestants typically have insisted that Christian
truth must be measured by the teachings of the Bible.
Classical Protestants said that the Bible is the norm,
while modern thinkers in this tradition are more likely
to say that the Bible contains the norm. Catholics have
allowed a place for Scripture and tradition as defining
Christian dogma. However it may be defined, every theology needs or has some way to determine what are true
and authentic teachings as compared to spurious, false,
or non-essential claims.

Correlated with the task of relating the message to
the needs of a particular group at some time and place
is what can be called the situational norm. Meeting
this standard means bringing contemporary reason and
experience into play in some fashion to determine what
is relevant to the human situation in a given setting.
Relevance has two ingredients: credibility and practic-
ality. A theology must be believable, must make sense.
It must be applicable to problems and needs that people
are actually facing in their lives. For example, Walter
Rauschenbusch in confronting the facts of an urbanized
and industrialized America at the turn of the century
announced the need for a "social Gospel" that would deal
with the corrupt institutions and corporate practices
which were destroying human lives. The demand for
social justice is the present-day implication of Jesus'
teachings about the coming of the Kingdom of God. Most
modern theologies are intentional about the requirements

of relevance that must be met if the church is to have any good news. In doing so, they are observing what is here being called the situational norm.

All theologians in some sense want to speak to the needs of the day -- to set forth Good News that is both true and practical. The crucial question has to do with the criteria by which relevance is to be determined. Hence, some theologians are suspicious of the deliberate effort to speak to the situation. The attempt to find a "point of contact" runs the risk of introducing culturally-defined criteria of truth and relevance. When the situation is deliberately made a source of questions or answers to be put alongside or correlated with Gospel truth derived from Scriptural revelation, the result is disastrous. What is relevant to the situation cannot be defined by the situation but can only be derived from the message and addressed to the situation in an appropriate way. This point was the burden of Karl Barth's theological method.

The situational pole can be and is taken into account a variety of ways. Hence, different weights will be assigned to cultural criteria derived from the contemporary quest for truth and relevance. Karl Barth and Henry Nelson Wieman represent the extreme options in recent thought. Barth urges us to attend solely to the Word of God. Only truth so grounded can be relevant to the needs of today or any day. Wieman argues that we are to accept only the best from the Bible and the Christian past. The "best" is to be determined by what contemporary reason and experience judge to promote the increase of human good here and now.[34] Between these polar positions are to be found a number of intermediate views. Tillich suggests that questions about the meaning of human existence derived from the "situation" are to receive answers provided by the "message." Revisionists seek to correlate the meanings discovered by an appropriate interpretation of classical Christian texts with the meanings arising out of an analysis of common human experience here and now, with the results tested and synthesized by philosophical criteria.

Paul Tillich points out that concrete and specific norms have arisen in every period of church history. These norms as he delineates them can be understood as uniting the universal and situational norms as they have been defined here. For the early Greek church it was salvation from mortality and error by the incarnation of Christ who brought immortality and truth. For the Roman church it was freedom from guilt and disruption by the sacrifice of Christ and its sacramental re-enactment. For classical Protestantism the norm was salvation by the grace of God through the atoning work of Christ. For liberal Protestantism it was the personal and social ideals of Jesus as found in the synoptic Gospels. We can add to Tillich's list another example from contemporary thought. For black theology, the norm is the liberating Christ who manifests God's saving action in freeing black people from suffering and oppression.[35]

Here it needs to be noted again that classical theologies did not make the explicit distinction between the universal and the situational dimensions of their thinking that is being made here. Not all modern theologians would be as clear as Paul Tillich is in differentiating between the eternal message and its situational embodiment. We may be sure that in teaching salvation by grace through faith Martin Luther and John Calvin did not think of themselves as speaking simply to their time. The message of grace and forgiveness was the Gospel for all ages. Using the terminology suggested here, they simply combined the universal norm and the situational norm into one material theme. The message they preached to their situation, in their eyes, was the universal Gospel taught in the New Testament. It was relevant then and now and always for everybody. Neither apparently did the Greeks and the Latins in developing their creeds at Nicea in 325 AD and Chalcedon in 451 AD have the sense that they were just trying to be relevant to their own day and time. This was it -- the Bible and all the great theologians have taught this, they said. They were unperturbed by the fact that the categories of Greek metaphysics which they unashamedly used were not the thought forms of the Bible.

Looking back we have a sense of historical relativity which they did not, the heritage to us of the liberal movement of the 19th century. Hence, we are aware that our own theologies are and should be situationally oriented. A new generation will need to make its own statement of the abiding Gospel in a tentative set of categories and themes. We must distinguish, as the classical theologies did not, between the universal norm and the situational norm.

To summarize thus far, two tests must be brought into play:

1. The universal norm which establishes and maintains the identity of the Gospel message through all ages. It is what makes a theology Christian.

2. The <u>situational</u> <u>norm</u> which establishes the relevance of a theology for a particular group under specific circumstances. It is what makes a theology credible and practical in meeting actual human needs here and now.

3. A third norm must now be stated. This is the <u>system-atic</u> <u>norm</u>. Meeting this norm means conforming to the requirements of logic, sound reasoning, and evidence. It guarantees the internal consistency and overall coherence of the total set of ideas. Does a theology hang together as a unified whole without internal con-tradiction or lapses in logic or reasoning? Does it work out its themes on the basis of its announced method, sources, and norms? Does it meet the rules of evidence applicable to religious thought? Does its content rest on the data correctly interpreted to pro-duce sound conclusions in accordance with some articu-lated procedure? This norm guarantees the rational character of theology in terms of both method and con-tent.[36]

Having elaborated two aims of theology to be measured by three norms in order to give them particular attention, it may be useful to say that concretely there is only one end: to state the Christian message for today. There are two dimensions of this single task: the "message" and the "situation." They are not to be separated into two parts of a theological system. They are aspects of a unified purpose: to proclaim the Gospel for here and now. Likewise, the three norms might better be thought of as dimensions of the one standard: Is this the Christian message for today? The universal, the situational, and the systematic aspects belong together to form a <u>Gestalt</u> - an organic whole. We can abstract from the one concrete test these three dimensions. Each is individually definable and relatively autonomous but the three are interdependent and mutually conditional. Each requires and completes the others. A theological perspective may be judged to be inadequate from these three standpoints. (1) Does it proclaim the one Gospel? (2) Is it fitting or appropriate to the situation of the audience being addressed? (3) Is it internally consistent and does it account adequately for all the evidence? Thus, these questions are dimensions of one integrated norm by which we measure whether the single task of articulating the Christian faith credibly and relevantly for a particular setting is being accomplished.

VII. Tensions in Theology

A study of the history of theology shows that two kinds of tensions develop in different theological outlooks.

A. UNITY AND DIVERSITY. On the one hand, Christians recognize one Gospel, one Lord, one faith, one baptism, one Bible, one Savior of us all. On the other hand, this one gospel is presented in many forms and expressions. It would be impossible to list all the varieties of Christian belief that have appeared over the centuries. Just think of a Pentecostal service in a snake-handling cult in the West Virginia mountains and contrast that with an Easter celebration in a Greek Orthodox church in New York City. Consider the difference between Karl Barth lifting up the free and transcendent Lord of the Bible, the Wholly Other, over against Shailer Mathews teaching that God is the concept we have of the "personality-producing factors in the universe."[37] Or, again, contrast St. Augustine referring to humanity as a "mass of perdition," each new baby inheriting both a sinful nature and guilt worthy of hell from Adam and Eve, with the evolutionary picture of Newell Dwight Hillis, an extremely optimistic liberal of the late 19th century, who sees humankind rising upward in inevitable progress toward universal sainthood.[38] Set the omnipotent predestinating God of John Calvin who from exalted transcendence determines in detail the course of history alongside the views of Edward Scribner Ames, who said that God was to religion what Santa Claus was to Christmas.[39] Amid all this diversity and contradiction, where is the unity to be found? In what does it consist? Must some expressions of "Christian" faith and practice be declared null and void so that some principle of unity and universality can be discerned and so that authentic belief can be preserved? Every theology needs some answer to these questions.

B. UNIVERSALITY AND PARTICULARITY. Christians generally hold to a "faith once and for all delivered to the saints." The Gospel is for all people everywhere all the time -- an ecumenical faith and fact. Jesus Christ is "the same yesterday, today, and forever." This is the universal dimension of the message and mission. Yet every embodiment of the Gospel -- every theological system -- is relative to time and place, a fact that is demonstrable easily enough by careful historical inquiry. The thought forms the language, the categories, the symbolic system, the music, etc. -- all these can be shown to be expressive of the surrounding culture. There are, of course, more universal features which endure through many social settings, if they are not completely culture-transcending.

One comparison may suffice to illustrate the tension between universality and particularity. Augustine's THE CITY OF GOD is one of the classic theological works of all time. It was produced in the 5th century toward the end of the Roman Empire. In 410 AD the Goths invaded Rome, who had ruled that part of the world for centuries. It was the Eternal City. The invasion came as a great shock. Many blamed Christianity, which had a century earlier been declared by Emperor Constantine to be the official religion of the Empire. Augustine set out to refute this charge. But after a start in which he tried to demonstrate the absurdity of the accusation, he began to write on the difference between two cities -- the earthly city symbolized by Rome and the heavenly City of God. In history the two are intermingled. He traces the whole history of the world from creation to consummation, from Adam and Eve in the Garden to the saints in the New Jerusalem enjoying the bliss of heaven while the wicked are tormented in hell. The point is that anyone who puts faith in Rome or any earthly city or anything less than God is ultimately doomed to failure, despair, and utter ruin. There are two loves -- the love of the temporal and the love of the eternal, pursuit of earthly glory and pursuit of eternal bliss in the presence of God. Christians have found much that is universally true in this great work. Hardly any book has been more influential outside the Bible in all of Christian history. Yet it clearly bears the marks of particularity and relativity in fundamental ways.

Walter Rauschenbusch lived in the late 19th and early 20th centuries. He experienced the rapid urbanization and industrialization of America with all the attendant social problems this generated, especially for the poor and the working class in the burgeoning cities in a day of crass and often cruel industrial practice. As a minister in a poverty-stricken area of New York City, he came to see the inadequacy of the individualistic piety of Protestant orthodoxy and revivalism. How can we save souls one by one for heaven when the social order is destroying them by the thousands here and now? The situation calls for a "social Gospel," an interpretation of the message of Jesus and the coming of a Kingdom of love which will transform the social structures and institutions of society. Rauschenbusch thought that the biological transmission of moral corruption and guilt from Adam and Eve to all subsequent generations was historically false and theologically repulsive. However, there are superpersonal powers of evil at work in the very fabric of society whose destructive effects are passed on socially from age to age. Hence, at least this remnant of the old doctrine of original sin could be preserved. The whole social order needs to be Christianized, especially the economic realm. The power of love can transform institutions as well as individuals. This remaking of society in accordance with the will of God would constitute the coming of the Kingdom of God--the central theme in the teachings of Jesus.[40]

Augustine and Rauschenbusch proclaimed the same good news of a loving God whose supreme purpose was to establish the City and Kingdom of God. But the common features of the Gospel centered in the same Christ are set within the framework of radically different theological systems. Universal and particular elements are intermingled in ways that both unite and distinguish these two theologies separated by 1500 years of history and theological reflection. Every theology seeks to preach the same Gospel of Jesus Christ -- the one universal message -- but to do so in ways that speak to the situation at hand -- the Gospel for a particular situation. Hence, both the universal norm and the situational norm must be brought into play to test every particular version of the one saving truth for all time.

VII. The Pattern of Theological Development

Fundamental to modern thought is the idea that theologies develop and change. This note has been prominent in the previous discussion. This theme can now be summarized and further spelled out by indicating a pattern in the way theologies arise only to be superceded by novel versions of the Gospel with different accents. A new theological perspective comes into being as a criticism of some established point of view as a result of an encounter with a changing cultural situation and a fresh examination of normative Christian sources, especially the Bible. The pattern is repeated in large and small manifestations. The last 500 years run something like this when terribly compacted and oversimplified: Amid rising currents of modernity, classical Protestant thought arose and later hardened into a scholastic orthodoxy only to be challenged by the appearance of liberalism in the 19th century which subsided as neo-orthodoxy flourished to be succeeded by a variety of outlooks on the current scene. Each of these transitions illustrates the pattern of theological development just stated.

Three assumptions underlie the operation of this pattern. (1) RELATIVITY. All historical phenomena bear the marks of particularity. They reflect the total cultural context in which they appear. A theological professor once remarked that he could listen to someone preach a few times and tell what seminary he or she graduated from and what year! The quip is overdone, but the point is obvious.

(2) DYNAMISM. Things change. What is humanly created can be humanly altered, and it frequently is -- especially in the modern world. Hegel, Marx, and Comte all thought they had discovered the pattern of historical change. Evolution and progress gave the clue to many 18th and 19th century theories of development. At any rate, that things change is a presupposition and expectation that lies deep in the psyche of Western people in the last few centuries.

(3) THE GESTALT DIMENSION. Each epoch or unit (large or small) does tend to have a kind of unity or whole-ness. Certain patterns of thinking tend to cluster together to form a Gestalt. We speak of the Enlighten-ment, the Renaissance, the Romantic movement, of liberal theology, neo-orthodoxy, etc. Without at all denying the diversity and complexity and countermovements in an era, more or less coherent climates of opinion do come and go.

Relativism and dynamism suggest change and diversity, an ever flowing stream. The Gestalt principle
indicates that the complex currents of historical forces
made up of many diverse and shifting tributaries do now
and then converge to form a configuration that has some
order, pattern, unity, and analyzable wholeness. In
this light we can understand the unity and variety that
are present in the Christian phenomenon in history. The
universal and particular elements that enter into each
theological outlook can be interpreted within this
frame- work. And this is why theologies must be tested
by reference to both a universal norm and a situational
norm. All of this is connected with and explains why
there is a two-fold task of theology: to proclaim the
message of the one Gospel and to relate it to some
particular cultural context.

The recognition of relativity, dynamism, and the
Gestalt factor is itself the legacy to us of the 18th
and 19th centuries. They form part of the historical
consciousness of modern human beings. The theological
significance that needs highlighting is the two-fold
consciousness that (1) all theologies are historically
relative and that (2) an enormous gap exists between the
thought world of the Bible and that of the modern age.
Much of the creative work of the past two centuries has
struggled with the implications of these two facts. The
problems they pose still constitute a central challenge
of theological method today.

The conceptual gap between the Bible and modernity
raises the question as to whether a modern person can be
a Christian. The relativity of all theologies chal-

lenges theology to say whether there is an abiding essence of Christianity. Each issue requires further examination.

A. CHRISTIANITY AND THE MODERN MIND. It is probably not an exaggeration to say that the fundamental question of theology since about 1750 has been the compatibility of Christianity and the modern mind. Can one be "an intelligent modern and a serious Christian"? In answering this question theology has faced a basic dilemma. It can focus on the situation and strive to be credible and relevant -- risking the loss of the universal message. Or it can focus on the message once and for all delivered -- risking loss of contact with the situation to which it is speaking. Modernistic liberalism and the death of God theologies illustrate the first danger.[41] Orthodoxy, fundamentalism, and even the sophisticated neo-orthodoxy of Karl Barth are subject to the second peril.

Recent centuries are filled with efforts to avoid both dangers and to state the universal Gospel in credible terms to the modern ear. Harry Emerson Fosdick suggested that we center on "abiding experiences" and live with the fact of "changing categories." Rudolf Bultmann proposed that we demythologize the New Testament by getting behind its supernaturalistic framework to discover the understanding of human existence before God contained in the out-moded pre-scientific myths of the ancient world.[42] Paul Tillich urges us to analyze the immediate cultural situation to discover the religious questions people are asking. Then we can go to the Bible and Christian tradition to get answers whose content can be stated in the form dictated by the culturally-posed questions. Karl Barth is the great dissenter in 20th century theology to the proposal of Tillich and others that we start with humanity and the contemporary scene. Instead, he urges us to let our cultural situation be the medium through which the Word of God comes to us, but not a second source of truth or even of questions alongside revelation. Both question and answer come to us from Beyond. The theological task is solely and wholly to listen to the Word to which the Bible gives witness. Natural theology, based culturally, can only produce idolatrous distortions. It expresses a sinful refusal of humanity to accept God's grace. Yet even Barth recognizes that theology can only be stated in culturally-produced forms of expression. Philosophy and reason can be servants of faith in articulating the Word from God. Moreover, the accents of his own theology have changed by his own admission because different emphases are needed depending on the circumstances.[43] Hence, in his own way he does take the situation into court.

B. IS THERE AN ESSENCE OF CHRISTIANITY? Most modern theologies assume that there is some universal essence of Christianity which can be abstracted from its original conceptual embodiment in the Bible and rephrased in contemporary idiom. The implication is that we can speak of the Gospel, some abiding core, some generic essentials of a universal kerygma which constitutes the faith once and for all delivered to the saints. But can we? What is it? How can it possibly be expressed in a way that does not become just one more historically relative statement? Can form and content be so neatly separated that the universal message can be set forth in innumerable expressions? Some have given up the quest as impossible in the nature of the case. Of these one group simply identifies Christianity with the history of its development. It is whatever it has become. This view was found in the history of religions school in Germany around the turn of the 20th century.[44] Shailer Mathews concluded that a Christian was anyone who had ever claimed to be.[45] John Cobb has urged us to give up the search for the content essence of Christianity. What is essential is not some abiding core of doctrines but the principle and process of "creative transformation" revealed in Christ. This is the universal element in the Gospel. On this basis the various world religions can go "beyond dialogue" and become open to being mutually transformed in quest of a more complete and whole truth not found anywhere in the past.[46]

Once again a dilemma is posed. If Christianity is simply identical with its history and is equally valid in all its expressions, then relativity seems triumphant. If there is no universal norm by which particular expressions can be judged, then Christian identity is lost. The unity disappears in the variety. But the ideal of a universal essence which can be defined and agreed upon by all does seem to be a hopeless quest which has never been and probably never will be realized. The New Testament itself does not explicitly set forth such a core of generic essentials and probably does not even contain such a unity, whether defined in terms of beliefs or anything else. The New Testament writers do agree on the formal proclamation that Jesus is the Christ. Morever, common themes do appear: the Old Testament promises are fulfilled, the New Age is breaking into history in the person and work of Jesus, and people are called upon to repent, accept the Good News, and be obedient to the righteousness of the dawning Kingdom. But these themes are variously stated, and contrasting theological interests, perspectives, and categories abound. Compare Romans with James or Revelation, the Gospel of John with Mark, and Luke with II Timothy. Moreover, every historical attempt to locate or define or even point to some universal essence represents in part the viewpoint of the interpreter and not a simple reading off of what is objectively and demonstrably there. What George Tyrrell said about Adolf Harnack, who made a popular effort to define the essence of Christianity around the turn of the century,[47] is true of all such attempts. Harnack, he said, looked deeply into the well of history to see what was at the bottom. When the waters got still, what did he see? He saw "only the reflection of a liberal Protestant face."[48] In part, at least, we always get out of our search for the generic features of the true Gospel what we put in.

Is there a third way between the futile quest for one pure unified objective essence and the dissolution of Christian faith in a morass of subjectivism and relativism? Perhaps it is enough to claim that the Gestalt of a contemporary theology is derived from the kaleidoscopic message of Biblical religion or that it participates in the differentiated complex of the New Testament witness. It is too much to claim that anyone's outlook reproduces the essence, as if there were such a thing anyway. But any representation of the Gospel must justify its Gestalt on the basis of the original set of witnesses to Jesus as the Christ found in the Scriptures. The norm is to be found in the center and vicinity of that source,[49] although it is not defined with singularity and precision there or anywhere else. Each interpreter here and now has to develop a functioning norm in the encounter of the Biblical witness and the contemporary situation. This is what has happened throughout church history, as Paul Tillich has pointed out. Every such norm will unite features found in the Bible with elements derived from the situation. Christians will doubtless still argue over what does or does not belong to or participate in the universal dimension of the Gospel message. But these debates will be more realistic if the idea of a single, pure, definable, objective essence is surrendered in favor of the idea of a variegated configuration of New Testament themes developed around the unifying confession that Jesus is the Christ. We all "have this treasure in earthen vessels, to show that the transcendent power belongs to God and not to us" (II Cor. 4:7 RSV). And the Bible is always there as the locus of the norm of authentic Christian thought. In the light of this universal point of reference, particular theologies can be created, judged, corrected, and recreated.

To summarize, the underlying assumption of modern theological methodology is this: SOMETHING ABIDES, SOMETHING CHANGES. Hence, the perennial question is WHICH IS WHICH, AND HOW DO WE KNOW?

The following chapters focus both on the abiding themes that Christians over the centuries have continually reaffirmed, while at the same time noting how both the form and the content of the Gospel have received numerous contrasting and even conflicting embodiments.

IX.   Theology, Belief and Faith

It may be useful at the end of this chapter to bring together a number of themes that have been introduced by taking one final look at what theology is and does. By now it is obvious how complex an enterprise theology is. No brief definition can take into account all of its facets, especially given the fact that the focus varies from one theologian to another. Most of the complications have now been introduced. It is now time to summarize and integrate many of these strands of thought.

A place to begin is to look once more at the short definition of theology given at the outset. Theology is the activity in which Christians reflect upon and express what they have experienced or believe. It should be clear by now that while this way of putting it is true as far as it goes, it is not totally satisfactory. It is certainly not complete. Experience is of something. Beliefs are about something. Reflection and articulation occur in a context. There are sources and there are norms of theological thought. A full delineation of what theology is and does has to take into account many factors. In the midst of it all are persons existing in communities who have faith in God as revealed in Jesus Christ and who are seeking understanding by the guidance of the Holy Spirit.

Four summary points can help put all this together. 1. Theology takes place in a community. Individual believers and theologians are surrounded by fellow Christians. Some of them are living, and others make up "the great cloud of witnesses" (Hebrews 12:1) who have gone on before. Theology takes place within the church with its inherited ways of believing. Even an individual reflecting alone in search of a personal credo is surrounded by these witnesses, the fellow believers past and present who reason about faith. To stray too far from this community and its beliefs is not only to become a heretic but to place oneself outside the Christian circle. This fact provides one way of defining theology. Theology is a work of the church by which it articulates its faith. But who is authorized to carry out this task? Individuals working alone under the guidance of the Holy Spirit? The church itself as a whole through its authorized teachers in an official capacity with an infallible Pope at its head? Or is theology the expression of the faith of a particular communion -- such as the Lutheran or Reformed Church? Theologians and church bodies could argue over this for centuries, although even Baptists have their communal confessions of faith while individual Catholic theologians take issue with the official teachings of the Church.

2. Theology is grounded in sources and tested by norms. Theological knowledge comes from somewhere and is measured by something. Theological perspectives divide over the authority to be assigned to revelation, to reason, and to experience. More particularly they divide over how to relate the "message" side with its

"givens" from revelation, Scripture, and tradition to the "situation" side formed by reason and experience operating within a given cultural setting. Where does one start, and how does one move toward the other? Karl Barth defines theology as the work of the church by which it examines its witness in the light of the revealed Word of God found in the Bible -- in any situation.[50] Paul Tillich urges us to start with the "situation" and then correlate questions that arise with the answers derived from the "message" contained in Scripture.[51] Hence, we get two basic definitions of theology: (1) It is a setting forth of the contents of Christian faith. (2) Or it is reflection on human existence and experience in the light of Christian symbols. Today it is typical to insist on the unity and interrelatedness of these two poles of theology.[52]

The recognition of the "situational" pole of theology is an indication that theology takes place in two contexts -- the church with its inherited givens of revelation, the Bible, and tradition and a particular societal setting with its own ways of understanding reality and human existence. As H. Richard Niebuhr puts it the believer has to relate the claims of "Christ" and "culture."[53] A Christian is both a "believer in the church" and a "self in the world." Reason and experience are shaped by the cultural consciousness of a given era. Each cultural epoch has its own mentality, its own characteristic ways of believing, feeling, valuing, and of measuring what is important. A culture has an ethos -- a qualitative feel for what matters as well as convictions about what is real. All the way through this book it will be apparent that the modern consciousness has brought about profound changes in theology. A revolution occurred in the 18th and 19th centuries which sets the modern period over against all previous forms of theological thinking. The reason why most people today are so horrified at Calvin's doctrine of predestination is not that the Bible has changed but that cultural consciousness has changed. The current search for feminine images of God and for equalitarian motifs in the Bible proceeds more from a culturally-aroused consciousness than from a belated discovery of what our forefathers have been telling us all along! In the whole of Christian tradition women are, with few exceptions, seen in a subordinate role. It may well be that the full equality of men and women and the rejection of exclusively male symbols of God are demanded by what is deepest and ultimately normative in Scripture, but the majority of Biblical texts teach otherwise. Slavery, persecution of heretics, and all sorts of cruelties have been justified by Bible-quoting theologians. The reason we reject these evils and assign different weights to a whole range of values, including sexual morality and the rights of sexual minorities, is in part that cultural consciousness has led us to a reevaluation of traditional and even Biblical practices. Theology, then, is always in conversation with culture, and the relationship would seem to be one of mutual transformation.

3. The ultimate reference points of theology are God, humanity, and the cosmos (creation). This is what theology is about. Hence, theology literally means reasoning about God -- the creative and redemptive acts of the Maker of Heaven and Earth. As Calvin said, true and substantial wisdom consists in knowing God and ourselves.[54] An investigation of either one leads to

the other and to the relationship between them. But theology is concerned with God, humanity, and the creation primarily from an existential or practical point of view and not as objects of disinterested inquiry. Theology deals with matters of ultimate meaning. It is concerned with salvation. Its theoretical inquiries are necessary, but they are instrumental to the elucidation of faith, hope, and love and their embodiment in the lives of people.

4. Theology presupposes individuals and communities of faith. Theology can be defined as reasoning about faith or as faith seeking understanding or as the explication of the contents of Christian faith. This important term requires definition. Three meanings need to be distinguished.

a. Faith, first of all, defines the personal relationship between the self and God. In this context it means trust, confidence, faithfulness, fidelity, loyalty -- the response of persons to a trustworthy, loving, gracious, forgiving, merciful God. It means surrendering one's whole being to God, who is experienced as worthy of this ultimate commitment. This is the fundamental meaning of faith from which all others spring.

b. Faith may also refer to what is believed. Here faith means the same thing as message, beliefs, ideas about God, humanity, and the world -- the conceptual content of Christian theology. In definition a, faith means "believing in," while in b, it means "believing that." Trust in God presupposes that there is a trustworthy God who actually exists, so that the statements "God exists" and "God is trustworthy" are true. But trust (belief in) and belief (belief that) are not the same. When theology sets forth faith as beliefs, it presupposes faith as trust.

c. A third meaning of faith concerns its epistemological status. It combines or shifts back and forth between the first two. Here we deal with the element of uncertainty that attends faith. Faith suggests that one can never be sure. Uncertainty can be attached to both trust (a) and belief (b). We cannot prove that God is trustworthy or that God is real. Hence, we trust and believe in the presence of uncertainty. So far, so good. But at this point things get complicated. Faith can be strong or weak or wavering. It can be mixed with or alternate with doubt in various combinations. We need some clarifications and distinctions. "Being sure" has two elements. On the one hand, it has to do with the degree of subjective confidence one has. This we can call <u>certitude</u>. On the other hand, it relates to the degree and possibility of objective demonstrability of actual fact -- the extent to which we can absolutely determine what is the case as truth about reality. Here we are concerned with the possibility of establishing correspondence between subjective beliefs and objective reality. This we can call <u>certainty</u>. Obviously, no degree of subjective confidence (certitude) can guarantee or establish absolute knowledge of objective truth (certainty). The possession of truth about God with apodictic finality transcends human possibilities. Religious belief is never quite synonymous with knowledge.

At the communal level tension arises between relativism and absoluteness. In the modern world communal faiths, whether Marxism, Christianity, Buddhism, or whatever, are regarded as ideologies of particular groups. Their truth is conditioned and relative, having no claim to universality or absoluteness. A kind of social subjectivism attaches to these communal credos. In previous centuries when Christian symbols provided the structure of truth for the whole culture as well as for the church, theidiosyncratic, particularistic, and relativistic feature of faith were not a part of the consciousness of the believer as is the case today.

To say, "I believe" is a complex phenomenon. It has become evident even in this brief discussion that faith occurs in the context of several polarities and tensions. (1) Communality and individuality. On the one hand, to be a Christian believer is to participate in and confess the common faith of the community. It is to identify oneself with the church and its faith. And it is to submit oneself to communal tradition, authority, and discipline. On the other hand, belief is an individual matter which expresses personal autonomy. It is a choice freely made which can be revoked. In this context a critical spirit prevails in which one claims the right to question church dogma and to work for revision of both belief and practice. In extreme cases, both the community and the individual may have to make decisions as to whether one is "in" or "out" of the church. When does heresy become intolerable? When does the constructive reformer become a destructive revolutionary?

(2) Absolutism and relativism. On the one hand, faith intends to be in correspondence with truth. One believes in God because God is real and trustworthy. In this sense faith makes universal and absolutist claims. Reality is what it is, and it is the same for everybody. On the other hand, modern Christians have an awareness that their faith is one among many belief systems in the world, none of which has sole claim to universal and absolute truth. Christianity is a particular religion relative to Western civilization. In this context we become consciously confessional and say, "Christ is final for me, the norm of truth for me, but I cannot say that other religions or philosophies are false."

(3) Certitude and doubt. On the one hand, at its heights faith is confident assurance. We <u>know</u> in whom we have believed. We believe that our beliefs are true. On the other hand, skepticism may enter as the consciousness dawns that subjective confidence cannot guarantee objective truth. As certitude weakens, doubt arises and may completely crowd out faith. Faith and doubt gradually replace each other in converse proportions along a sliding scale that moves from certitude toward uncertainty and back.

The awareness of the gap between certitude and certainty has given rise in some quarters tothe view that faith is belief that rests upon weak evidence. Belief is then contrasted with knowledge to the detriment of the former. Faith, on this view, is an act of will that moves the intellect to trust or assent to something where knowledge is not available. Assent may be given either in the absence of (or contrary to?) evidence or on the basis of unassailable authority --

Scripture, tradition, the church, or whatever. It is typical today to criticize this view of faith as false or inadequate. While this may be the case, who can deny that it may be descriptive of the way faith actually functions in the lives of some Christians? Faith may be strong where knowledge is not available or understanding is not possible.

It is possible, however, to interpret faith epistemologically as rational perspective rather than as unsupported belief. While religious truth cannot be universally demonstrated or proven beyond reasonable doubt to all competent inquirers, neither can any philosophy that deals with ultimate matters of faith. Faith can be rational in the sense of generating a set of beliefs that are internally coherent and that are congruent with available evidence. Faith is not belief that exceeds or contradicts evidence but is a rational perspective which is required by the evidence. Faith arises in an intuition in which all the available data fall into place around some organizing center in a coherent vision that accounts for all the known facts. As Augustine said, "I believe in order that I may know." Faith is illumination which provides reason with the interpretive principles and organizing insights that enable it to give a rational account of reality. It is not contrary to reason but is its underlying integrative center. In the Augustinian-Anselmic tradition, faith provides the clue to reality on the basis of which reason can do its work of giving a coherent interpretation of relevant facts. Christian faith, then, is a perspective on reality, an orientation to the world. The truth of this perspective can only be verified by those who stand within the circle of faith.

Metaphysical systems can be evaluated only from within some circle of faith and not from some universal perspective which transcends particular ideologies. Everybody has a point of view, from which every other set of truth claims appears to be false or inadequate. In this sense, everybody who speaks about God speaks on the basis of faith, that is, a particular orientation or outlook. Any judgment about the truth or falsity of a set of religious beliefs proceeds from faith, that is, some perspective which determines what the relevant criteria of truth are. Theology, then, which explicates the meaning and content of Christian faith does not violate the canons of rationality that are applicable to metaphysical philosophy. It only makes explicit its faith (point of orientation), whereas some allegedly rational philosophies hide or ignore their particular orientation by simply identifying their "faith" (perspective) with truth.[55]

To summarize and to end this discussion, theology can be defined as reflection upon and articulation of Christian belief. It can equally well be viewed as faith seeking understanding. The fundamental theme of Christian belief is the reality of God. The following chapter turns to that topic in an effort to set forth the understanding of God to which Christian faith gives rise.

CHAPTER II
GOD, CREATION AND PROVIDENCE

I.   The God-Problem

Why do people speak of God anyway? In a general way the answer is that they do so for theoretical reasons and for practical reasons.

A.   PHILOSOPHICAL-METAPHYSICAL. People sometimes make reference to God in order to complete an interpretation of reality. God is a theoretical requirement of reason in its attempt to give a full account of what is. Aristotle and Aquinas illustrate this point. Beginning with the observation that things move and change, they reasoned that it was necessary finally to posit an Unmoved Mover or a First Cause to explain the simple fact of motion and other changes in the observable world. Reasoning like this constitutes the cosmological argument for the existence of God. Others have advanced similar ideas to explain the fact of order and purpose in the world -- the teleological arguments which lead to the postulation of an Ultimate Designer. Underlying both types of reasoning is a larger assumption that finitude (the realm of ordinary, limited things) is insufficient to account for itself. A complete explanation of things requires reference to something infinite, eternal, unlimited -- some necessary, self-existent Being or Purposer. Again, there are those who claim that the very idea of God as a Being so great that no greater can be conceived includes and implies the existence of God. The most perfect being imaginable necessarily _is_. This is the ontological argument advanced in its classical form by Anselm and debated in nearly every century since. Immanuel Kant argued that the fact of moral obligation experienced by everybody requires the postulation of freedom, God, and immorality in order to give a rational account of it all. Moral arguments for God have been popular in modern philosophy and theology. In each of these instances philosophers have concluded that God is real because correct reasoning leads convincingly to that conclusion.

B. RELIGIOUS-EXISTENTIAL. In this setting people speak of God not out of theoretical considerations but for practical reasons. God is sought or responded to as One who saves life from fundamental threats of meaninglessness, sin, guilt, anxiety, suffering, and death. God is relied on for courage, hope, liberation, and ultimate salvation. The theoretical search of reason leads to the postulation of some Unconditioned Power or Supreme Being. The practical search of people has as its object some Powerful Redeemer or Ultimate Compassion -- the final source of human and universal good in the universe. God and humanity belong together as partners and companions. Augustine said in a prayer, "Thou hast made us for Thyself, and we are restless until we find our rest in Thee." Scrawled in almost illegible handwriting on the walls of a Georgia jail were these words, "There is no God." Surely this negative conclusion was not primarily the conclusion of abstract reasoning but emerged out of a sense of despair and hopelessness. There is nothing ultimate to rely on -- no ground of hope beyond ourselves in a Boundless Love, no Cosmic Friend on whom to call in the midst of misery, pain, and anguish. People who affirm or deny God in this context are speaking not as disinterested spectators who want to understand the world in a theoretical way but as involved participants in life whose quest is practical, existential, and religious. They may reason about God or look to their own experience or consult a sacred book such as the Bible or join a community of seekers or simply meditate, but their intention is to find salvation and hope in the midst of a dangerous or lonely world. Sometimes deliverance, faith, and courage find them and are experienced as a gift from Beyond. In this case the response may take the form of praise, joy, gratitude, and a desire to tell other people the good news or to express thanksgiving by loving and helping others in need.

The theoretical and practical dimensions of the quest for God are distinguishable for purpose of analysis, but they need not be separated in the lives of people. They may be, and the interest may be primarily in one or the other. Whitehead remarked that Aristotle did not go very far in producing a God "available for religious purposes,"[1] while in turn a critic questioned "the religious availability of Whitehead's God."[2] The Bible is full of language about God, but it is clear that the interest is primarily religious. Little or no disinterested speculation about ultimate matters of fact is in evidence. Theology, likewise, has as its starting and ending point the existential implications of the reality of God. If philosophy has as its task objective inquiry into the nature of ultimate reality as such, then theology asks about the meaning of God for us.[3] Obviously, however, the two interests are interdependent. Theology cannot do its work without examining the philosophical questions related to the factuality and nature of God as such. To take an extreme example, if there is no God, then God can have no meaning for our existence.

But let us note that whether the term God is used in a theoretical or practical setting, it functions as a FINAL REFERENT WORD. In the musical OKLAHOMA, the lyrics of one song said that in Kansas City they have "gone about as fur as they can go" -- seven storey buildings, cars that go 20 MPH, and things like that! In philosophy and theology, when you refer to God, you have gone about as far as you can go. There is nothing beyond God, since if there were, that which is beyond would be God. Generally speaking, in terms of its usage in Western thought, the term God is reserved for that supreme level of analysis, for that reality reference which is final, that which by definition there is no going beyond. To put it differently, God is the CATEGORY OF THE ULTIMATE. Hence, whether designated as the Creator, the One, the All, the Unconditioned, the Absolute, Being-itself, or some other name, God is the final and ultimate reality, transcending in eminence, power, and value everything else.

Central to Christian thought is the affirmation that the Supreme Reality (ultimate in being or power) is also the Savior (ultimate in goodness). The Creator and the Redeemer are one and the same. God (Omnipotent Power) is love (Perfect Goodness). The Gospel is that the Ruler of All Things has created a good world and intends to bring all of creation to a final Consummation at the end in which all evil is put down in a Kingdom of righteousness and happiness. A reading of Isaiah 40-45 and Romans 1-8 will show vividly how the idea of God as the sovereign Creator united to the idea of God as the gracious and loving Savior who has compassion on sinful and suffering humanity and takes steps to save them from

their own folly and pride as well as from their bondage
to oppressive powers. In Biblical religion, then, the
love of God revealed in Christ is the Ultimate Power in
the universe, so that saving faith is directed toward an
utterly reliable Savior (Rom. 8:18-39). In this sense
the Christian God stands at the end of both the
theoretical and the practical search for ultimacy.

II. Belief in God in the Modern World

Belief in God has become problematic for many
people in the modern world. In joy or despair or with
an indifferent shrug, God has been declared dead by
large numbers of learned intellectuals and ordinary
people. A few atheists, skeptics, and agnostics have
always been a part of Western societies, but in the last
few centuries their numbers have vastly increased. Many
have proffered the generalization of Dietrich Bonhoeffer
that beginning somewhere around the 13th century AD a
movement began which has brought about a situation in
which humanity "has learned to cope with all questions
of importance without recourse to God as a working
hypothesis."[4] People are no longer dependent on
religion, where religion means (1) a reference to God as
the ultimate explanation of matters of fact and (2) a
way of solving the existential problems of guilt,
suffering, anxiety, meaninglessness, and death. Note
that Bonhoeffer said that both the theoretical and the
practical reasons people have turned to God have ceased
to be compelling.

This is not the place to review in detail the loss
of the religious premise as the undergirding assumption
of Western culture. Suffice it to say that a secular

society has arisen as a combination of two interrelated sets of factors. (1) One configuration of intellectual forces led to the conclusion that belief in God is both incredible to the mind and irrelevant for life. (2) A companion cluster of movements resulted in a focus on this life as the locus of meaning and on humankind as the sole subject and agent of history. Roughly, these two generators of theoretical and practical atheism can be summarized under the headings of science and secularization.[5] Science seemed to imply that nature is a complex, non-purposive network of interacting causal forces which can be fully or at least satisfactorily explained without any necessary reference to a Transcendent Source or Purpose. From the Renaissance through the Enlightenment and beyond attention shifted away from an otherworldly focus toward the meaning and destiny of life in this world. Associated with this was a growing confidence that humanity could direct history toward a future of increasing prosperity and happiness. Science, technology, and the development of humane reason were the basic elements which undergirded the faith in progress. Nature as a purposeless or at least neutral and self-explanatory process and history as the realm of human autonomy -- these are the fundamental ingredients in the world-view produced by the interdependent forces of science and secularization.[6] August Comte, Ludwig Fuerbach, Karl Marx, Friedrich Nietzsche, Sigmund Freud, John Dewey, Albert Camus, Jean-Paul Sartre, Bertrand Russell, Julian Huxley, A.J. Ayer -- these influential names suggest the varieties of naturalism, positivism, humanism, and existentialism that have shaped the thought of Europe and America during the last 150 years. Hence, Henri de Lubac could write that "the peoples of the West are denying their Christian past and turning away from God."[7]

The following types of modern atheism suggest the variety that characterizes unbelief in the modern world. This list is illustrative but not exhaustive.

1. THE SCIENTIFIC, PRAGMATIC, TECHNOLOGICALLY ORIENTED PERSON. This type is practical, down to earth, more indifferent to religious questions than in opposition. Metaphysical debates, grand world-views, and religious beliefs are a waste of time. Life is a set of problems to be solved, not a set of mysteries to be explored. Science and technology are our best hopes for dealing with real life issues, while religion is irrelevant.[8]

2. THE SCIENTIFIC HUMANIST. This group is closely allied to the first but is more self-conscious about having a world-view. The only reality is nature, and the only way to know nature is through scientific method. God is an unnecessary hypothesis in this system. So naturalistic philosophy is wedded to a devotion to humanly created and achieved values and goals.[9]

3. THE EMPIRICAL PHILOSOPHER AND LINGUISTIC ANALYST. The word God is dead, since there is no empirical referent by which assertions about God can be tested. The only meaningful sentences about matters of fact are those for which some observation is relevant to the determination of its truth and falsity. Language about God cannot meet the test of empirical verification and so is just plain meaningless.[10]

4. THE ATHEISTIC EXISTENTIALIST. This group is more serious about life and flirts with despair in the face of a purposeless, cold, silent universe. Humanity makes itself by its free choices in a world into which we are inexplicably thrown for no reason. There are no objective standards of value or morality. All is humanly created in an otherwise meaningless world so that the fundamental question is whether we should commit suicide.[11]

5. THE ORDINARY, COMMON SENSE SECULARIST. A number of people strikingly different from each other have simply come to a point in which God, religion, church, and ultimate questions are a matter of indifference. God is dead in an experiential and practical way apart from any particular commitment to any specific world view. Life is just getting by and doing the best you can. The life situations and emotional dispositions may vary widely from poor to rich and from happy to sad, from optimism to pessimism, and so on. They agree in being able to live without any intentional reference to religion or God.

A statement by an imaginary composite of the "modern secular person" might run something like this:

> Why should I believe in God? Not only is there no agreement among the world's religions and philosophies about the existence and nature of God, but belief in God seems impossible and irrelevant in a scientific age. Why not just take the universe as it is without asking for further

explanation? Science can get along without the hypothesis of God, and philosophers have never proven anything. Besides, being religious does not seem necessary to achieving happiness and solving any real human problems. What does adding God to anything do to change what is happening anyway? Food is produced by soil, seed, and climate along with human effort. Weather is produced by scientifically known forces that are highly predictable. Wars are won by those with the largest army or the most efficient weapons. Diseases are caused and cured by natural processes that science can investigate. Mental illness can be diagnosed and treated. The world seems to run by itself affected only by natural and human forces. How does believing in God matter? What is God doing, if anything? I am committed to freedom, equality, justice and happiness for all people everywhere, I do my best to champion good causes. People need food and love and care, which people can provide by using their best knowledge. Does God plant any seed, cure any diseases, provide loving caring arms in addition to what happens by itself in nature or is done by human beings? I don't see that belief in God has any practical usefulness, and I can live my life fully and do my work without any reference to that word or reality. What can a theologian say to my questions?

In answering these questions, it is necessary to turn back to the previous chapter which showed how modern theologians have appealed to various combinations of revelation, reason, and experience as sources of truth about God.

The catastrophes of the 20th century have shaken the confidence in evolutionary progress which was the hope of the preceding period. But the underlying naturalism and humanism continue to be powerful. Recently some interpreters have begun to say that the science-based secularization of recent centuries is itself just one more historically relative epoch which too shall pass and not the culmination of a process whereby humanity has at last grown up to maturity.[12] 20th century science, whatever the case may have been earlier, neither requires nor implies atheism. Moreover, the experiential bases and need of humanity for sustaining relationship to the environing cosmos and its Ultimate Ground remain as the perennially valid foundations of religion. Finally, millions of believers do still find insight and inspiration in their faith. However, the impact of modernity on theology has been profound and lasting. This has already become apparent in the preceding chapter dealing with the sources and norms of Christian truth. It will be in evidence in every succeeding chapter as well. In particular, theologians have been concerned to develop doctrines of creation, providence, and prayer which do not offend the seemingly assured results of scientific inquiry. Supernaturalism, other-worldliness, and divine interventions into the causal order (miracles) have frequently been rejected out of a concern to be credible in a secular age. The question of how the God of the Bible who acts in salvific ways in nature and history can be interpreted to the scientific-secularized consciousness in ways which both preserve the "message" and speak to the "situation" is basic to modern theology.

This chapter will set forth Biblical and classical views of God. It will also indicate how the impact of the modern world has led to some basic changes in the traditional models.

III. Language About God

The "oddness of godness" creates notoriously difficult problems with respect to how people can speak of God. The "oddness" is found in the fact that God is not simply one more of the many finite things that make up the world of time and space. God is not just another being only bigger, better, stronger, and longer lasting. The difference between God and ordinary things -- or even the sum total of them in the whole universe -- is not just very great but infinite. God is a radically different kind of reality from everything else. In speaking of God we refer to another realm--the realm of ultimacy -- where the usual rules do not hold. Note some of the traditional distinctions. (1) God is self-existent, uncreated, independent - the aseity of God. Other beings are not self-existent. They are created, utterly dependent on God. (2) God is eternal, does not come into being or pass away. In fact, the usual view has been that God completely transcends time and unlike us does not live from one moment to another. Finite things are temporal. They have a beginning and an end. We have a past, a present, and a future. (3) God is not located somewhere in a particular space. In that sense God is nowhere. God transcends space, encompasses all places. In that sense God is everywhere. Other things are somewhere, in some local space. (4) God's being is necessary. God cannot not be. We are contingent. We are, but we might not have been. To summarize, God is the source, the ground, the underlying cause and reason for everything else, that on which everything else absolutely depends but which depends absolutely on nothing else. Such words as unconditioned, absolute, infinite, eternal, necessary, Being-itself, etc. have been used to refer to this unique reality. The point is that the Creator cannot be spoken of in the same way as the creation.

In fact, skeptics from Carneades to David Hume have claimed that theists are in an impossible dilemma.[13] They are caught between empty abstractions which preserve divine absoluteness and concrete references which finitize God. Is God-language limited to literal but formal designations empty of specific content, on the one hand, and non-literal categories which say something definite but whose truth status is vague and dubious, on the other hand? To say that God is ultimate, absolute, transcendent, unconditioned, and uncreated may be true but religiously of limited value. To say "The Lord is my Shepherd" is comforting to the believer, but in what sense is it true? The truth content or cognitive meaning appears to be problematic or at least vague. Is there any way out of this dilemma?

It is impossible to review all the ways this problem has been dealt with over the centuries. Some of the discussions get quite complex, subtle, and technical. But perhaps enough can be said to indicate the main options and some particularly noteworthy themes. Let us begin with the assumption that some high level abstractions can be used to designate the kind of reality God is or possesses which are literally true. They mean just what they say and do not point beyond themselves. Such designations at least distinguish God from other beings. They locate God properly in terms of the kind of reality God is. In that sense they are useful, meaningful and necessary. God is infinite, necessary, absolute, independent, uncreated, immutable, eternal. This doesn't say much that is concrete, particular, and specific. We need to say more if we are to know how God is related to us and how we can have a meaningful relationship to God. The religious life requires more than these relatively empty abstractions.

Thomas Aquinas developed the notion of analogy.[14] Analogy stands between univocal statements which have the same meaning in two different settings and equivocal terms which have completely different senses. To say that Plato is a person and that Aristotle is a person is to use the term person in a univocal sense. To refer to the King of England on the throne and the king on the checkerboard is to speak equivocally. King has two different meanings in that case. Aquinas thought there was a middle way which he called analogical predication. If we say God is rational or just or loving, the meaning is not univocal or equivocal but analogical. There is something in God and in us which is common to terms like rationality or justice or love, but the shared feature is possessed in different proportions. Likewise, there is proportionality between the necessary being of God and the contingent being of other things. The proper or primary designation of these terms is God. We are like God or reflect the perfection of God. God is being in the true sense. God's being is necessary. Our being is contingent and derivative. But being applies in both cases, so that there is an analogy between God and us which language can express.

Paul Tillich has stated a similar point of view.[15] Only one literal statement can be made: God is Being-itself. This statement and its equivalents (God is the Unconditioned, etc.) mean just what they say in a univocal way. All other statements are symbolic. They point beyond themselves, but at the same time they participate in the reality they symbolize. It is proper to speak of God as personal, as living, as related to us, and as acting, as long as we do not take the ideas literally and provided they are balanced appropriately with other symbols as the need arises.

At this point some other terms need to be introduced: myth, metaphor, and parable.[16] Myth in common usage may mean fictitious or imaginary. Among historians of religion, however, it means stories about the gods or God in relation to the world and human beings. Divine beings are spoken of in quite anthropo-morphic terms. They are born and die and may be reborn. They act, but often in supernatural or miraculous ways. They may even create and destroy worlds. Rudolf Bultmann referred to the importance of myth in the Bible.[17] Myth means two things here. (1) It is a pre-scientific way of thinking which assumes a three-storied world populated by supernatural beings--divine and demonic--who affect and interact with human beings. The creation stories of the Bible, the virgin birth, the bodily resurrection of Jesus, the last judgment and the end of the world, etc. are "mythological" in this sense. (2) But myth is also a way of speaking of divine transcendence in spatial terms, i.e., God is in heaven. Myth speaks of the other world in terms of this world. Bultmann proposes that we "demythologize" by discovering the religious and existential meaning contained in these myths. The myths are not literally true, but they tell us exactly what our relationship to God is like. In this connection Bultmann says that to speak of God is to speak of ourselves. To speak of God acting refers to events in our personal existence. Biblical myths are not to be interpreted as cosmic events which are true apart from our involvement in them. Their meaning and intent are practical and existential. Our speech about God acting is to be understood analogically. The relationships between God and humanity are in strict analogy with relationships between two human beings. Biblical myths teach us that God is related to us in a personal way. We are addressed, blessed, judged, confronted, loved, forgiven, etc. by God. These are real experiences of God here and now. In this sense, language about God acting is not symbolic. Rather the words are to be taken in their full and direct meaning. Biblical myths, while not literally true in a scientific or theoretical sense, clarify the nature of our relationship to God here and not in our own personal existence. In a similar fashion Reinhold Niebuhr is well known for his statement that eschatological and other myths in the Bible are to be taken "seriously but not literally."[18] They contain meanings essential to Christian understanding, but they are not factually true.

Metaphor simply means a term that suggests a likeness but not exact correspondence. The 23rd Psalm uses the metaphor of shepherd to speak of God's kind and caring relationship to us, but everyone understands that the words indicate a meaningful but non-literal comparison between a shepherd and the sheep and God and us. A parable tells an ordinary story that also has religious meaning. Symbol is used in a wide variety of senses ranging from a loose suggestion of a metaphor to a more technical frame of reference in which it becomes identical with analogy. In every case a symbol is something which points beyond itself.

What are the relationships among analogy, myth, and metaphor? Do they differ in cognitive status from each other? Is the difference between analogy and metaphor a real one? If real, is it a matter of degree or of kind? To put it differently, are there three classes of statements about God (literal, analogical, and metaphorical) or two (literal and non-literal with analogy, metaphor, and myth all being forms of symbolic speech)? What cognitive status do symbols, myths, analogies, and metaphors have? What kind of knowledge do they give us? In what sense are they true? Do they have theoretical validity, or do they simply have practical or existential value whose cognitive status is problematic, unknown, or null and void?[19] These questions are endlessly debated with inconclusive results.

Here they must remain as questions with the suggestion that we may not be able to say precisely how literally or accurately our language grasps the real being of God in a cognitive or theoretical sense. The task is to create a set of abstract categories and concrete symbols (analogies, myths, and metaphors) which best combine the theoretical and practical requirements of Christian faith. The goal is to find language which is most effective in stating the Christian vision of God, the world, and humanity. The aim is to develop a symbol system which is required by this vision as measured by its norms. In so doing we may proceed in the hope that our language is, minimally, the least misleading, practically useful and essential terminology available and, maximally, that it provides a valid perspective which grasps in a partial way the real being and nature of God. While every effort must be made to develop categories and symbols based on the best reasoning possible, the results will inevitably have a pragmatic and instrumental dimension. The final test is whether or not the language used creates a system of personal and religious meaning effective in relating believers to God in accordance with the norms and goals of Christian faith. Is God a Person? We cannot answer that question with any theoretical confidence. But that God is personal, i.e., related to us in the way that people relate to each other as suggested by terms like love, trust, loyalty, compassion, forgiveness, and reconciliation -- of that we can be sure if the Christian religion is true in any sense worthy of human attention and commitment. In the final analysis, then, the language we use about God is a matter of faith in the same way that the objective truth of the Christian message and vision itself is. We cannot transcend our categories and symbols to discover their objective validity, but neither can we have the truth of the Gospel apart from them. Language and objective referent are united in an indissolvable bond of mutual interdependence.

IV. The Reality of God in the Bible and in Christian History

Every attempt to present the fundamentals of Christian belief confronts the tension between approaching the subject historically or systematically. Should one start with the Bible and trace the development of Christian theology from the beginning to the present? Or is it better to analyze topics systematically, ordering them in some logical and comprehensive scheme, and then show how different options have been offered over the centuries? Obviously, the two approaches are complementary. Both are essential to a complete treatment of the issues. Every chapter in this book combines both historical and systematic perspectives in some fashion. The presentation of each topic will vary in this regard, an effort being made in each case to find the most intelligible and effective way to lay out the issues, the options, and the historical development of doctrine.

The concept of God is difficult and complex. Many different topics need attention. The method to be followed in the remainder of this chapter is first to give a brief overview of developments from the Biblical era until the present. This will be followed by a more systematic analysis in which references will be made to various historical points of view in order to illustrate the issues and options that come logically into view as each subtopic is dealt with.

A. THE BIBLE. No systematic doctrine of God ever appears in the Bible. Yet a number of themes combine to create a distinctive picture of the Holy One of Israel, incomparable in power, wisdom, and goodness, who creates and governs all things in accordance with a sovereign purpose (Gen. 1; Is. 40-66; Job 38:1-40; Ephes. 1:3-23).

1. God is One. At least from the time of Moses, if not earlier, Israel worshipped Yahweh (Ex. 3:1-15). It is difficult to know just when and how Yahweh became Israel's God or when Yahwehism became explicit monotheism. In the 8th century BC the prophets testified that Yahweh controlled surrounding nations (Is. 10:5-19). With II Isaiah in the 6th century it is clear that there is but one God, and God is Yahweh (Is. 40:18-46:11). The unity, supremacy, and sovereignty of God are everywhere presupposed in the New Testament though seldom dwelt on anywhere (Rom. 1:20; Mark 12:29-30; I Tim. 1:17, 6:15-16; Rom. 11:33-36).

2. God is the Holy One. As applied to God holiness refers to the radical otherness of deity, that which separates the Creator from all that is ordinary, earthly, or human. God is the mysterious, unanalyzable, unfathomable, awe-inspiring power, majesty, glory, and purity so exalted in incomparable splendor that mere mortals tremble in fear and fascination (Gen. 18:27; Ex. 3:1-6; I Sam. 6:19-20; Is. 6:1-13; Is. 40-45, 55:1-9, 57:15-21; Heb. 12:10; I Peter I:14-16; Rev. 4:8).

3. God is Living and Personal. The Bible is unashamedly anthropomorphic throughout and sometimes naively so (Gen. 3:8-10, 11:5, 18:20-21). Taken at face value, the language used in the Bible presents God as a Person who thinks, feels, and wills (Jer. 10:10; Zeph. 3:17; Lev. 20:23; Gen. 6:6; Ex. 20:5). God is an I, not an It, and is so referred to more than 1000 times (Is. 46:8-13, e.g.). Yet God is utterly different from human beings (Is. 55: 8-9; Job 9:32; Hos. 11:9; Is. 31:3).

God is that Inexhaustible Everlasting Living Energy by which the world and everything in it is created, sustained, and governed by a Moral Purpose conceived of as Personal Will (Ps. 104; Is. 40:12-55:13). God as King is the sovereign ruler of all things (Jer. 10:10) and as Father protects and cares for the chosen people in loving kindness (Ps. 103:13; Jer. 3:19; Matt. 6:8-9; Mk. 14:36; John 17). On some occasions God appears like a Mother Bird defending her young or a Mother giving birth to Israel or feeding Israel (Ps. 17:8; 36:7, 57:1,91:1; Is. 31:5; Deut. 32:18; Is. 49:15, 66:12-13).

4. God is supremely Good. A variety of terms is used to indicate the complex set of qualities which define God as morally perfect. An inner tension emerges between the jealous, holy, wrathful Judge, who demands honor, praise, and obedience, and the merciful, compassionate, loving Savior, whose concern for the salvation of the elect is boundless (Ex. 20:5-6, 34:6-7; Amos; Hosea: Is. 40; Rom. 1:18-2:11, 3:23-25, 5:6-11). The Psalms exalt God as one worthy of praise because of the steadfast love shown to Israel (Ps. 17:7, 25:10, 103:17-18, 106:7, 45). The compassion and tenderness of Yahweh persist despite Israel's sinfulness (Hos. 11:1-9). God's righteousness is seen primarily not in terms of judgment but as saving activity which rescues the oppressed and redeems the disobedient (Is. 45:21-23; Rom. 1:16-17, 3:21-26). In the New Testament the saving love of God is revealed supremely in Christ, who is the means divinely set forth to overcome the wrath of God and make forgiveness and reconciliation available (John 3:16; I John 4:8-10; Rom. 3:23-25; Ephes. 1:3-7, 2:1-9).

5. God is and has a Spirit. From the first chapter of the Bible to the last frequent reference is made to the Spirit of God or the Holy Spirit (Gen. 1:2; Rev. 22:17). The word for spirit (ruah) literally means wind or breath. As Spirit, God is an Almighty Invisible Power and thus utterly different from all that is material, limited, weak, and human (Is. 31:3: John 4:24). The Holy Spirit effects the will of God and manifests the divine presence and power in human life (Gen. 1:2; Joel 2:28-29; I Sam. 11:6, 16:13; Is. 42:1; Luke 1:35; Mk. 1:10-11; Rom. 8:1-27; I Cor. 11P1-12). In the New Testament Christ and the Spirit are the central manifestations of God's redemptive activity. Generally speaking, it may be said that what Christ objectively accomplishes is made subjectively effective in the believer by the Spirit (Rom. 3:21-25, 8:1-11). The intimate connection of God, Christ, and Spirit pictured in the New Testament left to the church the task of defining the triune character of the one and only Creator and Redeemer.[20]

B. CLASSICAL THEOLOGY. The religious thought of the Bible is essentially historical theology, i.e., a witness to the mighty acts of God in the crucial events of Israel's history and in the life, death, and resurrection of Jesus. As the church moved into the wider world, the doctrine of God was recast in the language of Greek philosophy. The Biblical Creator and Lord of History was identified with Absolute Perfect Being -- eternal, uncreated, immutable, immaterial, invisible, omnipotent, void of passion, and utterly transcendent to the finite, temporal, corruptible world of earth and flesh. One Biblical theme that was, however, carefully preserved from the second century Apologists to the medieval scholastics was the idea of

God as the Creator. Out of nothing, creatio ex nihilo, God made the world. This foundational motif denied the eternity of matter, denied the divinity of the world, and firmly established God's full control over everything. Positing an infinite gap between God and humanity in no way inhibited the notion of a universe populated with innumerable intermediate beings, i.e., angels and demons -- superhuman agents of good and evil.

The first five centuries of the Christian era gave birth to two enrichments or modifications of monotheism -- the affirmation of the full deity of Christ and the construction of the Trinitarian dogma. The Father was conceived as the Transcendent Creator whose unfathomable depth is given self-objectification and creative expression in the Logos, who is yet co-equal and co-eternal with the Father. The Logos was made flesh in the person of Jesus, who is fully human and fully divine. The Holy Spirit was in time also given equal status with the Father and the Son to complete the conception of one God existing eternally in three co-equal manifestations or modes of being. Thus was created the peculiar conception of God which all orthodox Christians were to affirm from that point.[21]

The medieval theologians built upon the contributions of Tertullian, Origen, Athanasius, and Augustine and completed a structure of thought about God which Etienne Gilson has called "Christian philosophy."[22] As embodied in the more Platonic scheme of Anselm and the more Aristotelian outlook of Aquinas, the central note is that God is Pure Being, Being-itself. This is Being so excellent that no greater can be conceived, and since even the conceivability of non-existence would be a mark of imperfection, Perfect

Reality necessarily is (Anselm). God is Pure Actuality -- actus purus in whom all potentiality has been eternally actualized (Aquinas). Yet the medieval thinkers did not hesitate to combine this notion of Absolute Being -- totally beyond time and change and hence not at all affected by what happens on earth -- with the Personal Lord of History who acts in time, interacts with people, and alleviates human pain in mercy and compassion.

The Protestant Reformers did not essentially change the main outlines of the Christian view of God they inherited. They accepted the Trinitarian and Christological doctrines without question. It is true that their reliance on Scripture led them to speak of God more in terms of sovereign Personal Will than of Perfect Absolute Being. Yet the God of Luther and Calvin was the all-controlling Will who totally preordained every event from eternity and governs with absolute authority. Hence, the Protestant God would appear to be, in fact, as unresponsive to earthly happenings and as unaffected by them as the Catholic God of the medieval theologians.[23]

C. MODERN THEOLOGY. The challenge of the modern world has given rise to numerous reinterpretations of the doctrine of God. Much of the remainder of this chapter will deal with these efforts. This is a long and complicated story. Suffice it to say here that among the elements that have led to modifications in traditional conceptions are the following: 1. The scientific picture of nature as an autonomous system of law-abiding causes and effects has made miracle and supernatural intervention problematic. 2. A cosmology in which both nature and history are developing, evolving, changing, and growing -- and thus introducing genuine novelty into the world -- challenged the static and immutable God of orthodoxy and led to the positing of a dynamic element or even change within deity itself. 3. The emphasis on human agency as giving direction to the course of history was seen to place limits on divine sovereignty and to give new potency to the problem of evil. 4. The recognition of historical relativity showed how culture-bound previous doctrines of God were, leading to efforts to create new models that were both Biblical (and less dominated by Greek metaphysics) and relevant to the new scientific, industrial, technological world.[24]

A major aim of 19th century liberal Protestants was to find a grounding in ultimate reality for moral values in the world of fact described by modern science. Philosophical alliances were made with various Kantian and post-Kantian philosophies which had the same purpose. Idealism posited as the foundational Reality some form of Mind or Consciousness or Spirit so that the world of phenomena described by science could be seen as a product or manifestation of an underlying Purpose. Hence, the law-abiding world of nature, though neutral with respect to value from the vantage point of empirical inquiry, could nevertheless be seen as the instrument or embodiment of Spirit. Absolute idealism as found in Hegel tended toward pantheism, while personal idealism spoke of an Infinite Person who creates finite persons and the phenomenal world of matter and nature.

Common to all liberal views was emphasis upon divine immanence. Liberals vehemently rejected the transcendent and tyrannical God of orthodoxy who from on high controlled all things, intervening arbitrarily but at will. God was now seen to work in and through natural processes and in cooperation with human freedom. This outlook combined well with the reigning concepts of the era -- evolution and progress. In liberal theologies God is the Immanent Spirit at work gradually bringing order out of chaos and leading the cosmos and human history to ever higher levels of value and achievement. From Schleiermacher through Ritschl and on to Walter Rauschenbusch, Shailer Mathews, and A.C. Knudson, the themes of immanence, evolution, and progress were given prominence. God is the Ultimate source and Ground of the gradual emergence of a society based on cooperation and love -- the Kingdom of God on earth.[25]

A major shift in thought about God, and yet one sharing many liberal and modern presuppositions, came about in the 20th century. Neo-orthodoxy arose in response to the monumental social evils of the period marked by World Wars I and II and the collapse of the theory of historical progress. The key figure was Karl Barth, who took as his theme Kierkegaard's notion of the "infinite qualitative distinction between time and eternity." God is "the Wholly Other" whose will and way are not to be identified with the course of history. The God of the Bible stands radically over against all that is human and finite as the Judge and yet paradoxically the Redeemer who speaks a forgiving word of grace despite the thundering divine "NO." This cannot be known at all except by a self-initiated revelation in the Word made flesh witnessed by Scripture. Most neo-orthodox thinkers were more moderate, but doctrines of divine transcendence and sovereignty centering on the Biblical Lord of History were central in all of them.

Yet they all criticized the static, immutable Absolute of Greek metaphysics and Christian orthodoxy. The laws of nature, the fact of real chance and contingency in the world, and human freedom were generally seen as limits to absolute divine control, although frequently this was seen as the acceptance of a voluntary or self-limitation on God's part. God permits a certain autonomy to nature and to human agency, yet somehow without negating divine sovereignty. Since human beings were thought in this outlook to be radically sinful and rebellious, the rule of God is hidden and can be affirmed only paradoxically by faith, while a final triumph of God can be affirmed only in terms of eschatological hope. The holy, wrathful, yet gracious, merciful God high and lifted up took the place of the more gentle God of the liberals who worked within the world process to win gradual spiritual victories. Emil Brunner, Rudolf Bultmann, H. Richard Niebuhr, as well as Reinhold Niebuhr, Paul Tillich, Gustaf Aulen and Barth carried on the polemic against liberalism and tried to find hope in the Sovereign Personal Lord of the Bible in a world shaken to its very foundations by totalitarianism, global wars, and other horrors springing from the evil lusts of prideful human hearts.[26]

A number of contemporary emphases can only be hinted at here. Eschatological theologians locate God not so much in the past as Creator or in the present as Providential Ruler but in the future as the Sovereign Ground of Hope. From "ahead" and "above" God comes and will come to fulfill the Biblical promises of a Kingdom of perfect righteousness (Wolfhart Pannenberg, Jurgen Moltmann).[27] Liberation theologians sound similar notes with much stress upon God's partiality to the poor and oppressed, who will be freed in God's own time from every form of dehumanizing bondage (Gustavo Gutiérrez, Hugo Assmann).[28]   In both of these overlapping theologies the eschatological note is strong, but interpreted in earthly, socio-historical rather than in otherworldly terms.   The Kingdom of freedom and universal justice will come in this world someway, sometime.   Black theologians also affirm the note of liberation, insisting that God is Black as a way of stressing the identification of the Sovereign Lord with the oppressed (James Cone, Deotis Roberts).[29]   W.R. Jones, a black humanist, poses sharply the theodicy question, wondering whether God is after all a White Racist.   Since the emancipation of blacks has not occurred even after centuries of white domination, it would appear that God is either not all-powerful, that black suffering is deserved, or that God is not concerned with black liberation, i.e., is a White Racist.[30]   Feminist theologians criticize the domination of male imagery in the traditional view of God and seek to construct non-sexist alternatives (Rosemary Ruether, Phyllis Trible).[31]   Process theologians describe a God who literally interacts with the world and with humanity in the effort to lure the creation toward higher levels of harmony, value, and enjoyment (John Cobb, Schubert Ogden).[32]   The process God, though unsurpassably perfect and absolutely immutable in essence is, in fact, a temporal being whose experience changes in content in response to the world.   God's power and knowledge, and thus the divine control over the world, are limited by the freedom of finite beings.   Such a God stands in sharp contrast to the eternally static, atemporal deity of the classical tradition who is absolute and immutable in all respects, while being relative and changing in none.

With the historical background in mind, we turn now
to a systematic analysis of the doctrine of God. Major
affirmations about God will be examined, and different
points of view will be outlined as a way of suggesting
both the unity and variety of Christian thinking about
the Maker of Heaven and Earth.

V. The Nature of God

A. BASIC AFFIRMATIONS;

1. God as the Holy One. Holiness pertains to
deity as such. It is the unique quality which separates
God from all else. Holiness indicates the Godness of
God and, as such, is simply identical with God. The Old
Testament frequently speaks of "the Holy One of Israel"
(Is. 40-45, for example). On the objective side
holiness refers to the radical otherness of God -- the
majesty, sublimity, purity, transcendence, power, glory,
and overwhelmingness of the Almighty high and lifted up.
Holiness points to the utter mystery of the "Supremely
Other." On the subjective side it indicates the
awfulness, the fascinating terribleness, the frightening
wonderfulness people feel in the presence of God. The
contrast between the smallness and impotence of human
beings and the overwhelming power, mystery, and glory of
God creates fear, trembling, and a sense of unworthy
puniness (Gen. 18:27 and Is. 6).[33]

Holiness is characteristically treated in one of
two ways by contemporary theologians. (1) Holiness may
be seen as the context or background in which everything
about God is to be treated. It defines the atmosphere

in which God is to be thought about. In this sense
holiness is the unique quality of deity which modifies
and affects everything. God's power is holy power,
God's being is holy being, God's love is holy love.
This way is illustrated by Paul Tillich and Gustaf
Aulén.[34] (2) Holiness is seen along with righteousness
and wrath as standing in tension with love, grace, and
mercy. In this framework holiness may be thought of as
God's demand to be recognized and honored as deity. It
is a quality of God which makes God jealous and wrathful
at those who do not obey the divine law or worship and
respect God. Holiness is God taking Self seriously as
God. Emil Brunner and many others take this approach.[35]

   2.   The Nature of the Holy One. The fundamental
affirmations that Christians have made about God over
the centuries in interpreting the Biblical witness can
be conveniently put under three headings: God is
Ultimate in Being; God is Personal in Nature; and God is
Perfect in Goodness. These characterizations can be
summarized by saying that in Biblical religion God is
the Sovereign Lord who is Holy Love. God is sovereign
-- ultimate in being. God is the Lord -- a Person who
when speaking says "I am the Lord" (Is. 41:4, etc.).
God is Holy Love -- perfect in moral goodness and
righteousness. Each of these needs to be examined in
some detail.

   a.   God as Ultimate in Being. In the Bible the
unrivaled supremacy of God among the things that are is
indicated by calling God the Creator. In the beginning
was God. God created all else (Gen. 1, Is. 40-45, many
of the Psalms, Job 38, and many other places). God is
related to humanity and to the whole universe as Creator
to creature. Theologians have used a wide variety of

terms to indicate the ultimacy of God. Aseity means self-existent or uncreated. God is unconditioned, absolute, actus purus (pure actuality with no unrealized potential), infinite, Being-itself, eternal, omnipotent, omnipresent, omniscient, immutable, the Wholly Other, necessary being, and on and on. All these terms suggest the transcendent otherness of God by which God is the Source, Ground, Creator, etc. of all else. Hence, God is real in a way that is qualitatively different from everything else. The gap between Creator and creature is infinite.

The religious or practical meaning of all this is that God has the power to save. God is able to keep promises, to bring about what has been purposed, to put down all enemies of righteousness, and to bring the world and all its people at last to a perfected Kingdom in which goodness will reign supreme. Hence, nothing can separate us from the love revealed in Christ, since God's love is undergirded with almighty power. God, then, is an utterly reliable Savior and Refuge.

b. God as Personal. In the Bible God is spoken of as a Person who thinks, feels, wills, and even has a change of mind. God is related to human beings and interacts with them as people engage each other. While some forms of theology have so stressed the transcendence of God as to render any personal conception of God ineffective, the main tradition has sought to preserve this basic Biblical theme. God is said to have intellect and will, to be just, loving, merciful, wrathful, and so on -- all attributes of persons. With the use of these human terms, it is possible to speak of God in relation to humanity, interacting with persons, judging and saving them.

c. God as Perfect in Character. The Bible is also quite consistent in representing God as supremely excellent in moral terms. God is the measure of perfect goodness. God is just, holy, merciful, kind, compassionate, patient, and caring -- utterly lacking in blemish or flaw, complete and perfect in every way. The supreme excellence of God is love. This note is especially prominent in the New Testament. Agape is the word most often used to describe the special kind of unconditional outgoing good will which characterizes God's attitude and actions toward humanity (Rom. 5:6-8, e.g.). Theologians have frequently distinguished between the metaphysical attributes of God, used to describe the being of God as ultimate and absolute, and the moral attributes, used to define the divine character. It is probably true to say that the terminology employed in the latter case has more often simply taken over the Biblical words -- such as love and mercy -- rather than resorting to the high abstractions which are frequently used to describe the being of the Almighty Creator.

B. TENSIONS WITHIN THE BEING AND NATURE OF GOD.

It is extremely difficult to combine the three affirmations just enumerated. Tensions inevitably arise. The character of the doctrine of God in a given theological system will depend in large measure on how these different attributions are made in relationship to each other. The tensions that arise can be put under two headings: those which arise between the basic characteristics of God and those which appear within a particular characteristic.

1. Tensions Between Basic Characteristics.

    a. Ultimacy and absoluteness versus personhood and relatedness. The classical Christian view of God was formulated in the first few centuries A.D. God came to be described as eternal (timeless or overarching time and so not living as we do from moment to moment), necessary (lacking in all contingent elements), immutable (undergoing no change), absolute (independent and unrelated to finite beings), and impassible (not affected by what happens in time, history, and human life). This notion of God as eternal, changeless, unrelated, unaffected, self-sufficient, utterly transcendent and alone continued as the dominant model right on through the Protestant Reformation and into modern times. Only in relatively recent decades has it been seriously challenged under the impact of modern consciousness. Obviously such a conception stands in contrast with the Biblical and hence Christian idea of a God who is personally involved with human beings. In the Bible God acts and people respond (Moses at the burning bush, Ex. 3). People act and God responds (David sins and God sends the prophet Nathan to rebuke him, II Sam. 11-12). Beyond these individual encounters is the larger drama of history in which God calls the people of Israel into covenant, judges and punishes them for their disloyalty, restores them, sends Jesus Christ into the world as the Word incarnate to die and rise again in a cosmic act of redemption, and finally directs history toward a final consummation in which all evil is put down. The very notion of divine love suggests that God knows and cares what happens to people and hence is affected and changed. Over the centuries several ways of dealing with this tension have been tried.

One way is to hide the contradiction in an appeal to the mystery and transcendence of God, to live with the paradox, or to ignore it altogether. To put it in this fashion probably represents a modern consciousness which the theologians of centuries past would find unfair. The problem did not appear to most of them as the acute contradiction that it does to most people today. The critics of the impassibility tradition like to quote Anselm at this point to indicate the conflict that this sensitive soul felt:

> How art thou . . . compassionate, and
> at the same time, passionless? For,
> if thou art passionless, thou dost not
> feel sympathy . . . for the wretched:
> but this it is to be compassionate.[36]

Anselm resolves this paradox (contradiction?) by saying that God is compassionate in terms of our experience but not in terms of the divine being. God, then, seems to feel compassion for the wretched but really does not.

John Calvin clearly continues the impassibility tradition.[37] In dealing with Genesis 6:6 and Isaiah 63:9 in the Commentaries Calvin says confidently that we know that God cannot really repent or feel anguish but "remains forever like Himself in His happy repose."[38] This is just a way of speaking for our benefit, an accommodation to our way of thinking. J.K Mozley concludes that the idea of the impassibility of God was not really questioned, with minor exceptions, until modern times.[39] In contemporary theology Karl Barth seems to handle the issue by simply affirming the paradox of absoluteness and relatedness as itself implied by the divine freedom.[40]

A second way of resolution, reminiscent of Calvin, is that proposed by Paul Tillich.[41] Language about God as related is symbolic and not literal. Symbolically, God is the living God who acts, interacts, knows, feels and wills. But all symbols point beyond themselves, and all finite categories are transcended and yet grounded in God as Being-itself. Strictly speaking, however, when we speak of loving God this really means that God is loving God through us, since God cannot be the object of an action by us as subjects. God remains subject.

A third approach is to assert that God is self-limited. God wills to be related to us, to interact with us, to be affected, to hear prayer, and to respond. It is in this connection that modern theologians teach that God really grants us freedom, so that we have a genuine but limited autonomy over against God. Hence, we interact with God. In these encounters God both affects us and is affected by us. For modern theologians who feel the contradictions in traditional thought, this is the most widespread way of resolving the issue. Emil Brunner is an example of this way of thinking.[42]

A fourth option is laid out by the process theologians under the influence of Alfred North Whitehead and Charles Hartshorne.[43] They criticize the "monopolar prejudice" in classical theism, according to which only one side of certain descriptive polarities can be attributed to deity:

Eternal-temporal   absolute-relative
immutable-changeable   necessary-contingent

Process theists want to apply both terms in each of these pairs to God. Central to their critique is the claim that only with a di-polar view can we give rational meaning to the love of God as both creative and responsive. A God who loves surely feels our joys and sorrows as well as seeks our welfare. In order to maintain this di-polarity without contradiction, a distinction is made between the abstract essence and the concrete actuality of God. This further involves the assumption that the primary designation of God is Becoming, not Being. Concretely, God is a process characterized by time, relativity, change, and contingency, while in abstract essence God is eternal, absolute, immutable and necessary. Hence, God literally enters into real relations with human beings and is affected and changed by the encounter. God's experience is continually enriched by this involvement with the world.

In this view God is absolute in some respects, relative in some respects, God's existence is necessary. God cannot not be. But contingent elements enter into God's experience in encounter with the world of time and history. God is perfect in power, knowledge, and love. These attributes are immutable and could not be more excellent than they are. God always has had these absolute perfections and always will. But God's power is limited by the actions of the creatures. God's knowledge is limited by the free decisions of finite beings, and God's love changes in strategy in response to changing circumstances. God is eternal (has no beginning and end), but God has a past, a present, and a future. In abstract essence God is perfect and absolute, but as a concrete (actual) process, God is changing as new elements enter the divine experience. And God is related to us literally as one whose love is both creative and responsive.

A similar tension arises between ultimacy and personhood. To declare that God is ultimate in being seems incompatible with the understanding of God as Person. To assert that God is a Person appears to rob God of transcendence and absoluteness. It threatens to finitize God by an unacceptable anthropomorphic image. Two basic options are available to ease this tension.

One way is to start with an affirmation of ultimacy and then proceed to show how this claim can be combined with the assertion that God is personal. Paul Tillich is the best known contemporary advocate of this approach.[44] God cannot be thought of as a being who is a person. This would illegitimately apply the category of individuality to God. But God transcends infinitely all the categories applicable to finite beings. God is Being-itself, the Ground of Being, the power of being in all things that resists non-being. After having said this, all else is symbolic. God is the ground of the personal and is not less than personal but is not a Person. God symbolically becomes a Person for us in prayer, worship, and personal encounter. In these contexts it is legitimate to speak of God in personal terms. Tillich points out that classical theology used the term person to speak of the members of the Trinity but not of God as one. God became a Person only in the 19th century under the influence of Kantian philosophy as a way to elevate God above the reign of impersonal natural law. But the kind of supernaturalism which defines God as existing in a heavenly realm above the world from which God acts in this world must be rejected as a finitizing anthropomorphism which robs God of ultimacy and absoluteness.

The second option is to begin with a definition of God as Person and then proceed to show how such a being can be ultimate. This group can be divided conveniently into those who take this approach on primarily Biblical grounds and those who make more use of philosophical arguments. Karl Barth and Emil Brunner represent the former group. Brunner asks, "What is the alternative to speaking of God as Person?"[45] It is to think of God as an It, an Impersonal Something, _actus purus_, the Unconditioned, Necessary Being, the Absolute, etc. Really now, he persists, are we really to think that the idea of God as Person is inferior to that? Besides, the personal God is not made in the image of humanity. It is rather the reverse. Only God is true Person. Only God is Absolute Subject always acting and never acted upon (except by divine permission). God is Personality-Itself. We are only images of personhood. It is we who are persons in a symbolic way, as the pale replica of God the Absolute Person. Thus does Brunner refute Tillich.

A.C. Knudson, a personalist philosopher, argues in similar fashion.[46] Personality in essence means self-hood, self-knowledge, and self-direction. A person is a conscious agent with freedom to act. So defined a person can be finite or infinite. God is an Infinite Person or Absolute Person, the self-existent being who is the causal ground of all else, including the natural world and the plurality of finite persons. Process theologians likewise argue for the legitimacy of speaking of God as both Independent-Individual Person and as the All-Inclusive Society (panentheism). Hence, God is ultimate and absolute, as well as being a Living Person.[47]

Related to these views but different from either of the options is the existential agnosticism of theologians in the Kantian tradition like Rudolf Bultmann and H. Richard Niebuhr. For Niebuhr ideas of God as ultimate and personal are postulates of the practical reason and not metaphysical theories of speculative reason.[48] We can speak of God only from the point of view of faith, saying what God means to us as persons in quest of meaning and fulfillment. From this orientation God is Being -- the transcendent and ultimate Power -- and God is Person -- One who can only be described existentially in personal images as trustworthy, loving, and loyal. Niebuhr unashamedly uses anthropomorphic language, but as existential images of the reasoning heart and not as theoretical concepts of the head.

Considerably removed from all of these more orthodox views is the naturalistic outlook of certain modernistic liberals of the Chicago school. For these thinkers God is neither a Person nor absolute. For Henry Nelson Wieman, God is creative event, the objective source in nature of human good.[49] For Shailer Mathews, God is the name we give to the personality-producing, personality-sustaining activities or factors in the universe.[50]

b. Ultimacy versus goodness. This tension relates to the problem of evil. Here it only needs to be noted that it is an apparent contradiction to believe that God is both supremely powerful and perfectly good in a world so filled with suffering, injustice, misery, and meaninglessness. This issue will be discussed in some detail under the question of providence.

2. Tensions Within Basic Characteristics

a. Goodness. It is frequently noted that there are internal complications in the conception of God's moral perfection. This can be indicated as follows:

```
holiness ..... love
righteousness..... graciousness
wrath ..... mercy
```

The first term in each pair seems in contrast with the second. Yet both are essential to the elucidation of divine goodness. As A.C. Knudson puts it, the left-hand group suggest God's concern for the divine law. The right-hand group refers to God's concern for the creature.[51] Sometimes this tension is so great that Christ's atoning death on the cross is thought to be necessary to satisfy the divine wrath or righteousness before the grace and mercy of God can be operative. So Anselm, Calvin, and many others have taught. Some theologians see holiness or wrath simply as the other side of love -- the divine reaction to those who sin against God (Nels Ferré, Paul Tillich).[52] Still others effectively eliminate the notion of wrath as a primitive expression of violence and insist that God is pure love (Ritschl and many liberals). But every time that position is stated, another rises to restate the case for including wrath as essential to the Christian view (Gordon Kaufman versus James Cone).[53]

   b.   Personhood.   This tension has to do with sexuality in God. Does God have masculine and feminine dimensions, or does the personal nature of God transcend any specifiable gender reference? This is a new issue for theology basically within the last two decades. In its current expression it would have been a surprise to the theologians of former centuries. The problem has been raised acutely by feminist theologians who are critical of the oppressive dominance of patriarchal images and values in the Bible and throughout Christian tradition right down to the present. It appears at several levels. 1. Pronouns and direct references to God are almost exclusively masculine. God appears as "He" all the time. 2. The imagery used to symbolize God is predominantly male. God is Father, King, Shepherd, although there are feminine metaphors here and there. Given the will, the first two could easily be corrected. 3. The more fundamental question is whether there is something intrinsic to the Biblical-Christian doctrine of God which is in some identifiable fashion masculine in a one-sided way? Is it sufficient merely to equalize the number and value of masculine and feminine symbols? Are those right, usually males in a defensive posture, who say, "The opposite of He is not She but It"? Is pronoun reference merely to indicate personhood not gender or sexuality? Or is there something deeper? That is the fundamental issue which must be but has not yet been resolved or even sufficiently defined. This is a task for the present and future.

To conclude, three possible resolutions presently suggested illustrate ways the problem might be dealt with. (a) God's personhood transcends sexuality, but symbolic references should be equalized. (b) God's being includes both feminine and masculine attributes in ways that can be identified -- the androgynous thesis. (c) The Trinity includes a feminine dimension.[54] The choice most often suggested for this role is the Spirit. As a basis for this it is noted that the Old Testament word for Spirit and its correlates are feminine. Finally, one impact of the feminist consciousness is reflected in that in this text no pronoun or gender designations are made to God whatsoever, except when the tradition is being referred to or other authors are being quoted.

A SUGGESTED SCHEMATIZATION OF THE ATTRIBUTES OF GOD

God, the Holy One, is the Sovereign Lord who is Holy Love.

GOD

THE HOLY ONE

The Godness of God   God's self-regard

Metaphysical attributes   Moral Attributes

is

SOVEREIGN	LORD	HOLY	LOVE
(Absolute in	(Personal in	(Perfect in Goodness)	
being)	nature)		

Attributes of the Personal Absolute	Attributes of Perfect Goodness	
self-existent	holiness	love
omnipresent		
perfect in power	righteousness	grace
perfect in knowledge	wrath	mercy
	wisdom	patience
absolute-related		
necessary-contingent		
eternal-temporal		
immutable-changing		

glory

The Sovereign Lord who is Holy Love

is the Glorious One.

VI.   The Trinity

It has been generally said that the trinitarian conception is the distinctive Christian view of God and essential to it.   From Tertullian (160-220) to Schleiermacher (1830) this was almost universally accepted as correct. In the 19th century among liberal thinkers the Trinity became a "doctrine of second rank," though still central to Protestant and Catholic conservatism.   The 20th century has witnessed a revival in neo-orthodoxy, notably in the thought of Karl Barth.

Nevertheless this doctrine does not have the prominent role in theology that it had in previous eras.[55]

Most non-conservative theologians would agree that the <u>doctrine</u> of the Trinity does not appear in the New Testament, but the <u>data</u> are there. The doctrine is the work of theological reflection and imagination based on the Biblical witness to God as Creator, Incarnate Word, and Indwelling Spirit. These three themes are central to the New Testament, and many passages explicitly tie them together (Matt. 28:19 and II Cor. 13:14, e.g.).

A. THE ROOT OF THE DOCTRINE. How does the doctrine of the Trinity arise? On what is it based? What is its root? What is its function? Is it essential to Christian witness? An examination of contemporary theological literature would reveal a wide variety of conflicting answers to these questions. It might be safely concluded that modern theology does not quite know what to do with it. The views of three recent theologians will be presented as representing the variety of answers that are being given with respect to the source and importance of the doctrine.

Karl Barth argues that the Trinity is the immediate implication of revelation.[56] The single ground of the doctrine is that in the Bible "God reveals Himself as the Lord." God reveals <u>Himself</u> in the Son. God reveals Himself in the <u>Son</u>. God reveals Himself in the Son by the <u>Holy</u> <u>Spirit</u>. This implies a Revealer (the Father), a Revelation (the Son), and Revealedness (the Spirit). Put otherwise, it implies a Subject of revelation (Father), the objective Reality of revelation (Son), and the subjective Reality of revelation (Spirit). From this single ground the doctrine the Trinity necessarily arises to work out the implications of the fact of revelation for the inner being of God. On this basis Barth proceeds to develop an elaborate doctrine in classical fashion.

J.S. Whale[57] agrees that the doctrine grows out of revelation itself. However, he sees it more as a synthesis of three basic elements given in Christian experience. It puts together in a monotheistic doctrine the three major axioms of early Christian thinking. They seem to be mutually incompatible, but all are essential in the revelation of God to humankind. First, the church inherited monotheism from the Old Testament. The Bible speaks of one true God as Creator and Lord. Second, the New Testament witnesses to the deity of Christ, God present in Person in human flesh (John 1:1-14). Finally, God is present as Spirit, calling, judging, renewing, and sanctifying. The Spirit is understood both as the Spirit of God and as the Spirit of Christ. The doctrine of the Trinity inevitably arises as the attempt to preserve monotheism but in a way that incorporates this three-fold experience of God.

C.C. Richardson[58] gives a much more negative interpretation. The Trinity is a very bad way to say two necessary but paradoxical things about God. On the one hand, God is absolutely above and beyond the world, independent, unrelated, beyond change, inaccessible. On the other hand, God is near, related, immanent, accessible, present in and to the world. Theology has tried to express this paradox by distinguishing between the Father and the Son, with the Holy Spirit added to complete the picture. Richardson proposes that we keep the symbols of Father, Son, and Spirit as expressing important aspects of our relationship to God but that we abandon the classical doctrine itself. The paradox of transcendence and immanence can be expressed in much better ways.

B. THE CLASSICAL DOCTRINE. The formulation of trinitarian doctrine in the first four centuries of the Christian era was the outcome of a long, complex, confusing process.[59] It was complicated by the fact that theologians in the East used Greek categories, while in the West Latin was used. Moreover, the basic terms used to distinguish between the unity of God and the three modes of divine existence had acquired different meanings and could be used to express conflicting ideas -- all legitimate given the history of their usage. Finally, political motives and personal rivalries were often mixed with theological concerns. Only the highlights of this complex story can be noted here.

The initial problem was to affirm the deity of Christ without compromising monotheism. In the 3rd century efforts were made to spell this out. Two schools of thought developed, represented by the Monarchians and the Logos Theologians.

THE MONARCHIANS: This group wanted to preserve the unity of God. Monotheism, they insisted, was essential and must not be compromised. They wanted to affirm the divinity of Christ without introducing the Logos as a second God, as they thought some were doing. Two kinds of Monarchianism appeared.

1. DYNAMIC MONARCHIANISM. Theologians in this group saved the unity of God by denying the full deity of Christ. Christ, they said, was a man who was endowed with a special gift or power which set him apart from other human beings. Adoptionism is another name for this view. God adopted Jesus as Son and filled him with a divine quality. God and Christ are one in will, purpose, and disposition, but they are not equal in being or essence. Christ is not God but inspired by God and endowed with divine powers. Paul of Samosata was condemned by a Synod at Antioch in 268 AD for holding such views.

2. MODALISTIC MONARCHIANISM. Theologians of this stripe took seriously the full deity of Christ as equal with God. God is one being who is manifest in three successive modes or manifestations. Father, Son, and the Spirit were one and the same God in different and sequential appearances. Sabellius is the name most frequently associated with this view. Critics quickly pointed out that this form of modalism involved Patri-passianism -- the Father was born, suffered, and died.

THE LOGOS THEOLOGIANS: The second line of thought proceeded by developing the implications of Christ as the Logos -- divine and yet somehow distinct from God (John 1:1). Origen inherited this way of thinking from the 2nd century Apologists and developed it in complex ways. After his death the right-wing Origenists asserted the equality of the Logos with the Father. The left wing thought in hierarchical terms in which Christ is the first and highest of created beings but inferior to God. In the beginning of the 4th century Arius appeared representing this view. Arius stressed an exalted view of God as absolutely unique and utterly transcendent. Christ is a creature, not co-eternal with the Father. There was once when He was not. But the pre-existent Christ, the first and highest of created beings, created everything else. Christ is a second and derived being, yet divine and worthy of worship. Athanasius argued against him that a creature could not save. Christ is Savior and must be and is equal with God, co-eternal with the Father.

The controversy was resolved at the Council of Nicea in 325 AD in favor of Athanasius. Christ is of the same substance (homoousios) with the Father, not just of like substance (homoiousios) as Arius had contended. Belief in the Holy Spirit was affirmed but not related to the statement concerning the full deity of Christ as eternal co-equal with the Father. This was done at a Council in Alexandria in 362 AD. Here what was to become the classical formula was foreshadowed. God is one being or essence or substance (ousia) existing in three subsistences or individual modes of being (hypostases). This formula was championed by the Cappadocian Fathers -- Gregory Nazianzus, Basil of Ancyra, and Gregory of Nyssa. they added the idea that each of the three has its particular characteristic or property, while being co-eternal and equal in essence. The Father is ungenerated; the Son is generated; the Spirit proceeds from the Father and the son. At the Council in Constantinople in 381 AD the formula of one ousia, three hypostases was confirmed -- one being or essence manifested in three co-equal, co-eternal ways of existence. This was the formulation in the East in the Greek language. Tertullian of Carthage in North Africa provided the West with the Latin version. His formula was una substantia, tres personae, one substance existing simultaneously in three persons (manifestations or roles or modes of being).

What do these fine words mean? We may think these highly speculative ideas stand somewhere between being unintelligible to the mind and irrelevant to life. The issues are bewildering in their complexity. Various thinkers put the emphasis in different places, while the same words were used with different meanings, meant one way and interpreted by others in another. Nevertheless, important issues for thought and life were at stake for those engaged in those ancient controversies. To summarize is to oversimplify, but some things may be said with confidence. Using the language available to them, these theologians of old were trying to steer between modalism on the one side and Arianism on the other in the attempt to enrich monotheism without falling into tritheism. Two truths must be held together.

1. God is one. Christ and the Holy Spirit are equal in essence with the Father, but there are not three Gods. There is no activity on the part of one hypostasis which is not the work of the other two. The "persons" of the Trinity mutually indwell and inter-penetrate each other (perichoresis or circumincessio), so that one God acts in Father, Son, and Spirit. 2. Real and eternal distinctions exist in the Godhead. These different modes are not temporary phases. That was the error of modalism. They are eternal, and they are internal to the being of God. Person or hypostasis means more than attribute or phase, less than

individual, self-conscious personality. Personae referred to masks worn by actors enabling them to play more than one role in a drama. There are not three centers of divine self-consciousness, yet God exists in not one but three modes. The attempt is to speak of one God without confounding the persons or dividing the substance.

C. FURTHER CONSIDERATIONS. Two further distinctions may be helpful.[60]

1. Immanent versus Economic Trinity. Some theologians affirm an immanent Trinity. This means that the three persons are eternal and internal distinctions within the being of God as such. They are objectively real in God. Others affirm an economic Trinity. In this case the threefoldness refers to the way in which God is known to us. We experience God in three ways. God is revealed in three ways. but God is one internally. The modalistic monarchians (Sabellius) and many liberals of the 19th and 20th centuries fall into this group. A typical liberal view would be that God is known to us in nature as the Creator, in history in the person of Jesus, and in our personal experience as Spirit. This leaves completely open the question of God's own inner life or reality, except that the God we know in these three ways is the one and only true God. The classical doctrine was, of course, of the immanent variety, but this would also include the idea that God appears to us or is experienced in three different ways. The economic doctrine strictly taken would not admit of trinity within the eternal and internal reality of God as such.

2. From Unity to Trinity and from Trinity to Unity. In the history of trinitarian thought of the immanent type, some tend to begin with the oneness of God as primary. Athanasius, Augustine, and Barth illustrate this approach. They tend to use psychological analogies based on the selfhood of one person. Augustine suggested that the presence of memory, intellect, and will in a human being might faintly resemble the divine triad. Others have begun with the individuality of the three persons and then have sought ways to preserve divine unity. The Cappadocian Fathers in the early church and some Anglican thinkers in recent times are illustrative of this approach. Leonard Hodgson uses a sociological analogy.[61] God is a society, three centers of self-consciousness. But the three are united organically in ways that transcend mere numerical oneness. An analogy might be the unity of an atom or of a living organism with many parts. The mystery of the Trinity is beyond our understanding, but it is hinted at more by sociological or organic analogies than by psychological ones.

D. THE TRINITARIAN PATTERN AND TRINITARIAN DOC-TRINES. A trinitarian pattern seems to arise inevitably out of Christian experience and reflection. We cannot say all we need to say about God without referring in some way to the Creator, the incarnate Logos, and the presence of the Spirit. This way of thinking about God is intrinsic and not arbitrary. But trinitarian doc-trines are many, debatable, conflicting, and secondary. The perennial problem of Christians, then, is to find the most appropriate doctrinal expression in which to articulate the trinitarian pattern. Probably most

people today are more comfortable with economic doctrines than with immanent ones. Whether a feminine
element needs to be included in whatever formulation may
result is debatable. More important is a way to
eliminate the offensive exclusiveness of masculine
images without losing vital Christian substance. This
may mean abandoning sexually-oriented terminology altogether rather than seeking to balance gender references
somehow. Even to make the Spirit feminine still leaves
it two to one in favor of the masculine. One could, of
course, seek to describe a masculine and a feminine
element in each member of the Trinity.

VII. Creation

We move now from a consideration of the being and
nature of God to the relationship of God to the world.
This is traditionally discussed under the headings of
creation and providence.

A. CLASSICAL THEMES. The Bible begins with these
momentous words, "In the beginning God created the
heavens and the earth" (Gen. 1:1 RSV). Classical
theology has interpreted this to mean that God made the
world out of nothing, creatio ex nihilo. Out of nothing
has negative and positive meanings. The negative
meanings are two: 1. It is a denial of dualism. God
did not simply shape or develop pre-existing materials.
Rather God absolutely originated both the matter and the
form of the world. 2. It is a denial of monism. The
world was not made from God's own substance (pantheism).
The world is not divine. It is something other than

God. The positive meaning of creatio ex nihilo is that
the world has real but dependent existence. The world
has no independent status or power. It originated from
nothing. But the world is not an illusion or mere
appearance. God created something real and gave it
being, status, and power. God made room for the
creature as something over against God. The idea of
creatio ex nihilo was important in the early centuries
to establish the sovereignty and transcendence of God
and to distinguish the Christian view of the world from
competing alternatives. Whether the Bible explicitly
teaches or requires creation out of nothing is debatable
in current theology. Neither is it clear that it has
the existential or religious significance for modern
people that it once had.[62]

By modern standards the world envisaged by
theologians prior to the rise of modern astrophysics was
relatively small, neat, and tidy. The universe came
into being a few thousand years ago. It was called into
existence by divine command in essentially the same form
as we now know it, populated from the beginning with all
the species of plant and animal life that were ever to
be. The earth was in the center of a cosmos that was
hierarchically ordered and teleologically organized.
Ranging from inert matter at the bottom to the celestial
angels at the top, each kind of being has its own nature
and end. Every species and material form fills a niche
in the total scheme of things -- a place for everything
and everything in its place. The world is a plenum in
which every potential type of existence has been
actualized. The created order, then, is an organized
unity of material and spiritual beings related to each
other in purposeful ways, with human beings constituting

the apex of earthly life. Humankind was made in the image of God and commissioned as God's appointed agent to tend and to dominate the subhuman world. (Gen. 1:26-31; 2:15). The earth is the scene of the historical drama which began with Adam and Eve in the Garden of Eden and will end with the saints in the New Jersalem at the end of the age, with the fall into sin and the rescue by Christ in between (Rev. 21:1-4). This ensemble of themes was given its classic expression by Augustine in THE CITY OF GOD in the 5th century AD. The basic framework which he laid down was to shape Christian thinking about the creation for approximately the next 1400 years.

Genesis 1 teaches not only that God created the world but also that the creation is good. This can be interpreted in various ways. The world is good because God made it. God's motives in creating are ultimately unfathomable. Perhaps it was for God's own good pleasure, a manifestation of love. But in any case, it was a free act of will and not a necessary outcome. The world as made is whole and complete. Everything in it has its own intrinsic though finite and mutable excellence, so that whatever is is good. Goodness is correlative with being. As it comes from the hand of God, the creation is without flaw in any of its parts. Mosquitos and poisonous reptiles, perhaps noxious from the human point of view, contribute to the wholeness and perfection of the created order. Nature and history embody divine purpose and are the scene of God's revealing and redemptive activity. Augustine was especially insistent that no flaw or evil taint is present until free will enters to spoil the harmony of creation. Even then, evil is not real in itself but only as a corruption of what is inherently good. Existence is intrinsically positive and excellent. More precisely, creation is essentially and potentially good, although it is existentially and actually a mixture of good and evil given the world's present fallenness. Taking the theological tradition as a whole, the essential (though corruptible) goodness of the creation can be spelled out in several ways:[63]

1. The world embodies an intelligible order and is a fit subject for human inquiry, knowledge, and control.
2. No dualism of value exists between body and soul, the material and the spiritual. Life is a unity such that the whole range of humanity's bodily and natural existence is included in God's concern.
3. Evil and sin are not essential or intrinsic to the world but are intruders in a creation that is naturally good. When they do appear, they are potent and threatening but not ultimate. Since they are intruders, they can be overcome. Divine resources are available which give meaning and hope and promise of ultimate victory of goodness.
4. History is directional, meaningful, and goal-directed -- the scene of God's purposeful activity and of an ultimate perfection (Consummation).

B. CONTEMPORARY EMPHASES. A number of themes are characteristic of recent theology. Three in particular are noteworthy.[64]

1. A distinction is made between the scientific and theological dimensions of the creation story in Genesis 1. This is a result of the impact of modern science on theology. Those who retain the doctrine of creatio ex nihilo do not mean that once upon a time several thousand years ago the world was made by divine fiat as recorded in Genesis. That story is a myth and not literally true. Its theological meaning is that the world depends absolutely on God for its origination and continuation.

2. Creation continues. The modern world is impressed by the importance of novelty, process, evolution, growth, development, and the emergence of new forms of life and potential over billions of years. Hence, it is said that creation was not once and for all long ago but a continuing reality and possibility. This emphasis further tends to reduce the importance of creation out of nothing once upon a time.

3. Theologians today tend to interpret creation Christocentrically. The place to begin is John 1:1. The intent is to connect the Creator and the Redeemer. Creation is an act of love in and through the Logos. The Creator is the Parent of Jesus Christ. The power of the Creator is interpreted through the love of the Redeemer, while the love revealed in Christ is undergirded by the power of God manifested in creation. In this way we see most clearly the religious significance of the doctrine of creation. It affirms the Sovereignty and Goodness of God in relation to the world and human life. It is the theological foundation of Romans 8 and Psalm 139. The Creator is the Savior and has the resources to fulfill the promises of love.

VIII. Providence

Providence refers to the divine governance of the world. God acts purposefully to order all things and direct the whole cosmos toward an ultimate consummation. Creation is origination. Providence is continuing governance. God rules in macroevents (Is. 40-42) and in microevents (Matt. 10:29-31), directing the destinies of nations and numbering the hairs on our heads.

A. CLASSICAL THEMES: How does God rule? In the Bible God has a direct and immediate relationship to every event large and small. As G.K. Chesterton said, "It is as though God said to the sun every morning, `Get up and do it again'." A distinction is made between God's ordinary way of governing in the regularities of nature, the alternation of night and day, seed time and harvest etc., and extraordinary means of accomplishing the divine purpose, such as the rescue at the Red Sea. But no secondary order of autonomous natural law stands between God and the world.[65]

The classical theologies of the past declared the sovereignty of God in unqualified terms. The divine rule over all things is without exception complete and thorough. If one is to generalize, it would have to be said that traditional theology in effect asserted that God controls and ultimately determines everything that happens on earth in nature, in history;, and right down to the details of human life. The meaning of this gets complicated, subtle, technical, and fraught with contradictions both apparent and real.[66] The problem is not so great as long as we talk about the rule of God in nature over inanimate things and even over animal life. But it becomes acute when we come to human beings, since the apparent omnicausality of God seems to conflict with free will. Is God the cause even of evil and sin, of misery, suffering, and wrongdoing?

To understand these issues, we have to take into account the theory of the double perspective. At one level God controls the world and accomplishes the divine purposes by working through the natures, structures, and processes of finite beings. God makes trees by seeds produced by other trees, etc. In human life this means that God works through our freedom. God gives people the power to choose, so that when they make decisions, it is they who are acting, and yet at another level it is God who is doing it. Thomas Aquinas referred to God's rule through worldly events and antecedent finite causes (including human freedom) as "secondary causation." In addition, there was the "primary causation" by which God made the world and gives the finite beings the natures, powers, and capacities to act as "secondary causes."[67] So far so good, for it appears that human beings then are really free to choose, even though they do so as "secondary causes" relying on God as "primary cause" of everything.

However, when we press further it appears that even in the free choices of people, God is still in ultimate control so that nothing whatsoever happens that God does not actually will to come to pass. How can this be? The answer lies in the meaning given to freedom. It does not mean basically the power to originate an event,

to be creative of something genuinely new in history as
the real source of novelty. Generally speaking, what
traditional theologians have meant by finite freedom is
voluntary action, choices that proceed from the person
who willed it.[68] The willing is genuine, uncoerced by
external forces. The sinner really wants to sin. Sin
expresses what a person is, has become and chooses.
Hence, at one level human choices are voluntary. Yet
when we look at the matter closely, it turns out that
these "free choices" end up accomplishing what God has
actually and finally willed. Consider the pen that
writes and the hand that moves the pen. What makes the
marks on the page? It is not partly the one and partly
the other but wholly the pen and wholly the hand.[69]
James Ross uses the analogy of the author of a novel who
determines what the characters in the book do, and yet
they act freely.[70] The butler murders the mistress of
the house by voluntary choice, yet the author of the
book "makes" the butler do it.

This account is oversimplified as it must be in
dealing with centuries of thought. Yet in its essentials, it describes the views of Augustine, Thomas
Aquinas, and John Calvin -- than whom there are no
higher peaks in Christian thought. Much could be quoted
from their words that would seem to contradict this
analysis. They certainly affirmed that people were
responsible for their own acts. Yet the bottom line is
that finally God is in complete control of the world
right down to the tiniest details of everybody's daily
life. God uses the free choices of people as instruments of the divine purpose. God rules by overruling,
by working in and through and around and in spite of us.
God's will and ways are mysterious, hidden from our

view. Events may seem fortuitous, contingent, and even chaotic to us. But in the end nothing happens that God did not one way or the other intend.

Running right through the tradition from Augustine through Calvin is the idea of predestination. God determines by a secret and unfathomable counsel of the divine will to save some from the damnation which all deserve as a result of the fall of Adam and Eve. The rest are deliberately consigned to hell or left to their own devices, which comes to the same thing. A good deal of the thought about providence has to do with the ways in which the elect are mercifully brought to salvation by the unfailing workings of divine purpose in history.

Is God, then, the author of sin and evil after all? The Protestant Reformers come closest to giving a positive answer. It was here that the unqualified sovereignty of God was set forth in its ultimate extreme. Hulrich Zwingli unabashedly said, "Yes, God does everything, including what we call evil, but we cannot apply human standards of morality and justice to the Almighty."[71] Calvin seems more reluctant and squirmy but explicitly agrees that God really makes the sinner sin.[72] But when he wants to hold people responsible for their acts, he also insists that the sinner willingly commits the sinful deed.[73] Calvin distinguishes between God's "secret will" and God's "commanding will." We are, he says, deserving of damnation because we have freely (voluntarily) violated God's "commanding will" although God's "secret will" makes us do what we do![74] Calvin also says that God hates the reprobate because they do not have the Holy Spirit. Of course, the reason the damned do not have the Holy Spirit is that God has deliberately chosen to withhold this gift from them.[75] Nowhere is the difference between post-Enlightenment consciousness and classical theology more acute than at this point. It baffles us to think that anyone with the slightest compassion or sensitivity could call a God good who would deliberately damn those to everlasting torment whom God has caused to sin. To his credit, we must note that at one point Calvin did say, "The decree is dreadful indeed, I confess."[76] Martin Luther held essentially the same views as Calvin. The highest degree of faith is believing God merciful when God damns so many and saves so few, believing God righteous when appearing to be unjust and thus worthy of hatred instead of love.[77] Like Calvin, he insists that we must not question God's ways. Given the transcendent mystery of God, is it not reasonable that God's justice should be incomprehensible? Luther can be quoted and interpreted in contradictory ways but explicitly in some writings denies the existence of free will altogether.[78]

On the surface Augustine and Aquinas appear to take a different line. Augustine frequently and vehemently denied that God was the author of sin. Evil proceeds from the free will of angels and of people.[79] Yet he is ambiguous and sometimes even self-contradictory.[80] In order that the divine decree of predestination be carried out, Augustine makes God's control of events so complete that he finally ends up not far from Calvin's subjection of human freedom to divine determinism.[81] Aquinas attributes sin not to God but to deficient secondary causes, including the human will in particular. God permits but does not cause evil. He further complicates the matter by distinguishing between foreknowledge and foreordination and between God's "antecendent will" and God's "consequent will" in order to soften the contradiction involved in God's apparent condemnation of what God has caused to happen on earth.[82] Augustine and Aquinas, given their assumptions about the nature of God, cannot avoid the conclusion that God finally is the author of everything whatsoever that happens, all their subtle efforts to absolve God from being the cause of sin notwithstanding.

It is clear to these theologians of the past that God has made a world and rules over it in such a way that nothing, not the least detail, can get out of hand. They were adept in quoting Scripture and really believed that the Bible required the unqualified sovereignty the affirmed. Many passages certainly seem to support their interpretations. But perhaps even more important is the fact that they were in the grip of philosophical assumptions which inevitably led to their conclusions. Once the absolute perfection, omnipotence, omniscience, atemporality, immutability, and simplicity of God are assumed as unquestioned presuppositions, it is doubtful that meaningful human freedom can be consistently asserted. This is certainly the case if freedom means the real power of contrary choice and the capacity to originate an event as a relatively autonomous and creative source of genuine novelty in history. To allow this kind of finite freedom requires some qualifications of God's absoluteness either as a divinely chosen selflimitation on or as a given metaphysical fact. Moreover, without some such reinterpretation, evil must be finally attributed to God and/or viewed as only apparent and not genuine. Since traditional theologians did not allow the qualification of sovereignty or any reinterpretation of absoluteness, we may feel that their affirmations of freedom are trivial, inconsistent, or merely verbal. If choice is real in some initial fashion, it finally seems so over-ruled that it becomes in the end ineffective, if not null and void. The Westminster Confession (1643) states succinctly what is intended to be a paradox beyond human comprehension but which the modern consciousness can scarcely avoid regarding as a contradiction: "God from all eternity did, by the most wise and holy counsel of His own will, freely and unchangeably ordain whatsoever comes to pass. Yet so as thereby neither is God the author of sin or is violence offered to the will of the creatures" (Article III).[83]

B. MODERN REINTERPRETATIONS: In the 17th and 18th centuries the Western world was presented with two different versions of God as the atemporal, immutable, omnipotent Sovereign. In the Catholic version God was Pure Absolute Being, while Protestants spoke more of the Almighty Personal Will.[84] Both asserted the all-embracing rule of God in which even the rebelliousness of finite subjects was ultimately if not immediately made to serve the good intentions of an ultimate purpose. A number of developments in the modern age have combined to generate revised estimates of divine sovereignty and human freedom.

1. Science for three centuries provided a picture of nature as a complex network of interacting events governed by inexorable and mathematically exact law. At worst this new cosmology seemed to describe an autonomous order in which the reality of a Transcendent Purpose was either unnecessary, incredible, or irrelevant, except perhaps as a remote First Cause now

inactive in daily affairs. Minimally, it provided the context within which providence must now be interpreted. Miracles and supernatural events which had been prominent in traditional conceptions now became problematic instead of a probable proof of divine action.[85]

2. The Enlightenment set forth the rights and dignity of humanity in ways that challenged the oppressive rule of tyrants both human and divine. Democracy was in the air, and even God was not exempt from the demand that ruling authority respect the rights of the governed. The insistence that religion be both rational and humane generated skepticism about the supernatural and miraculous elements in traditional piety and questioned whether a benevolent deity would predestine the majority of humankind to eternal torment.[86]

3. A growing historical consciousness asserted the autonomy of human subjects as the real agents in creating and directing history and strengthened the demand for either sole control or at least a partnership with the Almighty in shaping human destiny. Since the locus of meaning had been shifted from the next world to this one, humanity as the source and subject of historical advance assumed even more importance. Science with its views of an evolving nature and the growing faith in progress demolished the old static, closed, hierarchical world and gave impetus to a dynamic conception of reality that moved forward and upward in time to exhibit both novel forms of biological life and changing social institutions. History is malleable to human purpose and creativity.[87]

In the face of this emerging thought world, orthodoxies persisted to defend and restate the old views of providence. But liberal theologies arose to take modernity into account by generally moving away from tyrannical Calvinist determinism to softer views in which human freedom was taken more seriously. The harsher notes of predestination and everlasting punishment of the wicked were moderated or abandoned altogether. God was seen to be the immanent purpose and power within nature guiding the upward course of evolution and inspiring humanity to make progress toward the Kingdom of God on earth.[88] Post-liberal theologies, including neo-orthodoxy, generally have affirmed non-supernaturalistic modes of divine activity and have preserved the liberal rejection of tyrannical and unloving views of providence. But neo-orthodoxy in particular, in the midst of such 20th century horrors such as the Holocaust and the Bomb , vehemently rejected the idea of moral progress. In its extreme forms general world history was seen to be so chaotic and so morally ambiguous that divine sovereignty could only be affirmed paradoxically and by faith's vision alone, while ultimate hope was beyond history.[89] God's grace was experienced internally as a word of courage, meaning, forgiveness, and hope in the midst of chaos and absurdity (Barth and Bultmann). Milder versions represented by Reinhold Niebuhr found tangents of meaning in history, which are best interpreted by the parable of the wheat and the tares in which good and evil grow side by side while awaiting a final judgment at the End.[90] Current eschatological and political theologies (the theology of hope, etc.) see God's rule somehow proceeding not so much from the past by divine determination or from above in the present but from the future, which peculiarly defines the locus and reality of God.[91] But how God works from the future backwards into the present to bring about the good and perfect reign of righteousness is not always clear. Liberation theologies find God at work in liberating the downtrodden from oppression.

What is more clear is that while miracles and supernatural occurrences have not been entirely abandoned by all modern theologians, by and large the rule and activity of God are seen in and through the structures and processes of finite reality (nature, history, and human freedom) rather than in supervention of them. Providence is seen in the outworking of the inner-directedness of teleologically ordered beings (Tillich)[92] or paradoxically by faith in a stream of events otherwise fully interpreted by scientific methods (Bultmann).[93] Process theologians depict God as luring the world forward by persuasive love by evoking the free response of the creatures.[94] Increasingly, theologies of the last two centuries have granted a real if relative autonomy to nature and humanity in which contingency, chance, creativity, and freedom have qualified the absolute sovereignty of God. God is reinterpreted as either being selflimited and/or as including a dynamic dimension in which contingency, temporality, potentiality, and relatedness are affirmed as at least symbolically real (Tillich)[95] or declared to be a metaphysical fact (Hartshorne).[96] Actus purus is not in style today. Moreover, as compared to previous centuries of thought, the rule of God appears in modern theologies to be more clearly the sovereignty of love rather than the sheer control of events by absolute power. Even Karl Barth, who in most ways reinstates the classical views of God's all-determining rule, insists that providence is nothing more than the reign of pure love and grace. He rejects the idea of two divine elections -- one to salvation and one to damnation. In Christ we know of but one will. God elects that all be saved.[97]

IX. The Problem of Evil

If God is all-powerful, supremely wise, and perfectly good, how can we account for so much pain, suffering, misery, injustice, and evil in the world? With this question skeptics have taunted believers for centuries. It would appear that God cannot or will not prevent or remove suffering. If we say God cannot, the divine competence (power and wisdom) is impugned. If we say God will not, the divine goodness is put in jeopardy. If evil is real, then it seems that God is either too weak, too dumb, or too indifferent to do anything about it. This is a statement of the problem of evil -- the theodicy question. It is a part of the doctrine of providence, but it assumes such importance for modern people that it merits separate treatment.

A. CLASSICAL THEISM. We have already seen that traditional theology is filled with tensions that may be contradictions on this point. It can plausibly be argued that the only consistent (though not necessarily adequate) conclusion to which classical theism leads is that evil is only apparent and not real.[98] Once it has been assumed that God is pure simplicity, absolutely perfect, immutable, omnipotent, and omniscient, it follows that human freedom is, in effect, overruled, so that God is actually the cause of every event whatsoever.[99] Distinctions between foreknowledge and foreordination, between divine permission and divine causation of sin, between primary causation and secondary causation and all the other rationalizations which seek to preserve human freedom and absolve God of responsibility of sin finally fall away, given the conceptual model of God which is never questioned.[100] The only conclusion remaining is that God is really the cause of sin, but since God is perfect, this cannot be unjust. God could have prevented evil but didn't. Hence, sin and evil must finally be justified as contributing to and making possible a greater good than would have been possible without them. If this is the case, what appeared to be evil is only apparently so since it becomes an instrument of God in achieving maximum good.

This interpretation is prominent in the writings of many classical theologians. In particular, the greater good thesis runs right through the tradition. Though surrounded with many other claims, reservations, complications and qualifying themes with respect to human freedom and responsibility, the idea that suffering and sin are only apparent and not genuine evils would appear to be the only non-contradictory rendering of the logic of classical theism.

Another prominent theme is that we cannot finally understand or question the ways of God, who, after all, is perfect and thus cannot be either incompetent or immoral. Obviously there are questions here that can be debated endlessly.

B. THE BIBLE AND SYSTEMATIC THEOLOGY. The
remainder of this section will look at Biblical themes
regarding suffering and conclude with a brief analysis
of major themes developed by theologians relating to
theodicy.

Little systematic reflection on the problem of evil
will be found in the Bible. No solution is anywhere
offered. Injustice and suffering are dealt with in
numerous places but usually in a specific context. A
wide variety of settings and experiences provides the
occasion for the enunciation of a particular theme. The
sovereignty and goodness of God are everywhere assumed.
Evil and suffering are recognized as a part of life.
The sinfulness of humanity is often the subject of
prophetic declarations along with the pronouncement of
divine judgment and a call to repentance. Particularly
noteworthy is God's concern for the poor, the oppressed,
the outcasts, the sick, and the suffering. The Bible
can be quoted on both sides of the divine sovereignty
versus human freedom question.[101] God's control over
all events and doctrines of predestination is plainly a
part of the record. Yet people are clearly held
accountable for their wrongdoing.

With regard to suffering in particular, it may be
helpful simply to list some of the many themes contained
in the Bible without interpreting them in relationship
to any overall scheme.

The Old Testament

The good people always win. This theme is prominent
in the Deuteronomic
philosophy of history

	found in Judges, for example. If you are obedient, things will go well. If you sin, you will be punished.
<u>Take the long view</u>.	The unrighteous may flourish now, but in due time they will fall, and God's people will triumph. Psalm 73, Hab. 2:1-4. Sometimes what seems evil now turns out for the best later on. Gen. 45:1-15.
<u>Soon God will rescue us.</u>	Now the wicked are in charge, but God will very shortly intervene supernaturally and es-tablish an otherworldly Kingdom. The Book of Daniel.
<u>Its too difficult for you to understand</u>.	The mysteries of good and evil are beyond human comprehension, so people should not get impudent with God. Job, especially chapter 38.
<u>The suffering of some saves others</u>.	Suffering can be vicar-ious and redemptive. Is. 53.
<u>God is the source of everything, including evil.</u>	God is the Almighty

Creator who creates light and darkness, weal and woe. Is. 45:7.

God is a source of strength in times of trouble.

Trouble is all around, but God is near to provide comfort and deliverance. Many of the Psalms, e.g., 18 and 46.

The New Testament

There is a purpose in what happens.

God works for good everywhere. Rom. 8:28.

In the midst of suffering we are secure.

Nothing can separate us from God's love. Rom. 8:31-39.

The hope of heaven will carry us through.

The sufferings of this age cannot be compared to what lies beyond. Rom. 8:18-27.

Who are you to question God?

God is the potter, you are the clay. You have no right to be God's judge. Rom. 9:14-24.

Demonic powers wreak havoc with the world now.

Satanic beings are the source of much evil, suffering, and spiritual

God __will__ __intervene__ __very__
__soon__.

Suffering __disciplines__
and __tests__ __us.__

bondage. This is as-
sumed nearly everywhere,
but see I Cor. 2:7-8;
Ephes. 6:12; Luke 5:31-
36.

The end of the world is
near. God will soon
appear to vindicate the
righteous and put all
evil down once and for
all. This is generally
assumed, but see the
Book of Revelation.

God works through our
suffering to perfect us.
Heb. 12 and I Pet.

From these and many other passages that could
be noted, it is clear that a righteous and loving God is
clearly in charge of things, though often working in
mysterious ways beyond our understanding. God provides
comfort in times of distress and ultimately will deliver
the righteous, either in a future on earth or in heaven
beyond. Suffering may be educational for us and
redemptive for others, but God's love is never absent.
God's providental care is evident, and God's people live
confidently in hope of spiritually transcending present
suffering while they await a final victory here or
hereafter. If there is a solution to the problem of
evil in the Bible, it is plainly a practical one. With
God's help we can overcome it. No theoretical
explanations or interpretations or resolutions are

offered, perhaps because they are not needed when the practical triumph in life is assured.

Theologians over the centuries have reflected upon the issues in a systematic and theoretical way. A brief survey of these reflections will conclude this section. First of all, some distinctions are needed.

1. <u>Natural</u> <u>evil</u> refers to pain and suffering that spring from the nature of things involving no human irresponsibility -- unavoidable accidents, disease, storms, deformed babies, floods, etc. <u>Moral</u> <u>evil</u> is the suffering caused by people acting irresponsibly involving either bad intentions or carelessness, i.e., sin.

2. A distinction is helpful between <u>apparent</u> <u>evil</u> and <u>genuine</u> <u>evil</u>. Some suffering may not be evil, if it is the necessary means to a larger good. Genuine evil is suffering that is pointless, gratuitous and destructive. The world would have been better off without it, all things considered. As we have seen, one thread of thought in classical theology is that all sin and suffering are only apparently evil from the largest possible perspective of God's ultimate purpose in creation.

Some prefer to distinguish between relative and absolute evil. To call some suffering only apparent evil may trivialize it or unjustifiably take away its badness. <u>Relative</u> evil is suffering that is partially, wholly, or more that compensated for by an accompanying or subsequent good, especially which we could not have had without the suffering involved. <u>Absolute</u> <u>evil</u> is suffering that is purely destructive, unnecessary, and without any redeeming compensation in the short or long run.

In its classical form the problem of evil can be stated systematically as follows: Can one affirm that God is both omnipotent and perfectly good while acknowledging the reality of genuine or absolute evil without falling into contradiction? Two ways of dealing with this question can be noted. The first takes the form of appeals in the attempt to show that no necessary contradiction is involved. The second acknowledges that logic and truth require that one or more of the terms be qualified. Either the goodness or power of God or the reality of evil must be denied or reinterpreted if contradiction is to be avoided and an adequate interpretation of God in relationship to evil is to be discovered. Both lines of thought will be examined briefly.

One group of theologians believes that there are considerations which taken singly or in combination can preserve both divine omnipotence and divine love despite the presence of real evil in the world. Five of the most common appeals follow.

1. The appeal to sin. Some suffering may be the result of wrong-doing, either as divinely ordained punishment or as the unavoidable consequence of violating the moral order of the universe. Suffering that we bring upon ourselves by our misdeeds does not implicate the goodness or power of God. Yet this appeal

surely has limits, for suffering does not seem to be distributed in proportion to sinfulness but often quite arbitrarily. Sometimes the righteous suffer while the wicked prosper.

2. The appeal to ignorance and paradox. Finite beings cannot understand the intricacies of the world in relation to God's purpose. Hence, we are incapable of solving the problem. Some theologians would insist that it is a paradox. We must affirm the goodness of God and the reality of evil. But we cannot work out a satisfactory theoretical solution. Sometimes this is connected with the idea that God has provided a practical resolution in Christ, who on the cross participates with us in our suffering and offers the assurance of God's love here and now and an ultimate victory by and by.[102] But are there limits to this appeal too? Mystery may be involved ultimately, but surely the combination of revealed truth about God and the insights of reason can throw some light on the subject. Theologians do not seem inhibited in speaking with confidence about many other equally mysterious realities. Hence, the appeal to ignorance in this case may seem to be arbitrary.

3. The appeal to freedom. God has given us the precious gift of freedom, but this carries with it the possibility of its misuse.[103] Much suffering is caused by people harming, exploiting, and neglecting each other. But freedom is essential to our humanity and to the creativity and love which make life worthwhile. Hence, the gift of freedom is worth the risk of its possible and actual misuse. Surely there is truth here, but is freedom such an absolute value that it justifies

all the cruelty that might result? Would it have been better if God had limited or redirected Hitler's freedom in order to prevent the murder of 6,000,000 Jews during the Holocaust? Moreover, reference to freedom can deal with moral evil, but it does not account for natural evil, unless much more is said about how moral evil can be the cause of natural evil.

4. The appeal to divine purpose. Suffering may be willed or permitted by God because it is essential to the development of human beings as moral personalities.[104] The world is a laboratory of soul-making. Suffering and even injustice may have disciplinary, educational, and redemptive values which are so important that the world is better off on the whole than would be the case otherwise. How can this important dimension be acknowledged while noting that suffering is often destructive and not redemptive or educative? Is not much suffering simply pointless, meaningless, and absurd without compensating gains? And is the enormity of suffering far in excess of what is needed to accomplish its positive values? And is it distributed so unfairly, so disproportionately and randomly, that its redemptive possibilities are outweighed by its negative features?

Other thinkers develop the idea of the world as a place of adventure which adds zest to life while unavoidably involving danger. The universe embodies the most appropriate combination of law and freedom, predictability and precariousness, order and contingency, necessity and chance, promise and peril. This makes possible learning, evokes creativity, offers challenge, and develops us into mature, fully actualized moral beings. The risks are necessary and instrumental to the goal. God made the world the way it is with all this in mind.[105]

5. The appeal to the nature of finitude. The possibility of evil is the inevitable and unavoidable implication of our existence as finite beings.[106] An experiencing subject capable of enjoyment and pain is an organized unity of structures and processes which must function together in harmony and mutual support in order to sustain the organism. This means that something can go wrong. Things happen that disrupt organic functioning. To be finite is to be vulnerable. The brain, for example, is a highly complex organ with marvelous abilities. But the very fact of this complicated organization which makes it work also means that it is very delicate and easily damaged. A slight blow to the head might destroy it.

Moreover, we live in interdependence with other beings in a total system of things governed by natural laws and causal relationships. In this context contingencies arise which can be the source of pain, disruption, and death. Yet life and learning and creative actions would be impossible without this interdependence within natural, organic, and social settings. The world is made up of a plurality of relatively autonomous chains of causation and events. Sometimes they collide with devasting results. A man and a woman left a restaurant. A maid cleaning a room upstairs accidently knocked off a flower pot from a window sill which fell down and killed the man walking past underneath. Different chains of activities intersect in accidental ways which are destructive. This is the way things are. But without these separate and intersecting streams of activities in an interdependent, law-abiding universe, valuable features of our world would be lost.

In summary, the very structures, processes, and interdependent relationships which make enjoyment and fulfillment possible when they work harmoniously are the very same factors that cause pain, suffering, and destruction when they go wrong or collide with each other. We cannot have the possibility and actuality of goodness in such a world without having the possibility of evil. God's choice was not (1) whether to create a world with the possibility of evil in it or one that had only good but rather (2) whether to create a world with the possibility of both good and evil or no world at all.

If the valid elements of these five principles are combined, they go a long way in showing how God can be omnipotent and loving in a world in which real evil occurs. Some theologians do not believe that the problem can be resolved without contradiction within this framework. They insist that some of the terms must be redefined or modified. One could, of course, avoid contradiction by denying that real evil exists. All prima facie instances of pain, injustice, and misery turn out upon full consideration to be only apparent evils. This view has its defenders. Or one could question the divine goodness and love. A few reluctantly take this alternative. The remaining option is to limit the power of God and question omnipotence. The theory of the finite God has attracted a few theologians. E.G. Brightman argued that God is perfectly good but not omnipotent. An all-powerful God would have created free finite persons who always freely choose the good, and there would be less non-humanly created suffering. God is limited by what Brightman calls "the Given" -- something just there inside of deity which God neither willed nor approves. He likens this internal non-rational factor in God to what sensation, emotions, disorderly desires, instinct, and impulse are for us. This passive element helps to account for both moral and natural evil. God struggles to overcome "the Given" hindrance to the production of value, and there is hope for progress if we cooperate with the divine will which aims at the good.[107]

Process theologians also modify the terms of the equation.[108] They deny or at least redefine omnipotence. God cannot unilaterally bring about any desired state of affairs, since other beings have some power to resist God. Hence, the possibility of evil is a given metaphysical fact. However, God does have perfect power, i.e., all the power and the kind of power that a perfect being can have. And a perfect being exercises primarily persuasive rather than coercive power. A further step is taken by recognizing two forms of evil: disharmony and triviality. The former is evil in itself, the latter by comparison with what might be. Likewise, there are two forms of good: harmony and intensity. God, then, has two aims: overcoming disharmony and achieving more complex harmonies, i.e., more intense, rich, fulfilling experiences. But if the attempt to bring about complex harmony fails, then more suffering is introduced into the world. If it succeeds greater good results. God faces a dilemma: remain with trivial harmonies with the possibility of small evils (e.g. a one-celled organism) or seek more intensive harmonies with the possibility of greater evils (e.g. by creating human beings). God wants to go beyond triviality and to avoid discord, but these two aims are in tension. Is the risk of creating greater good worth the chance of introducing greater (genuine) evil, given the fact that God's persuasive love cannot guarantee the outcome? Process theologians say yes. While redefining omnipotence in terms of perfect power and taking away its coercive elements, process theologians agree with those more traditional modern theists who assert that the possibility of genuine evil is a necessary correlate of the possibility of goodness. Even a perfect God cannot make a world in which the creation of good does not run the risk of introducing evil.

X. Miracle and Prayer

Two additional subjects related to divine providence must be treated briefly: miracles and prayer. In the Bible supernatural occurrences abound. The Red Sea waters stood up like walls so that the Israelites could escape Pharaoh's army (Exodus 14). The Savior was born of a virgin (Matt. 1) and was raised from the dead (Matt. 28). Many other signs and wonders signify the sovereignty of God over nature. Classical theology took Biblical miracles at face value, never questioning their literal factuality. Since the rise of modern science, miracles have become problematic.

Prior to the 20th century science seemed to describe a universe that was law-abiding in a strict and exact mathematical way. Miracles implied a violation of these regularities, a breaking in from above which

contradicted scientific knowledge. 20th century physics
defines nature in much less deterministic, mechanistic,
and materialistic terms. The world has a more organic,
dynamic, creative character in which rigid law has been
replaced by statistical averages. Nature seems more
like an organism with life-like characteristics than a
dead machine.[109] Hence, it would appear easier to make
a place for human freedom and divine purpose given the
conceptions of nature found in 20th century physics than
was the case in prior centuries, as Whitehead has so
persuasively argued.[110]

Nevertheless, two questions must be dealt with by
theologians today as before. 1. What is the nature of
nature as science conceives it? 1. However nature is
thought of, whether in Newtonian or post-Newtonian
terms, does God always without exception work in and
through the general structures and processes of the
cosmos, or does God on occasion miraculously transcend
them by acting directly on the world from above in
supernatural, interventionist fashion? Hence, it is not
enough merely for Brunner to attack Bultmann because his
science is out of date, that is, allegedly wrong on
point 1 above.[111] It is still necessary to ask the
second question. Here Bultmann is correct that science
has not thrown overboard its methodological assumption
that nature is an autonomous realm requiring no supernatural or mythological principles to complete its
interpretation.[112] Miracle as supernatural intervention
has no more place in 20th century physics than prior to
relativity theory and quantum mechanics and the other
innovations introduced by Einstein, Heisenberg, and
others.

However, in all fairness it should be noted that contemporary theologians who insist on the possibility of miracles as direct and immediate acts of God do not necessarily think in terms of intervention or intrusion into natural processes. Since God is at work in the general processes of nature as well as in miraculous occurrences, the distinction is between ordinary and extraordinary modes of divine activity. It is only when nature is considered to be an autonomous realm with its own self-possessed mechanisms and principles that miracles are seen as violations of natural law. Even the term "supernatural" is ambiguous, since from a Christian standpoint all events in creationto -- miraculous and ordinary -- have their ultimate source in the nature-transcending power and purpose of God. Yet in common usage "supernatural" with respect to miracle refers to acts of God which do constitute exceptions to -- if not violations of -- natural causality. This usage is followed here.

No consensus can be found relating to miracles in contemporary theology. Some theologians have no hesitation in affirming the possibility and reality of occasional interruptions of the ordinary course of events.[113] Such happenings are described in the Bible and may occur today. Other thinkers, who have imbibed deeply of the ethos of science and the secular mentality, see God as working without exception in and through the universal structures and processes of nature and human freedom. The crucial issue here has to do with the modes of God's purposive action. One group wants to maintain the reality of an occasional or extraordinary breaking in of God's power from above as essential to Christian belief. The Bible teaches it, and miraculous actions would seem to be an implication of the freedom and sovereignty of the Almighty Creator.[114] The other group believes that experience does not validate the reality of supernatural interventions into natural processes. God does not interrupt the general order of nature.[115] Cosmological miracles belong to a pre-scientific age and have no place in modern thought. Moreover, supernaturalism raises moral questions about the love and justice of God. If nature miracles occur as a part of God's providence, then how can we account for their relative rarity and their seeming arbitrariness?[116] Why does God answer some prayers and deny the request of others? Why does not God mass feed starving children in the midst of widespread famine? A God who acts sporadically and according to some whim or secret purpose appears to violate norms of both morality and rationality. An interventionist God acting arbitrarily disrupts the rational structure of reality and is an offense to reason.[117]

While these two contrasting views are easily identified and real, the total theological spectrum cannot be described by simply saying that some theologians believe in miracles and some don't. Neither is it strictly a matter of controversy between fundamentalists and all the rest. The attitude taken toward miracles depends on the character of a theological outlook taken as a whole. All these complexities and variations of belief cannot be detailed here. Some theologians could be called skeptical about the reality of supernatural miracles but want to remain cautious and openminded. It is important for them to affirm that God stands in a free and purposive relationship to the created world. God is not a slave to natural causation nor locked out of the finite realm of nature and history. The world is so structured that the divine purposes can be accomplished. Whether God ever acts in ways that transcend the law-abiding character of the world known to science is an open question. Particular Biblical miracles must be examined one by one, with most credence usually being given to the healing miracles of Jesus. The tendency is to doubt obvious cosmological wonders, but a dogmatic position is not taken.[118]

Liberal theologians emphasize divine immanence. God works in and through all things in a creative and evolutionary way, so that supernatural miracles lose some of their importance. Some neo-orthodox theologians stress the transcendent freedom and sovereignty of God to such an extent that miracles are not out of the question. Barth so affirms the priority of God's unqualified Lordship that problems raised by science are by-passed or ignored. He does affirm both the virgin birth and the bodily resurrection of Jesus as signs of the reality of revelation. But the relationship of these events known in faith to the observable world order is complex and ambiguous. Barth urges that we cannot say how the "miracle of Christmas" and the miracle of the empty tomb occur. He does add that the virgin birth is in no way a "psycho-erotic" matter. Barth is not intimidated or even very interested in what scientists or secular historians have to say about these matters.[119] Brunner teaches that the Incarnation was a unique and miraculous act, but the deity of Christ was invisible to the ordinary eye of the dispassionate observer. Cameras at the tomb of Jesus on Easter would have recorded no objective wonder. The resurrection took place in another order from that which science can detect. Brunner rejects the virgin birth and a physical or bodily resurrection on both historical and theological grounds. However, the big MIRACLE of the incarnation is associated with visible wonders in the objective order, as a stone dropped into the water might send ripples into the surrounding areas. Moreover, exceptional events still happen in our time.[120] Barth and Brunner, then, affirm the reality of miracles but in a sophisticated, modern framework. They are neither orthodox nor liberal but neo-orthodox and Kantian. From their standpoint empirical science deals only with the phenomenal order, not with things as they are in themselves. Hence, faith may discern a supernatural order of things in which God is active in ways which transcend or escape scientific methods.[121]

Many modern theologians prefer to redefine miracle so that the term can be preserved without offending science. Schleiermacher thought of miracle as an event which has revelatory significance.[122] Tillich uses the term with the same meaning.[123] Revelation occurs in miracle received in ecstasy. A miracle is an astonishing event which unveils the mystery of being. This is the fundamental meaning in the Bible itself. Neither thinker believes that these revelatory occurrences involve any breach of natural causality. Many theologians would deny that there is a supernatural order which breaks into the natural world open to ordinary experience. However, they would urge caution in defining the boundaries of the natural and argue against being dogmatic about what can or does happen.

Against this background petitionary or intercessory prayer can be examined. Prayer has many functions and meanings. It is a form of praising God, giving thanks, and seeking a deeper faith and a more intimate experience of divine presence. Here the concern is with those petitions which "ask God for something." Does it do any good? Does it change things? Will God change the course of objective events, heal bodies, deliver from natural disaster? The prayer-answering, miracle-working God is extolled every Sunday morning by television evangelists. In a more thoughtful and responsible fashion some conservative and liberal theologians contend that a sovereign God certainly can and on occasion very likely will intervene in the ordinary course of events to change things in response to the earnest intercession of the faithful.[124] At the opposite pole are theologians who maintain on rational and theological grounds that we should never expect God to reorient the factual order on request.[125] Genuine prayer, says Paul Tillich, is a surrender of a fragment of existence to God. In that sense prayer has power to change things. Presumably, this means that those who surrender to God are transformed and through them other events are affected. Still others want to affirm the intimacy of a sovereign God with seeking believers in ways that unite the divine loving will with the valid hopes of finite wills in a shared providential governance of the world.[126] Frequently, however, they are vague about what this really means in terms of changing the stream of external events in more or less miraculous fashion. The tendency is to want to move beyond mere self-induced psychological change but to stop short of nature miracles. The favorite middle ground is the healing of the body, while gross suspensions of natural law are ruled out. Critical openness is the stance that defines this cautious yet positive view of prayer.

A frequent note is that the highest form of petitionary prayer is "Thy kingdom come, Thy will be done on earth as it is in heaven" (Matt. 6:10 RSV). Hence, while personal needs are not to be excluded from intercessions, the result of true prayer may be a surrender of individual desire to divine purpose. While prayer is not likely to invoke supernatural nature miracles, it may lead us into cooperative ventures uniting divine and human creativity so that the world is changed in surprising ways. Earnest intercession may clear away the barriers that inhibit divine creativity and thus open us up to the working of divine aims so that the fullest potential for good that is really present may be actualized. Since the body is our nearest and most intimate natural environment and hence most open to spiritual influences, organic healings and the actualization of human potential may be the point at which petitionary prayer is most effective.[127]

This concludes the consideration of the nature of God and of the relationship of God to the world. The next topic examines the highest form of created life on earth -- a creature made in the divine image, but fallen from the potential of that high estate, yet capable of being renewed and fulfilled in a perfected destiny by an everlasting love.

CHAPTER III
HUMANITY, SIN AND SALVATION

I.

Humanity as a Problem

Discussions of this topic typically begin with the assertion that we are our own greatest problem. Who are we? What kind of being is a human being? How shall we understand ourselves? Humanity itself is the most vexing puzzle facing us.

1. Are human beings best understood from "below" in terms of their connection with nature, the animals, and their bodies? Are we just a more complex edition of the chimpanzees, and is our behavior most adequately explained by our primeval origins in the evolutionary process? Or are we best thought of from "above" as minds or souls or spirits? Are we fundamentally different from the animals and from nature by virtue of our freedom, reason, and imagination? Or are we some sort of composite creature with citizenship somehow in both worlds?

2. Is our predicament that we cannot sufficiently bring our impulses, drives, and instincts under the control of reason, or is the human spirit itself corrupted by nature or choice, poisoned by some defect in our own freedom?

3. Are we fundamentally determined in our behavior by our genes and by social conditioning, or do we rise above nature and society with the power to choose our own destinies?

4. Is there a "human nature" which all of us as individuals exemplify, or are we infinitely malleable products of heredity, environment, and choice with no fixed or universal characteristics?

5. Is life a "one-shot" deal in which we live and die as a particular individual once and for all, or is this life just one of many incarnations of an immortal soul? And if we live only once, is death the ultimate end, or is there a life beyond that never ends?

This list could be made much longer and the questions indefinitely expanded. But even this sketchy outline will serve as a reminder of the complexity of the human problem and of the contradictory views of our nature and predicament which this self-inquiry has produced over the centuries. It is the purpose of this chapter to survey the Christian understanding of humanity. This inquiry will reveal the unity and the variety, the particular and the universal features, which a previous chapter described as characterizing Christian thought on every issue it takes up.

As a way of indicating the basic structure of Christian thinking regarding humanity, the chapter will be divided into three basic sections: Humanity as created, humanity as fallen, and humanity as the subject of redemption. To put it differently, the human story is a drama in three acts. (1) Human beings were created in the image of God from the dust of the earth. (2) By

their own folly and choice, they fell into sinful
disobedience, alienated from themselves, each other,
from nature, and from God. (3) Humanity has been
redeemed from its predicament by a divine saving act in
Jesus Christ for an everlasting and perfected destiny in
glory. In one sense these three can be seen as
successive phases and have so been presented in the
Bible and much traditional theology. The first eleven
chapters in Genesis tell the story of the creation and
fall of the human race. Genesis 12 begins the history
of salvation with the call of Abraham. With some justification the rest of the Bible right through the last
chapters of the Book of Revelation can be seen as the
story of God's efforts to save humanity. When the story
of Adam and Eve was taken literally as a historical
fact, the sequential treatment of creation and the fall
of humanity was especially pertinent, since the disobedience of the primal pair was thought to implicate all
succeeding generations in this "original sin." But even
in modern theological systems in which the dramas of
Eden are regarded as mythological embodiments of universal truth about the human predicament, it is still the
case that the saving action of Christ is in the past,
while ultimate fulfillment lies in the future. Hence,
temporal and sequential dimensions do remain in the
Christian understanding of sin and salvation.

Yet creation, fall, and redemption can also be seen
as headings under which the essential Christian
teachings about humanity can be articulated. Existence
in the divine image, alienation from essential human
nature, and restoration to wholeness are interrelated
dimensions of the human condition which are descriptive
of every moment of the believer's life. At any rate,

whether considered as sequential stages or as coexisting characteristics, Christian theology has not said all that it believes about humanity until all three of these perspectives have been developed.

II. Humanity as Created

Beginning with the Bible itself the theological tradition has been consistent in viewing humanity in a double perspective. While much more will need to be said, it may be sufficient initially to say that a human being is a unity of soul and body. It may be more useful to use the more metaphorical Biblical categories of "breath of life" and "dust of the earth" to indicate the duality and complexity of human being in Christian understanding. Under these headings various conceptual models that have appeared over the centuries can be developed.

A. BIBLICAL AND CLASSICAL CONCEPTIONS OF HUMANITY: The Bible nowhere presents a systematic or technically precise conceptual model of the human being. Various terms are used to describe the makeup and functioning of a person. If one is to generalize, perhaps it is fair to say that a human being is a duality but not a dualism of body and soul. Body and soul are not separable or independently existing parts which are combined. In particular, the soul is not an immaterial, immortal substance or entity which inhabits the body temporarily. That is a way of thinking associated with the Greeks but not with the Hebrews. In Hebrew thought, according to H. Wheeler Robinson, a person is conceived of as "an animated body not an incarnate soul."[1] A human being is

a living body with spiritual capacities -- an inseparable unity of biological and psychic constituents and
functioning. A person is an indivisible whole.

   Much that traditional theology has said about
humanity as a created being is based on Genesis 1-3.
The classical text for understanding humanity as a unity
of body and soul is the statement that God "formed man
of dust from the ground, and breathed into his nostrils
the breath of life; and man became a living being" (Gen.
2:7 RSV). Humanity (adam) was made from dust (adamah).
When the breath of God was breathed into Adam, he became
a living creature or soul (nephesh). Nephesh is the
principle of life, the animating vitality that is found
in animals as well. Ruach (spirit) is frequently used
as an equivalent of nephesh, but its distinctive meaning
relates to the human capacity for relating to God in
trust and obedience. The important thing is that there
is no sharp separation of body (basar) from soul
(nephesh) or of soul from spirit (ruach). The meanings
of each flow into each other to form a wide range of
overlapping designations. The words for flesh, body,
and soul can all be used to refer to the whole person
viewed from a particular perspective, as well as having
a variety of more limited or specific meanings. In
general, body or flesh is the tangible, material
dimension that people share with other living beings.
Soul is the life principle that animates human beings as
well as animals. Spirit (literally, wind or breath) is
the unique human capacity to be empowered by the Divine
Wind (Spirit) and to interact with God. Yet all these
dimensions are integrated into an indivisible unity of
being and functioning which constitutes a person.

The anthropology of the New Testament does not differ in essentials. The terms body (soma), soul (psyche), and spirit (pneuma) pretty well correlate with their Hebrew counterparts. Soma and psyche may each refer to the whole person as a unity. In the New Testament, as well as the Old, flesh (Heb., basar; Grk., sarx) may also refer to a person or to the whole of humanity. In its restricted meaning flesh refers to the outer parts of the physical organism of people and animals, but in its extended reference flesh indicates a mode of finite existence that stands in contrast with the life of God. As flesh, humanity is weak and mortal (Is. 31:3, 40:6) and, in the New Testament, sinful. In Pauline thought sinful life "according to the flesh" is not primarily the victory of unruly passions or bodily desire over rational control but a self-centered life of pride, rebellion, and sensuality which springs from a disordered and corrupted mind or will (Rom. 8:1-17). Flesh as creaturely reality and sinful possibility is contrasted with the life-giving energy of the Spirit which issues from the goodness and power of God. The body and the flesh may fall under the power of sin and evil, but they are, as created aspects of human existence, not evil in themselves nor are they as such the source of sin.

Humanity has a unique status as a creature made "in the image of God" (Gen. 1:26-27). What the original writer had in mind is hard to tell. Perhaps the implication is that humanity is a free, creative, purposive, intelligent being with a knowledge of good and evil who can interact with God. The nearest thing the text itself suggests is that human beings share in the rule of God by having dominion over other living creatures in a way that "images" the sovereignty of God over the whole creation.

Humanity, then, is a thinking, feeling, willing creature made "in the image of God" from "the dust of the earth" who exists and functions as a psychosomatic totality. Three other aspects of humanity as created are worthy of notice. Human existence is good, temporal, and social. (1) GOOD: Creatureliness suggests dependence, weakness, and subjection to all the infirmities of the flesh, including sickness, pain, and death. But there is never a suggestion that finitude is evil as such, nor is it the source of evil. The essential goodness of human existence is a part of the general conviction in Biblical thought that whatever God creates is good. Sin, as we shall see, springs from freedom not creatureliness. (2) TEMPORAL: Human life is set within time and history, bounded by birth and death. But individual existence takes place in a community which lives between memory and hope. Meaning to life is provided by the revealing and saving acts of God which constitute the history of salvation, beginning with an originating creation and moving toward a final consummation in which the divine purpose will be brought to a glorious fulfillment. In between are the convenant with Israel and the new convenant in Christ. These decisive events occurring in time and history give meaning and purpose to life and point toward an ultimate fulfillment in the future. Time, then, is the essential framework within which life and destiny are understood. (3) SOCIAL: Individuals belong to groups, and this communal dimension is not accidental or superficial but basic. Organic conceptions of society prevail in which meaning and fulfillment are experienced in terms of membership in the corporate body. In the Old Testament, as well as the New, the view is that individuals are "members one of another" (Rom. 12:5 RSV), related to each other as parts of the human body are to the whole organism.

In summary, the Bible stresses both the creatureliness of humanity as a frail, dependent, weak being made of dust and the unique dignity and status of humanity existing in the image of God.[2]

The main line of Christian thought through the centuries has more or less preserved these Biblical themes. However, some motifs have been threatened in different eras and cultures by the mixture of ideas from secular culture and philosophy. In particular, the use of Greek concepts has been pervasive and often corruptive of the Hebrew inheritance. Eastern Christianity, for example, was prone to identify sin and evil with the finitude and mortality of human existence. Origen taught that the mutability and corruptibility of earthly life was a punishment for a preexistent rebellion against God. Greek Christianity generally saw sex as a special symbol and manifestation of sin and regarded the lust associated with reproduction as an obvious necessity of the bodily life. These tendencies, springing from Platonic and Hellenistic sources, threatened to disrupt the Biblical notion that human life is finite and dependent yet essentially good. Yet while extremes can be found in which the body is even regarded with horror as the locus of sin, death, lust, and corruption, it cannot be said that the main line of classical thought ever lost its firm rootage in the Biblical outlook. Gnostic, Manichaean, neo-Platonic, and other dualistic views were regularly condemned. Origen's teaching that bodily life is a punishment for a pre-Adamic Fall was rejected by the mainstream. A high view of the body was maintained, even though the suspicion of sex as peculiarly identified with sin permeates Christian thinking right down to very recent times. Contemporary theologians typically regard the negative views of sex as an influence from Greek thinking and not as an authentic presentation of Biblical conceptions, despite some Pauline passages which seem to lend credence to ascetic values and scorning of the flesh.[3]

It is fair to say that the conception of humanity that dominated Christian thought from the 2nd century until modern times was a mixture of Hebrew and Greek thinking.[4] The typical view of theologians through the centuries has been that a human being is a combination of two distinct parts -- a rational, immortal soul and a physical, mortal body. Death is a punishment for sin. Nevertheless, the Biblical notion of the life in heaven as involving the resurrection of body was preserved. Theologians under the influence of Platonic philosophies from the early centuries onward were especially prone to see body and soul as separate elements temporarily joined together. Aquinas, under the influence of Aristotle, presented a more unified view in which the soul is the form while the body is the matter of the person, constituting a single substance. Yet he in the end, still reflecting Aristotle, asserted that reason has an eternal quality that distinguishes it from the body in such a way that it (mind or intellect) exists as a subsistent form independent of the body -- a note seemingly in contradiction with the view that soul and body in unity constitute the single substance of humanity. The dualistic note is present also in Martin Luther and crystal clear in John Calvin. Humanity consists of two substances, the soul and the body. The soul is "an immortal yet created essence"[5] which dwells in the body "as in a house."[6] While we ascribe properties to the whole person that cannot be attributed to either alone, body and soul are two distinct parts, each with its own nature. Calvin repeated the familiar Platonic arguments for the immortality of the soul.

Likewise, the traditional interpretation of the imago dei represents an ingrafting of intellectualistic elements from Greek thought. Generally, the image of God is identified with the presence of rational soul. However, nearly always there is an additional notion of a capacity for relating to God in love and obedience which goes beyond the ability to think logically and reason discursively. This is especially true of Augustine, who develops out of his neo-Platonic heritage a notion of self-transcending spirit with powers of introspection, memory, intellect, will, and imagination such that only in God can humanity find a home. Based on a probable misinterpretation of Gen. 1:26, Irenaeus made a distinction between image and likeness which was developed further by Thomas Aquinas. The image of God is the rational nature of humanity with its capacity for the natural virtues of wisdom, courage, justice, and temperance. The likeness is the supernaturally added set of virtues consisting of obedience to God in faith, hope, and love. Only the latter virtues are lost in the fall, while the former abilities remain to distinguish humanity from the brutes. This distinction became official Catholic doctrine.

At the time of the Protestant Reformation John Calvin continued the traditional view that the image of God is located primarily in the powers of the rational soul, along with the added capacity for a faithful and virtuous relationship to God. Yet the whole of the human person, including the body, reflects in a special way the rays of divine glory. Calvin, following some of the theologians of earlier centuries, even sees the upright walking position of humanity in contrast to that of the animals as an aspect of the total meaning of the imago dei. For Calvin the main emphasis is two-fold: (1) The divine image refers to a unique set of capacities possessed by humanity, especially the powers of reason, will, moral judgment, and spiritual discernment. (2) It also refers to a state of original perfection, integrity, virtue, and right understanding which Adam and Eve possessed before the fall and which is now lost.[7] Martin Luther particularly emphasized this latter point. He defines the imago dei primarily by contrast with the present condition of sinfulness. The original perfection of humanity is now so marred and obscured that it is almost wholly lost. Luther went on at some length to extoll the intregity and excellence of that former state, including highly adorned descriptions of the moral and physical perfections of Adam.[8]

To conclude this section, one additional controversy needs to be introduced. Theologians over the centuries have debated the question of the origin of the soul. Traducianists take the position that the soul, as well as the body, originates from the parents. In the early church Tertullian affirmed this view.

<u>Creationists</u> argue that each new soul is created <u>ex</u> <u>nihilo</u> and infused with the body at conception or birth. This view was predominant in the Greek church, and many of the Latin thinkers also took this position. Traducianism was thought by many to afford the best explanation of the transmission of original sin. Augustine leaned toward this option but in the end confessed to being baffled by the question. The fact that both Pelagius and Calvin were creationists indicates that the doctrine of transmitted corruption does not necessitate one theory or the other. Traducianism has been regarded as heretical in the Catholic Church. Aquinas was a creationist, while Luther favored the traducianist position.

Modern theologians are not particularly exercised over the issue, though traducianism would seem to fit most naturally with scientific and evolutionary views, as well as with as Hebrew psychology. It is a speculative question, and the position one takes is dictated more by philosophical commitments than by any essential theological interests. Emil Brunner calls the dispute a pseudo-problem, it being obvious to him at least that a human being is derived from the parents <u>and</u> a new creation of God.

B. CONCEPTIONS OF HUMANITY IN MODERN THEOLOGY: The confrontation with the modern world resulted in significant transformations in the understanding of humanity, just as it has with all other doctrines. This is a complex subject which cannot be traced or described in detail. Major features of these reformulations can be dealt with under six headings.

1. A characteristic feature of modern theologies is that they no longer take literally the creation stories in Gen. 1-3. Adam and Eve are not historical figures who lived once upon a time somewhere in Mesopotamia. These accounts are myths which nevertheless contain truths essential to Christian thinking. The decisive factor in this reformulation was the theory of evolution developed by Charles Darwin in THE ORIGIN OF SPECIES (1859), although geology had already made it evident that the account of the earth's origin in the Bible was not compatible with scientific findings. One consequence of this is that modern theology has returned to the Old Testament view that death is a natural part of human creatureliness, not a consequence of the rebellion in Eden.

2. A major shift occurred in the "turn to the subject" which took place in modern philosophy beginning with Descartes. In classical thought every kind of being was thought of as a substance with its own identifying nature or essence. Humanity was a special entity composed of soul and body. Like other beings, humanity had its own distinctive end or purpose. The world was made up of the sum total of substances arranged in hierarchical order from the lowest to the highest, with humanity at the apex of the earthly realm. Beginning with Descartes attention was focused away from humanity as a being with a special essence or nature toward the self as a center of consciousness and action. A person is not a being with a unique essence but a subject with a structure of consciousness shaped by history and decision. This turn was in part a reaction to the threat implicit in the supposed materialistic and deterministic implications of a scientific cosmology

which was shattering the teleologically-directed cosmos of medieval thought. In the new world-view the objective world consisted of particles of matter ordered by efficient causes in accordance with inexorable law. But in addition to the objective world of things, there is the subjective world of persons. Hence, modern thought struggles with the relationship of the known world to the knower -- the subject who inquires and acts.

Immanuel Kant is the focal point at which this revised way of thinking entered into the stream of theological thought. He envisioned a moral self, somehow transcendent to the phenomenal stream of nature, legislating duty in obedience to a categorical imperative. Associated with this was a "Copernican revolution" in thought in which the mind, instead of reading off the patterns existing objectively in the world itself, imposes form on the chaotic mass of sensory data. Soren Kierkegaard -- a 19th century Dane who was the father of 20th century existentialism -- heightened this emphasis on the self as subject. A person is "an existing individual" made dizzy and anxious by the reality of a radical freedom in the presence of the dreadful threats of the moment and the terrifyingly open future. The individual must choose a way of life and make commitments in the context of objective uncertainty. Becoming a Christian involves a leap of faith -- a sheer decision of will -- in a state of heightened subjective passion in the midst of rational absurdity (the claim that the Infinite was incarnate in the finite in the historical fact of Jesus Christ). Hence, "Truth is subjectivity."[9] From Descartes to Heidegger and Whitehead and through many intervening and associated forms of idealism, existentialism, phenomenology, pragmatism, and process thought, centering on the experiences, choices, and actions of subjects became the dominant way of organizing thought about the human way of being. Associated with "the turn to the subject" is a focus on history as the locus and focus of human existence. History is the realm of meaning created by persons as free, creative, imaginative subjects. The title of one of Reinhold Niebuhr's books sums up the center of concern in modern theology -- THE SELF AND THE DRAMAS OF HISTORY.[10]

3. A good deal of modern theological thought arises as a response to the challenge of scientific materialism and other reductionist philosophies. In the Augustinian and medieval worlds of thought humanity was a finite purposer in a system of interrelated, harmonious purposes in which every being had its distinctive end, ordered and directed by a sovereign Purpose. In this neat, relatively small universe humanity was at home. Modern science presented a vast impersonal cosmos which by the 18th century looked like a machine in which efficient causes had replaced final causes. The only place for freedom and value seemed to reside in the human mind and perhaps in the mind of the Machine-Maker envisioned by deists. An increasing number of scientists and philosophers followed LaPlace in finding no need for the hypothesis of God. When humanity itself turned out to be the product of an evolutionary process in the Darwinian discovery, human dignity was further threatened by the growing power of materialism, naturalism, and determinism. Karl Marx offered a picture of the world determined by economic forces and in which the intellectual and moral creations

of the mind are ultimately generated by impersonal material forces. Hence, much thought is simply rationalization dictated by the necessities of the class struggle. Sigmund Freud described humanity as driven by the chaotic drives of the id over which the rational ego has limited control. Hence, whether humanity is ultimately economically determined (Marx) or biologically determined (Freud), little remains of the Biblical view of a free and responsible creature made in the image of God. Among many intellectuals a naturalistic humanism flourished in which nature as known by scientific methods is the only reality, and moral values are purely human creations in a Godless universe (John Dewey, e.g.).

Liberal theologians attempted to appropriate the empirical conclusions of the growing sciences without succumbing to the atheistic conclusions which many were drawing. The evolution of humanity from lower forms of life over billions of years was regarded simply as God's way of creating. By referring to the unique qualities of mind and spirit found only in persons, humanity could be acknowledged to be a child of nature without giving up the conviction of Christian theology that humankind was also a child of God and of infinite worth.

Against the background of evolutionary theology and the impact of naturalistic and reductionistic philosophies, a central problem for the liberals was to interpret the relationship of personhood to nature. Albrecht Ritschl, one of their most influential number, wrote, "In every religion what is sought with the help of the superhuman power reverenced by man is a solution of the contradiction in which man finds himself as both a part of nature and a spiritual personality claiming to dominate nature."[11] In trying to articulate the Christian view of humanity as a moral subject or spiritual personality transcendent to nature, theologians appropriated a variety of philosophical models, particularly those found in Kantian and post-Kantian forms of idealism. Idealism saw mind or spirit as the clue to reality and as the creative source of the phenomenal world of nature studied by the sciences. Hegel interpreted humanity as finite Spirit in the context of a cosmic history in which Absolute spirit was dialectically evolving to achieve self-realization. In addition, romanticism was an ally by virtue of the emphasis upon the reality and importance of the inner world of spirit with its feelings and intuitions of things sublime. Alfred North Whitehead interprets the romanticist movement as a protest on behalf of value in reaction against reductionistic implications of scientific materialism. Liberals of the 19th and early 20th centuries most often turned to the idealists and the romanticists in their efforts to acknowledge the embeddedness of humankind in nature without giving up the idea of the imago dei. In Germany Schleiermacher, Ritschl, and Harnack made use, in various combinations, of these outlooks, while in America the same influences could be found in William Adams Brown, A.C. Knudson, Walter Rauschenbusch, and many others. Shailer Mathews and Henry Nelson Wieman of the Chicago School turned more to naturalism and the empirical sciences. But in all varieties of liberalism the emphasis was on humankind as a moral personality evolving out of nature with spiritual capacities to choose between good and evil and with a potential for intimacy with God. Liberals generally had a high estimate of humanity as a potential coworker with God in bringing the creation to completion in a universal Kingdom of love, harmony, and peace.[12]

The influence of existentialism along with a recovery of the authority of Scripture and the Augustinian tradition characterized the neo-orthodox effort to state a Christian view of humanity. The notion of humanity as "finite freedom" (Paul Tillich) epitomizes an emphasis frequently heard. As finite, human beings are weak, mortal, and dependent creatures embedded in a network of biological and social forces which limit and condition their existence. As free creatures, aware both of their limitations and their creative powers, they are anxious and tempted toward irresponsible and destructive attempts to achieve security. Reinhold Niebuhr found in the heights of creative freedom, which he called the capacity for self-transcendence, the clue to the image of God. Using insights from the Bible, Augustine, and Soren Kierkegaard, Niebuhr developed a powerful polemic against the secular philosophies of the modern world. He urged that only the Biblical view of humanity as both creature of nature and free spirit transcending nature could account for both the "grandeur and misery" (Pascal) of the human drama.[13]

Secular views of humanity continue to challenge Christian thought. Behaviorism in psychology (B.F. Skinner) maintains a reductionist and deterministic picture of human beings.[14] Sociobiology (E.O. Wilson) turns to the evolutionary orgins of homo sapiens for explanations of social practices and even ethical tendencies.[15] Perhaps more important than specific philosophies is a pervasive secularism which sees the sciences interpreted on the basis of naturalistic assumptions as providing all we need to know about personhood. Such a view sees the self as a product of nature (genes) and society (prevailing social institutions and ideologies) as modified by the responses and actions of the individual. Such a self, whether regarded as determined or free, is an autonomous subject who exists as the sole creator or personal meaning and historical destiny. Recent Christian thought has made use of phenomenology, process, philosophy, humanistic and transpersonal psychologies, as well as existentialism, in the attempt to restate in a modern conceptuality the Scriptural view of humanity as both flesh and spirit, a frail creature of "dust" who reflects the "image of God." Without denying the rootage of humanity in the evolutionary processes of nature and the conditioning power of social institutions, Christian theologians seek to exhibit the truth of the "'religious dimension' present in everyday and scientific experience and language."[16]

4. Much modern theology, especially in the 20th century, has been concerned to recover the depth dimension of personality. This is a reaction against the emphasis on rational consciousness and simple moral will as the center personality -- views represented in Descartes, Calvin, and modern industrial society generally. The central theme of this outlook is that selfhood is centered in and directed by conscious rational choice. Marxism, existentialism, and depth psychology (Freud) have been particularly important in helping theology to recover the irrational, unconscious sources of behavior, to acknowledge the profound

conditioning of economic forces and social institutions, and to take into account the dreadful anxiety, guilt, doubt, and meaninglessness which threaten "finite freedom." These deep sources and forces beneath the surface and beyond the control of conscious moral choice underlie the tragic conflicts and alienation which attend the human condition. Incorporating these insights puts theology back in touch with Augustine and other classical diagnosticians of the soul. Moreover, it helps to overcome moralism and superficial views of sin by acknowledging the dark irrational side of human existence beyond immediate conscious control. The work and influence of Paul Tillich are especially worthy of mention in this connection.[17]

5. Considerable attention has been given in 19th and 20th century thought to the purging of Greek and Hellenistic influences which were thought to distort Biblical anthropology. Particularly important has been the attempt to recover the psychosomatic unity of the self against the dualism of Greek thinking which assumed the union of an immaterial soul with a physical body. An associated emphasis has been the attempt to overcome the denigration of the body and the suspicion of sexuality as a peculiar locus of sinfulness. A healthy hedonism and an appreciation of the sexual life characterize much contemporary theology and ethics, though excessive bodily indulgence and destructive, self-centered, exploitative sexuality are regularly condemned. The single most controversial point at the moment has to do with whether homosexuality can be a responsible form of sexual love. An increasing minority of theologians is inclined to answer in the affirmative.

6. Finally, but by no means least, is the confrontation with sexism. Much of the Bible and nearly everything in Christian tradition treats women as inferior to men. The devaluation of females is a horrendous blot on the Christian conscience, the immensity of which has only begun to penetrate the thinking of the church. Feminist theology in its critical function calls the idolatry of one-sided patriarchal values and the domination of women by men in church and society into question and demands redress and a revolutionary change of belief and practice.[18] On the constructive side it has not yet become clear what the implications for a new anthropology are to be. It can be stated that the issues call for fundamental, permanent, and radical revisions of theological conceptions, the language of worship, and the ministry of the church. Full equality of men and women in every area of life, thought, and practice is the emerging norm among an increasing number of Protestant and Catholic thinkers, though the power of traditional views is still strongly entrenched.

III. HUMANITY AS FALLEN

So far attention has been devoted to humanity as created. Christian thought has been consistent in seeing human beings under the headings of creatureliness and the image of God. Humanity is flesh and body imbedded in and arising from nature as a weak, mortal, dependent creature. Yet, as made in the divine image, humanity is a being of great worth with marvelous capacities of freedom, reason, imagination, and creativity. As a unity of body and soul (spirit), humanity is potentially and essentially good. Finitude is neither evil nor the source of sin. No dualism of value is allowed between body and soul, flesh and spirit. Yet that is not the whole truth. For humanity is actually and existentially fallen. A gap exists between what human beings can and should be and what they are here and now. Sin intrudes to corrupt the intended harmony of creation. How does evil enter the good world? What is the nature of sin, and what are its sources and consequences? Why were Adam and Eve cast out of the paradise of Eden? What is the nature of the human predicament? This is the subject of the second act of the Christian drama regarding humanity. We must now examine humanity as fallen.

A. BIBLICAL AND CLASSICAL VIEWS OF HUMAN FALLENNESS: Sin may be taken as the comprehensive term symbolizing the conflict, injustice, estrangement, and suffering which human beings bring upon themselves by their foolish and perverse choices. The Bible is quite clear that humanity fails to move toward its intended destiny because of acts of free will. While the human situation may be such that temptation is powerful and while the human frame may be frail, in the last analysis people are responsible for their deeds. Sin may not be an act of sheer perversity, utterly unconditioned by mitigating circumstances, but neither does it follow from necessity or from causes too powerful for the weak will of tempted humans to resist. Humanity falls by choice. Yet sin is usually taken to be universal. Hence, a tension arises which challenges all Christian thought to preserve responsibility while acknowledging that all have sinned, without making sin necessary.

The Bible has a rich vocabulary to indicate the nature of wrongdoing. A large number of terms, images, and conceptions appears. A brief account is inadequate to explore all the nuances of meaning, but the main import can be indicated. While elements of taboo can be found in the Old Testament (Lev. 19:9, 19), fundamentally human perversity is set within a moral and religious context. By far the most important idea that sin is a violation of the nature, intent, and revealed will of God (Is. 59:12-13; Rom. 1:18-32). Sin is a revolt, a rebellion against God (Gen. 3). It is willful disobedience proceeding from an evil heart (Gen. 6:5; Jer. 11:8, 18:12; Is. 29:13). Sin is a state of inner corruption and perverse intentionality which issues in specific acts of disobedience (Rom. 1:1-32). In its nature sin is personal estrangement from God and other people, the very opposite of loving God with all one's heart and one's neighbor as oneself (Luke 10:25-28). Toward God, sin is faithlessness, disloyalty, idolatry, and lack of trust and honor. Toward others, it is injustice, exploitation, neglect, cruelty, and oppression. To be a sinner, then, is to live in a wrong relationship with God and others rooted in a deliberate refusal to honor and obey the Creator and to live in harmony with one's fellows.

Little speculation is to be found in the Old Testament regarding the origin of sin. The story of Adam and Eve tells how sin began (Gen. 3), and subsequent chapters report its spread and universally destructive consequences (Gen. 4-11). However, nothing is made of the rebellion of the primal pair elsewhere in the Old Testament. A few references can be found to demonic influence (I Sam. 16:14) and to the temptation of Satan (I Chron. 21:1), but generally the origin of sin is sought simply in an evil and perverse heart -- a self-chosen corruption of the will. Yet sin is universal, involving all people from the beginning of their lives in a tragic and destructive destiny (Ps. 51:5, 14:1,3; Eccl. 7:20). It involves the whole person and the whole race. Individuals and the nation are mutually implicated. The nation sins (Is. 1:4), the wrongdoing of a leader of a family or state involves all members in guilt (II Kings 9:8). The organic solidarity of self and society extends over the generations (Lam. 5:7). While Jeremiah and Ezekiel protested on behalf of individualism (Jer. 31:29-30; Ezek. 18), the corporate implications of sin were contained in a proverb: "The fathers have eaten sour grapes, and the children's teeth are set on edge."

The solidarity of the race in its fallen condition appears in the New Testament also. All are together in a state of rebellion and disobedience, individually and corporately falling short of the glory of God (Rom. 3:23). Occasional references are made to the rebellion in Eden (II Cor. 11:3; I Tim. 2:14). It is, of course, Paul who makes most of the Genesis story. In Pauline thought sin is a principle and power that dominates this age. Adam is the symbol, head, and progenitor of the reign of sin and death which now prevails, from which Christ -- the second Adam -- delivers us (Rom. 5:12-19). In the New Testament generally the present age is under the domination of principalities and powers of darkness -- supernatural agents of evil (John 3:19-21; Ephes. 2:2; I John 5:19; Col. 1:13). Within this context the rebellion of humanity fills the world with ungodliness, lawlessness, and evildoing. Yet the fallen state and its slavery to demonic powers is not a tragic fate over which individuals have no control but a freely chosen life which results in suffering, death, punishment, and a realm of disorder in which the intended harmonies of creation are fundamentally disrupted. So serious and universal is the predicament of humanity that only the saving power of God's love revealed in the triumphant death and resurrection of Christ can deliver the world and its inhabitants from the historical and cosmic consequences of this revolt against the Creator (Ephes. 1:16-2:10).[19]

In the early centuries following the New Testament era, particularly in the East, sin took on a far less profound and menacing appearance. Several tendencies emerged. One was to define the human predicament in terms of ignorance, weakness, error, bondage to demons, and the fact of death. A related theme focused on the power of the flesh expressed in sensual indulgence, especially the pursuit of sexual pleasure. Sensuality (concupiscence) is the special mark of sin. While the descendants of Adam may have inherited a powerful bias toward sin along with a corrupted environment, nevertheless no guilt attaches to us from that primal fall. Free will remains sufficient to resist actual sinning. We somehow participated in the original sin and are one with Adam. Its legacy to us is more like a wound or a sickness which makes it more difficult but not impossible to serve God. Strictly speaking, we are responsible (guilty) only for our own defections. A more somber view developed in the West among the Latin thinkers such as Tertullian and Ambrose, but it was not until Augustine that the full blown doctrine of original sin emerged as a fundamental tenet of Western orthodoxy.[20]

In the 5th century a controversy arose which was to define the terms of the debate about the human predicament, at least in Western Christianity, for all subsequent centuries. Somewhere around the year 405 Pelagius, a British monk, now teaching in Rome, set forth a high doctrine of freedom and responsibility. We are fully capable of keeping the law of God if we choose to do so. Three elements enter into human action: the power (posse), the will (velle), and the realization (esse). The first comes from God exclusively. The latter two belong to humanity. The descendants of Adam have no inherent bias toward sinning as a result of the Fall. Each child is born innocent, though granted the social environment has been polluted by the example of the first parents and the sins of their offspring. Sin is the deliberate violation of laws that we are perfectly capable of observing. Celestius put the logic of the Pelagian position with vivid clarity: if sin proceeds from necessity, it is not sin; if it proceeds from choice, it can be avoided. Sin, then, is a conscious choice of evil, an act of perversity that breaks a commandment known to the perpetrator. It is generally agreed that all post-New Testament Christian thinkers before Augustine were more or less Pelagian. Little indication of an enslaved will can be found during this period.

Augustine stated the polar option to Pelagius in classic form. As created, humanity was an unflawed specimen of virtue, integrity, intelligence, health, and beauty -- unmarred by any physical, moral, or spiritual blemish. Existing in the image of God, the self was perfectly ordered, endowed with a will oriented toward the good. The body was subject the soul, the carnal appetites to rational will, and the will to God. The will was free in the sense of possessing the ability not to sin (posses non peccare). Hence, the first pair was endowed with such abilities and such divine grace that sin need not have occurred. But it did. Why? The fall was the result of free choice, an act of will. The internal motivation of the rebellion against God was pride, an inordinate love of self in which the soul substitutes itself for God who alone is due worship. The prideful exaltation of self (superbia) issues in revolt against God and disobedience of the divine command. Such a turning was a momentous loss of being and status, not only for Adam and Eve but for all their descendants. Speaking out of his neo-Platonic background, Ausustine thought the fall resulted in a lapse of being, a metaphysical fall in the direction of non-being. Moreover, the whole self was now disordered and corrupt. Since God is both truth and goodness, a will not centered on God will lose both in a state of ignorance and concupiscence. The fallen soul exists in a state of confusion and insatiable craving without satisfaction. The whole being is disordered. The emotional life ranges from elation to depression, and sexual life even in marriage is marked by irrational passion, lust, and shame. This corrupt nature is passed on to subsequent generations through the uncontrollable carnal excitement which accompanies conception. In the fallen state humanity is incapable of doing good or of remedying the dreadful state into which Adam's defection cast the whole human race. Every child is born into a mass of perdition with a corrupt nature and guilt inherited from the primal parents. Each in turn passes

on this original sin to the next generation. Only the
unmerited love of God expressed in a creative act of
saving grace will suffice to restore the will from its
dreadful corruption. Doomed to death and worthy of
eternal hell, the human race is helpless to save itself.
Worthy of note is Augustine's view that we all were
seminally present in the reproductive power of Adam.
Hence, we participated in the fall and are co-
responsible for it. Adam and Eve were the human race.
They embodied human nature. Their fall was everybody's
fall. In every life actual sins proceed inevitably from
the original sin -- the inherited depravity -- which
unites us to Adam and Eve in the universal ruin of the
whole race.[21]

The Council of Carthage (418 AD) clearly denounced
Pelagianism. The Council of Orange (529 AD) basically
took Augustine's side but modified his views on the
irresistibility of grace, denied that we are predestined
to sin, and insisted on the necessity and possibility of
human effort to complete the process of salvation. In
some such qualified form the Augustinian position became
a part of Roman Catholic orthodoxy. In the East
Augustine had little impact. The view of Aquinas that
only the likeness (the supernaturally added virtues of
faith, hope, and love) but not the image of God (the
capacity for the classical virtues of temperance,
courage, justice, and wisdom) enabled him to modify the
more thorough-going conception of depravity found in
Augustine. But Aquinas agreed that pride (inordinate
self-love) is the root sin and the underlying source of
concupiscence (devotion to mutable good). Formally, sin
is loss of original righteousness. Materially, it is
concupiscence. As the comprehensive name for sin

concupiscence is the result of turning away from God (pride). It refers to the evil desires residing in a corrupt heart which get expressed in disobedience of the divine law and in a voracious craving for selfish pleasures.

The Protestant Reformers returned to a purer form of Augustinian thought in their attempts to refute the semi-Pelagian doctrines of Catholicism. Martin Luther delighted in contrasting the present state of corruption with the original righteousness and the perfection of Adam before the fall. Only a mere shadow of the image of God remains. So marred and obscured is it by perversity of will that it is almost completely lost. John Calvin defines original sin as an inherited depravity evoking the wrath of God and corrupting the soul in all its parts.[22] Both Reformers agree in affirming total depravity. By this they meant, not that fallen sinners can think or do no good at all, but that every dimension of the self is infected with the taint of rebelliousness, self-love, and evil desire. The center of personality itself -- the will -- is vitiated, so that humanity cannot rescue itself but is entirely dependent on God's saving grace. Some orthodox Protestants in the next century went further, even to the point of making sinfulness the primary defining characteristic of the self. Flacius, a Lutheran scholastic, said that the very substance of fallen humanity was original sin. The suggestion that not only the behavior but the very being of humanity was bad was rejected as bordering on Manichaeism.[23]

B. MODERN REINTERPRETATIONS OF SIN: It was in liberal Protestantism that Pelagian doctrines received their most powerful revival.[24] A new theological _Gestalt_ emerged as liberals sought to modernize orthodoxy in the interests of both credibility and a recovery of what they regarded as genuine Biblical ideas obscured in traditional formulations. The rationalism and optimism of the Enlightenment plus the new framework offered by evolutionary philosophies were decisive. The orthodox doctrine of original sin is an offense to reason in that it condemns individuals for a corrupt nature and inevitable sinning over which they have no control. It is irrational to hold people accountable for actions they cannot avoid. Moreover, the fall was not a literal happening anyway. Hence, the story is neither factually true nor is the Augustinian interpretation of it theologically sound. Finally, the estimate of the human predicament is far too pessimistic.

The liberal view of sin assumed that human beings emerged from an evolutionary background. Their problem is that the nascent spirit with its basically sound impulses toward the good is dragged down by the animal passions which still rage within. Shailer Mathews spoke for many when he said that human nature is not corrupt but atavistic. Sin, then, is _the victory of nature over spirit_. Ignorance, inertia, the corrupting power of evil social institutions, and the sheer difficulty of living in accordance with high moral standards means that sinful living is easier and more likely than righteousness. Sin is the organization of life around the motives of the lower self -- the surging animal passions and the preference for selfish pleasures -- rather than around the potential of the higher self -- the spirit with its ideals of altruism, justice, and love. The will is not so much corrupted by a self-chosen defection from God rooted in pride and rebelliousness as weak, lazy, and undeveloped. Guilt emerges when the will gives consent to the lower motives and selfish impulses and when it chooses to violate known ideals which demand that the soul struggles upward toward moral perfection. Sin is less prideful rebellion against God than it is selfishness in all its forms, from harmful pleasure-seeking to neglect and exploitation of others. Sin against self and neighbor is sin against God. The one point at which a connection with the old doctrine of original sin remained was in the affirmation of the solidarity of all people in a corrupted environment. "Sin," said Schleiermacher," is in each the work of all, and in all the work of each."[25] Sinful practices are transmitted socially and institutionally from one generation to another, creating a powerful network of "superpersonal forces of evil" (Rauschenbusch) to which individuals add their own wrongdoing.

Liberalism flourished during a time of general cultural optimism about humanity and its future. The view of human nature reflected this outlook. For liberal theologians human reason and freedom are basically on the side of virtue. Sin is more a matter of weakness than of a fundamental self-chosen corruption at the center of the self. Will and spirit wrestle with the drag of nature in the pursuit of goodness with great hope for increasing success for progress toward the reign of justice and love in human affairs. Underlying and surrounding this optimistic vision is a theology of divine imminence which sees the cosmos and history being gradually infused with the qualities of a Creative Spirit whose purposes are mirrored in the person of

Jesus of Nazareth. Hence, the inertias of nature are progressively to be overcome as the human spirit wins its battles with the lower impulses of sensuality and selfishness.

This optimistic outlook was shattered by the catastrophes of the 20th century. In reaction theologians turned again to the Pauline-Augustinian tradition in order to speak to a culture whose very foundations were being shaken. Neo-orthodoxy revived the doctrine of original sin but disavowed the literalism of the drama in Eden and the notion of inherited corruption based on it. Adam and Eve become the mythological story of Everyone. Karl Barth, Emil Brunner, and Paul Tillich could well be taken as representative of this point of view, but Reinhold Niebuhr stands out above them all. According to Niebuhr, humanity is both involved in the necessities, contingencies, and vicissitudes of nature and, at the same time, transcendent to nature through reason, freedom, and creative imagination. Spirit reaches its height in the power of self-transcendence -- the capacity to make the self the object of the self as subject. Existing at the juncture of nature and spirit, humanity is anxious. Anxiety is not sin, but as the internal precondition of sin (Kierkegaard), it constitutes temptation. Hence, sin is not a matter of sheer perversity. Ideally, anxiety might be resolved by faith in the power and goodness of God. Actually, everyone responds sinfully. Sin posits itself (Kierkegaard), leaps into the situation as an inevitable but unnecessary choice as the self seeks to overcome anxiety in a combination of two perverse ways. Here Niebuhr reproduces the familiar Augustinian analysis. 1. The root of sin is unbelief -- lack of trust in God -- which on its reverse side is pride -- undue exaltation of self. Unbelief/pride is the attempt to resolve anxiety by attaining invulnerable security for the self, an effort which fails. Nevertheless, the result is injustice toward the neighbor as the self exploits the other out of self-interest. 2. Sensuality is the other dimension of sin. It is, on the one hand, an alternative strategy for ridding the soul of anxiety by immersing oneself in the pursuit of worldly values in an attempted escape from freedom. Sensuality is, on the other hand, a further extension of self-love in a life of pleasure seeking. Neither strategy singly or in combination works to bring tranquility of soul, but the futile attempt fills the world with violence, oppression, destructive self-indulgence, and/or anesthetic loss of self.[26]

With the special assistance of Soren Kierkegaard, Niebuhr restated the Pauline-Augustinian assessment of the human predicament. Several points are worthy of note: (1) The self is vitiated at its very center by a perverse and self-corrupting act of will. Hence, salvation can come only from beyond the self in an act of divine grace. Niebuhr rejects the Pelagian and liberal view that sin is simply the drag or inertia of nature against the more inclusive moral ends which reason entertains. (2) Though denying inherited corruption and guilt, Niebuhr falls into the familiar logical absurdities of Augustinian thought by affirming that sin is universal and inevitable but not necessary. The paradox of responsibility despite inevitability indicate the inability of mere logic to comprehend the complexities of experience. This point illustrates his dialectical method according to which truth is found by holding contrary points in a balanced tension, not resolvable in a more inclusive synthesis. (3) Sin is ultimately mysterious, proceeding from the unfathomable depths of the human spirit. It is an act of anxious, tempted freedom and hence not a matter of sheer perversity. Yet sin is an inevitable choice but only because the situation in which it occurs is falsely and freely though universally misinterpreted. (4) Niebuhr agrees with modern theology generally and with Celestius that death is a natural fact, not a punishment for sin. The nearly unanimous voice of the whole Christian tradition has held that had Adam and Eve not sinned, they would have lived forever. The Genesis account and the Old Testament as a whole would appear to support Celestius and Niebuhr, but Paul apparently accepted the common rabbinic teaching of his day that mortality resulted from the defection of Adam.

Niebuhr's account has been deeply and widely influential despite some suspicion, reflecting the persisting power of Pelagian rationalism, that his paradoxes may actually be contradictions. Theologians of many persuasions have adopted major elements of his views of sin and their implications for social ethics. However, in recent years he has been attacked because his alleged excesses of realism are thought to inhibit the fervor for revolutionary change that is both necessary and possible. Liberation theologians, among others, have voiced this fear.[27] Feminist theologians, in particular, have attacked all forms of Augustinian theology because it is said to be sex-biased. The description of sin as prideful rebellion against the sovereignty of God and aggressive exploitation of others

may well define the perversity of men as occupying the
positions of power in church and society. But it is
inadequate to explain the sin of women and other
relatively powerless groups. Their estrangement from
God, self, and others is more likely to proceed not from
pride and self-elevation but from passivity and self-
abnegation. Sin here is the failure to affirm the worth
and dignity of their selfhood, to accept timidly their
inferior status and devaluation by patriarchically
defined rules. This may include collaboration with the
oppressor in the interests of secondary gains and to
avoid conflict and perhaps humiliation.[28] Clearly an
agenda has been set to which both men and women must
give serious attention. Blacks, other minorities, and
women have reason to make common cause on this issue.
But perhaps the universal and ultimately crucial issues
have to do with the differences between those who have
power and those who do not. This means that any
definable differences in the sinful tendencies of men
and women or between whites and blacks arise out of the
peculiar historical and current inequalities of power
that characterize their relationships and not out of any
inherent genetic differences between the sexes or races.

IV.   HUMANITY AS REDEEMED

One point remains with respect to the Christian
understanding of the human condition and prospect. By
tragic and universal choice humanity fell from or failed
to rise to its intended estate as an essentially good
creature of God made in the divine image. The
possibility of redemption from this estranged condition
inheres in the fact that sin came into the picture as an

adventitious intruder. The fallen state is a contingent fact, even if a universal one, not a necessary outcome or an expression of the givenness of human nature. The alienation from self, nature, other people, and from God defines the existential condition not the essential being of humanity. Hence, salvation is possible. Moreover, deliverance and healing involve a fulfillment of the potentialities inherent in creation not a liberation or escape from the world. The whole person is to be saved as a unity of body and spirit, and the whole cosmos is to be redeemed along with humanity (Rom. 8:18-23; Rev. 21:1-5). The creation and the human race that are now engulfed in conflict, disorder, suffering, and confusion are fallen from a potential and essential goodness which can be reclaimed and brought to the glorious fulfillment of an intended, possible, and promised destiny.

The eschatological dimension of salvation will, for reasons of convenience and systematic neatness, be taken up in another chapter. Moreover, in discussing the nature of redemption, the saving work of Christ will be presupposed but elaborated later. Christian thought is an organic whole in which each part presupposes and implies every other segment. But not everything can be said at once. Thus, some logic of organization must be imposed which is in every case somewhat arbitrary and/or conventional.

A. BIBLICAL AND CLASSICAL CONCEPTIONS: The Biblical vocabulary for salvation is as rich and varied as is the terminology used to describe sin. Any brief synthesis will inevitably leave out important dimensions of the total picture. One consistent note is that God is Savior (Is. 45:21). In the most comprehensive sense salvation refers to divine deliverance from any and all ills of humankind. This includes the suffering which springs from creatureliness such as pain, sickness, and death as well as from the bondage to sin and demonic powers resulting from the rebellious disobedience of a perverse will (Ps. 103; Ephes. 2:1-10). In the Old Testament, in particular, the central references are historical, concrete, and social -- the liberation from Egyptian bondage in a special way but including deliverance from all political threats from invading enemies in subsequent centuries (Ex. 15; Deut. 33:27-19,; Ps. 44:1; Is. 40). Beyond this is the promise of a good and perfected future, a final and permanent victory in which all the evils springing from both finitude and freedom will be overcome (Is. 11:1-9; Daniel). In the first instance, then, salvation is an all-embracing term referring to God's intervention into history by which the people of God are rescued from every threat to their health, prosperity, freedom, and well-being. The New Testament is dominated by an apocalyptic framework in which salvation refers to the deliverance of believers from the realm of darkness, sin, demonic bondage, and death into the new age of light, righteousness, and immortality -- an inbreaking whose effectiveness is already decisively felt but which will soon be brought to completion in a cataclysmic intervention of God at the return of Christ.

In a more restricted sense redemption refers to the restoration of right relationships with God and other people which sin disrupted. In this context God is both Judge and Savior. The anger of God is hot against the rebellious spirit and evil heart of humankind which fill the world with violence, depravity, and injustice (Amos; Rom. 1-3). But the Bible is eloquent throughout its pages in proclaiming not only that God is gracious, merciful, and ready to forgive all who repent but that God takes the initiative to make salvation available (Ps. 32; Micah 7:18-20; Hosea; Mk. 1:15; Rom. 5:6-11).

Any summary will suffer from oversimplification, but at least three interrelated dimensions of the restoration to right relationships can be discerned. (1) First is the gift of forgiveness by which transgressions are blotted out, cancelled, remembered no more (Is. 6:7, 43:25; Mk. 6:12; Rom. 4:7). The larger idea here is the reconciliation of God and humanity, overcoming the estrangement that sin wrought (II Cor. 5:18-20). Paul's distinctive term for this is justification -- God's gracious acceptance by which we are absolved of guilt and pronounced righteous (Rom. 3:21-26; Gal. 3:23-29). God's declaration comes as a free gift to be received in faith. A related aspect of the process of salvation which leads into and overlaps the second dimension is suggested by the term repentance. It refers to a change of mind, to sorrow and regret, but most importantly it means a turning back to God and away from sin. It is closely related to conversion and indicates the beginning of a new life (Deut. 4:30; I Kings 8:33; Matt 3:8; Mk. 1:14-15; Acts 3:19, 26;; Luke 22:32; II Cor. 7:10; Heb. 6:1).

(2) A second dimension has to do with a transformation of the inner springs of action within the self so that the sinful nature is replaced with a new heart or orientation of will. This idea in its fullest sense is mostly absent in the Old Testament except in

the promise of a new heart that is to be given individuals in the coming age when the new covenant is introduced (Jer. 32:31-34; Ezek. 36:25-27), though a few passages approach the idea (Ps. 51:5-7, 10: I Sam. 10:9). The idea of regeneration or a transformation of nature is most prominent in Paul and the Johaninne literature. For Paul the believer has a new life in Christ, no longer carnal or according to the flesh but according to the Spirit (Rom. 6; 8:1-11; I Cor. 2:14-3:3; Gal. 2:30). In John salvation is basically the infusion of life involving a change of nature through union with Christ by which one is born from above (John 3:1-10, 5:24, 10:10, 15; I John 3:6-10). The term regeneration appears rarely and mostly late in the New Testament period. It refers to being reborn by the Word and Spirit into the eschatological age already present and shortly to be consummated (I Peter 1:3-5, 23-25; Titus 3:3-7). Sanctification, as a process of growth in holiness (Godlikeness) and love inspired by the Holy Spirit, overlaps the idea of regeneration and leads into the third dimension of salvation (Acts 2:38-40; 26:18; Rom. 6:19-22; I Cor. 1:2; I Thess. 5:23; Heb. 2:10-11).

(3) The life that has been turned around and reoriented toward God will be rich in the fruits of obedience and love. God requires justice, kindness, and steadfast love (Amos 5:24; Hos. 2:19-20; 6:6; Micah 6:8). The righteous take delight in the law of God (Ps. 1). A typical pattern in the Epistles of the New Testament begins with the proclamation of the Gospel and a call to repentance followed by a description/prescription of the ethical qualities of the new life in Christ (Rom. 12:12-15; Gal. 5-6; Ephes. 4-6; Col. 3-4), chief among which are love, humility, self-denial, and service

of others. Paul calls these virtues the fruits of the Spirit (Gal. 5:16-24). Salvation is an accomplished fact, a process, and a goal to be reached. The new age has broken into history with power sufficient to overcome the demonic grip of sin and death and to insure the victory proleptically enacted in the resurrection of Christ.

Biblical summaries of the normative existence of the righteous and the redeemed show a two-fold reference which is the exact opposite of sin. Toward God the ideal life is praise, loyalty, reverence, love, trust, humility, and gratitude. Toward others it is joyful obedience expressed in acts of justice, compassion, and loving service of the neighbor in mutual helpfulness (Ex. 20:1-17; Deut. 6:4-5; Lev. 19:19; Ps. 18:1; Micah 6:8; Matt: 5-7; 25:31-48; Luke 10:25-28; Rom. 12-15; I Cor. 13). Throughout the Bible the framework for understanding the reclaimed good life is the intention of God to create and perfect a loyal and royal people. The old covenant with Moses and the new covenant in Christ are the concrete, corporate manifestations of the saving purpose of God, whose Kingdom is both the first and last word about history. The sinful rebellion of humanity presupposes and disrupts the goodness of creation, while the saving work of God reclaims the fallen world and directs it toward a glorious consummation in which all the evils which threaten the elect people of God will be abolished in a universal triumph of divine sovereignty and love (I Cor. 15:10-14, 24-28).[29]

Over the centuries Christian theologians have incorporated various configurations of Biblical themes into distinctive understandings of salvation. Each thinker and era tends to create a particular <u>Gestalt</u> uniting Scriptural motifs with culturally-influenced and situationally-relevant conceptions of the human predicament and its resolution. In the early church, among the Greek thinkers especially, redemption was viewed in terms of the light, truth, and immortality which come from union with Christ and which overcome the ignorance, error, weakness, and mortality of humankind in its present fallenness. The saving knowledge which Christ brings as teacher, law-giver, and example is not simply a matter of receiving information in a cognitive sense but a matter of existential participation and inward appropriation. Salvation comes primarily by being united with Christ through the power of the Holy Spirit or through a sacramental union with the Incarnate Word "who became what we are that we might become what he is" (Irenaeus). According to Athanasius human nature was "deified" when assumed by Christ in the incarnation. For Ignatius the Eucharist is "the medicine of immortality." While salvation comes from God, a high view of freedom prevailed in which human participation, cooperation, and even initiative are required by a will which -- though wounded, weak, and under demonic influence -- can still choose between life and death.

A doctrine of salvation by grace from a sinful condition of guilt and corruption so total that the will on its own is completely unable to do good or return to God awaited the work of Augustine in the 5th century. The grace which Pelagius insisted was necessary for salvation consisted mainly in what was provided in creation itself -- free will and reason -- and in such purely external aids as the law of Moses and the teachings and example of Jesus, along with the forgiveness of sins in baptism. Predestination can only mean that God treats everybody in accordance with the merit the divine foreknowledge anticipates they will have. People even after the fall in Eden can live up to the law of God if only they will take advantage of the assistance available to all in creation and in Christ.

For Augustine salvation is a matter entirely of God's grace and work from start to finish. The Spirit operates in us in a secret, wonderful, and ineffable way to effect the restoration from the moral and ontological lapse in being and goodness precipitated by the fall of the entire race in Adam. Prevenient grace initiates the turning around of the will toward God and goodness. Cooperating grace assists and continues the process once begun. Efficient grace enables the chosen saints to will and to do whatever is required to bring them at last to glory beyond this life. All this is a free gift of God presupposing no merit on our part. Good deeds are the outcome of saving grace not its prerequisite. Grace in no way, however, annihilates or even overrules the human will. Rather it works in and through the human spirit enabling the will freely and spontaneously to do good. Grace energizes, revitalizes, and infuses the will with the power to do what it could not do under the bondage of sin. But grace is irresistible in those to whom it is give. Out of infinite mercy God predestines from all eternity a certain number to be saved, no more and no less than are required to replace the number of fallen angels. The rest are destined for everlasting hell to manifest the divine justice. God so arranges all things so that what has been predestined for each of the elect will inevitably come to pass without fail. The choice of God resides in mystery beyond our comprehension in a will that depends on nothing other than itself for its inscrutable operations. Faith, by which grace is accepted, is prior to works, and while all the good that the elect do is made possible by the operation of grace in them, nevertheless, the merit resulting from obedience and deeds of living service to others is a necessary component of the process of salvation.

A modified Augustinian view of redemption prevailed in the Roman Catholic Church of the medieval period, though the resulting doctrines are usually referred to as semi-Pelagian. A movement in the opposite direction took place in the Protestant Reformation. In some ways Martin Luther and John Calvin went even further than Augustine in stressing the role of grace and the priority of faith. In fact, justification by grace through faith alone was their central theological principle. The theology of the Reformers constituted a radical break with centuries of Christian thought and with the Roman Catholic way of belief and practice. At the heart of their revolution was a return to Biblical modes of thought in which salvation is a personal relationship between God and human beings. Luther and Calvin cut through the whole complex ecclesiastical system in which grace was channeled into life through the sacraments administered by a set-apart priesthood with a superior official status. All this machinery was thrown out and replaced by a personal relationship to God which was immediate and direct and required no mediation by a sacerdotal ministry, since all believers are priests.

For both Luther and Calvin salvation comes of necessity by the mercy and grace of God, since fallen humanity unaided is totally unable to return to God and goodness. Grace comes only to the elect who have been predestined to receive it, and it is irresistible in its operations. Here the Reformers are in full agreement with Augustine. For Luther the heart of the matter is justification of God's imputed righteousness which comes as a free gift to be received in grateful trust (faith). Justification is the forgiveness of sins based solely on God's mercy and not at all on our merit. As a result of this gift the believer is transformed so that henceforth the whole orientation of life from its center outward is radically changed. Joy and gratitude expressed in loving service of the neighbor are the heart of the Christian life. Yet sin persists in the life of the redeemed in a fundamental way, so that repentance and forgiveness are continuing features of the believer's existence. Hence, we live in a paradox, simultaneously justified and a sinner (simul justus et peccator). Good works do not save in any way. They are the outcome of the new life in Christ made possible by the Holy Spirit at work in the believer. Faith itself is not a good work in this sense, but it is simply the acceptance or appropriation of God's imputed righteousness. The appropriation is itself the work of grace in us, though it is also our own act as enabled by God.

Calvin's views were similar. The awareness of the gift character of salvation is the underlying existential basis of the doctrine of predestination. Justification is the imputation of the righteousness of Christ given to us by the grace and mercy of God received in faith, which the Spirit awakens in us.

Justification is also regeneration (repentance) by which God creates in the believer a love of righteousness by the power of the example of the divine holiness and the communion of the elect with Christ. Regeneration results in a process of sanctification by which the saints are led progressively into a renewing of the divine image which had been lost in the fall, though the believer is never free from the power of sin on this side of heaven. The Christian life is a disciplined but joyful pilgrimage of self-denial by which the elect subject themselves to the sovereign will of God and live in dutiful but loving service of others in all humility, patience, and persistence.[30] Like Luther he believed that we are not saved by good works but for good works by which faith becomes active in love. But in Luther one detects a more ecstatic quality to the Christian life which comes from an overwhelming sense of gratitude and joy in the presence of the paradoxical wonders of divine love -- a response which spontaneously leads to loving acts of compassion. A sterner emotional tone comes across in Calvin who, while stressing the joyful side, gives more of an impression of steady duty, discipline, and effort in well doing as the marks of Christian obedience.

The Reformers made another radical break with Catholic teaching in their understanding of the Christian life. Just as they rejected the difference of objective status between priesthood and laity, so they also rejected the notion of two levels of obedience. Catholic thought distinguished between commandments and counsels, the first for all Christians and the second for monks and nuns and partly for priests. Love toward enemies is a counsel of perfection but not a commandment for everybody. Asceticism is likewise a counsel not a universal commandment. Moreover, a distinction was made between mortal sins and venial sins with different punishment for each. Luther and Calvin wiped all this out. Faith is not a quantitative relationship that has various levels and degrees. It is a total orientation to life, qualitative in nature. The believer's relationship to God is a personal one in which one is either rightly related to God or not. Moreover, all Christians are on the same level. The whole law of God applies to all equally. The effect of this latter view was to sanctify all of life and to give the secular realm a status equal with that of the special service of God supposedly performed by those who aim for spiritual perfection. The work of the housewife and the laborer in the field is just as worthy a calling as the priesthood or life in the monastery. Virginity is not superior to marriage as a way of life.[31]

Where things stood theologically between Catholics and Protestants as far as salvation is concerned can be seen by examining the Council of Trent (1545-1563). Against the Protestant notion of salvation by God's grace received in faith alone, the Council stated a complex position in which human choice and good works are also necessary for salvation. It is true that in adults the initial stage comes by the operation of God's prevenient grace entirely apart from merit. But then free will must decide whether to accept the salvation that is offered and which now has become a possibility. Moreover, justification is not simply _imputed_ righteousness but _imparted_ righteousness by which the recipients are made really just and able to fulfill the commands of God. Justification is increased and completed in good works; faith is completed by hope and love. Grace is necessary, but the more we cooperate in faith, hope, and love, the more grace is given and increased. Salvation, then, comes by divine grace <u>and</u> human works in a cooperative venture. The theology of the Reformers rejected entirely the moralistic, legalistic, and quasi-magical elements of Catholic thought and their embodiment in the sacramental system of the church. The Council of Trent interpreted faith as intellectual assent to doctrine rather than as an act of trust on the part of the whole self. Hence, the Council could say that saving grace might be lost though faith would remain, except in the case of infidelity in which both grace and faith were lost. Moreover, Catholic thought contrasted sin with virtue, whereas the Reformers contrasted sin with faith. Thus, salvation is a relative matter in the thought of Trent, since different degrees of virtue, dependent in part on human effort, are present in different degrees in the redeemed. For the Reformers faith is an all or nothing matter, and since it is given and sustained in the elect by the Spirit of God, it is never lost. Clearly a great gulf existed between the Catholic Church as defined by the Council of Trent and the new vision presented by Luther and Calvin.[32]

Two further developments especially important for American Protestantism are worthy of note: Arminianism and John Wesley's doctrine of sanctification. To the five points of scholastic Calvinism -- the so-called TULIP theology -- five corresponding themes derived from the thought of Jacobus Arminius (1560-1609) can be briefly summarized: (1) God predestines to salvation those whom God foreknows will repent and believe. (2) Prevenient grace is bestowed on all, enabling them, if

they will, to respond in faith, but only those who do so
by their own choice are saved. (3) Christ died for all,
not just for the elect. (4) Grace is not irresistible;
it can be refused. (5) It is possible to fall from
grace. John Wesley, under the influence of Arminian
thought and the pietist movement, is especially known
for his doctrine of entire sanctification. Luther had
stressed the paradox of being justified and a sinner as
characterizing the continuing life of the believer,
though obedience in love is spontaneously generated out
of joyful gratitude to God. Calvin agreed that sin
persists in the life of the redeemed but made a place
for growth in holiness in a process of disciplined
obedience to divine law. Wesley stressed regeneration
as a transformation of moral and spiritual nature which,
simultaneously with justification, begins a process of
sanctification which can lead to perfection of motive
and complete purity of heart before God. This does not
imply that the believer is completely free from error of
any sort or ceases to stand in need of divine grace. It
means that those who have attained it no longer
willfully break the law of God and that they act out of
an intentionality defined by love. Perfection is rarely
achieved but is a goal to which every believer should
aspire.[33]

B. SALVATION IN MODERN THEOLOGIES: Consistent
with its view of sin, Protestant liberalism developed a
theory of redemption as essentially the victory of
spirit over nature. The great concern of liberals was
with the development and perfection of moral personality. The human spirit is basically good but weak,
held back and dragged downward by the threats to
finitude (pain, sickness, suffering, and death) and the

inertia and untamed passions of a human nature that has
not transcended its evolutionary heritage of animal
impulses. What human beings need is moral and spiritual
power to energize consciousness and inspire the will to
achieve its higher possibilities. The historical Jesus
is the norm of moral personality. The teachings,
example, personality, and sacrificial death of Jesus
infuse those who come under his influence with transforming energy. Salvation, then, is basically a process
of moral and spiritual renewal in which forgiven
sinners, now reconciled to God, are reoriented from the
pursuit of selfish ends to the ideals of Jesus, whose
supreme virtue was unselfish love. The emphasis on
morality as the heart of religion reflects the influence
of Kant and was superbly represented by Albrecht
Ritschl. Friedrich Schleiermacher, coming from a romanticist and pietistic background, emphasized the mystical
dimension. According to Schleiermacher, saving power
comes from a spiritual communion with Jesus whose perfected God-consciousness is communicated to us through
the medium of the Christian community. Walter Rauschenbusch united both moral and mystical elements into his
interpretation of the new life.

In keeping with the dominating principle of continuity, liberals did not generally distinguish sharply
between the religious and moral dimensions of salvation,
nor between justification and sanctification, nor
between divine grace and human effort. Likewise,
liberal thinkers typically abandoned the sharp
distinction between the saved and the lost which
Protestant orthodoxy had assumed. They tended to think
of a continuum ranging from the lowest possible level of
moral failure and beastly behavior to the perfection of

Jesus. Most people are in between. Doctrines of predestination in the Calvinist sense were condemned as irrational and unworthy of the God revealed in Jesus of Nazareth. Salvation is a process of moral and spiritual growth which will continue perhaps even beyond death until perfection is reached. These evolutionary ideas pertained also to society. The liberal hope was that the whole of society including all its institutions and values would gradually move toward a Kingdom of love and justice on earth. However, some,like Rauschenbusch, realized how deep and stubborn the evil tendencies of humanity are.[34]

The liberal sense of harmony, continuity, and progress informed by doctrines of divine imminence was shattered by the events of the 20th century. Neo-orthodoxy arose with theologies filled with paradox, discontinuity, and dialectical tension expressing a radical view of human sinfulness and a renewed stress upon the transcendence of God. Within this framework Pauline-Augustinian-Reformation notions of salvation by grace seemed appropriate once more. Justification by grace through faith became the key to resolving the human predicament of a will self-perverted by pride, rebellion, and disobedience. Only the mercy of God expressed in the free gift of the forgiveness of sins is sufficient. With this theme at the heart of neo-orthodox doctrines of salvation, the basic problem had to do with the place of sanctification in individuals and society, that is, the extent to which the whole of life can be brought into conformity with the Christian vision. Luther's doctrine of _simul justus et peccator_ was popular, along with a rejection of the idea of social progress and liberal hopes for the coming of the

Kingdom of God on earth. Salvation tended to take on a strong inward, eschatological, and transcendental cast.[35] To be saved is to find meaning and hope that sustain the inner self and the community of believers in the midst of an external world that is chaotic, even absurd, and full of injustice, violence, and suffering. It is to experience reconciliation with God and with others through forgiveness, though love for God and neighbor is still more an intention than a sustained or growing reality in actual life.[36]

New Testament apocalypticism with its dualism of the old age and the new age paradoxically interwoven here and now, existentialist interpretations of the inner self as threatened by meaninglessness, anxiety, and death in a hostile world, and the pervading sense of massive historical evil symbolized by world wars -- all these factors contributed to the neo-orthodox interpretation. They saw salvation as forgiveness, hope, and courage coming from beyond and effective inwardly despite outward appearances and worldly events. Saving truth is grasped by faith and stands in tension with worldly wisdom. The Gospel provides a new self-understanding which takes away guilt and the fear of the future (Bultmann), enables one to have the courage to be (Tillich) or assures one of God's gracious "Yes" despite the wrathful "No" against all human works and prideful self-assertion (Barth). Clearly Christian faith unites one with a transcendent realm of being and meaning, but the relationship of salvation experienced in faith to secular events and the external life of the believer in the world is ambiguous and paradoxical.

Neo-orthodoxy was a complex phenomenon combining both orthodox and liberal themes. The gift-character of salvation was emphasized, but predestination was rejected or given an Arminian cast. While it is not clear how much human autonomy and spontaneity remain in the Swedish Lutheranism of such theologians as Anders Nygren or in the implied universal election of all to salvation in Karl Barth, freedom was generally affirmed in terms more Arminian than Calvinistic. Neo-orthodoxy was often focused on the meaning of the Gospel for social ethics and the interpretation of history, thus not preoccupied with individual salvation in the older sense. Like the liberals, thinkers in this widely diverse camp were disinterested in dividing the world into the saved and the lost -- so conscious were they that all stood constantly in need of grace and that unbelievers were often more devoted to justice than church members. Yet the difference between unrepentant sinners and those who live by faith is crucial.[37]

A form of neo-orthodoxy more balanced than some of the European varieties was elaborated by Reinhold Niebuhr -- the most influential of the Americans.[38] Salvation is both pardon of sin (justification) and power to live a new life (sanctification). These themes must be held in paradoxical tension. No prior limits can be put on the extent to which love can become the principle of individual life or to which justice can be achieved in society. Yet simul justus et peccator is never transcended by moral perfection or social progress. Neither can a steady process of growth in love and justice be predicated as the truth of sanctification. Niebuhr was informed by an existentialist view of time in which the decision of faith had to be renewed in every moment -- each choice being a possibility for a renewed expression of pride and self-love. Neither Catholic thought, Luther, Calvin, Wesley, Barth, or Brunner fully mastered the dialectical interplay between "the indeterminate possibilities of realizations of good in individual and collective life" and "the realities of sin which appear on every new level of virtue."[39] Niebuhr admitted that the subtle, multidimensional, and paradoxical relationships involved are difficult to state without offending some part of the truth of experience and/or the canons of logic. Every "yes" has to be balanced with a "yes, but."

Writing at mid-century, Daniel Day Williams was not happy with either liberalism or neo-orthodoxy. Neither had an adequate doctrine of redemption. The liberals lacked a proper view of sin -- too Pelagian. The neo-orthodox were deficient in their views of regeneration and sanctification -- too much *justus* et *peccator* and not enough place for growth in grace and moral progress in history. Between the excessive optimism of the one and the timid hopes of the other, Williams sought with the aid of process philosophy to state a more balanced view of divine grace and human hope.[40]

Liberation and eschatological theologies have combined in a distinctive way liberal and neo-orthodox themes but in an eschatological framework that is peculiar to themselves.[41] The focus on inwardness, subjectivity, and individual faith in existentialist theologies is rejected, along with otherworldly versions of eschatology which leave secular history perpetually unredeemed. Christian hope expects a perfected socio-historical future on earth to be enacted more by God's transcendent power or revolutionary transformations than by a process of gradual progress. The present as marked by injustice and oppression is sharply contrasted with the eschatological transformation that is imminent. Hope is grounded in the promise of God, who is the power of the future. Salvation is not limited to economic, political, and social liberation, but secular well-being is included along with redemption of believers from guilt, anxiety, sin, and death. Social utopia and the Kingdom of God are not identified but neither are they separated.

Illustrating once again how difficult it is to keep realism about sin and the hope of redemption in proper balance, Langdon Gilkey has sought a synthesis of "the emphasis of the liberation-eschatological theologies on social liberation in history and the neo-orthodox emphasis on the continuity of sin and so the need for justification and reconciliation. . . ."[42]

V. SUMMARY OF CONTINUING ISSUES

This sketchy history of Christian reflection on the human predicament has revealed a cluster of issues in which a dialectical tension between opposing but essential motifs seems to preclude any final systematic resolution. Rather each theologian and school of thought creates a distinctive Gestalt, usually to refute a prevailing perspective in the interests of situational relevance and Biblical authenticity. Four of the perennial problems can be briefly analyzed.

A. UNIVERSALITY AND INEVITABILITY VERSUS FREEDOM AND RESPONSIBILITY: Pelagian doctrines approach universality empirically, i.e., by counting noses to see if everybody has actually sinned. Hence, inevitability is avoided, and universality is affirmed in terms of probability. The strength of this approach is that it uncompromisingly maintains freedom and responsibility, but it appears to miss the deeper realities of tragic estrangement which arise at the center of the human spirit. Augustinian views stress the universality of profound existential alienation but obscure the goodness of creation and the reality of freedom by seeming to make sin into an unavoidable destiny. Is it possible to elaborate a view of sin as a contingent but freely chosen occurrence which is universal without falling into contradiction? Augustine distinguished between original goodness and the fall by relating them to successive stages in the career of the primal pair. A modern Augustinian like Paul Tillich contends that the fall is not something that happened once upon a time. Rather it symbolizes the fact that the leap from essence to existence is not a structural necessity but nevertheless is universal. Creation is potentially and "essentially good but if actualized falls into tragic estrangement through freedom and destiny." Hence, "actualized existence and estranged existence are identical." The end of creation is the begining of the fall. Hence, theology must simultaneously affirm the "tragic universality of estrangement and man's responsibility for it."[43] Reinhold Niebuhr thinks this philosophical theory implies that sin is an ontological necessity, a conclusion which a more dramatic Hebraic interpretation can avoid. Yet neo-liberals like Daniel Day Williams and Robert Calhoun suspect that Niebuhr's own version implicates the goodness of creation and

compromises human freedom by making sin inevitable.[44]
Moreover, rationality is offended by asserting inevitability but denying necessity. Augustinians seek
religious and existential depth of analysis while
Pelagians defend freedom and moral responsibility. Can
both interests be combined in a conceptual model that is
comprehensive and coherent? Given the circumstances
that surround choice -- the anxieties, the sheer difficulty of moral perfection, the urge toward self-realization, the power of psychosocial conditioning, genetic
predispositions, etc. -- perhaps the best we can say is
that the emergence of idolatrous, selfish, and sensual
patterns of life is an overwhelming spiritual probability.

B. GOD'S INITIATIVE AND HUMAN RESPONSE IN
SALVATION: An opposite puzzle arises in relating divine
grace to human freedom. Sin is said to be a universal
fact but a free human act which in no way implicates God
or the goodness of creation. Salvation is said to be a
work of God which nevertheless does not offend or
override freedom. Classical Augustinians stress divine
grace but in connection with doctrines of divine
determinism which overrule freedom in the elect and
unilaterally damn the non-elect. Pelagians put so much
stress on human effort that grace is reduced to
universal factors present in creation or to purely
external aids such as the educational role of law and
teaching and the inspirational power of the example of
Jesus. How can salvation be a work of grace in us but
not a matter of divine determinism? And why do some
respond to the Gospel and others do not? Is it that
divine grace is not given to them or that they refuse to
receive the gift? Predestination suggests the former

alternative, while the efforts to state the latter view seem to end up making salvation a matter of human choice and effort rather than or, as much as, a gift and deed of God. Augustine, the Reformers, the Council of Trent, the Arminians, liberals, the neo-orthodox, and current theologies wrestle with the issues but always seem to leave something out that opponents find essential.

By making virtue essential to the fulfillment of the work of grace, Catholic theories conceive of salvation in quantitative, relative terms and partly dependent on human effort. But making us responsible for our own eternal destiny increases anxiety and insecurity. In the attempt to avoid works righteousness, the Reformers viewed the opposite of sin as not virtue but faith, which comes solely from God. Faith, as the appropriation of justifying grace, depends on predestination. Moreover, by making faith an all or nothing matter, so that one is either saved or lost altogether, the incredible variety of life-stances among people is obscured. Both faith and virtue, justification and sanctification, appear from the human side, when viewed empirically, in a nearly inexhaustible array of patterns, levels, and degrees. Is justification, like pregnancy, something that either happens altogether or not at all? Is not faith mixed with doubt and unbelief, at times at least, in the same way that virtue is mixed with vice? Can the saved and the lost be divided strictly into separate groups whether salvation is dependent on faith alone (Luther and Calvin) or on faith and virtue (Catholic thought)? Granted, it would be a misconception of Reformation theology to think of faith as just another kind of "good work" that merits salvation. But even if we define faith as trust and understand it, in Tillich's terms, as our acceptance of God's acceptance of us, surely, once we abandon predestination, it is partly a human decision or act. As such faith can waver, alternate with unbelief, or finally die.

Paul stated the matter in a paradox when he urged his readers to "work out your own salvation with fear and trembling; for God is at work in you, both to will and to work for his good pleasure" (Phil. 2:13-14 RSV). Here are the essential poles, but how are they to be combined in a systematic scheme? Perhaps the best we can say is that what only grace can make possible, only freedom can make actual. The analogy of "falling in love" -- in which we are powerfully (irresistibly?) drawn to what we spontaneously choose -- may be the best way of relating the initiative of grace to the response of freedom. But surely both faith and the good works which follow from faith are variables which suggest the liberal pattern of a continuum with relative differences among people rather than the strict division between those destined for hell and those who are on the way to heaven -- a view found in both classical Catholicism and Protestantism.

C. GROWTH IN GRACE DESPITE THE PERSISTENCE OF SIN: Forgiveness of sin without a change of life is inadequate to Biblical teaching and Christian experience. Yet a life free from the power of sin seems impossible. The problem is how to connect justification with sanctification by an appropriate understanding of regeneration. But how? Reinhold Niebuhr subjects the major theories of the Christian life to a brilliant analysis.[45] He displays an uncanny ability to ferret out the flaws in each. Luther is too pessimistic and in so stressing the fact that all are sinners before God obscures the important differences between relative rights and wrongs, especially in the social and political arena. Catholic views are too optimistic and prone to moralism, legalism, and a new works righteousness. Liberal theologies are superficial and utopian, while Wesley and the radical sects are beyond the pale of realism in so far as they are perfectionist about individual and collective life. Calvin is more precise and balanced, but even he nearly fell into Catholic error by suggesting that fundamental self-love can be overcome so that only remnants of incidental sensuality (carnal desires) remain -- an error which tempts the redeemed toward a new self-righteousness. All these criticisms are compelling.

Yet when Niebuhr gives his own paradoxical views, he manages to rise above the errors of others only by stating contrary positions held in dynamic tension but incapable of being incorporated into a larger synthesis. This strategy is perhaps more useful in exposing the errors of more straightforward alternatives than it is for constructive theorizing. Yet who can state a superior position, one that is both conceptually consistent and true to the varieties of Christian experience? Maybe it is impossible to capture the whole truth about everybody in a single theory. In the final analysis each individual exhibits a peculiar _Gestalt_ -- patterns, habits, and styles of life which general and abstract concepts of justification and sanctification, faith and works, can describe only in inexact fashion. Without neglecting the universal features of the

Christian life, an adequate view must allow for a wide variety of actualities and possibilities for growing in grace and for falling back into grievous sin.

These three fundamental issues have been and are a perennial challenge to Christian imagination. No doubt the future will continue to produce a variety of alternatives, each of which may have more value in correcting the excesses or limitations of some prevailing outlook than either has in stating a final view of universal truth.

D. AUGUSTINIAN VERSUS IRENAEAN PERSPECTIVES: This summary just given, particularly the first two points, has more or less assumed a Pelagian-Augustinian context. As a result of the influence of John Hick, attention has been given recently to an "Irenaean model" as a quite different scheme of thought.[46] Based on the thought of Irenaeus, two main differences from the Augustinian framework are worthy of note. 1. Augustine assumed a perfect state followed by the fallen state in temporal sequence. The Irenaean view sees the created Adam as naive, immature, and childlike, not a mature, perfect embodiment of virtue. God's purpose is to develop the primal pair and their descendants as moral personalities and to lead them toward an ultimate perfection in the eschaton. 2. The Augustinian tradition seeks to exonerate God from any responsibility for sin and evil by blaming humanity exclusively. The Irenaeans see sin and evil as virtually inevitable given the immaturity of the infant human race and the conditions of existence in this world. Moreover, God permits or ordains sin and evil, since they are essential to the perfection of human beings as moral agents and spiritual beings.

Since sin and evil lead to a greater good, they can even be seen as necessary means to a justifying end -- moral perfection in glory with God. Hick sees Schleiermacher as reviving the Irenaean alternative. Liberals frequently exhibited Irenaean assumptions, though the 19th century exponents were, in Hick's view, naive and superficial, generally speaking. Given a deeper view of the radical sinfulness of humanity and of the massiveness and persistence of suffering in the world, Hick offers the Irenaean orientation as a superior alternative to the Augustinian model. It would seem to be more compatible with evolutionary assumptions about the origin and destiny of humankind. Many prominent theologies in the present have strong Irenaean features. Teilhard de Chardin, Gordon Kaufman, and the process theologians may be offered as examples.[47] Paul Tillich's description of the mythical pre-fall state of Adam and Eve in terms of "dreaming innocence" is set over against the Augustinian notion of the first pair as fully mature moral decision makers. The Irenaean overtones of the Tillichian revision are apparent. However, the Irenaean model has its own set of difficulties relating to human freedom, the inevitability of sin, God's responsibility for evil, and the interaction of divine initiative and human response. It is not at all clear that these problems are any less formidable or that some of the assumptions involved are any less questionable than those posed by the Augustinian tradition. Nevertheless, it is a way of looking at creation, sin, and salvation that is worthy of examination. Augustinian and Irenaean motifs can, of course, be variously combined.

The Christian understanding of salvation stands in strict correlation not only with a doctrine of sin but with the saving work of Christ. What has so far been presupposed can now be developed in some systematic and historical detail. The next chapter will examine the person and work of Christ as Mediator, Lord, and Savior.

CHAPTER IV
THE PERSON AND WORK OF CHRIST

With Christology, we arrive at the center of Christian faith. While all doctrines are organically related to each other, there is a special sense in which the understanding of Jesus as the Christ is the focal point of Christian truth. This does not mean that everything that the church believes can be deduced from Christology. Christians know something about God, humanity, church, history, and eschatology apart from Christ. But the specific, distinctive meaning to each of these doctrines is given in and through the special revelation Christians find in Jesus as the Christ. All beliefs are interpreted by reference to Christ. Hence, everything that has been said so far presupposes what must be set forth explicitly regarding the person and work of Jesus believed to be the Christ. Incarnation and atonement are at the heart of Christian faith.

A useful way of locating Christology in the logic of the Christian message is to view Christ as the mediator. Speaking functionally, Christ stands between God and humanity. A two-fold movement or duality of relationships can be discerned. On the one hand, Christ points us, leads us, relates us to God. On the other hand, Christ brings God, reveals God, manifests God's saving power, relates God to us. As the go-between, Christ mediates in this double way -- from humanity to God, from God to humanity. Once this two-fold relationship is seen, the pattern of Christological doctrine becomes apparent. We must speak of one person with a duality of nature, role, or function. The perennial task of Christology is to show how Jesus, as one of us, leads us to God and how, as one sent from heaven and thus unlike us, he brings God to us. This is another way of saying that Jesus is both human and divine.

What does Christ mediate to humanity? The brief answer is that he provides both true knowledge of God and saving power. To use New Testament terminology, Christ is both the wisdom of God and the power of God (I Cor. 1:24); truth and grace come through him (John 1:17). Revelation and redemption are centered in Jesus as the Christ. The clearest disclosure of the nature, will, and purpose of God is manifested in the wisdom, the truth, the revelation given in the life, the personality, the deeds, the death, and resurrection of Jesus. But Jesus as the Christ also saves. He makes possible the restoration of fallen humanity to a state of salvation and wholeness in right relationship to God.

It is conventional to treat Christology under two headings: the person of Christ (incarnation) and the work of Christ (atonement). This pattern will be followed here. A strong tradition in Protestant thought affirms that we must approach the person through the work. We can only know who Christ is by what he does. As Philip Melanchthon said, "to know Christ is to know his benefits." The early church, however, had no hesitation in beginning with incarnation and moving on to atonement. In fact, in the Greek-speaking church, Christ saves us by becoming incarnate and thus "deifying" human nature. Surely, in the largest framework person and work are interdependent. Christ had to be who he was in order to save, and he was who he was because of his saving deed. At any rate, as a matter of convenience and systematic logic, incarnation will be treated first, followed by atonement.

I. The Person of Christ

Christian thought has affirmed from New Testament times until now that Jesus Christ is the mediator between God and humanity who has fully revealed God and truly redeemed humanity. In making this claim, the church has found it necessary to make two sorts of statements about him which are extremely hard to combine. To mediate between God and humanity, Christ must be related to both parties and yet himself be one being or person. This means that somehow one must say that Jesus the Christ is one person who is both human and divine. He is both God and man. Regardless of the philosophical framework or theological context it is set within, a doctrine of incarnation is finally inadequate unless it can preserve both the unity of his person and the duality of his nature or of his relationship to us.

Donald Baillie has pointed out five inadequate ways of affirming the incarnation, given the viewpoint of classical Christology.[1]

1. The incarnation does not mean that Jesus was not a man but God or a god. He was a human being not a deity. Only one God exists. Orthodoxy has asserted that Jesus as the Christ shares the divine nature and in that sense is God, as well as man, but it is not proper to speak of Jesus simply as God.

2.　It is inadequate to say that Jesus was some kind of intermediate being, neither fully god nor fully human. This is the Arian heresy.

3.　It is not correct to say that Jesus was simply God or the Son of God inhabiting a human body, so that while the physical organism was human, the mind or spirit was divine. This is the Apollinarian heresy. This makes Jesus only partially human. Orthodoxy has asserted that both complete humanity and true divinity are present in him.

4.　The main line of the church has not been content to say that Jesus began by being only a man and then grew into divinity or was endowed with a divine status. Broadly speaking, this is adoptionism. Orthodoxy affirms that Jesus Christ was from the beginning the eternal Word of God who became flesh in the person of Jesus.

5.　Finally, it must not be said that God changed into a man for about thirty years. God cannot change in this way but is forever God and only God. Moreover, deity and humanity are not successive stages but co-exist simultaneously in Christ.

The church has wanted to say that Christ is both God and man united in one person. Divinity and humanity have been interpreted in many thought forms, from the Greek metaphysics of classical orthodoxy to the Kantian and historically-oriented language systems of modern

Protestantism. But whatever philosophical or theological concepts are used, if it can be shown that a doctrine makes Jesus less than fully human or if it does not account for the uniqueness of Christ as the divine Son or if it divides his person, then it must be declared inadequate. This is the fundamental challenge of Christology in every age: to state the reality of two natures (or histories or relationships or functions) in one person.

A. THE NEW TESTAMENT BACKGROUND: The primary data for Christology are provided by the New Testament. No clearly worked out doctrine is to be found there. The incarnation is clearly taught in many places, but the exact relationship between the human and the divine is never stated. The New Testament contains a variety of witnesses using widely differing categories, all pointing to the centrality of Christ as the climactic event in the history of salvation. Two concepts are particularly important: the new age and the Messiah. The New Testament sees Christ as the fulfillment of the Old Testament promise of a specially appointed agent whose coming would introduce the Kingdom of God in its fullness (Is 9:1-7, 11:1-9). Christ by his redemptive work initiated the beginning of the new age. This is the heart of the kerygma (the preaching or proclamation): the new age has dawned, the promises are fulfilled. Repent and believe in Christ and receive new life. This is the good news (Mark 1:14-15).

The New Testament uses numerous titles to indicate the status and function of Jesus. Scholars debate the question as to which categories Jesus employed to refer to himself. No detailed consideration of the messianic titles can be provided here. The main categories can be listed. Jesus was regarded as prophet (Mk. 6:4, Luke 13:33), teacher (Matt. 4:23), and lawgiver (Matt. 5-7). He is the High Priest (Hebrews), the Suffering Servant of the Lord (Mk. 10:45; Luke 24:13-27; Acts 8:26-39), and the Lamb of God (John 1:29; Rev. 5:6) - all of which indicate that Jesus died for our sins to make a vicarious atonement according to the Old Testament Scriptures (Is. 53). Jesus is, of course, everywhere regarded as the Messiah (Grk: <u>Christos</u>, anointed). Related titles are Son of David (Luke 1:30-33), and King (John 18:33-37) -- all indicating Davidic descent and the fulfillment of prophecy.

In the synoptic Gospels Jesus refers to himself as the Son of Man (Mk. 2:28, 10:45, 14:62; Matt. 25:31-46). The background is the developing apocalyptic tradition in which this title refers to the Man from Heaven who will come at the end of the age as Judge and Deliverer (Daniel 7:13-14, and the Similitudes of Enoch). A more widespread designation is Son of God, a unique relationship of intimacy and authority which qualifies Jesus as representative of God (Luke 3:22; Mk. 12:1-11, 13:32). By his resurrection the Son has received all authority (Rom. 1:1-6), having been sent as the redeemer (Gal. 4:4-6). In John the unique Sonship of Jesus is stressed, along with a virtual equality with God which is eternal (John 1:14, 3:16, 10:30, 14:9, 17:1-10). Closely related to the idea of Sonship in John is the notion of Christ as the Logos or Word which is pre-existent, eternal, the agent of creation, and the very embodiment of deity (John 1:1, 14). Jesus is also called Lord, a term everywhere suggesting authority and at times approaching an identification with God (Mk.

11:3; Matt. 7:21-22; John 20:28; Acts 2:36, 10:36; I
Thess. 5:2; I Cor. 8:5-6). Lord is one of the most
widely used appellations for Christ, and it is Paul's
favorite term. In Acts 1-12 Lord is used to refer both
to God and to Jesus, and in about one-third of these
cases it is difficult to know which is meant. This
close association of Jesus with God by calling him Lord
clearly indicates that he exercises divine authority
(Phil. 2:5-11).

Christ is called Savior only a relatively few
times, mainly in the later writings of the New Testament
(Acts 5:31; Luke 2:11; II Peter; Jude; Titus 2:12).
Like Lord, the term is sometimes used of Jesus and
sometimes of God. In four passages Jesus is referred to
as God, but with the exception of John 20:28, either the
text or the meaning is uncertain (John 1:18; Titus 2:13;
II Peter 1:1). Perhaps the writers of these passages
were influenced by the use of the term "God" in emperor
worship. Many other images, phrases, and concepts are
used throughout the New Testament to indicate the high
status and unique function of Jesus as the Christ, the
bringer of salvation and the inaugurator of the new age
who will soon return to judge the world and put down all
enemies of God once and for all. In Revelation, Christ
shares with God many titles and attributes such as "the
Alpha," "the Omega, and "the Living One" (Rev. 1:8,
22:13, 1:18, 10:6).

Jesus entered a situation filled with messianic
expectations. As he came to be recognized as the
fulfillment of these hopes, some of the available titles
were applied to Jesus. The result was a two-fold
process. On the one hand, Jesus was interpreted in the

light of the messianic ideas and religious conceptions
available in the Jewish and Hellenistic worlds of the
expanding church. On the other hand, the available
designations were transformed in the light of the
message and ministry of the remembered Jesus. Moreover,
the use of Jesus' words and deeds in a variety of
settings in the early church brought about modifications
in their meaning which passed into the oral tradition to
be finally recorded in the Gospels. The outcome is a
rich and diverse body of materials filled with an
amazing variety of conceptions, images, and titles which
cannot possibly be synthesized into one systematic
doctrine of the person of Jesus as the Christ. Yet they
all add up to a unified witness to the exalted and
unique status and role of Jesus as the long-awaited
Messiah of Israel whose coming marks the culminating
event in the history of God's revealing and redeeming
activity in the world.

A doctrine of the relationship of divinity and
humanity in the person of Jesus is nowhere developed in
the New Testament. No attempt is made to say how or in
what way he is both a man and yet an embodiment of
deity. But the data are there which clearly teach both.
The humanity of Jesus is a pervasive assumption, more
taken for granted than explicitly stated. We are told
that he was like us in every respect, except he was
without sin (Heb. 2:17, 4:15). He was born of woman,
born under the law -- the two marks of manhood in Jewish
thought (Gal. 4:4). He grew, developed, and learned
(Luke 2:52); he experienced weariness (John 4:6),
compassion (Mk. 8:2), thirst (John 19:28) and anguish
(Luke 22:44); and he died (Matt. 27:50). Yet he is also
assigned a unique status and function so exalted that

only the highest superlatives and titles available in the culture of the time would suffice to indicste his special relationship to God. Clearly while Jesus is on earth, God is still in heaven. Jesus obviously prays to someone other than himself. Yet the unity of Jesus as the Christ with God in status and function isexplicitly taught. He is equal with God (John 5:18; Phil. 2:6). He is in the form of God (Phil. 2:6), one with God (John 10:30, 17:21), the very image of the invisible God (Col. 1:15), the agent of creation (John 1:1; Col. 1:16; Heb. 1:2), the first born of all creation (Col. 1:15), and bears the very stamp of God's nature and upholds the universe by his power (Heb. 1:3). As the pre-existent Word, Christ was with God in the beginning and was God, so that God and the Word are both identified and distinguished (John 1:1-2). In Christ the fullness of God dwelt bodily (Col. 1:19, 2:9). In reading the high Christological passages such as John 1:1, Phil. 2:5-11, Col. 1:15-17, II Cor. 4:4 and Heb. 1:1-4, it is difficult to avoid the conclusion that while Christ is not God as such without any qualification, he has a status equal or nearly equal with God, though he remains the Son of the Father and the Word of God. Christ shares in the fullness of deity with God.

The virgin birth and the resurrection, marking the beginning and the culmination of his life, also indicate that Jesus is no ordinary mortal. The relationship between the pre-existence of Christ and the virgin birth is interesting in that no writer teaches both. Matthew and Luke speak of virgin birth but not of pre-existence (Matt. 1:18-25; Luke 1:26-35). John and Paul teach pre-existence but make no mention of virgin birth. Mark has neither. The resurrection of Christ from the dead is, of course, universally taught or assumed. The preaching of the resurrection was the focal point of the message of the early church, offered as the culminating act of God's saving work and the sure sign that Jesus was indeed the promised Messiah (Acts 2:14-36, 4:5-12, 5:29-32, 10:34-43; I Cor. 15). Both virgin birth and resurrection epitomize the character of New Testament Christology as a whole. We are presented with a history of God's saving activity in Christ -- a story in which Jesus of Nazareth is the central figure. Christ, who existed in heaven with God from the beginning, was sent to earth as the promised Messiah and the Agent of salvation. He was born of a virgin and exercised a ministry of healing and teaching centered in the proclamation of the final inbreaking of the Kingdom of God. He was crucified and buried, but God raised him from the dead. He has been exalted to heaven and will soon return at the end of the age as Judge. He has reconciled us to God by his death, overcome the demonic powers that hold humanity in bondage, and will in the end put down all enemies including death. Such is the composite drama that is told in various ways throughout the New Testament. While titles, concepts, and images with theoretical content are employed to say who it was who did all this, the center is the telling of the story of salvation and the call to repentance and faith. If we try to abstract a conceptual model of the person of Christ from the New Testament witness in all its variety and with its diverse images, phrases, ideas, and complex terminology, it is clear that we must affirm that he was both a real human being and the incarnation of deity whose saving activity was God's own accomplishment. He was not simply doing God's work. God was at work in and through him (II Cor. 5:16-21).[2]

It was left to the church to render intelligible, precise, and consistent the meaning of the incarnation. This attempt became necessary as people asked questions and as versions of the Gospel arose which threatened both the spirit and the substance of the New Testament witness to Jesus as the Christ. Thus, in order to give a clear witness and to counteract heretical and destructive theories of the person of Christ, the church found it necessary to state as accurately as it could what it meant to confess that Jesus was Lord. To that story we now turn.

B: THE FORMATION OF THE CLASSICAL DOCTRINE: In the first three centuries the main line of the church affirmed both the divinity and the humanity of Jesus, althoughthe details of this were not precisely worked out. However, very early heretical trends developed which spurred the development of clearer definitions. Three deviant trends are worthy of notice. (1) Ebionism denied the divinity of Jesus. Members of this sect repudiated the virgin birth, though they regarded Jesus as the Messiah who would return to reign on earth. Jesus was a man like the prophets of old. The Ebionites were an offshoot of Jewish Christianity. One group called the Nazaraeans were orthodox in their Christology, although they continued to obey the Jewish law. (2) Docetism denied the humanity of Jesus. He only appeared to have human flesh and attributes. In the background was an assumption of divine impassibility and the inherent impurity of matter. Docetism was not so much a heresy in its own right as it was a tendency or element in other outlooks such as Marcionism and Gnosticism. (3) Adoptionism is the view that Jesus was a man who was especially endowed by the Holy Spirit with powers and qualities that enabled him to function as the Messiah. He was an adopted Son of God. This outlook was previously examined in connection with the Trinitarian controversy. It is associated in Paul of Samosata with an extreme form of monarchianism. Ignatius, Justin, Irenaeus, and others developed more orthodox views. In the West Tertullian provided the formula that was to become normative when worked out in more precise detail. Jesus was one person in two substances or natures, being both God and man.

The next major step took place at Nicea in 325 A.D. Here it was decided against the Arians that the Logos (Word) is of the same or equal substance with the Father (homoousios). Once this was established, the question of the relationship of the deity of Christ to his humanity came into the forefront of discussion. Only the highlights of this long, complicated, and controversial story can be told here. Two schools of thought came into conflict, conventionally, if not always altogether accurately, associated with Alexandria and Antioch.

1. The Alexandrian School. The Alexandrians sponsored Word-flesh Christologies which taught that the eternal Logos assumed human flesh (body) or humanity rather than being joined to an individual man. In the background is the Platonic theory in which an immortal, immaterial soul is united with a mortal, physical body to form a person. The Word-flesh school went through two stages. The first stage became heretical when Apollinarius was condemned by the Council of Constantinople in 381 AD for teaching that the eternal Logos (Word)

took on or assumed a human body but not a human soul. In this view the Word took the place of the human soul in Jesus. The second stage assumes a full human nature for Jesus, including body and soul. Cyril of Alexandria was the key figure here. He repeated the Apollinarian theme of the "one incarnate nature of the Divine Word." Two natures before the incarnation are united to form one nature in the incarnate Word. Nature (<u>physis</u>) here means "concrete individual." To say it differently two <u>hypostases</u> (divinity and humanity) united to form the one concrete individual who is Jesus Christ. Cyril's favorite analogy was the union of soul and body to form one real human being. Or consider a piece of black charcoal that is heated until it becomes red hot. Clearly charcoal and heat have been united so that both are present in one entity. The Eternal Word assumes human flesh animated by rational soul. God takes on full human existence while remaining God. Hence, the metaphysical subject of the incarnation is none other than the Word. This view seems to fit John 1:14. It preserves well the unity of person. But it does not go well with Luke 2:52, which speaks of Jesus gradually learning. And it does not preserve the full humanity of Jesus as a real, individual man.

2. <u>The Antiochene School</u>. The Antiochenes sponsored <u>Word-man</u> Christologies in which the incarnation is viewed as the indwelling of the Word in the man Jesus. The background here is the Aristotelian view of the self as a psycho-physical unity in which the soul is the form, while the body is the matter of a person. Hence, a real individual must have both body and soul. This school began with the historical Jesus as a real individual who was born, grew, learned, and died. The

incarnation means that the Word indwells the man Jesus as a person lives in a house. This outlook fits well with Col. 2:9 and with John 2:19, but runs into trouble with I Cor. 2:8, which says that the Lord of glory was crucified. It obviously preserves the reality of the humanity and keeps the divine and human natures separate and unconfused. However, it runs the danger of affirming that there were two persons involved, one living in the other. To affirm that there were two Sons is to be guilty of the Nestorian heresy. However, it is not at all clear that Nestorius was a "Nestorian." Yet his inability or vagueness in saying how humanity and divinity were united to form one person (prosopon) left him open to the charge that in the incarnate Lord were two persons in a voluntary or moral rather than in a real or metaphysical union.

To summarize, Cyril emphased the unity of Christ the God-Man and sought the distinctions within the one nature. Hence, the unity and the distinctions are sought at the same level. Nestorius, on the other hand, stressed the distinctions and located the unity at one level (the person) and the distinctions at another level (the natures). Each position moved toward the other but from different starting points. Since the two schools had contrasting theological interests and used different conceptual models, conflict and misunderstanding were inevitable.

At stake in this controversy were at least three vital concerns: (1) consistency with other established theological conceptions, (2) consistency with the teaching of the New Testament, and (3) a theory of the person of Christ adequate to ground the saving work of

Christ. The theology of "the hypostatic union" held by the Alexandrians was concerned to protect the unity of the person of Christ and to guarantee salvation understood as "deification" through union of the soul with the Word. Yet their theory seemed to imply that God suffered and died -- a violation of divine impassibility. Moreover, humanity appears to be absorbed into the Word and thus without independent individuality and reality. The theology of "the indwelling Word" put forth by the Antiochenes was determined to assert the reality and individuality of the man Jesus and to defend the impassibility of God. The difference between the divine and human natures is clear, but the unity of person is obscured. Each party was ingenious in finding ways to make its basic assertions compatible with unquestioned dogmas and with New Testament passages which apparently contradicted its theory. The problem was complicated by the fact that key terms like <u>physis</u> (nature), <u>prosopon</u> (person) and hypostasis (individual existent) were used with different meanings by the adversaries, resulting in misunderstanding and confusion. For example, for Cyril nature meant "concrete being," but for Nestorius it meant "assemblage of essential traits or characteristics." In the course of the controversy, <u>hypostasis</u> was associated with both "person" and "nature."

3. <u>The Chalcedonian Settlement and Afterward</u>. It was apparent that a conceptuality that went beyond both of these alternatives was necessary if any resolution were ever to be possible. The Latin West was not so speculative, but it had long consented to the full humanity and divinity of Christ united in one person -- the formula provided by Tertullian. Under the influence

of the famous Tome of Pope Leo this formulation received the official endorsement of the general council held at Chalcedon in 451 A.D. The definition adopted there affirmed several essential points: (1) Jesus Christ is one Person. That one Person is the Word, who is the metaphysical subject of the incarnation. (2) Jesus Christ has two natures. Each one is full and complete. In the incarnation they exist without confusion, change, or division. The properties of each nature remain and all are fully operative without qualification. The Two natures unite in one prosopon (person) and hypostasis (real individual being.)

The definition of Chalcedon did not itself resolve all of the disputed issues. It did not even state a position on all the subtle and technical controversial points. What it did was set the boundaries and the requirements of orthodoxy. Any correct teaching must affirm one person and two full and complete natures. Jesus Christ is truly God and truly man but is one unified being, a single real individual. It is not at all clear that the language they were using was capable of saying what was needed without falling into ambiguities or contradiction or into meaningless verbiage. It is not at all evident that any language ancient or modern can state how one being can be God and a human being, somehow eternal and immutable and also temporal and changing. To many modern minds the task seems impossible, since contradictory assertions must be made of one person.

Nevertheless, the formula was decisive for the Latin West. In the East controversy continued as the monophysites (those teaching the one nature of the incarnate Lord) persisted in arguing their case. An Alexandrian twist was given to the Chalcedonian Creed by the interpretation provided by the Second Council of Constantinople in 553 AD. The Council approved the thesis of Leontius of Byzantium, who offered an interpretation of the Chalcedonian notion that the human nature of Jesus did not have its own independent hypostasis. He proposed, however, that instead of being without hypostasis (anhypostasis), the concrete attributes or traits of the human Jesus were anchored in the hypostasis of the Word (enhypostasis). The Individual Being (the metaphysical subject) is the Word, so that "humanity" was present in Jesus Christ but not "a man." The "manhood" of Jesus belonged to the individual reality (hypostasis) of the Word. This appears to be essentially the position on Cyril of Alexandria, or at least a more precise rendering of what was implied in his teachings. A more Antiochine direction was taken by the Third Council of Constantinople in 681 AD. This Council decided in favor of the view that there were two wills in Christ, although the human will was always subject to the divine will and in harmony with it.

The Chalcedonian Creed defined orthodoxy for Western Christianity for all future centuries. Neither Aquinas, Luther, nor Calvin questioned it. However, Reformation theologians did revive themes reminiscent of the controversies between Alexandria and Antioch. Lutheran theologians stressed the unity of natures, while Calvinist thinkers focused on the distinction between them. The unity of natures was essential to the Lutheran position on the presence of Christ in the Lord's Supper. Unless the properties of the divine nature, especially ubiquity, could be communicated to

the human nature, Christ could not be bodily present in
the bread and wine. Calvinists insisted that the body
of Christ was localized, dwelling at the right hand of
God. Hence, it could not be present in a literal bodily
fashion in the elements of the Supper. None of the
disputants challenged the Chalcedonian formulation
itself. Hence, it remained the hallmark of orthodoxy
for Protestants as well as Catholics.[3]

C. CHRISTOLOGY IN MODERN THEOLOGY: A number of
developments in the post-Reformation period, particularly in the 19th century, put the question of Christology in a new intellectual setting.[4] Reconstruction
was called for.

1. The rise of the historical-critical approach to
the Scriptures called attention to the variety present
in the New Testament witness to Jesus affirmed to be the
Christ. The New Testament does not contain one pure
system of doctrine as classical orthodoxy had assumed
but reflects the diversity of backgrounds and the
various theological interests of the Biblical writers.
The modern theologian is a bit bemused observing the 4th
and 5th century thinkers squirm when confronted with New
Testament passages that contradict their conceptual
models of the person of Christ. The ingenuity exhibited
in making exegesis fit theory is impressive. But it is
not acceptable to the historical-critical view of the
Bible which frankly recognizes both the lack of
technical precision and the diversity of perspective
which characterize the New Testament. The categories
employed to speak of Christ are historically relative
and culturally conditioned. Hence, they cannot be
absolutized as conceptual models, though the unity of

witness to Jesus as Lord and Savior is definitive for Christian thought.

It follows that the creeds of the early centuries -- Nicea and Chalcedon in particular -- will also be seen as relative to time and place and not binding on modern Christians. Greek metaphysics is not a sacred language but an instrument which served its purpose then but is not necessarily the required or universal tongue of theology. Contemporary Christians need to find thought forms and conceptual models relevant to their own culture and experience. The recognition of the diversity and relativity of traditional conceptual models of Christ, reflected even in the New Testament, stimulated a desire to get behind the theology about Jesus to the man himself, described particularly in the synoptic Gospels.

2. The 19th century was characterized by an intense historical consciousness. The historical-critical approach to Scripture and tradition arose out of this fascination with history. This interest carries with it the assumption that the best way to understand any idea, institution, or movement is to trace it back to its origins. (a) For Christology this reinforces the desire to get behind the creeds to Jesus himself as he really was. (b) The focus on Jesus as an object of historical study -- one phenomenon of the past among many others -- raised the question of history and faith. What is the relationship between the person known by the objective, dispassionate historian and the Savior and Lord known in the witness of the church? Jesus as object of historical study and Jesus as object of Christian faith -- no issue has been more central or

more often debated in modern theology than this one. This distinction between "the Jesus of history" and "the Christ of faith" has taken the place of the contrast between the human nature and the divine nature of Jesus Christ in much post-Kantian Protestant theology.

3. The rise of new philosophies also had its impact on Christology, as well as on other doctrines previously noted. In particular, the shift to thinking of a person as a subject with a structure of consciousness instead of as a substance with a nature or essence was decisive. The philosophy of Immanuel Kant was of particular significance in this regard. For Kant a person is a center of moral decision-making, not a static, impersonal essence. Kant also questioned the possibility of attaining metaphysical knowledge, that is, knowledge of things in themselves as they really are. This skeptical attitude has been shared by many theologians of the 19th and 20th centuries. It obviously throws doubt on the objective validity of the Chalcedonian categories. The result has been a widespread tendency to view the divinity of Christ as the moral perfection of his personality, not as the indwelling of supernatural existence in a human being. Walter Rauschenbusch typified this attitude in saying that the social gospel has "more interest in basing the divine quality of his personality on free and ethical acts of his will than in dwelling on the passive inheritance of a divine essence."[5] Moreover, for those who accepted the metaphysical skepticism of Kant, Christology takes the search for a practical or functional approach in contrast to the ontological outlook for Chalcedon. In this framework the person of Christ is seen in terms of the meaning Jesus has for us

as moral personalities. Jesus is the clue to the meaning of history, the prime example of normative human existence, and the supreme revelation of the will, character, and purpose of God, etc. Albrecht Ritschl, following Kant, said that the affirmation of the divinity of Jesus is a practical or evaluative judgment rather than a theoretical or factual assertion. Jesus, he said, has the "value of God for us," i.e., functions for faith in that pragmatic way by initiating us into the Kingdom of God.[6]

The consequence of all these influences has been to shift the language with which the church confesses its faith in Christ away from impersonal, static, metaphysical categories of substance, essence, and nature toward personal, dynamic, moral categories. The center of attention is on history as the locus and focus of human existence in which selves search for and create structures of meaning and purpose. Philosophies as widely different as various forms of idealism, existentialism, phenomenology, and process thought have viewed persons as subjects and agents with a structure of consciousness shaped by history and decision. The self as creative moral agent who must decide how life is to be ordered is a focal point of much modern theology. Jesus as the Christ becomes the normative revelation of the meaning of selfhood and the goal of history and thus serves the function of relating us to God, who both creates the self and directs the historical process toward its proper destiny. Within this context theology has the task of articulating a conceptual model in which the Jesus known by historians can be related to the Christ known in faith in a way which exhibits in modern language the reality of both his divinity and humanity.

While this paragraph would not accurately describe all the varieties of modern Christology, it does point to a widespread tendency in Protestant thought since the time of Friedrich Schleiermacher (1830).

a. The Liberal Reconstruction of Christology: In the 19th century new ways of stating the meaning and significance of Jesus for faith emerged which can be put under the rubric of liberalism. Some of the main features of this reconstruction can be briefly indicated.

1. A major interest of liberal Christology is suggested by the phrase "the quest of the historical Jesus."[7] An effort was made to get behind the creeds and the Christologies to the man himself. Attention was centered on his life, his deeds, his teachings, and especially his personality. Jesus the man becomes the center of theological interest and the norm of moral and religious truth. A distinction was sometimes made between the religion "about Jesus" and the religion "of Jesus." Liberals generally wanted as little of the former and as much of the latter as they could get.

2. Stress on divine immanence allowed liberals to identify the perfect moral personality of the man Jesus with his divinity. God is at work in all nature, history, and human life but is uniquely present in Jesus. Hence, we can speak of the real presence of God in him in a full and complete way. Schleiermacher used the category of "God-consciousness." In other people the awareness of God is wavering, partial, and weak. The "God-consciousness" of Jesus, however, was steady, full, and perfect, constituting "a veritable existence

of God in him."[8] Liberal theologians, then, tended to identify the supreme degree of the immanence of God in Jesus with the idea of incarnation.

3. In keeping with the principle of continuity -- pervasive throughout liberal thought -- the difference between Jesus and other people is one of degree, not an absolute gap in status. Jesus is the prototype of what God intends all human beings to be. Hence, the liberal could move with ease from ordinary folks, to the human Jesus, and on to the divine Christ.

In summary, Jesus was seen as a perfect moral personality whose spiritual excellence constitutes a unique presence of God in him. His teachings rightly instruct us, his example inspires us, and the total impact of his personality communicates to us his own moral and spiritual qualities. In this way Jesus is the Savior of humanity and the Son of God. William Adams Brown was typical of the liberal estimate of the founder of the faith. Christ is, he says:

True man.   Jesus was completely human, a citizen of his time, like all other people around him.

Unique man.   His uniqueness consists in his authority and saving power. He is our authority by virtue of his moral and spiritual excellence, and he saves because of his ability to communicate that excellence to us.

God in man.   This means that God is everywhere

and always like Jesus. Jesus
reveals the true nature and
intention of God in all nature and
history.[9]

b. <u>Neo-orthodox</u> <u>Trends</u> <u>in</u> <u>Christology</u>: A number
of developments in the 20th century called the liberal
reconstruction of Christology into question and brought
forth new perspectives.

1. The work of Johannes Weiss, Albert Schweitzer,
and others re-established the apocalyptic framework of
Jesus' teachings. Jesus was concerned with the coming
of the new age, the consummation of the Kingdom of God
in a special and climactic act of God in history.
Liberals often removed the apocalyptic element,
attributing it to the early church. For 20th century
scholars this view was no longer tenable. Jesus himself
expected a sudden, supernatural intervention of God, and
he thought it was about to happen. This introduces a
dualism between the present evil age and the future
consummation. Hence, the liberal view of the Kingdom as
a gradual transformation of history bringing about the
reign of love on earth did not fit the New Testament
pattern. Neither did it seem credible in an era of
world wars, economic collapse, and totalitarianism.

2. Form criticism in New Testament studies was
insisting that the Gospels are primarily expressions of
the faith of the early church which do not provide the
biographical materials needed to reconstruct the life
and personality of the historical Jesus. Not all that
much can be known with certainty about his deeds and
teachings. The life-situation depicted in the Gospels

is that of the church, not of Jesus. Hence, the accounts we find there represent the interpretation of the meaning of Jesus for faith in the life of the church, not bare memories of facts about him. This means that the quest of the historical Jesus is historically impossible.[10]

3. New Testament studies were revealing that the heart of the Gospels was not the biography of the man Jesus but the kerygma (message, proclamation). The kerygma does not focus on the human personality but on the role of Jesus as the Christ who constitutes the eschatological occurrence by which the new age breaks into history. The New Testament, including the Gospels, is a witness not to the historical Jesus but to the kerygmatic Christ or to the Christ-event -- the culminating act in the history of salvation. This means that the quest of the historical Jesus is theologically illegitimate. It misses the real point of New Testament teaching.[11]

4. Along with these developments in New Testament research were shifts in systematic theology. Neo-orthodoxy expressed an emphasis on the transcendence of God and a loss of confidence in humanity and historical progress. These new notes mean that Christology will show a concern for the deity of Christ as the heaven-sent Savior. God, the transcendent Lord, breaks into history from Beyond to save those who are hopelessly lost apart from God's redemptive act of grace in sending a supernatural redeemer. For Christology this brought about a revival of the dualisms and paradoxes of Chalcedon in place of the smooth continuities liberalism had articulated. But there is a difference between neo-

orthodoxy and the classical models of previous centuries. Neo-orthodox theologians generally shared with the liberals a metaphysical agnosticism and a disdain for impersonal Greek categories. We can speak of a shift of attention from two natures to two histories and two modes of knowing.

Jesus stands in two histories. One is the ordinary, objective, observable stream of general world events which the historian can record and interpret. The other is sacred history (Heilsgeschichte) in which God acts to reveal the divine nature and to redeem humanity -- a saving act known only to faith shared in the Christian community. The historical Jesus is the completely human being known by objective, factual knowledge. The Christ of faith is the divine redeemer whom the believer knows by a personal grasp of meaning appropriated in decision and commitment. This general approach manifested itself in two distinguishable but closely related ways among neo-orthodox thinkers.

1). Some, especially the existentialist theologians, pointed to one series of events making up the life of Jesus and suggested that these happenings can be known from two different perspectives: (1) the objective, critical view of the secular historian and (2) the standpoint of personal faith. Rudolf Bultmann's distinction between Historie and Geschichte and Richard Niebuhr's contrast because "external history" and "internal history" exhibit this approach. The divinity of Christ refers to the existential meaning which Jesus has for the believer.

2). Others, who were more "orthodox," seemed to think of two orders of reality which confront the Christian, one accessible to objective reason and the other knowable only to faith. Both Karl Barth and Emil Brunner, for example, affirmed that God is ontologically present in Jesus. He is fully God and truly human. However, his deity resides in a superhistory which is visible only to faith. The early Barth said that the incarnation touches history like a tangent touches a circle, that is, without touching it. There were no observable manifestations of the deity of Christ as such, said Brunner, although smaller miracles surrounded the superhistorical MIRACLE -- just as ripples move out from a stone that falls into a pond. Barth, however, does speak of the virgin birth and the bodily resurrection of Jesus as signs pointing to the reality of the incarnation.

Neo-orthodox theologians continued the liberal emphasis on the humanity of Jesus. As D.M. Baillie pointed out, modern theology has finally put an end to the subtle docetism that haunted the orthodoxy of previous centuries.[12] Whatever else may be said about Jesus, he is completely and truly human in every respect. However, neo-orthodoxy did show a considerable reduction of interest in the historical Jesus as critical study reveals him. The focus of attention was not on the man Jesus, on his life, teachings, deeds, and personality, but on the divine Christ who constitutes the eschatological event by which the new age irrupts into history. The early Barth once remarked that the Jesus of history was an ordinary, itinerant Rabbi whose human life was more a concealment than a revelation of God.

Neo-orthodoxy also shied away from the easy harmony between revelation and reason which liberals had espoused. For the latter the Christian estimate of Jesus could be validated in various ways. Jesus offered the world the highest ethical ideals known to us in all of history, and these teachings correspond to the finest human intuitions growing out of our own experience and imagination. William Adams Brown, for example, taught that faith in Jesus as the Christ is a value judgment which is verified by the actual results which follow from believing in him. Neo-orthodox thinkers were suspicious of these appeals to the "best" in human nature and to the course of history as the tests of truth. Faith in Christ involves a leap, a decision of the will, which is not easily verified by appeals to reason and experience as shaped by secular culture. Discontinuity, rather than liberal continuity, was the fundamental underlying intuition informing neo-orthodoxy. This orientation moved a long way from the liberal view that Jesus is the concrete embodiment of an Immanent Power and Purpose which is at work in nature and history transforming the actual structures of social existence into an ideal society on earth -- the Kingdom of God. Neo-orthodoxy tended toward a two-dimensional view of history in which the human Jesus is the manifestation of a divine reality and intention known only to the community of faith in its internal confession -- a revelation that escapes worldly wisdom altogether. The Kingdom which Jesus disclosed is an eschatological reality to become enacted fully only beyond this life and history, though tangents of meaning and even instances of progress may be in evidence here and now.[13]

Reinhold Niebuhr offered a practical or moral interpretation of the person and work of Christ along Ritschlian lines, except in a neo-orthodox framework. Christology has to do with "the disclosure and the fulfillment of the meaning of life and history,"[14] not with how the divine and the human can both be ontologically and objectively present in one person. Metaphysical doctrines which attempt to assert both deity and finitude of Jesus are absurd as philosophical claims. The story of God coming to earth in the person and flesh of Jesus is not to be taken literally. It is a myth which illuminates the nature and activity of God, the norm of human existence, and "the possibilities and limits of history."[15] As myths, incarnation and atonement have profound moral and practical meaning by disclosing the love of God which both transcends history and yet, paradoxically, is involved in history.

In God there is a harmonious coincidence of ultimate power and perfect love. But the divine goodness can be revealed in history only in a human life as it becomes powerless on a cross. The agape of Jesus is a revelation both of the nature of God (the divinity of Jesus) and of the moral norm of human existence (the humanity of Jesus). Only powerless love on a cross can accomplish this double symbolization. Agape (sacrificial, self-giving love heedless of the interests of the self) stands above history as an "impossible possibility."[16] Any attempt to embody it in actual practice compromises its purity by mixing it with the claims and counterclaims of relative values which are in tension with each other. Even the historical Jesus could not escape the ambiguities, relativities, and compromises involved in particular moral issues, so mixed up are right and wrong in the complexities of actual life. Only powerless love which rises above the rivalries of competing groups can symbolize pure, disinterested love by a refusal to get involved in conflicts between relative values. The cross, then, is the paradoxical disclosure of a divine agape which stoops to participate in history and a human agape which rises above history in an act of total self-sacrifice. "The `essential,' the normative man, is thus a `God-man' whose sacrificial love seeks conformity with, and finds justification in, the divine and eternal agape, the ultimate and final harmony of life with life."[17]

Paul Tillich, who stands "on the boundary" between neo-orthodoxy and liberalism, developed a Christology that reflects both the influence of Schleiermacher and existentialist philosophy. He rejects the quest for the historical Jesus. The focus of Christology is not the human being from Nazareth as such but the "New Testament picture of Jesus as the Christ."[18] We cannot go behind this portrait of faith to discover the man Jesus as he really was. Every such quest yields only probable and tentative results. Neither faith nor theology can rest its case on such a shifting and uncertain foundation. Yet believers can be sure of the reality of the incarnation as the appearance of the New Being, since this reality has created faith in those who have been transformed by it. Faith cannot deny its own foundation. Believers, then, can be certain on the basis of their immediate experience of salvation that a personal life really did appear in history in which estrangement was overcome with saving power for others. However, this does not guarantee any particular factual details of the life of Jesus reported in the New Testament.

To say that Jesus was both human and divine means that we find in him the union of essence and existence under the conditions of existence. Essence means human life as it ideally and potentially is and ought to be. Existence means human life as it actually is here and now in its universally fallen state. In everybody else existence is estranged from essence, but in Jesus they are reunited in an actual human life living in real history. Jesus as the Christ lives in perfect unity with God, experiencing all the threats and anxieties of this life but conquering them by a total commitment to the divine will and purpose. In this sense, the New Being appeared in Jesus as the Christ. By participating in the power which overcame estrangement in the Christ, believers can experience healing and reunion with essential being in themselves. The classical doctrine that a divine and a human nature were united in one person must be replaced with "the assertion that in Jesus as the Christ the eternal unity of God and man has become historical reality."[19] The notion of a static essence is given up in favor of "dynamic relational concepts."[20] In a real human life Jesus as the Christ faced all the fears, temptations, sufferings that life has to offer and yet conquered all that was negative and potentially destructive, thus exhibiting perfect harmony and unity with God. In this sense he was divine, and because of this fact he can be and is the embodiment, symbol, and mediator of salvation.

c. Recent Currents of Thought: A few distinctive notes of recent reflection about Christ can be indicated.

1). Mid-century saw a renewal of concern with the man Jesus -- "a new quest of the historical Jesus" (James Robinson).[21] Neo-orthodoxy has stressed the "Christ-nature" of Jesus as the saving event of God's action proclaimed in the kerygma. The "new questers" were fearful that lack of attention to the "Jesus-character" of the incarnation might result in a mythological Christ not sufficiently rooted in the actual facts of history. In renewing concern with the man from Nazareth, they hoped to show that the proclaimed Christ of faith was indeed a legitimate interpretation of the real Jesus -- his person, his message, his ministry, and his intentions. Otherwise, the gospel would loose its anchorage in history. A modern form of docetism would threaten the reality of the Word truly made flesh in the earthly Jesus.

2). Process theology embodies a variety of themes that differ from one interpreter to another. David Griffin sounds "liberal" when he speaks of Jesus as perfectly actualizing the divine aim for his life. Because of the special excellence of this aim, Jesus becomes the decisive revelation of God to humanity.[22] John Cobb refers to Christ as the Logos manifested in the life of Jesus. He identifies the Logos with the principle and fact of "creative transformation" -- a process that can be seen universally at work in all positive reformations of life and history which lead toward truth, goodness, and beauty.[23] Schubert Ogden sounds like a continuation of Rudolf Bultmann in that he sees "the point of Christology" as existential. This means that the proclamation of Jesus as the Christ is not about Jesus only but also about God and humanity and the normative relationship between them. As the Christ, Jesus clarifies God's will and purpose, the meaning and destiny of human existence, and the way of salvation. To preach Christ is to confront people with the decision as to whether they will order their lives in accordance with the normative vision disclosed in the New Testament withness to Jesus as the Christ.[24]

3). Liberation theology in its various forms has interpreted Jesus to be the Christ in so far as he is God's Liberator. Liberation theologians protest the captivity of Christ to the ideology and interests of ruling classes, dominant majorities, and oppressive races. In these theologies Christ is a tool of classism, sexism, and racism. The Christ of the ruling classes is an ideological invention and not the Biblical Lord. Liberation theologians want to develop a Christology from the point of view of the poor, the oppressed, and the outcasts to whom the Gospel was originally given. The meaning of the Good News is freedom from bondage. Jesus is the bearer of that message. As the Christ, Jesus is the Word and Deed of God's liberating action in history. Liberation means deliverance not only from sin and death but also from every form of psychological, political, economic, and social bondage which demeans human existence. The favorite texts of these theologies is Luke 4:16-20. James Cone proclaims the Black Christ as the liberator of black people.[25] Feminist theologians stress the special ministry and equalitarian themes of Jesus with respect to women.[26] Third World theologians see Christ as promising freedom to the impoverished masses held in slavery to domestic and foreign elites who exploit them for economic gain and keep them powerless.[27] Liberation

Christology has revolutionary implications in that it beckons the oppressed to struggle against their chains and to become the subjects of their own destiny by the authority and power of the Christ who means freedom. Privileged classes who profess faith in Christ are called upon to surrender their unjust benefits and to identify themselves wholly with the struggles of the oppressed.

Liberation Christologies may be set within a variety of theological perspectives. They may be conservative or liberal, Catholic or Protestant. They may begin with the historical Jesus (Heyward, Sobrino, Ruether)[28] or with the Absolute who appears in time within the frame work of "the orthodox Catholic vision of the Incarnation" (Gutiérrez).[29] Liberation theologians, in short, may take a variety of positions on the standard Christological questions. But in all of them the distinctive and identifying mark is the centrality given to the theme of liberation -- whatever theological form a specific theologian may give to the understanding of Jesus as the Christ. The importance of Jesus Christ is as the preacher and practicer, the source, norm, and ground of liberation as a concrete reality in history -- whether it is the Word made flesh or the prophet from Nazareth who is the focus of theological attention. However, it is not surprising to find a great deal of attention is being given to the identification of Jesus with the poor and the outcasts during his earthly mission. Liberation theology is in the midst of its creative phase, so that it is not yet clear what types and themes of Christological thinking will finally emerge.

D. SUMMARY AND ANALYSIS OF CONTINUING THEMES: The
central motif of all mainline Christology is that Jesus
Christ is one person who is both human and divine.
Unity of person and duality of nature, role, or function
-- this is the pattern that keeps reappearing through
the centuries. It may help to suggest two different
forms which this witness has taken. A basic division
can be seen between what can be called ontological and
functional approaches to the person of Christ.

1. Ontological. In these Christologies both
divinity and humanity refer to objective ontological
facts. Jesus Christ is in and of himself God incarnate
in a human life and history. He does not merely reveal
God or represent God or do a divine work. He is God,
and he is man. The thought of classical orthodoxy took
this form. The Council of Chalcedon asserted that
humanity and divinity are objectively and ontologically
present in the person Jesus Christ -- the God-man.
Luther, Calvin, and Protestant orthodoxy reaffirmed
these themes. Karl Barth and Emil Brunner elaborate
ontological Christologies in modern dress. Both reflect
19th and 20th century tendencies in that neither speaks
of deity as a static essence in the Greek metaphysical
sense. Their language is more oriented toward history
and toward action. Jesus Christ is the Word and Act of
God manifest in the culminating Event in the history of
salvation. On the current scene Wolfhart Pannenberg
agrees with Barth and Brunner in regarding the
Chalcedonian formulation as correct in stating that
Christ is both true God and true man. Even more so, too,
his position is stated in a historically oriented frame
of reference. For Pannenberg vere deus, vere homo is to
be understood, however, not as the unity of two natures

but simply as the fact that this man Jesus is God. From the perspective of the resurrection he is one with God and is God. As the risen Lord he is -- and will be revealed to be -- the eschatological Ruler who exercises the omnipotence of God over the whole world process as the mediator and reconciler of all things. Since things are (in essence) only what they become, from the Endtime view humanity and the cosmos were created through Jesus, the Word of God (John 1:1).[30] In summary, then, from New Testament times until now, one strand of thought maintains that Jesus Christ is both God and man in an objective, ontological sense.

b. Functional. Many modern theologians have sought ways to speak of the person of Christ which are true to Christian experience and to the New Testament witness but which do not involve the literal attribution of deity to the historical figure who lived on earth. Skepticism about all metaphysical claims in general and the recognition of the historical relativity of the Greek categories employed at Chalcedon have played a part. Conceptual equivalents to the traditional language have been sought which express the special and unique place of Jesus in Christian faith without maintaining that Jesus Christ was actually God or the Son of God (Logos) in some objective and ontological sense. Many modern theologians would agree with Reinhold Niebuhr that it is rationally absurd to assign both deity and humanity to one being. Instead, many 19th and 20th century theologians have focused on the role or function of Jesus in revealing God or in saving humanity. In so doing, they shifted from the static language of nature, substance, and essence to the dynamic language of history, personal existence, and

action. In many cases, the divinity of Christ is viewed
in terms of the perfection of his humanity. It is this
special and unique excellence which makes it possible
for Jesus to serve the function of being God for us in
history and human existence.

A few examples will suffice to illustrate this
approach to Christology. Functional views were common
in the liberal theology of the 19th and nearly 20th
centuries. Schleiermacher saw the divinity of Jesus in
terms of the perfect God-consciousness achieved in his
human life. Jesus becomes Savior by communicating the
power of his own God-consciousness to us. William Adams
Brown and other American liberals simply meant that
Jesus revealed God to us, that God is everywhere like
Jesus in character and intention. Paul Tillich
discovered the divine aspect in the paradoxical fact
that Jesus in his human life united essence with
existence under the conditions of existence, thus
becoming the source of the New Being whereby the
estrangement present in everybody else is overcome.
According to Reinhold Niebuhr, the powerless Jesus on
the cross symbolizes both the perfect love of God and
the perfect human love which is the norm of historical
existence. D.M. Baillie speaks of the paradox of grace
whereby the good that Christ does as a human is at the
same time the consequence of the fullness of divine
grace in him. This is what it means to say that in a
fully human life, God was fully present.[31] John Knox
means by the divinity of Christ the fact that through
the man Jesus, completely human in every respect, God
has accomplished the salvation of humanity.[32] For David
Griffin and other process theologians, Jesus became a
normative revelation of God for us by fully actualizing

the special aim which God set before him. Some
theologians standing in a Kantian and/or existentialist
tradition see the humanity in terms of the historical
facts about Jesus and the divinity in terms of the
evaluation or decision that Christians make in reference
to the man Jesus. Albrecht Ritschl said that Jesus has
the value of God for us. Rudolf Bultmann and H. Richard
Niebuhr in similiar fashion contend that statements
about the divine nature of Christ are judgments of the
practical reason and not of theoretical reason. For
them the divinity of Jesus refers to the meaning the
historical Jesus has for faith as the Word and Deed of
God by which reconciliation is achieved. All of these
Christologies, and many more that could be listed, seek
a functional equivalent of Chalcedon by finding in the
fully human life of Jesus a unique presence of God, a
normative revelation of God, and a decisive saving act
of God. But for these perspectives it is not true to say
that in his divine aspect Jesus is God in the literal or
ontological sense which classical and modern orthodoxy
has asserted.

II.   THE WORK OF CHRIST

Much that relates to the saving work of Christ has
already been stated or implied in dealing with the
meaning of salvation and with the definition of his
person. However salvation is conceived, Jesus as the
Christ is the source of it. Moreover, the person of
Christ can hardly be described apart from what he
accomplished as Savior. This fact was evident in the
preceding section. The focus here will be on the death
and resurrection of Jesus as the events in which God has

provided a way of salvation. Put otherwise, we shall be dealing with what is traditionally referred to as theories of atonement.

A. THE NEW TESTAMENT FOUNDATIONS: It can scarcely be doubted that the death and resurrection of Jesus are seen by the New Testament writers as the focal point of God's saving action. The Gospels themselves, which report the life of Jesus, have aptly been called passion stories with an extended introduction. Hence, however important the teachings and example of the man Jesus may be for the Christian believer, it is clear that cross and resurrection take center stage in the New Testament witness to the importance of Jesus for the redemption of the world. Basically, this witness takes the form of a narrative. Christ, a pre-existent divine being, becomes incarnate in human flesh through the womb of Mary. Jesus begins a short ministry of preaching, healing, and teaching, all centered around the inbreaking of the new age which is soon to be consummated in its fullness. Jesus dies on the cross as a sacrifice for the sins of humanity and by his death and resurrection overcomes the demonic powers which bring sin and death. Jesus ascends to heaven from whence he will return at the end of the age, fully victorious over all evil. Writers of the New Testament concentrate on different portions of this story and offer a variety of interpretive images and concepts to fill out the meaning of these crucial events by which salvation has been accomplished. But there can be no doubt that death and resurrection are the focal point of God's victory over sin and death. The New Testament overflows with a rich profusion of metaphors, principles, and ideas drawn from the Hebrew and Hellenistic environments to express the conviction.

However, the sum total of the convictions expressed do not add up to a single, unified systematic theory of atonement in any precise or technical way.

The New Testament is unanimous in the claim that "Christ died for our sins in accordance with the scriptures" (I Cor. 15:3). This was the way God had chosen to break down the "dividing wall of hostility" (Ephes. 2:14) which separated sinners from their Maker. Forgiveness of sin and reconciliation to God are made possible by the self-giving obedience of Christ upon the cross (Mk. 10:45; Rom. 5:10; I Peter 2:24; Heb. 9:28; Ephes. 2:13). Instead of precise systematic theories what we find are themes or motifs associated with metaphors drawn from various legal and religious practices current at the time. The sacrificial system of the Old Testament is certainly in view at times (Heb. 10:12; Ephes. 5:2). The shedding of the blood (the surrender of life, Lev. 17:1) of an animal victim is a sacrifice acceptable to God and thus effective for the atonement of sins. The Letter to the Hebrews sees Jesus as both the High Priest and the sacrificial victim (Hebs. 7:27, 9:12, 25-28). Jesus is the "Lamb of God" (John 1:29), a ramsom to secure release (Mk. 10:45; I Peter 1:18), an expiation for sin (Rom. 3:24-25), the price paid for redemption of those in bondage (Ephes. 1:7; I Cor. 6:20). The idea of the Suffering Servant who suffers vicariously for others in order to save them is in the background of much New Testament thought regarding the sacrificial death of Jesus (Is. 53).

The death and resurrection of Jesus, however, are not only historical events which affect humankind. They are cosmic occurrences which alter the whole creation.

In particular, the death of Jesus constitutes a victory over the demonic forces -- the principalities and power -- which hold humanity in bondage (I Cor. 2:6-8; Col. 2:15; I Peter 3:18-22). The cross is a continuation and culmination of the battle Jesus had begun in his earthly ministry (Mk. 1:23-34). While the decisive battle has already been won, the final victory awaits the Endtime when all enemies, including death itself, will be put down once and for all (I Cor. 15:24-28).

It is the Apostle Paul who developed in the fullest detail the theme of the saving work of God in the incarnation, death, and exaltation of Jesus. For him the Gospel is nothing other than the "word of the cross" (I Cor. 1:18), and he decided to preach nothing but "Jesus Christ and him crucified" (I Cor. 2:2). He combines a variety of motifs in explicating the meaning of the salvation wrought by Christ. 1. His death is an expiation (means of atonement) for sin in terms of Jewish sacrificial practice (Rom. 3:23-25, 5:9; I Cor. 11: 24-25). 2. It is a vicarious sacrifice (Gal. 3:13; II Cor. 5:14). 3. Jesus' death is a ransom paid to secure redemption and freedom from the curse of the law (Gal. 3:13; I Cor. 6:20, 7:23). 4. The death of Christ is seen in analogy with the death of a god in the mystery religions in whose dying and rising one participates (Rom. 6:1-10; Gal. 3:27-28). 5. Incarnation, death, and exaltation are seen as a saving event in which a divine redeemer, perhaps patterned after the Gnostic redeemer mvth, comes down from above to rescue souls from darkness and bondage (Phil. 2:5-11). The demonic powers have been overcome so that the old age has passed away and the new has come (I Cor. 2:6, 7:31; II Cor. 5:17). Christ is the new Adam who brings life

and righteousness to overcome the age of sin and death
introduced by the first Adam (Rom. 5:12-19; I Cor. 1:21-
22, 45-50). Believers participate in the death and
resurrection of the divine Redeemer and are one with him
(II Cor. 5:14; I Cor. 15:20-22, 12:12; Phil. 3:10-11; II
Cor. 4:7-12).[33]

B. HISTORICALLY DEVELOPED THEORIES OF ATONEMENT:
We have no creedal decisions to define the orthodox view
of the saving work of Christ corresponding to Nicea and
Chalcedon which formulated the classical doctrines of
the Trinity and the person of Christ. Instead we find a
wide variety of formulations which take up various
motifs in the New Testament, frequently integrated with
prevailing cultural ideas and institutions. It is
possible to define certain types of atonement theory
which have dominated Christian thinking at one time or
another. For a long time histories of doctrine tended
to classify views of the work of Christ under objective
and subjective theories. Objective theories point to
something outside the believer pertaining to the nature
of God or the requirements of forgiveness which had to
be and was changed by the death of Christ. Anselm was
the primary source of such views. Subjective theories
point to a change wrought inside the believer by the
impact of the life and death of Jesus on the mind and
heart and will. Abelard was the classical exponent of
this approach. Since the publication of Gustaf Aulén's
CHRISTUS VICTOR (1930),[34] it has become customary to
include a third type centering on the liberation of
humanity from the bondage of evil powers by the death
and resurrection of Christ. While a classification of
major motifs can be useful in helping to simplify and
systematize the history of Christian thought, it is

important to recognize the richness, variety, and complexity of the ideas that get expressed in a given period or individual thinker. Many themes may be inter-woven and only loosely coordinated, as is the case in the New Testament itself. Hence, one must be careful not to force a rich complex of ideas present in a theo-logian into neat preformed categories. Nevertheless, for the sake of convenience a typology will be employed in the clear recognition that the concrete reality of thought overflows any imposed boundaries.

The traditional categories which distinguish between objective and subjective views will be used to set forth three main types of atonement theory that can be abstracted from the history of Christian thought. Within this framework some attention will be paid to other themes that do not fit the main classifications.

1. Objective Theories: The main conviction embodied in this approach is that something has to be done objectively so that humanity can be saved. Something in the nature of things has to be changed. There is a real and inviolable moral and spiritual order which prescribes conditions that have to be met. Christ saves because he accomplishes whatever must be done to set things right. Two major examples of this orientation can be outlines.

a. The Christus Victor Theme. The presupposition here is that humankind is enslaved to evil powers -- the law, sin, death, Satan, etc. The death and resurrection of Christ win a victory over these alien forces and set humanity free to live in reconciliation with God and to achieve fulfillment of life. God out of grace and love and mercy sends Christ to do this saving work and thus is the ultimate author of salvation. This theme is present in the New Testament. Aulén maintains that various versions of this approach were dominant during the first 1000 years of Christian history. This may well be true, but certainly other motifs were present as well. In fact, in every era, if not in every major thinker, elements, if not a fully developed example, of the main types of atonement theory can be found. In addition, there are distinctive features that do not fit well with any of the three to be highlighted here. In the early centuries, for example, notions of Jesus as teacher, lawgiver, and example are prominent (Clement, Justin). Christ the Logos brings truth, light, and immortality. Many taught that the incarnation itself is the primary means of salvation in that it unites the eternal Logos with humanity, thus "deifying" the believer and saving us from the mortality and corruption of finite existence. "He became what we are that we might become what he is" (Irenaeus, Athanasius). In these early theologians too are found numerous references to the idea of the death of Christ as a vicarious sacrifice who brings expiation from sin by the shedding of his blood. But in and among these themes is the central motif of the death and resurrection of Christ as a victory over the Devil and the demons which liberates humanity from bondage.

Aulén takes Irenaeus to be a clear and consistent example of the Christus Victor theme as well as the fountainhead of much of the best thinking that was to follow. Christ came down from heaven to "destroy sin, overcome death, and give life to humanity." What was lost in Adam has been recovered in Christ. Irenaeus explains this by his theory of "recapitulation." Christ retraces or reproduces in his own being and career each of the steps and dimensions of life which had been corrupted by sin and at each point heals, restores, and reclaims what has been lost. He sums up all things (Ephes. 1:10). By his obedience and by the shedding of his blood, he overcomes the Devil and reconciles up to God by propitiating the Father. Thus interpreted, Aulén denies the view of some liberal Protestants (Harnack, e.g.) that Irenaeus should be seen primarily as an example of the "physical doctrine of salvation." That is the theory that salvation is the bestowal of immortality through the incarnation -- a view in which sin is secondary.

Some exponents of the <u>Christus</u> <u>Victor</u> theme spoke of Christ as a ransom paid to the Devil as the price of release for the souls held in bondage. Crude images were used involving deception. A favorite set of metaphors pictured the human nature of Jesus as bait which the Devil greedily swallows thinking that an easy prey has been found. However, the hook of the divine nature captures the Devil. Gregory of Nyssa, who used this analogy, also thought the Devil had acquired rights over humanity by virtue of the fall and thus could claim a ransom price which the death of Christ paid. While all agreed that humankind had been released from demonic bondage by the power of Christ, not all accepted the notions of deception or of the rights of Satan to claim a ransom. Not surprisingly, many modern interpreters have been put off by the crudity of the images involved and even more by the mythological framework suggested by the acceptance of literal ideas concerning Satan and cosmic conflict.

Origen brings together most of the ideas that we have so far encountered. 1. First, he espouses the physical or mystical theory whereby human nature is progressively "deified." Christ as Logos is teacher, lawgiver, and model. By union with him we come alive and lose the irrationality and corruption of fallen existence. 2. Second, he holds that Christ overthrew the powers of darkness and death, overcoming the Devil and liberating humankind. 3. Finally, he teaches that the death of Christ was a vicarious or propitiatory sacrifice by which reconciliation is achieved. He was the first to develop this idea in detail. J.N.D. Kelly maintains that these three themes constitute the primary motifs of the early centuries as it relates to the saving work of Christ. Further, he concludes that it was the "recapitulation" theory of Irenaeus that provided the framework which the early thinkers used to unify these seemingly disparate themes. Christ as representative of the whole human race has restored what was lost to Adam's progeny. By participating in his life, death, and resurrection, believers can share in his victory over sin, death, and the demonic hosts whose rule is ended.35

The "physical theory" or the "deification" idea was most prevalent in the Greek-speaking church of the East. The sacrificial theory of vicarious atonement developed more in the Latin West. The Christus victor theme appears to be well nigh universal. In the 5th century it was Augustine who for the Latin church summed up the major developments and led the way into the theories of Anselm and Abelard which came into prominence in the Medieval period. All the previous motifs are present in

Augustine, but the center around which the others revolve is the idea of a substitutionary, vicarious sacrifice which appeases the wrath of God. Christ is innocent, but takes our place and by his death renders satisfaction to God. In this way Christ is the mediator who brings about the removal of our guilt and deserved punishment and hence reconciles us to God. Moreover, in .an unprecedented fashion Augustine stresses the impact of the example of Christ upon the sinner. Christ reveals the wisdom and love of God in a way that should evoke our love in return.[36]

b. Satisfaction theories. Anslem is the central figure here as we move into the medieval era. However, this motif had been anticipated already, in part by Tertullian and even more by Augustine. The general idea of an expiatory sacrifice was common from the beginning. It is so much a part of the New Testament witness that it could hardly be missed. But it is one thing to include the idea as one among others. It is another to develop a precise and detailed rationale which makes the idea of satisfaction the heart and center of atonement. This was left for Anselm to do in his famous CUR DEUS HOMO? (Why Did God Become Man), written in 1098 AD. Sin, he says, is failing to give God what is due. The sinner offends God's honor by not rendering perfect obedience. God must either punish the sinner, or the divine honor must be satisfied. Only God can make satisfaction since it is divine dignity that has been injured. But only a human being ought to make it since it is humanity that has sinned. Thus, God sends the God-Man to make satisfaction so that the divine will to perfect the creation can be accomplished. Christ rendered perfect obedience to God, which he owed, but he did not deserve to die. He, though innocent, gave up his life willingly to God. The death of the perfect man is a good of such immensity that it suffices to satisfy the honor of God for all the sins of the whole world. The benefits of his death are freely offered to all people by Christ and accepted by God as due satisfaction for all sinners. In short, humanity has offended God by breaking the divine law. But the law is holy and can suffer no violation without recompense. Christ provides the satisfaction required by his innocent suffering and thus wins acquittal for all. The legal structure which undergirds this outlook comes directly from the feudal system then in effect and would have made perfect sense to those who viewed his theory in that context.[37]

The Protestant Reformers, especially John Calvin, stressed this general view.[38] Christ bears the wrath of God on behalf of and in place of the sinners who deserve it. Thus, justice is vindicated. Forgiveness and reconciliation are now objectively possible. Calvin actually develops a concept of the three-fold office of Christ. In addition, to the office of priest in which Christ makes a substitutionary, vicarious sacrifice to God, he is also prophet and king. As prophet, Christ preached the Gospel and revealed the law of God in both word and deed. As king, Christ rules the church as well as individual believers and shares with them all his royal benefits.[39] Martin Luther also set forth a version of the satisfaction theory, although the Christus Victor theme is prominent too. In fact, Aulén -- a Swedish Lutheran -- maintains that the great achievement of Luther was that he not only reclaimed but deepened the understanding of the work of Christ in terms of his victory over the law, sin, and death.[40] Luther did exult in this motif, even reviving some of the cruder images. With gusto he spoke of the Devil's deception and defeat in terms of the bait-fishhook analogy. But here, as well as in interpreting earlier theologians, Aulén has a tendency to play down any motifs other than the favored one in his heroes. The satisfaction theory dominated the Protestant orthodoxy of the 17th and 18th centuries in both Lutheran and Reformed schools of thought.

In short, a line of thought can be traced from Tertullian, Cyprian, Augustine, and Gregory the Great in the early centuries right on through to the Catholic and Protestant orthodoxy of recent times which espouses the general idea of the death of Christ as a satisfaction for the sin and guilt of humankind. The main line of medieval thinkers followed Anselm's basic idea with variations in detail. However, later thinkers did not generally accept his conviction that the incarnation and atonement were rational necessities dictated by the structure of reality. Rather they tended toward the view that the way of salvation provided in Christ was a matter of divine choice. It could have been otherwise if God had so willed. Wherever orthodoxy is dominant, even in modern theology, the satisfaction theory remains attractive. Fundamentalist sts and conservatives in the 20th century still make the idea of a substitutionary atonement an essential mark of right thinking. Emil Brunner and Karl Barth among the neo-orthodox sponsored a version of this point of view, though both include the Christus Victor theme and subjective elements as well.[41]

2. Subjective Theories: Views of this type focus on what happens in the sinner to bring about a change of mind and heart. In their strict form they may deny the claims of the objective theories completely. No demonic powers have to be overcome. No satisfaction needs to be made to divine justice in order to preserve the integrity of the objective moral order. All that is required is that sinners turn from their wicked ways, change their attitudes, and seek forgiveness. God is ever willing and ready to have mercy and enter into a new relationship with humanity. Those who hold to objective views may, of course, insist that the subjective response of the sinner is an essential part of the total process. Hence, objective and subjective motifs may be combined, although the emphasis may be on one side or the other.

Alelard (died 1142 AD) is the name most frequently associated with what is sometimes called "the moral influence theory." He was not the first to state the idea by any means. Anselm regards the theme as one of the views of antiquity. The notion was prominent in Augustine. However, it was Abelard who made this view so central and so attractive that his name has subsequently been identified with it. He, like Anselm, rejects the idea that Christ's death was a ransom paid to the Devil. But he also rejects Anselm's claim that God's honor must be satisfied before the divine mercy can become effective. God could have chosen to forgive sin apart from the passion of the God-Man. Was not the God of the Old Testament a forgiving God, and did not Jesus forgive sinners during his earthly life? Moreover, when people crucified Jesus -- a sin far greater than the disobedience of Adam, would that not have increased God's wrath against humanity rather than bringing about reconciliation? "How cruel and unjust it appears that anyone should demand the blood of the innocent as any kind of ransom, or be in any way delighted with the death of the innocent, let alone that God would find the death of His Son so acceptable, that through it He should be reconciled to the world!"[42] Abelard offers instead the proposal that the life and death of Jesus are a demonstration of God's love so powerful that it evokes love in the sinner for God. Jesus' teaching and example are effective in melting the stony heart of the disobedient and in bringing about a change of attitude and motivation. On the basis of our rekindled love for God brought about by the impact of Christ, God forgives sin. Abelard quotes Luke 7:47 where Jesus says, "Therefore I tell you, her sins, which are many, are forgiven, for she loved much; but he who is forgiven little, loves little" (RSV). Abelard's intention, it appears, was to reduce the whole process of salvation to one principle: God's love for us in Christ brings about a responsive love.

This view, of course, made it difficult for Abelard to interpret the necessity of baptism. In the case of infants he had to admit that remission of sin was independent of the kindling of love. In adults he conceded that forgiveness was not effective until baptism even though love might be present prior to that. Moreover, passages can be found in which Abelard does speak in the traditional way of the death of Christ as a sacrifice. Also, he makes use of the idea of merit which Christ's obedience earned as efficacious for us. Nevertheless, the main tendency of Abelard was elsewhere.[43]

The Abelardian approach to the work of Christ was not a major influence in either Catholic or Protestant orthodoxy. It was in modern liberal theology that Abelard triumphed. Friedrich Schleiermacher, the father of Protestant liberalism, defined the divinity of Christ as the perfection of his God-consciousness. The saving work of Christ consists in his power to communicate that God-consciousness to us. Schleiermacher seems to envision an infusion of moral energy into the believer through a mystical union with Christ which is mediated through a participation in the Christian community in which Christ dwells and reigns. He sees this doctrine as identical with the Christ-mysticism of the Apostle Paul, who spoke of the union of Christ with the believer. As a Reformed theologian, Schleiermacher developed his views under the traditional three-fold heading. As prophet, Christ preached and ushered in the Kingdom of God. As priest, Christ took upon himself the sins of the world. His sinless perfection was a judgment on the world and evoked the hostility of sinners, and thus he died. By his sufferings he introduced a new possibility into the world -- forgiveness, reconciliation, and love. As king, Christ rules the church and provides all necessary spiritual benefits to the believing community.[44]

Albrecht Ritschl developed a more strictly ethical view of the work of Christ. Jesus mediates the forgiveness of sins and initiates us into the Kingdom of God. Contrary to the objective theory of Anselm, God does not need to be reconciled to us. He agrees with Abelard that we need to be reconciled to God. God is purely and simply love. Justice and wrath have no place in Ritschl's view. Hence, nothing in God's nature requires satisfaction. As pardoned sinners who have been brought into an awareness of God's forgiving love through the life and death of Jesus, believers are introduced into the Kingdom of God in which the new life is expressed and consummated. The Kingdom is an earthly community to be progressively realized in history in which persons serve each other in love. As the bearer of divine love Jesus saves us by being the instrument of both justification (forgiveness) and reconciliation (the coming of the Kingdom).[45]

C. ATONEMENT THEMES IN 20TH CENTURY THEOLOGY: A general remark may be made about atonement thinking in liberalism, neo-orthodoxy, and current theologies. The literal, mythological, quantitative, legalistic elements of previous theories are rejected. Frequently no specific technical theory of atonement will be offered at all. However, certain common features can be noted. The model for talking about atonement is taken from personal relationships. What is required to restore right relationships between God and humanity? What has to happen for reconciliation to occur between a personal God and finite persons? Moral and psychological language tends to predominate over legalistic conceptions. The idea that Christ was punished in our place to satisfy the wrath of God has little place outside conservative theologies in recent thought. The basic concern is with Christ as the revealer of divine love which overcomes guilt and brings about reconciliation. Within this basic framework a variety of themes are introduced.

In liberal theology Abelardian themes were dominant. As A.C. Knudson said, liberalism focused neither on the Devilward side (the patristic ransom theory) nor on the Godward side (the Anselmic satisfaction theory) but on the humanward side (the Abelardian moral influence theory).[46] In such thinkers as William Adams Brown, Walter Rauschenbusch, Harry Emerson Fosdick, as well as Knudson, the subjective elements were highlighted repeatedly.[47] The mystical approach of Scheiermacher and the moral approach of Ritschl were primary influences.

The neo-orthodox and neo-liberal theologies of the last half century have been respectful of classical motifs, though they are never simply affirmed in their traditional or literal meanings. The symbolic meanings are adopted as elucidating essential elements in the process of reconciliation. In this framework both objective and subjective dimensions are included. Reinhold Niebuhr saw all the classical theories of atonement as attempts "to state the paradox of the divine mercy in relation to the divine wrath."[48] As implausible and absurd as some of them are, they do make it clear that the final reality is not wrath but love. The cross is the supreme revelation of the meaning of history and of life by disclosing a divine mercy that transcends judgment and hence leads to an ultimate fulfillment of human existence despite sin. However, it is not enough simply to say that the cross reveals a love so powerful that sinners are led to repentance and to love God in return. Sin is serious, and forgiveness is costly. There can be no simple abrogation of wrath in favor of mercy. God suffers as an inevitable consequence of human sinfulness and by voluntarily accepting and bearing the results of pride and injustice in the divine heart. The wrath of God is the essential structure of reality reacting against the corruptions and destructive tendencies introduced by sin. It is love as the law of life responding to the defiance of that law by human egotism. Mercy represents the freedom of God over law and wrath, but not the freedom to abrogate law. God saves us by taking the consequences of wrath upon Self and bearing them in a suffering heart so that mercy and love can issue in forgiveness and reconciliation for repentant sinners.[49]

Paul Tillich finds symbolic meaning in all three of the classical theories, though each has limitations as well as strengths. A complete theory requires both objective and subjective elements. Atonement is a divine act which must be humanly appropriated. Without the experience of the love of God, the symbolic imagery of the victory of Christ over demonic forces is lacking in existential grounding in human life and thus becomes a drama so external to humanity as to lose its power. The betrayal and defeat of Satan, however, symbolizes the fact that evil has no independent power and lives only from the positive which it corrupts. Hence, evil cannot be ultimate but is overcome by the power of the New Being in Christ. Abelard's view provides an essential element but is psychologically inadequate. The assurance of divine love by itself is not enough to overcome the anxiety and guilt of sinners who are conscious of having violated justice and thus are deserving of punishment. The sacrifice of Christ satisfies the wrath of God and makes it possible for God to have mercy without violating justice. Hence, the sinner can appropriate forgiveness knowing that Christ has suffered in his/her place, thus preserving the integrity of an objective moral order. While the psychological symbolism of this theory is powerful in dealing with deep and often hidden realities of guilt, the legalistic framework of Anselm's theory must be rejected, along with the notion of a quantity of merit which the suffering of Christ earned. In short, the traditional theories must be interpreted in terms of their symbolic meaning for divine-human relationships and not seen as literal descriptions of cosmic transactions. The principles which should govern any future doctrine of the atonement see reconciliation as a divine act in which God symbolically participates in and overcomes human estrangement, taking the suffering of the world into the heart of deity, thus honoring the reality of justice which preserves the structural intregity of love. Believers must participate in the sufferings of God, existentially appropriating the atoning work and being transformed by it.[50]

The themes developed by Niebuhr and Tillich are widespread today, not only in American but in British[51] and Continental[52] theology as well. The emphasis tends to be on cross and resurrection as disclosures of the nature of God, the reality of human sinfulness, and of God's suffering with us, for us, and because of us in order to save us. Symbolic meanings are discovered in these events which illuminate life and empower us to respond to God in faith and obedience. The traditional theories are taken as attempts to express in outmoded language and categories what is better put today in personal, moral, existential, and psychological terms. They do convey something that is really true about God's being and activity, but the images, concepts, and metaphors are not to be taken literally as expressing cosmic events that happened once upon a time which alter the objective situation of humanity on earth. Demythologizing, deliteralizing, delegalizing, and rein- terpretation in contemporary existential and (sometimes) metaphysical terms is necessary.

The Christus Victor theme may be useful if the mythology of demonic powers can be translated into psychological, political, economic, and sociological terms to indicate the structural forces which oppress humanity. Neurotic patterns cause suffering in individuals which they cannot overcome by simple rational choice. Deep, irrational, unconscious forces shaped by destructive life history and wrong decisions affect behavior and do damage to self and others. At the societal level "superpersonal forces of evil" (Rauschenbusch)[53] get institutionalized in social structures (slavery, segregation, and unjust economic systems, e.g.) which oppress certain groups. The poor, the outcasts, and the weak in such cases are indeed enslaved to demonic forces -- structural and institut- ional powers of evil. If Christ can be seen as liberator from these objective patterns and destructive relationships, then the New Testament and patristic testimony to his victory over Satan and the demonic powers can be given contemporary meaning.

The Anselmic approach testifies to the gravity of sin and the costliness of forgiveness. When anyone truly forgives another of a grave offense, suffering occurs in the one who forgives. The hurt, the betrayal, and the wrath of the offended person must be borne in and burned out in a suffering heart before genuine reconciliation can occur. Think of what must happen before the Jews can forgive Hitler. Forgiveness is not

easy. It is costly. It comes at the price of suffering. And only great love that overcomes justifiable
wrath can bring it about. That is the symbolic meaning
of the cross. God suffers when people sin and bears the
cost of forgiveness.

The Abelardian orientation witnesses to the fact
that what is objectively made possible by the victorious
and atoning work of Christ can become actual only when
it is subjectively appropriated in repentance, faith,
gratitude, and love on the part of the beneficiaries.
The person who is forgiven must suffer in sorrow at the
offense sin has caused. Genuine love must be born or
reborn in the heart of the offender before
reconciliation is complete. In Pauline language one
must die to an old life and rise to a new existence by
participating in the cross and resurrection of Christ.
Put all together in contemporary language, the meaning
of liberation, reconciliation, and moral transformation
can be given vital meaning as ways of understanding the
victory of Christ over sin and death.

III. Concluding Reflections

All Christians are united in confessing that Jesus
is the Christ -- the unique revealer of God and supreme
redeemer of humanity. It is this conviction, of course,
which makes people Christians. The preceding pages have
made it clear that this basic faith shared by all
Christians can be stated in an astonishing variety of
ways. The New Testament itself contains many ways of
expressing the faith that Jesus is the Messiah, the
Deliverer, and Lord of Life who will in the end conquer

sin, evil, and death once and for all. Subsequent theologians have centered on particular motifs, images, and concepts derived from this witness, thus creating a variety of conceptual models. Developing a Christology, however, is never simply a matter of reproducing New Testament themes in a certain configuration around some organizing focus. Elements from the situation of the interpreter also enter into the final product. This may be the language of Greek metaphysics taken from the surrounding culture -- as in the case of the early controversies resolved at Chalcedon (451 AD). It may be legal concepts and societal ways of thinking -- as in the case of Anselm's theory of atonement. It may be the theme of liberation from oppressive social structures growing out of the yearning of the poor and the downtrodden -- as in the case of contemporary liberation theologies. Christologies, then, unite universal (New Testament) themes with situational (contemporary) ideas and concerns.

Every new generation in its own particular setting will have to answer for itself the question Jesus put to his first disciples, "Who do you say that I am?" Creative thought is being given to this question even now. Three currents of thought in the present-day may be highlighted as having the potential to bring forth new light on this old question. 1. It remains to be seen what the outcome will be of the attempt to see the significance of Jesus in a consistent and single-minded way from the point of view of the poor, the outcasts, and the oppressed in all the contexts in which injustice and misery prevail. Liberation theologies may have much more to say in this regard. The consequences of this understanding of Jesus for privileged peoples still has to be faced more profoundly than has yet been the case. Can the Logos made flesh or the Man from Nazareth be the source of creativity and new forms of human expression and fulfillment where oppression is not the dominant or only reality that has to be dealt with? In a society of equals does Jesus have any significance?

2. Feminist theologians (whether male or female) may have more important insights than have yet been forthcoming on the understanding of Jesus in relationship to sexuality as a defining characteristic of human beings. Does it matter that Jesus was a man? Are sin and salvation different for women and men in any way that matters? Does Jesus in his essential ministry, message, and saving work transcend gender altogether, or is there something missing which has to be supplied from elsewhere in order for Jesus to be a relevant Savior for women?

3. Renewed thought is being given to the question of the finality and universality of Christ. In a world that is increasingly interdependent and yet pluralistic, is it reasonable to claim that Christ is or should be the "way, the truth, and the life" for everyone? Or must Christians be content to believe that while Jesus is ultimate for them, other paths may have an equal claim of validity for others? Should Christians become open to allowing the truth they have to be supplemented or even transformed by the truth that Buddha may have disclosed?[54] Does the whole truth about Reality and salvation lie ahead yet to be discovered rather than given once and for all in the past? These are ancient questions, but they are alive today in a new way. The coming years may well produce novel and quite untraditional answers.

The consequence of the impact of Jesus received as the Christ was the coming into being of the church. It was in this community of faith that the memory of Jesus was preserved, celebrated, and transmitted to future generations. Attention must now be turned in the following chapter to the ways Christians have understood themselves to be the Body of Christ.

CHAPTER V
THE SPIRIT AND THE CHURCH

I. The Spirit

This presentation of Christian doctrine has a trinitarian structure, as do many systematic theologies in this and previous centuries. The logic of this arrangement is not difficult to discern. Theology is faith in action seeking understanding. Faith is directed toward God the Almighty Creator, the ultimate source of all things. Hence, the first person of the Trinity (traditionally called Father) is an appropriate starting point for presenting the content of Christian belief. After all, we confess that in the beginning God created the heavens and the earth (Gen. 1). The apex of creation on earth is the appearance of human beings made in the image of God. However, humanity fell from the potential of this high estate and intended destiny into a state of alienation. Thus, the development of the Christian understanding of the human condition follows as a next step. But God intervenes into the estrangement of persons from their essential being by sending Jesus Christ into the world to become the author of salvation. The presentation of the person and work of Christ naturally follows. Incarnation and atonement have to do with the earthly appearance of the second person of the Trinity (traditionally called the Son). The activity of Christ resulted in the formation of the church and the beginning of the culminating phases of the Kingdom of God. This brings us to the present portion of the outline of this text. Central to the exposition of the nature of the Christian community and of history in light of the Kingdom is the immanent presence of God in human life here and now. In this connection we address the function of the third person of the Trinity (traditionally called the Holy Spirit). The Spirit is God in us, with us, and for us in our personal lives and in the church. Yet the Creator, the Redeemer, and the Companion are not three Gods but one and the same Lord functioning in three modes of being and activity. In Chapter II it was argued that "the trinitarian pattern" is essential and unavoidable in giving an exposition of the Christian experience of God. Here the point is that "the trinitarian pattern" provides a useful and orderly way of organizing the presentation of Christian belief.

The Spirit has often been the neglected dimension of the reality of God. At Nicea in 325 AD the focus of attention was on the relationship of God and Christ. At the conclusion of the creed, which went to some length in spelling out the full deity of the incarnate Logos, a simple statement was appended: "We believe in the Holy Spirit." While later Councils did affirm the full deity of the Spirit as an equal partner in the Godhead, no Council ever spelled out an orthodox view of this doctrine in detail and with precision. We have no Council which devoted the same attention to the nature and function of the Spirit as Nicea (325 AD) and Chalcedon (451 AD) gave to the divinity and humanity of Christ.

The root meaning of "spirit" in nearly every language is wind or breath. Not surprisingly,the term was used to indicate the life force, the vitality, the animating energy of human beings. It is the unseen power which makes people alive and which vanishes when the breath is gone and death comes. In Biblical thought spirit, as a dimension of personality, is the capacity of relating to God, for being inspired and energized by the Divine Wind. The Spirit of God is the active and effective power and presence of God at work in the world and in human life. It was the Spirit which effected the work of creation (Gen. 1:2). The Spirit endowed prophets and kings with the capacity to accomplish their tasks (I Sam. 11:6, II Kings 2:9, 15). Jesus' ministry was inspired by the Spirit (Mk. 3:29). As the symbol of Invisible Personal Power, Spirit can be used to indicate and define the reality of God as such (John 4:24). God is Spirit -- the Divine Wind with attributes of Personality.

In the New Testament church the Spirit is closely associated with Christ. The Spirit renews the presence and continues the work of the exalted Savior. The Book of Acts tells of the descent of the Spirit like a inrushing wind on the day of Pentecost, which in some ways is the birthday of the church (Acts 2:1-21). Acts recounts the work of the Spirit in inspiring the life and ministry of the Apostles in preaching, healing, and organizing the growing Christian community. In fact, the summary statement of the New Testament conception would be that the Spirit gives rise to everything that is distinctly Christian in the church and in the lives of individual believers. It is given at baptism (Acts 2:38; I Cor. 6:11), freeing the recipient from the powers of the old age that is passing and providing a foretaste of the age to come (Heb. 6:4-5; II Cor. 1:22,

5:5). The Spirit is the source of the new life in
Christ by which faith becomes active in love in contrast
to the old life "according to the flesh" (Gal. 5:13-12;
Rom. 8:1-17). The Spirit bestows miraculous gifts of
prophecy, healing, speaking in tongues, insight, moral
power, and so on (I Cor. 12:1-11; Rom. 12:6-8). The
conception of the Spirit is complex and not without
tensions. It is given to everyone (I Cor. 12:13). It
is a permanent possession but also comes upon people on
particular occasions (Acts 4:8, 31; 13:9). It is both
the source of the normative moral virtues and of insight
and truth and also has ecstatic and miraculous dimensions such as speaking in tongues and the performance of
supernatural deeds (I Cor. 12:1-31). It is a gift which
is bestowed from above and yet a certain attitude is
needed to bring it about or to strengthen it (I Cor.
12:31, 14:12, 39; Acts 13:2). Yet always the Spirit is
the energizing vitality that gives life, power, and
direction to Christian existence. Above all, it is
God's gift to the church, which is the special arena of
its presence and work.[1]

II. The Nature of the Church

A. NEW TESTAMENT CONCEPTIONS: The church is the
community of the Endtime called into being by the
redemptive work of Christ. It is the congregation of
those who have been introduced into the new age and who
await the final consummation of the purpose of God at
the return of Christ. The church is God's people made
up of persons of all races and languages who have
responded in faith to the good news of salvation through
Jesus Christ by the power of the Spirit (Acts 2:1-47).

The church is also the body of Christ (I Cor. 12:12-13; Rom. 12:5-6). The church is also a fellowship of the Spirit. The Spirit knits together the body and is the gift-giving power which creates and sustains its life and vitality (Acts 2:1-21; I Cor. 12:1-13).

The New Testament is rich with images which illuminate the nature of the Spirit-filled body of Christ constituted by the people of God. The church is made up of the saints who have been called and gathered by the will of God to be the elect, the chosen ones (Matt. 24:22; Ephes. 1-4; Rom. 8:28-30). The church consists of those who have responded in faith and who are faithful (I Cor. 1:2; Matt. 28:19; Acts 11:26). Members of the Christian community are said to be slaves and servants of God (I Thess. 1:9; Rom. 6:18; Titus 1:1). The church is also spoken of in terms of institutions central to the life of Israel: kingdom and temple -- priests, kings, a royal people, citizens of a city and so on (Rev. 1:6, 5:10; I Peter 2:9; Heb. 12; I Cor. 6:16; Rev. 21-22). The list goes on: household and family (Rom. 9:26; I Peter 2:5), the new exodus (James 1:1; I Peter 2:9-11), salt of the earth, light of the world (Matt. 5:13-14), and many, many others.

One enters the church by baptism on profession of faith, thus receiving the Spirit (Acts 2:38). Baptism is a participation in the death and resurrection of Christ by which one begins to walk in newness of life (Rom. 6:3-4). The central act in the cultic life is the celebration of the Lord's Supper, by which believers are nourished by the body and blood of Christ received in the bread and wine (Mark 14:22-25; I Cor. 11:17-32; I Cor. 10:16-17). The mission of the church is to preach the Gospel to all (Matt. 28:18-20), to celebrate the unity and mutual love of believers (Ephes. 4:1-16; I John; John 17), and to serve one another in humility and joy (Rom. 12-15). In carrying out these functions, members are to exercise the spiritual gifts they have received (I Cor. 12:1-31).

Forms of organization and ministry evolved to meet changing conditions and needs under the guidance of the Spirit. The role of the twelve apostles Jesus chose to assist him (Mark 3:13-19) was unique. They had participated in the mission of Jesus, had been commissioned by him, and were witnesses of the resurrection. At first they were the sole leaders of the church, assisted at first by the "seven" (Acts 6:1-6) and later by the elders or presbyters (Acts 11:29-30, 14:23) in helping with the Lord's Supper and the distribution of supplies. This enabled the apostles to devote themselves to "prayer and to the ministry of the word" (Acts 6:4). Paul had been given a status equal to that of the "twelve." Paul refers to the elders (presbyters) at the church at Ephesus also as bishops (episkopoi, overseers) or guardians (Acts 20:17-28). Bishops also appear in Phil. 1:1, along with the first mention of deacons. In the pastoral epistles, representing a later period, reference is made in some detail to bishops (I Tim. 3:1-7; Titus 1:7-9), elders (I Tim. 5:17-22; Titus 1:5-6), and deacons (I Tim. 3:8-13). The duties and rank of each office in distinction to the others are not always clear in the New Testament. Some identity of function, however, may be assumed for elders (presbyters) and bishops (episkopoi), who are responsible for preaching, teaching, and general oversight. In Ephes. 4:11 pastors and teachers (doctors) have similar functions to elders and bishops. The work of deacons is administration and assistance. It is possible that late in the New Testament period there was one bishop for a congregation with special functions (I Tim. 3:1-7), although Titus 1:5-7 probably identifies bishops and elders. In addition to these three offices numerous other roles are mentioned for those who have been given the gifts for them by the Spirit (I Cor. 12:1-31; Rom. 12:6-8; Ephes 4:11; I Thes. 5:12). The conclusion we can draw is that while some more or less uniform functions and divisions of labor were emerging, forms of organization and leadership were not fixed but varied according to changing situations and local needs.[2]

B. HISTORICAL AGREEMENTS ABOUT THE CHURCH: While individual theologians over the centuries have developed interpretations of the nature of the church, the most important agreements and disagreements are those which are held in the various branches and denominations which have emerged since the writing of the New Testament. Moreover, rather than undertaking a sequential account of the emergence of the various ecclesiastical bodies, a typology will be presented which offers a systematic account of the underlying motifs which shape doctrines of the church. This account of ecclesiology will proceed in two steps. First, a list of themes will be presented on which all Christians more or less agree. The second step will be to show what the major disagreements are and to offer an interpretation of how and why these differences arise. The first part is heavily dependent on Walter Marshall Horton's interpretation of the ecumenical consensus which emerged in this century.[3] According to Horton, there are six major themes which unite all Christian churches.

1. All Christians are agreed in tracing the origin of the church back to God's calling of a chosen people in the Old Testament. The church is not something absolutely new. The Greek word ecclesia is used in the Septuagint to translate the Hebrew Qahal, which means "the assembly of the congregation of Israel." It expresses the conviction that Israel is the chosen people, the elect community especially set apart by the divine will for a peculiar purpose. Christians began to use ecclesia for the community of faith that arose as a result of the ministry, death, and resurrection of Christ. This means that the early Christians saw themselves as the true people of God, the fulfillment of the promise to Israel. The church is the new Israel, the elect nation, the true inheritors of the promises given to Abraham.[4]

2. Christians are united in the conviction that the decisive act of God in forming the church was the death and resurrection of Christ. We sing: "The Church's one foundation is Jesus Christ her Lord. She is the new Creation by water and the Word." Many New Testament metaphors teach the unity of Christ and the church: the foundation and superstructure of a temple (I Cor. 3), the vine and the branches (John 15), the bridegroom and the bride (Rev. 19:7-9), and the head of the body and its members (I Cor. 12).

At this point it may be useful to raise the question as to whether Jesus himself founded the church at some point in his own ministry. To be more specific, two questions must be distinguished. a) Did Jesus establish the church in the sense of originating an institution with a definite structure and organization? When the question is put this way, a great deal hinges on the interpretation of Matthew 16:17-19. If this passage records actual words of Jesus, then he used some equivalent of ecclesia and gave specific instructions about its organization and leadership. Scholars are divided about its authenticity. Some see it as coming from the early church and not from Jesus. Others attribute the words to Jesus but affirm that the foundation is Peter's confession of Jesus as the Messiah not Peter himself. Another group accept it as genuinely a word from Jesus and conclude that he did give to Peter a certain priority. All Protestants, of course, agree that the traditional Roman Catholic interpretation of the passage cannot be sustained. Even if Peter is given a certain priority, nothing is said about the transfer of his authority to his successors. b) Did Jesus intend to establish a community to carry out his work? Are the disciples the nucleus of a fresh new religious fellowship with a distinct message and ministry? One might rule out Matthew 16: 17-19 and still affirm that Jesus established the church in this second sense.[5]

In summary, the act of God in Christ is the foundation of the church in the theological sense in that the faith of the church is centered on him as the author of salvation. Whether the historical Jesus originated the church is a matter of dispute. The establishment of a new community would certainly seem to be implicit in the whole nature and intent of Jesus' ministry.

3. An ecumenical consensus also is apparent in the conviction that the church is the community of the Holy Spirit. The church came into definite reality on the day of Pentecost when the Spirit through the preaching of Peter called persons of many nations to faith in Christ (Acts 2). From that moment a definite historical movement can be traced. Wide agreement could be found with J.R. Nelson's listing of the four functions of the Spirit in the church: a) The Spirit makes the presence of the Glorified Christ a reality to persons in all generations. b) The Spirit calls persons to faith and leads them as children of God. c) The Spirit gives to believers the fruits of Christ-like character. d) The Spirit binds believers together in a common fellowship.[6]

So far the discussion has related to the divine nature and foundation of the church. Not surprisingly it has a trinitarian pattern: The church is the elect people of God. The church is the body of Christ. The church is the community indwelt by the Holy Spirit. Leslie Newbigin argues that this three-fold characterization provides a clue to the three primary answers given in history to the question of the nature of the church.[7] The first sees the church primarily as the people of God -- the congregation of the faithful. One becomes a member of the community by responding in faith to the proclaimed Word of God. The emphasis is on the preaching of the Gospel as the call to personal repentance, trust, and obedience. The faithful responders constitute the people of God. This is typically the Protestant view of the church, perhaps best represented by classical Lutheranism and Calvinism. Sacraments are important, and stress is put upon the endowment of the Holy Spirit. But the primary emphasis is on the church as the community of faith called into being by the preached Word. The pulpit is likely to be in the center of the altar, symbolizing the importance of the Word and the preacher. Salvation is by grace through faith.

The second view sees the church primarily as the body of Christ. The church is an organic community moving through history, incorporating persons into its divine life by the administration of the sacraments by which grace is channelled into human life. The emphasis is on the sacramental side of the church. Persons are saved by the spiritual nurture given them through the sacraments. This is the "catholic" conception of the primary nature of the church, found in Roman Catholicism, Eastern Orthodoxy, and in the Anglican Church. There is room for the preaching of the Gospel and for the personal response of faith. The sanctifying role of the Spirit is not absent. But the main stress is put upon the continuous sacramental order of the church by which one generation and then another is ingrafted into the supernatural body of Christ. The altar on which the eucharist is performed is central in church architecture rather than the pulpit, making clear the priority of the sacraments over the sermon.

The third perspective sees the church primarily as the community of the Holy Spirit. The church is a fellowship of persons indwelt by the living presence and power of God in the hearts and lives of believers. The center of the religious life is the holiness of the members of the community. The emphasis is not so much on faith as it is on the fruits of faith. Not much concern is shown for order, tradition, and historical continuity in comparison with the "catholic" outlook. The stress is on the free reign of the Spirit here and now. The radical Protestants belong here. Anabaptists, Mennonites, and the early Baptists exemplify many points of agreement with this type. Quakers, of course, are the classical example of the religion of the Inner Light which needs no sacramental system or priests to administer it. Pentecostal churches such as the Nazarenes, the Church of God, the Assembly of God, and various Holiness denominations embody the motifs of this third type. Among the Pentecostals the stress is not upon faith in response to preaching or upon the sacraments as life-giving acts but on the personal sanctification, the moral perfection, of the individual -- the Spirit-filled, Spirit-led life. Speaking in tongues, the gift of healing, and other ecstatic endowments are common. Enthusiasm and zeal are characteristic of church members.

4. While all Christians agree that the church is a divine institution, they also hold in common that it is a human community. As such it bears the marks of sin and error. The relationship between the divine foundation and the human expression of the church is a perplexing one. It would be difficult to state this relationship in a way that would satisfy everybody. Generally speaking, the Roman Catholic tradition is more disposed to speak of the divine and therefore sinless nature of the church. The Protestant tradition is more conscious of the human and therefore sinful element in the church. However, Catholics admit that individual members of the church are imperfect, although the true church is Christ himself present and at work in and

through his divine body. One cannot, of course, ascribe sin to Christ. Protestants, on the other hand, know too that the church is a transcendent reality in which Christ and the Spirit are present, although constant guard must be taken against absolutizing any particular historical institution.

An examination of some of the ways that have been employed to speak of the church may help to illuminate the relation between the divine and the human elements which constitute it.

(a) One traditional phrase defines the church as "one, holy, catholic, and apostolic." These are the marks of the church:

> One, because there is one Lord, one faith, one baptism.
> Christ is one and therefore his body is one.

> Holy, because of the presence on the Holy Spirit calling, cleansing, renewing, and sanctifying.

> Catholic or ecumenical, because the church has a mission to all the world and significance for all people.

> Apostolic, because the church's message is based upon the witness of the apostles, and it continues to preach the Word first proclaimed by them.

When we look at the church, however, what we see is something quite different:

> The Church is not one but many. There are Catholics and Protestants and on and on. Divisions, hostilities, walls of separation and suspicion abound, separating one group from another. What we see is not one church but many denominations.
>
> The church is not holy but impure. Other spirits than the Holy Spirit are present. Churches as institutions are involved in the corporate sins of the society.
>
> The church is not ecumenical but sectarian, bound by local traditions, practices, and modes of thought. Just look at the names: Roman Catholics, Southern Baptists, Missouri Synod Lutherans, The Anglican Church, and on and on. The geographical designations betray the provincial nature of the churches.
>
> The church is not apostolic but is tossed about by many conflicting "winds of doctrine" (Ephes. 4:14). Much that is proclaimed represents additions, corruptions, and eccentricities of later or local origin.

Hence, it would appear that the church both is and is not one, holy, catholic, and apostolic -- depending on the meanings given to the terms.

(b)   Another phrase in frequent use is this: "The church is the extension of the incarnation." If the church is the body of Christ, continuing the ministry he began in the flesh, it would seem legitimate to speak in this way. The idea is understandable when used by Roman Catholics, Anglo-Catholics, and Eastern Orthodox, but a surprising number of Protestants have also defended the notion. Others, however, reject it because it does not take into sufficient account the difference between Christ as the head of the church and the present community which is his body. It is the humanity of the church and its consequent sin, weakness, and error which make the concept suspect.

1)   It seems to call into question the idea of the once-and-for-allness of the incarnation. The New Testament teaches that Christ came and dwelt among us, died once and for all, and was exalted to heaven. While we must speak of the spiritual presence of Christ in the church, to say that the incarnation continues in the visible body of the present community is inappropriate.

2)   P.T. Forsyth has argued that the logical outcome of identifying the church with a continuing incarnation is the traditional Catholic doctrine of the mass and of an infallible Pope. The sacrifice of Christ is repeated, and the church and its teachings are infallible.

3)   Leslie Newbigin urges that the phrase contradicts the notion that the church witnesses to Christ as the Lord of the church. If the church is the

extension of the incarnation, then the church need only witness to itself.

4) The humility of the church is put in jeopardy by the idea. The claim constitutes too great a temptation to pride. Christ was sinless. The church today is not, and believers need to be aware of the difference.[8]

In summary, the persistent use of the term indicates that it has some theological validity. It grows out of the need to preserve the organic intimacy of Christ with the church, which in some sense continues his ministry. The objections arise out of an awareness of the differences between the ministry of the Lord on earth and the works of the fallible, sinful, divided human institution we know in our experience.

c) One final set of terms may be mentioned. Theologians have often distinguished between the invisible and the visible church. The concepts have been given a variety of meanings in church history. It may be useful to begin with the teachings of John Calvin on this point. For him, as for Augustine, the invisible church is the total number of the elect, those living, dead, and yet to be born, known only to God. The visible church is that community of believers on earth who profess worship of one Lord and Christ, whose members are known to one another. The visible church is the true church, the mother of believers, without whose external aid one ordinarily could not become a Christian. However, in the visible church are many false professors of faith. The wheat and the tares grow together. However, this pertains to the actual manifestations of the visible church, not to its essential nature. The main point is that the visible church is the real church, not something different in principle from the invisible church. It is simply that part of the total number of the elect now living. The admission that there are some pretenders in the institution is a secondary point with Calvin.[9]

This is important since in some circles influenced by pietism and moral perfectionism the terms have been given a different meaning. In this framework the invisible church refers to the true spiritual community made up of genuinely regenerated people. The visible church is the larger group including both believers and the unregenerate. The image is that of a smaller circle within a larger circle, the church within the church (ecclesiola in ecclesia), which makes the visible church a mixed body in principle.

Another interpretation of these terms springs from Martin Luther. For him the visible and invisible church are not two groups but different dimensions of the same reality. The invisible church is the inner, spiritual reality which can be discerned only by faith. The visible church is the outward, empirical manifestation of the people of God in institutional, organized form. The contrast is between inner reality and outward expression. The point is that the essence of the church as the people of God is no more visible to the detached observer than is faith in the individual believer. In contemporary terms we might distinguish between the church as a spiritual community of believers defined by its beliefs and values (its theological reality) and the church as an institution like other organizations that can be studied by the social scientists (its sociological expression).

Various other meanings could be outlined, leaving
the situation so confused as to lead Gustaf Aulen to
urge that the terms simply be dropped from usage. But,
as J. Robert Nelson points out, other distinctions would
have to be introduced in order to interpert the full
reality of the church in all its dimensions.[10]

5. Christians generally agree that the church is
positively related to the Kingdom of God but not
identical with its full and complete reality. It may
help to define the question more precisely. Are the
church and the Kingdom identical in the sense of being
coextensive as historical realities? Or is the Kingdom
a more inclusive reality, including the church but not
coextensive or identical with it? Both of the
alternatives may find support in Augustine. History is
the story of two cities -- the city of God and the city
of earth. The city of God (Kingdom) is present in the
church but the latter is a mixed body containing both
those who are citizens of the Kingdom and those who are
not. On the one hand, the church represents or is the
Kingdom on earth. On the other hand, it is not the
Kingdom as such, since the church is made up of non-
believers as well as the elect. The hierarchy of the
church mediates between the two aspects. Through the
official leaders of the church, Christ rules and is
present. Given this ambiguity in Augustine regarding
the relation of the church to the Kingdom,
interpretations could be developed from either side of
his thought. One line developed in the Catholic church
which identified the church with the Kingdom. Another
line developed in Protestantism distinguished the church
and the Kingdom.[11]

Both views may be found in contemporary thought.
T.O. Wedel, an Anglican, follows the Roman Catholic
line. According to him, "The Church of God is the
Kingdom after Pentecost but before the final judgment.
It is the Kingdom of God in history."[12] More typical of
20th century Protestantism is the view that the Kingdom
includes more than the church. The Kingdom is the rule
of God with respect to every aspect of historical life
-- the political, social, and economic orders included.
Wherever the will of God is obeyed and human liberation
and fulfillment are found, the Kingdom is present. The
church is the religious focus of the Kingdom in which
the Gospel is preached, the sacraments are administered,
and people confess their sins and devote themselves to
the service of God. In that sense the church is the
point at which the Kingdom is most visible in history.
The Kingdom is a reality within the church, but it is
more extensive. Moreover, the church is frequently so
identified with the injustices of the prevailing social
order that the Kingdom stands in judgment of the church
and in fact may often be more present in the witness of
justice-seeking outsiders than within the community of
faith itself. These notes are present in both neo-
orthodoxy and in current liberation theologies. But
Protestant liberalism is perhaps the clearest example of
this point of view. Among the liberals the Kingdom was
the primary reality and the focus of attention. The
church was most often seen by the social gospel wing as
the agent of the Kingdom. Its function is to promote
the realization of the rule of God in every area of
personal and corporate life. But other institutions may
also serve this function in so far as they contribute to

justice, harmonious social relationships, and the increase of love, i.e., an ideal social order on earth. Walter Rauschenbusch was the most effective exponent of this view of the relation of the church to the Kingdom.[13]

6. All churches agree, finally, in teaching that the church has been given a mission in the world and in carrying it out has been provided with an established ministry and appropriate means of grace. The church in some sense carries on the work begun on earth by Christ. The commission is to go into all the world and preach the Gospel. We may distinguish between an internal and an external dimension to this mission. Internally, the church is to nourish the fellowship of believers by providing worship, the sacraments, preaching, and pastoral care in all its aspects. Externally, the church is to evangelize the world by proclaiming the good news of salvation through Christ and to serve humanity through deeds of loving service.

To carry out the mission, the church has a ministry. Nearly all communions recognize a specialized and ordained ministry, while also insisting on the role of all the laity. The Roman Catholic Church with its priesthood endowed with a special status, authority, and power and the Quakers who have little or no place for an ordained or specially set-apart ministry represent the extreme views. Moreover, the church has been endowed with means of grace. Nearly all churches provide for baptism and the Lord's Supper as particular means by which the Christian life is generated or symbolized and nourished. Churches differ on the number, nature, proper administration, and effect of the sacraments.

C. FUNDAMENTAL DIFFERENCES AMONG THE CHURCHES: So far attention has been focused on the consensus of opinion regarding the nature of the church, though variety has already been encountered. It is time now to look at major points on which Christians disagree. Here again we may follow Horton's outline of the issues. He points out three fundamental points which are at stake.[14]

1. What are the limits of the church? Where is the true church and what are its boundaries? Who is included? Two typical answers are forthcoming. Traditionally, the Roman Catholic Church, the Eastern Orthodox, and some sectarian Protestants have said, "We are the church." Some Anglicans have made a similar claim, asserting that the church exists in several branches but these include no non-episcopal communions. The other and more frequent reply is that "The church is found where the grace of Christ is operative." This is the view of most Protestants and of the ecumenical movement.

2. What is the correct form of the church? How is it to be organized? Is there a divinely-given church order? With respect to government, three major positions are held. a) In episcopal churches the bishops are the locus of unity and the office through which continuity is preserved by way of apostolic succession. In the Roman Catholic Church an elaborate hierarchy exists centering finally on the Pope (the Bishop of Rome), who is thought to be successor of Peter the apostle to whom the keys of the Kingdom were given (Matt. 16:17-19). Eastern Orthodox, Anglican, and

Lutheran Churches exhibit a variety of patterns with respect to how authority is shared among the episcopacy and with local congregations. b) The presbyterian form of government involves a representative democracy in which authority is divided between local churches and presbyteries or synods. Reformed and Presbyterian churches are governed in this fashion with variations in detail among different groups. c) In the congregational form of government the local church has autonomy and operates as a democracy. Each congregation chooses its own minister and is self-governing, although ministers may be ordained by local councils. Delegated authority from congregations makes possible corporate actions in mission and education. Some conservatives in each type of church may insist that theirs is the one and only true form mandated by divine authority manifested in Scripture and/or tradition. A more prevalent view is that each of these forms can find some basis in New Testament teaching but that no one has exclusive claim to validity.

3. How is the continuity of the church preserved? The great problem here has to do with the meaning and importance of apostolic succession. Roman Catholic, Anglo-Catholic, and Eastern Orthodox churches affirm that God has established a visible, institutional line of authority from the first apostles to the present. Only those churches that stand in that visible, historical succession from Jesus through the apostolic succession are truly ordained and can validly administer the sacraments. At the other extreme are those radical Protestants who emphasize the free reign of the Spirit who works when and where the Spirit wills to call and to authenticate congregations and their ministries and

ministers as valid expressions of the church. A continuity of faith and message is thought to unite such churches with the apostles rather than a line of visible, historical, institutionalized succession.

4. This last point leads into what may be called the deepest difference among the churches. The argument over continuity is intimately related to the fundamental principles in terms of which the churches divide. An approach to an understanding can be made in terms of certain polarities. The Edinburgh Conference of 1937 spoke of a basic contrast between "authoritarian" churches holding to "a divine givenness in the Scriptures, in orders, in creeds, in worship," and "personal" churches who stress "the individual experience of divine grace, as the ruling principle of the `gathered' church." The Amsterdam Assembly of 1948 pointed to the same contrast by distinguishing "catholic" churches, emphasizing "the visible continuity of the Church," from "protestant" churches, stressing "the initiative of the Word of God and the response of faith."[15] It is best to regard these contrasts not as absolute dividing lines but as the two ends of a polarity with a continuum between which a church may combine the two principles in varying ways.

The contrasts already proposed can be incorporated in a more systematic scheme involving two pairs of polar emphases connected by a continuum.[16]

Objective Pole

Emphasis upon the givenness
of the church and the
priority of God's action in
Christ in establishing
certain relationships and
institutions.

Subjective Pole

Emphasis upon God's present
and immediate action in the
Holy Spirit and the personal
response of the believer.

Corporate Principle

Individuals are primarily
members of a social body which
is prior to them and into
which they are incorporated.

Individual Principle

The corporate body arises as a
voluntary covenant made by
individuals with each other
and before God.

It can easily be seen how the two pairs of
polarities above relate to the contrasts made in
Edinburgh and Amsterdam.

"authoritarian churches"   (Edinburgh)   "personal churches"

"catholic"   (Amsterdam)   "protestant"

Every church wants in some way to account for the principles indicated by both sides of the polarities, although in extreme cases the opposite pole may not get much attention. The differences lie in which side is given priority and in how the two poles of emphasis are combined and related to each other. The major church bodies can be located somewhere at a point along the continuum that runs between the two extremes.

The Objective Pole	The Subjective Pole
The Corporate Principle	The Individual Principle
"authoritarian"	"personal"
"catholic"	"protestant"

Roman Catholic	Anglican	Methodist	Disciples	Pentecostal
Eastern Orthodox	Lutheran		Baptists	Quakers
Anglo-Catholic	Reformed		Congregationalist	

The location of some groups is arguable in terms of their positioning in relation to others. Anglicans and Methodists, for example, are difficult to place because they combine various motifs in complex ways. Nevertheless, in a general way such a typology may have useful though limited validity in indicating the differences among them as being based on the way they unite fundamental but contrasting motifs into a doctrine of the church, ministry, and sacraments. In particular, three points may be located on this continuum, one toward either extreme and one more or less in the middle:

Catholic   Classical Protestant   Radical Protestant

It can be seen that these three views of the church correlate fairly well with Leslie Newbigin's distinctions among three primary definitions of the church.

The Body   The People   The Fellowship of

   of Christ   of God   the Spirit

This basic typology can be filled out by examining a variety of views of the church, the ministry, and the sacraments.

(1)   THE CHURCH

The "catholic" churches -- Roman Catholic, Eastern Orthodox, and Anglo-Catholic -- define the church as a supernatural body moving through history incorporating individuals into its corporate life by channeling grace to people through the sacraments. The church is a visible institution with a definite and required structure extending through time, connecting finally with the apostles in a line of historical, institutional succession. An episcopal form of the church government prevails.

Toward the middle are the classical Protestant views of Martin Luther and John Calvin. Here is to be found a balance of polar emphases. The church is a community of faith created by response to the objective and prior Word of God. Visible order and historical continuity are important. It is proper to speak of a given structure in church government and of the right administration of the sacraments by an appropriately ordained minister. Apostolic continuity is primarily a matter of message and faith rather than an institutional fact. The church is present where the Gospel is rightly preached and the sacraments are rightly administered. The emphasis is on justification by faith rather than on sacramental grace. But the corporate emphasis is clear in the practice of infant baptism in which the newly born are initiated into a community that is real and prior to the individual. A presbyterian form of polity tends to dominate, although Lutherans in their various branches have combined episcopal and presbyterian structures.

Moving toward the extreme of the radical Protestants, Baptists define the church as a fellowship of believers. Churches are organized into particular congregations as a gathered body created by a covenant among individuals. Personal faith and conversion come first. Then the church emerges as a body of baptized believers. Little concern is shown for institutional continuity. Emphasis is placed on the present vertical relationship of faith in response to the Spirit's call as the authenticating factor which makes the church valid. A congregational form of church polity is operative. The pentecostal churches put even more stress upon the Spirit at work in the hearts of believers and less emphasis on outward form and institutional validity. Quakers are also little concerned with visible order and historical continuity. Among them the free reign of the Spirit prevails. Attention is focused on the direct and immediate experience and the intimacy of fellowship made possible by the Spirit -- the Inner Light. No sacramental observances or specially ordained persons are needed to mediate or symbolize the grace of God, since the believer is immediately in touch with the Spirit.[17]

(2) THE MINISTRY

Closely connected with the polarities developed above, T.W. Manson points out the two main lines of thought about the church and its ministry.[18] On the one hand, the ministry is defined in terms of a hierarchy with strictly graded duties and carefully differentiated powers -- all determined from above. On the other hand, the ministry is defined in terms of particular duties performed in obedience to the call of God and by the appointment of a particular congregation. The form emphasizes orders and ordination. The latter emphasizes "calling."

Roman Catholics, Eastern Orthodox, and Anglo-Catholics represent the organic or hierarchical view of the church and its ministry. The church is a divine society, a supernatural organism, the visible body of Christ on earth. It has existed in direct historical continuity from the days of the apostles through the medium of the historic episcopate. A generation ago the Anglo-Catholic view of the ministry was stated in THE APOSTOLIC MINISTRY.[19] The thesis of the book reproduces the claim of Bishop Charles Gore that Jesus Christ constituted in the church an "authoritative ministry in the person of His Apostles" which was intended to be permanent and which did in fact propagateitself in various grades, so that the three-fold ministry of church history is ,in fact, by succession the only representative of the original apostolate, and all who desire to adhere to `the Body of Christ' must adhere to this (episcopal) ministry."[20] For the churches in this group apostolic succession is essential to the visible church, and traditionally they have insisted that those bodieswhich do not possess it are outside the visible church.

A majority of Anglicans rejected the conclusions of THE APOSTOLIC MINISTRY. T.W. Manson, for example, argued that no transferable authority from apostles to successors can be defended on New Testament grounds.[21] The church continues the ministry begun by Christ based on the pattern found in the teachings and examples of Jesus and undergirded by the presence of the Spirit. Ministers are called by Christ through the Spirit. The church is apostolic in the sense of continuing the ministry of the apostles which they received from Christ. The only test of validity is the presence of the signs of the apostles -- works of power and evidences of changed lives and new communities living out the Gospel. No essential forms of church government are required or mandated. Stephen Neil rejected the thesis of Kirk and his colleagues on theological grounds.[22] The Anglo-Catholics obscure the doctrine of justification by faith affirmed in the Thirty-nine Articles, and they seem to limit the operation of the Holy Spirit to rigid forms and traditions.

Toward the middle of the spectrum, and closely allied with the majority of Anglicans, are the views of Lutheran and Reformed theologians. The givenness of the ministry and the importance of tradition are recognized. Apostolicity is also central but not in the Roman

Catholic, Eastern Orthodox, and Anglo-Catholic sense. Lutheran Gustaf Aulén speaks of the ministry as the servant of the Word and of the sacraments. As such it is one of the constitutive elements of the church. As Jesus sent out apostles, so the church today must send out new messengers. Legitimacy is established by whether or not the message they preach is the apostolic message and whether the sacraments are administered as instituted and mandated by Christ.[23]

Daniel Jenkins, speaking from the Reformed tradition, takes essentially the same point of view. The Catholic church exists where Christ is present. We know Christ by the testimony of the apostles recorded in the Bible and interpreted through the Holy Spirit. That ministry is apostolic which accepts and continues this testimony. The ministry belongs not to the essence but to the fullness of the church, existing as the servant of the Word and sacraments and enabling all members of the body of Christ to hear the Word of God. As such it is a self-conscious, deliberate, professional ministry, but it is purely functional. The ministry derives its authority by the legitimacy of its message not by virtue of the office itself. Tradition is important in that there is need for interpretation, but it must never take precedence over the living Word.[24]

What we have in this middle position is an effort, on the one hand, to stress the givenness of the ministry and the importance of tradition and historical continuity and, on the other hand, to preserve the Reformation emphasis on the priesthood of believers without falsely objectifying the ministry in a particular institutional office or limiting the operation of the Spirit to certain prescribed institutional forms. The church is present where the Word is rightly preached and the sacraments are rightly administered. When ministry performs these functions, it is apostolic in every sense that matters.

Toward the other end of the spectrum are views which have little or no concern with the church as a supernatural, grace-filled organic community moving through history as the repository and dispenser of essential sacramental grace by a ministry that is validated by institutionally-based apostolic succession. Instead, the emphasis is on the congregation of believers who constitute a priesthood one and all by virtue of having been justified by grace through faith and by the calling of the Spirit. The ministry is a gift of the Holy Spirit through "the Call" and not an office that is institutionally validated. The purpose of ministry is to serve the congregation through the preaching of the Gospel, the administration of the sacraments, and the providing of pastoral care. No difference, apart from "calling," is recognized between ministry and laity. H. Wheeler Robinson, a Baptist, remarks, "In the wider sense of the New Testament, all Christians are called upon to minister, according to their `gift'; whatever they are able to do for the service of the community and of the world they are called to do. . . . There is nothing which a `minister' in the professional sense is called upon to do . . . which a layman as such is debarred from doing."[25] Hence, in the Baptist view no distinction exists between clergy and laity which implies a difference of status and privilege. The distinction is totally one of function and service based on the gifts and calling of Spirit.

The "call" to the individual is acknowledged and given external authority through ordination by the congregation or by larger units such as a conference or association. Ordination confers ministerial functions which no individual can properly take upon her/himself but is simply an acknowledgment by the congregation that the "call" is recognized and authorized. The immediate call from Christ through the Spirit is viewed as an authentic commission. Little or no concern is shown for institutional continuity. The concept of apostolic succession is foreign to this side of the polarity, except as a concern for the continuation of the apostolic message and ministry. In short, this position, as stated by Robinson, "is an emphasis on the inner, spiritual, and intrinsic nature of Christian ministry, its particular forms being accidental and occasional, evolved to meet particular needs as they were felt, such as the ministry of the seven at Jerusalem."[26]

It has already been noted that the Quakers go even further with an emphasis on the immediate authentication of ministry by the present and direct work of the Spirit. They find no need for an ordained ministry as such, relying upon the spirit to move, to call, and to send persons where need arises.

In conclusion, it should be noticed, as Leonard Hodgson points out, where the basic cleavage lies. It is not to be found between those who differ as to the nature of the visible continuity of the church. Rather, it lies between those who insist that there must be some sort of institutionally guaranteed historical continuity and those who do not.[27] This fundamental division is rooted in two basically different ways of thinking about the church, and it will not be easily overcome. Nevertheless, moves have been underway for a long time in this century to explore ways of healing the breach. Already a generation ago some Presbyterians were speaking of forms of the "corporate episcopate" through the presbyteries which confer ministerial standing. Some British Congregationalists at mid-century proposed the development of explicit congregational forms of episcopacy.[28] F.W. Dillistone made a distinction between "organic" and "covenantal" conceptions of the church which parallels the polarity being employed here. Three decades ago he expressed the hope that the structure of the Christian community might be conceived broadly enough so that a living organic society could be flexible enough to incorporate within itself vigorous convenanted fellowships, while convenanted federations might include growing organic societies.[29] This proposal illustrates a continuing movement by which diverse groups attempt to incorporate within themselves traditions and values from other groups which will both enrich them and break down some long standing barriers among different Christian communions.

(3) THE SACRAMENTS

As previously noted, all churches believe that sufficient means of grace have been provided whereby the Christian life can be generated and nourished. Nearly all focus on visible and material symbols and acts as the divinely-ordained channels or signs of God's effective presence. The churches have disagreed over the number, meaning, and efficacy of the sacraments and the necessary conditions of their valid observance. At no point have they been more divided than with regard to the understanding of how the outward and visible signs are related to inward and spiritual grace. The major cleavages can be derived from the basic motifs which give rise to the polarity which has been set up. Two issues are of major importance: 1. Do the sacraments actually and objectively convey grace, or are they signs of realities which occur in the personal relationships of God and believers? 2. Is the historic episcopate essential to the authentication of the priestly ministry by which the sacraments are validly administered?

Toward the "catholic" side of the polarity the emphasis is on what God objectively does through the sacraments. Something is done, accomplished, enacted by their valid celebration. They not only signify but convey or impart grace. As developed in medieval Catholicism the sacraments confer grace ex opere operato, that is, by virtue of what they are and of being done when the requisite conditions are present. A subjective element is present in that contempt for or positive disbelief in them or the presence of unforgiven mortal sin may set up an obstacle to their efficacy. In this context baptism was thought to wash away the guilt of original sin in infants. In the mass the bread and wine become the body and blood of Christ, and the sacrifice of Christ is repeated. Traditionally, seven sacraments have functioned to channel grace into human life: baptism, confirmation, marriage, ordination, penance, the eucharist, and extreme unction. Roman Catholicism exemplifies the objective emphasis that is found also in Eastern Orthodoxy and among Anglo-Catholics. For all of them, in the words of Angus Dun, "The Church does not talk to people chiefly; it acts upon them or for them. It takes them up into its life."[30] All of these churches insist that the only really valid sacraments are those administered in accordance with their understanding of church order, which includes the condition that the celebrant be ordained by a bishop in the apostolic succession.

Most Anglicans, along with Lutherans and Calvinists, have located themselves more toward the center. They have sought a balance between objective efficacy and institutional validity, on the one hand, and symbolic reference and personal faith in the recipient, on the other hand. Luther and Calvin made the Word primary over the sacraments, though they belong together. Justification by grace through faith was the central principle of the Protestant Reformation. The sacraments are the visible Word of God. According to Luther, the same Word is conveyed in preaching and in the sacraments, and the latter are never to be observed without the former. For Calvin sacraments are seals or confirmation of the promises of God which we know through the Word of God announced in Christ and Scripture. They supplement the Word and assist us in our weakness. Lutherans and Calvinists have insisted on the importance of traditional forms but are not willing do define validity simply in terms of particular institutional guarantees.

D. Mackenzie, a Reformed thinker, makes a distinction between "efficient validity," which depends on the faith, love, and godly devotion in those who take part and "institutional validity," which depends on the use of forms which can be traced back to the institution of Jesus.[31] Daniel Jenkins, of the same tradition, maintains that the essence of the church is defined by the presence of Jesus Christ, while the possession of proper liturgical form is made a secondary mark of the church.[32] Gustaf Aulén, a Lutheran, wants to keep an objective view of the sacraments, but he denies that any particular institutional guarantee is necessary for their validity. After defining the sacraments as "the self-impartation of divine love in the form of action," he insists that we must avoid a "realistic" extreme in which the sacraments are regarded as working _ex opere operato_, and a "symbolic" extreme, by which emphasis in so put on subjective factors that the sacraments lose their character as divine gifts and deeds of grace. The sacraments are symbolic, but this does not deny the real and effective presence of the divine will and activity.[33]

Moving toward the other side of the polarity, R. Newton Flew, speaking as a Methodist, says, "the only `valid' sacrament is one where the promised blessing is given and received, where the risen Lord grants and renews that personal communion with Himself to the believing soul for which the soul was made. In this sense the word `valid' really means `effectual.'"[34]

H. Wheeler Robinson, a Baptist, concentrates on the confessional values of the external symbols and refers to them as "acted parables." Baptism by immersion, symbolizing the death, burial, and resurrection of Christ, and the broken bread and poured-out wine, symbolizing the body and blood of Christ, both proclaim the cardinal verities of the evangelical faith and testify to the historical foundation of Christianity. Their real efficacy depends solely on the faith of the participants.[35] At this point on the continuum valid ordination is usually regarded as a prerequisite of proper administration. This is a matter of congregational authorization under the immediate guidance of the Spirit and does not depend on apostolic succession or any historical continuity of an institutional sort whatsoever.

The Quakers do not see the need for any symbols at all. Why, they reason, do we need symbols when the realities symbolized are experienced immediately and directly by the presence of the Spirit in the hearts and lives of the faithful?[36]

In addition to these general issues relating to the nature of the sacraments in general, further attention is needed with respect to baptism and communion.

(a) Baptism

All churches agree that baptism marks the initiation of persons into the Christian life through a participation in the death and resurrection of Christ associated with the forgiveness of sins and the gift of the Holy Spirit as the source of new life. Controversies aplenty arise over the interpretation and elaboration of that basic statement. Moreover, with respect to the mode of baptism three practices have prevailed: pouring, sprinkling, and immersing. More important is the question of the subject of baptism. Here the basic division is between those who baptize persons of any age (infants and adults) and those who baptize only adults or at least persons who have made a conscious profession of faith, technically known as the dispute between infant baptism and believers' baptism.

This controversy, like many others, can helpfully be viewed in terms of the polarity between those who begin with the objective pole and the corporate principle, on the one hand, and those who begin with the subjective pole and the individual principle, on the other hand. For those who start from the former pole of emphasis, becoming a Christian is like being born into a family. At birth one is given the family name with the hope and expectation that having been nurtured in the beliefs, values, and practices of the family, the child will in time confirm them in his/her own life by conscious commitment. This would appear to illuminate the logic of those churches who baptize infants into the Christian family and later make a place for a rite of confirmation. For those who practice only believers' baptism, becoming a Christian or joining the church is like getting married. Two people enter marriage on the basis of a personal covenant and commitment, having consciously decided to unite their lives in a lifelong relationship. So, the reasoning goes, only those who have professed faith in Christ by a personal decision should enter into the covenant by which the church is created. Obviously both images have much to commend them and can be undergirded with strong Biblical and theological arguments.

A basic problem arises for Protestants who try to combine infant baptism with a doctrine of salvation by grace received in faith. In what sense can an infant be said to have faith? No such problem arises for those "catholic" churches for whom sacramental grace is objectively efficacious and in which baptism functions ex opere operato in washing away the guilt of original sin. The New Testament nowhere explicitly mentions the baptism of babies, although some have tried to make inferences based on the baptizing of entire households, which could have included children (I Cor. 1:16). The justification of infant baptism has to be on theological grounds, not on the basis of explicit New Testament practice. Those Protestants who do defend it seem never to be far away from the "being born into a family" image, whereby baptism is a sign of the entrance of persons into the covenant community -- the people of God. An analogy is frequently made between circumcision in the Old Covenant and infant baptism in the New Covenant.

Beyond that the defense of infant baptism tends to be that it clearly proclaims that salvation is by grace, that is, by divine action. Martin Luther says that, of course, faith is indissolubly connected with faith but that does not mean that faith on our part must precede baptism. By God's initiative and act faith is bestowed. To deny baptism to infants would imply that the power of baptism depends on our power to receive it -- a new version of justification by works. [37] Gustaf Aulén, a contemporary Lutheran, makes the same point. He contends that infant baptism is the highest form of the rite because it, "more than any other form, demonstrates the reality and is the result of God's prevenient and unmerited love."[38] Membership in the church is based totally on God's loving will and not at all on the caprice and effort of people. John Whale argues in similar fashion, declaring, "Now the Sacrament of Baptism, administered almost exclusively to infants, and unrepeatable, obviously emphasizes the objective givenness of the Gospel of Redemption."[39] Aulén admits that faith is essential to church membership and arises by God's work in us. But faith is secondary to the "objective" [40] gift of baptism. P.T. Forsyth claims that "baptism unto faith has as good a right in the principle of the Gospel as baptism upon faith."[41] Whale declares that the baptism of infants has no efficacy apart from faith, but the faith is that of the church.

None of these arguments by which infant baptism is reconciled to the doctrine of justification by faith is convincing to groups such as the Disciples and the Baptists. A.C. Underwood contends, "Infant Baptism obscures the fact that salvation is by faith alone, independent of all priestly administrations and ecclesiastical rites."[42] H. Wheeler Robinson, a Baptist, remarks that only believers' baptism is "strictly and primarily an ethical act on the past of the Baptized."[43] We become members of the church by "being consciously and voluntary baptized in the Spirit of Christ."[44] Karl Barth added his voice to the insistence on believers' baptism. The one essential element in baptism "must be the responsible willingness and readiness of the baptized person to receive the promise of the grace directed toward him and to be a party to the pledge of allegiance concerning the grateful service demanded of him."[45] No infant can meet these requirements.

Between the insistence on the primacy of God's prevenient grace and the objective givenness of salvation, on the one hand, and the stress on the necessity of a conscious and voluntary acceptance of grace through personal faith and commitment, on the other hand, no easy reconciliation is possible. Moreover, since baptism is administered only once, a decision still has to be made as to whether entering the church is more like being born into a family or more like getting married.

The classical views of baptism can be lined up along the continuum illustrating typical positions as follows:

Objective Pole	Subjective Pole
Corporate Principle	Individual Principle

Catholic Stress on Sacramental Grace	Protestant Stress on Personal Grace	
	← Salvation →	
	by grace	through faith
Objective act of regeneration	Effective sign of divine gift	Visible symbol of spiritual realities
Roman Catholic	Classical Protestant	Radical Protestant
	Lutheran	Baptist
	Reformed	

(Infant Baptism)	(Believer's Baptism)

(b) The Lord's Supper

Christians generally agree that the Lord's supper is a communion with Christ and each other involving a memory and participation in the saving acts of the past and an anticipation of the fullness of the Kingdom yet to come. It involves thanksgiving to God for the love manifested in the gift of Christ, and it invokes the Spirit to renew and to sustain fellowship with God and with the community of faith. The Lord's supper nourishes the Christian life by a renewal of faith, hope, and love. Controversies have flourished around the particular meanings of communion, the centrality and frequency of observance, and the conditions of its valid administration. An especially deep and persistent division has concerned the real presence of Christ in the elements and event of the Supper.

The basic question is not whether Christ is present but in what way. All Christians believe that they are in communion with Christ in this central act of worship, praise, and renewal. The theories of the real presence range from objective doctrines in which Christ is literally there in body and blood in the bread and the wine to subjective doctrines in which the elements symbolize a presence of Christ in the hearts of believers through the effective work of the Spirit. These doctrines line up along the continuum between the polarities that have been employed throughout this presentation.

Beginning on the objective-corporate pole, a literal doctrine of the bodily presence is found in the medieval theory of transubstantiation formulated by Thomas Aquinas and others. This doctrine is based on Aristotelian metaphysics, according to which a distinction is made between the underlying real being (substance) of a thing and its attributes or properties (accidents). Transubstantiation means that at the moment of consecration the substance of the bread and wine become the body and blood of Christ, while the accidents (the visible, tangible properties) remain unchanged.

The Eastern orthodox church has been equally insistent on a real, objective and literal presence but has regarded this as a mystery beyond human understanding. The Thirty-Nine Articles of the Anglican Church reject transubstantiation (Article XXVIII). Anglicans have generally held to one of three views: (1) a real and objective presence in the bread and wine, (2) a presence in the hearts of believers, and (3) a real presence in terms of power and effect rather than in substance.[46] The traditional Lutheran view has been called consubstantiation -- the body and blood are present in, with, and under the material elements which themselves remain what they are.

The views of John Calvin stand close to the center of the continuum. He rejected Catholic transubstantiation and Lutheran consubstantiation. The body of Christ is in heaven and is not locally present in the elements of the bread and wine. However, there is a real communion of Christ with believers in which they virtually feed on his body and blood by being joined to him by the Spirit. Christ is objectively present in terms of power and effect through the work of the Holy spirit in a mysterious communion beyond comprehension -- a virtual presence.[47]

Hulrich Zwingli stands somewhere between Calvin, for whom Christ was present in the Supper in terms of spiritual power, and the Quakers, who represent the subjective extreme of the polarity in speaking only of spiritual realities in the inner life needing not even symbolic representation. For Zwingli the Lord's Supper is an act of the congregation in which the death of Christ is remembered with thanksgiving and joy. "This is my body" means signifies or stands for or represents "my body." Christ is present in the elements symbolically not bodily.[48] The views of Baptists have ranged between those of Calvin (in the early period) and of Zwingli (in the 19th and 20th centuries, especially in the United States). Some movement can be seen recently back toward Calvin.[49]

Presbyterians, of course, have officially followed Calvin, although much actual belief and practice sound more like Zwingli.[50] John Wesley had a high sacramental view of the objectively real presence, more like Calvin and many Anglicans than like Luther. However, Methodist practice and theology have, like the Presbyterian tradition, moved between Wesley and Zwingli, especially in the liberal thinkers of the 20th century.[51] These brief pointers cannot, of course, indicate the richness and variety of actual denominational belief and practice as represented in individual theologians and congregations. A generalization might be that frequently the founders and early thinkers of such groups as Baptists, Methodists, and Presbyterians have had a higher or more objective view of the real presence of Christ than later thinkers and congregations, especially in the 19th and 20th century expressions of these denominations.

In summary, the classical views of the Lord's Supper can be lined up along the proposed continuum:

Objective Pole		Subjective Pole
Corporate Principle		Individual Principle

Transubstantiation	Calvinist Virtualism	Quakerism
Consubstantiation		Zwinglian Memorialism
Real but Mysterious Presence		

Bodily Presence in the elements	Virtual Presence (Spiritual Presence) in the elements	Symbolic Presence in the elements	Spiritual Presence in participants (no elements)

Aquinas		Zwingli
Luther	Calvin	
	Wesley	

Roman Catholic
Eastern Orthodox
Lutherans

Anabaptists

Presbyterians
Methodists

Baptists   Quakers

Anglicans

III. Contemporary Ecumenical Discussions

The preceding interpretation has focused on classical views of the church, ministry, and the sacraments and their development down to the present. The intent has been to display the agreements and to set forth the differences. With respect to the disagreements, an effort has been made to uncover the underlying theological motifs and to develop the logic of the positions which result from the application of these motifs to specific issues. A polarity with a continuum between has been found useful to illuminate historic and contemporary doctrines regarding the basic nature of the church, apostolic succession, infant baptism versus believers' baptism, the real presence of Christ in the Lord's Supper, and so on. The attempt up to this point has been to set forth the basic logic and inner meaning of these doctrines that unite and divide the churches without much regard to the period of church history in which they first appeared.

The story would be incomplete, however, without taking note of the enormous effort that has gone into ecumenical attempts during the last half century to overcome these historic differences and to gain consensus on basic issues. The attempt has not been fully successful, since major differences with deep historic roots still divide the churches along the lines already indicated. Yet what is most surprising is the unity that has been achieved. It is startling to read some of the statements of apparent unity made by Roman Catholics, Anglicans, and Lutherans, even by individual Roman Catholics and Baptists, on such topics as baptism, eucharist, and the ministry. Remarkable agreements are taking place that alter the terms of previous conversations and make some historic controversies obsolete.

The literature is vast, and only a small sample can be discussed here. Two observations are worth noting from a purview of some of the consultations and consensus statements that have emerged. The first is that the meetings of individual theologians from diverse communions have produced far more agreement or potential agreement than has been adopted by churches in official action. The second is that consensus statements often give the appearance of having been framed in carefully chosen language that sometimes seems to be as successful in covering over disputed issues as in setting forth agreement. Yet even with these two reservations, the progress toward unity or belief is real and is continuing despite great obstacles yet to be overcome. Brief reference will be made to some representative consultations among theologians and churches and to a 1982 document of the Faith and Order Commission of the World Council of Churches dealing with baptism, eucharist, and ministry. Finally, the question of the ordination of women will be examined.

A. RECENT CONSULTATIONS: Among churches toward the "catholic" side of the spectrum, the meaning of the eucharist and the conditions of its valid administration are of central importance. Recent changes in Roman Catholic theology regarding the meaning of transubstant- iation have made it possible for consultations between Catholics and Lutherans and Catholics and Anglicans to conclude that the real presence need no longer be an issue in dispute.[52] In contemporary Roman Catholic theology transubstantiation is an affirmation that Christ is bodily present in the bread and wine, not a dogmatic and essential statement about how that mystery takes place. On this basis the controversies of the 16th century among Catholics, Anglicans, and Lutherans over the mode of Christ's presence seem outmoded, although different ways of affirming that fact may still persist within a framework of agreement about the essentials. It may be possible that the Calvinist view can also be brought into this consensus, according to some theologians. Christopher Kiesling, a Roman Catholic scholar, sees the Roman and the Reformed approaches as complementary, the former stressing objective presence in the elements and the latter stressing a real existential encounter with Christ in the sacramental event.[53] Obviously churches and theologies toward the Zwinglian and radical Protestant side of the spectrum cannot easily, if ever, be included within the theological consensus.

Roman Catholics, Lutherans, and Anglicans seem also to have reached unity on the essentials regarding the eucharist as sacrifice. All affirm that the redemptive act of Jesus Christ in his death and resurrection was a unique, once and for all event, which was a sufficient sacrifice for the sins of the whole world for all time. There can be no repetition or addition to that saving act. In the eucharist believers remember and participate in that sacrifice in ways that make it effective here and now.

Even among the high sacramental churches -- Eastern Orthodox, Roman Catholic, Anglican, and Lutheran -- where theological agreement on the essentials of eucharistic theology may now be possible, intercommunion is a more difficult goal not yet within reach. Full eucharistic sharing would involve such matters -- differing among various churches -- as mutual recognition of ministries, acknowledgement of the full and true ecclesiality of each church by the other, overcoming of other doctrinal disputes, and so on. For Eastern Orthodoxy intercommunion would involve their recognition of "true ecclesiality" (full status as a true and valid church). No official act of that church grants such acknowledgement of any other group, although some steps have been taken which seem to open up that possibility. Ancient disputes about the procession of the Holy Spirit and of the primacy of the Bishop of Rome (the Pope) still constitute formidable barriers for the East.[54]

For Lutherans the main prerequisite of intercommunion is "agreement in the doctrine of the Gospel," but widely different views are held regarding what this means. Missouri Synod Lutherans require strict doctrinal agreement about detailed matters. Most Lutheran and all non-Lutheran churches fail to meet their standards. Swedish Lutherans, at the other extreme, are satisfied with minimal agreement. Lutherans, of course, still have major problems with the Roman Catholic Marian dogmas (the Bodily Assumption and the Immaculate Conception of Mary), the primacy of the

Bishop of Rome when claimed as a matter of divine right rather than by voluntary human acceptance (by human right), and other teachings.[55] In the Fall of 1983, however, a Consultation of Lutherans and Catholics concluded that substantial and essential agreement now exists with regard to justification by faith! From the Catholic side reservations about Lutherans have traditionally centered on the lack of a ministry standing in valid apostolic succession, as well as doctrinal agreements about the eucharist, etc. Recent Catholic-Lutheran consultations have produced recommendations from the participating theologians that their respective churches mutually recognize each other as true and authentic churches of Jesus Christ having validly ordained ministries which rightly, truly and fully celebrate the eucharist in which the body and blood of Christ are present.[56]

Roman Catholic-Anglican discussions have encountered some of the same barriers that the Lutheran consultations did -- the Marian dogmas, the primacy of the Bishop of Rome, papal infallibility, and the problem of the Roman recognition of the validity of non-Roman ordination. The Second Vatican Council declared that the true church is not co-extensive with the Roman Catholic Church and that other churches may be found fully valid, except lacking the "visible manifestation of full Christian communion which is maintained in the Roman Catholic Church."[57] From the Anglican side the participants who issued THE FINAL REPORT of the Anglican-Roman Catholic International Commission seemed willing to abandon previous objections and to agree that "the primacy of the bishop of Rome can be affirmed as part of God's design for the universal koinonia in terms which are compatible with both our traditions."[58] Stubborn problems remain on many counts, and, of course, the Roman denial of validity to Anglican orders (APOSTOLICAE CURA, 1896)[59] will have to reappraised. The Commission found no insuperable barriers to ultimate organic union of the two communions.

To generalize about what is a much more complicated situation than has been hinted at here, the more distance there is between churches on the continuum between "catholic" and "protestant" types, the more difficult intercommunion is to achieve. The Eastern Orthodox are most traditional and least open to this possibility. Rome recommends shared eucharist with the Orthodox, but the Orthodox still officially reject it. Between Roman Catholics and Protestants the most that is recommended even by the consultations is limited, occasional, discriminate, and guarded eucharistic sharing. Many Protestant and Catholic theologians are willing to plunge ahead. Catholic theologian Leonard Swidler summarizes that the greatest "resistance apparently comes from Rome."[60] Yet since Vatican II the Roman Catholic Church has entered the ecumenical era, and though the authorities in Rome have sometimes been hesitant even to carry out the decrees issued there, a direction has been set.

Churches representing the span between classical Protestantism and the radical Protestant movement have less difficulty in engaging in full and free eucharistic sharing. Differences about apostolic succession and the distinctive claims and doctrines of Roman Catholics do not arise as effective barriers to mutual recognition of ministries and of the acknowledgement of the presence of

Christ at work among them all. Lutherans generally have been most insistent on doctrinal agreement and are more reluctant than most other Protestants to engage in intercommunion, although great differences exist among them in this regard. Among other Protestants, excluding the most conservative among them, communion takes place freely in practice with no theological inhibitions intervening. There are exceptions, of course. Some Baptists, for example, insist that only baptized (immersed) believers be admitted to the Lord's table. But among moderates and liberals (non-conservatives) in Protestant churches, intercommunion is based on the conviction that a unity of personal faith in Christ and agreement on the essentials of the Gospel are a sufficient basis for full and equal sharing of ministries and sacraments, despite differences in the particulars of theological expression. The greatest barriers to intercommunion have long been between those churches which make the historic episcopate essential to the validity of the ministry and of the sacraments. Where this is not an issue, other doctrinal differences are less difficult to deal with, except in those churches which insist on strict dogmatic or confessional standards.

B. FAITH AND ORDER COMMISSION STATEMENT ON BAPTISM, EUCHARIST, AND MINISTRY (1982): In Lima, Peru, January, 1982, the Faith and Order commission of the World Council of Churches approved a statement dealing with baptism, eucharist, and ministry.[61] It was an attempt to state agreements among the churches that had been achieved without claiming consensus. It acknowledges continuing differences in the midst of growing unity of belief. It can be used to indicate where things stand at the present in ecumenical theology. No attempt will be made to summarize the entire document. The focus will be on those areas of controversy which historically have divided the churches. Many of the agreements expressed in the document are identical with those that have already been pointed out in the earlier parts of this chapter.

1. Baptism

Baptism is a sign of new life in Christ. Its meaning includes a participation in the death and resurrection of Christ, the forgiveness of sins, and the reception of the Spirit, incorporation into the body of Christ, and entrance into the Kingdom both present and to come. It is a divine gift but requires a human response of faith. It is acknowledged that both infant baptism and believers' baptism are legitimate practices. The former emphasizes corporate faith and the promise of the Gospel. The latter stresses the confession of the believer who responds to divine grace. The differences between them become less sharp when it is recognized that all churches confess both God's initiative of grace in Christ and personal faith as essential to the fullness of baptism. Recognition of the legitimacy of both forms of baptism is urged upon the respective churches, along with an admonition to make efforts to incorporate the values symbolized by the form not practiced.

2. The Eucharist

The Lord's Supper is a gift of God which provides communion with Christ through the power of the Holy Spirit. By this meal faith is renewed and nourished by the body and blood of Christ. By the effective working of the Spirit a foretaste of the coming Kingdom is experienced. The eucharist involves:

1. thanksgiving to God for all that has been accomplished in creation and redemption;
2. a memorial of the unique, once and for all saving act of Christ which becomes effective for us by our participation in it;
3. an invocation of the Holy Spirit by which the promises of God are fulfilled in this life and in the world to come;
4. a communion of the faithful in which unity with all believers is experienced, a symbol of the impetus toward reconciliation and justice among all people; and
5. a meal of the Kingdom which celebrates and anticipates the renewal of the world which has begun and which will be consummated at the end of the age, a victory of which the ministry of the faithful must witness in solidarity with the outcasts and the oppressed.

The presence of Christ is real, living, and active in the eucharist. While the real presence does not depend on the faith of the individual, faith is required to discern the body and blood of Christ in the bread and wine. It is acknowledged that different theories have been proposed to interpret the mystery of the reality of

Christ in the supper. It is also pointed out that some do not link the presence of Christ so definitely with the signs of bread and wine as do others, who say that the elements become the body and blood of the risen and living Christ. The statement then leaves it up to the various churches to determine whether their own beliefs are expressed in or can be accommodated to the convergence sought in the text.

3. The Ministry

In the largest sense the whole people of God are called to witness and to work toward the end that the saving deed of Jesus Christ may benefit the whole world. The Holy Spirit provides the necessary gifts to carry out this mission. Ordained persons are especially set aside to be publicly and continually responsible in a special way to do and to guide the ministry of the church. The tasks of preaching, teaching, pastoral care, and sacramental administration are central to the work of the ordained. They have an authority in the church which must neither ignore the whole community of the faithful nor be dependent on the common opinion of all. While there is no single New Testament pattern of leadership, the three-fold ministry of bishops, presbyters, and deacons became the accepted pattern in the early centuries. However done, a ministry of episkope is needed to express and safeguard the unity of the church. The functions of the episcopate, the council of presbyters, and of the whole congregation of the faithful must somehow be included as essential to the order of life in a reunited church. In the largest sense apostolic succession refers to the continuation in the whole church of the message and ministry of the apostles. In a narrower sense it refers to a continuity mediated through the ordination by bishops who stand in a direct line of historical and institutional connection. Episcopal succession may be a sign to all of the apostolicity of the whole church, though churches who do not continue in a line of the historic episcopate cannot accept the suggestion that their ministries are invalid apart from and until brought into some chain of connection with the apostles. Different patterns of ordination are practiced, and no one of them can be singled out as exclusively valid. Churches who practice episcopal succession and those who do not but have apostolic ministries are called upon to move toward a recognition of the validity of the other. Some churches ordain women as well as men, while others ordain only men. This is a source of deep division which is simply acknowledged in the text of the statement without any attempt at normative resolution.

C. THE ORDINATION OF WOMEN: The role of women is a matter of deep controversy in the contemporary church, especially as it regards ordination.[62] A generalization is that the further a church is toward the "catholic" side of the polarity, the more it is likely to refuse ordination to women out of regard for historic practice and tradition. Churches standing in the center and toward the "protestant" side are more likely to ordain women, although resistance to their functioning meets continuing but lessening resistance.

The prevailing position of the Eastern Orthodox Church is clear. The question was never raised in the

ancient and undivided church. Hence, there is no reason
to consider it now.[63] The official Roman Catholic
position also forbids ordination to women. The Pope
recently warned (Fall, 1983) that this fact was not to
be regarded as a sign of unjust discrimination or
oppression but as a matter of correct doctrine. Many
Orthodox and Roman Catholic theologians seek a
Christological basis for the exclusion of females from
the office of ordained pastor. The argument is that the
ordained minister directly represents Christ. Hence,
for the sake of this symbolic correspondence between
Christ and the representative of Christ, the ordained
pastor must be male.[64] A growing number of Roman
Catholic theologians question the traditional arguments
and regard the exclusion of women as a cultural tradition which has no sound theological basis. The very
fact that some Roman theologians look favorably on the
ordination of women is an obstacle to discussions with
the Orthodox who are not generally open to any
reconsideration of the question.

Anglican churches in Hong Kong, Canada, and the
United States now ordain women to the priesthood. Those
branches of Anglicanism which do not have the problem of
deciding how they will relate to those who do as well as
to the women priests themselves. Major breaches of
communion have not occurred. The trend toward the
ordination of women does raise questions for further
Anglican/Roman Catholic and Anglican/Orthodox conversations.

Some Protestant groups do not ordain women, but
most now do. The major problem for those who do ordain
women is to bring about the necessary changes in
attitude among clergy and laity which will lead to their

full and equal employment as pastors. A further
question yet unresolved is whether men and women may
bring different gifts to ministry. Will the whole ethos
of leadership and authority be changed as larger numbers
of women assume greater responsibility at every level
and in every facet of church life? Only sufficient
experience with the leadership of women can determine
whether men and women have complementary talents or
whether individual differences, regardless of sex, are
more important to the diversity of gifts provided by the
Spirit.

D. CONCLUDING REFLECTIONS: How can we account for
the "remarkable degree of agreement" of which the Lima
statement of 1982 speaks? Granted that consensus has
not been reached on many fundamental issues and that
stubborn differences persist to divide the church, what
is responsible for the movement toward unity that has
occurred? Surely many factors are involved, but several
are worthy of note.

1. Modern methods of Biblical study and modern
views of Biblical authority have paved the way toward a
candid recognition of the diversity of theological
perspectives contained in the New Testament itself.
Acceptance of this fact means that divine authority
cannot be claimed for one particular tradition to the
exclusion of the others. Truth and error are not
simple opposites. Rather many perspectives may contain
partial and essential elements without any embracing the
whole range of insight and value. Yet contrasting
traditions in the New Testament, all of which may not
fit together in some one coherent scheme, uniformly
witness to the saving deed of God in Jesus Christ.

2. The rise of historical consciousness has created a similar attitude toward developments in Christian history. Patterns of theology and church polity exhibit particularities and diversities which are historically conditioned and culturally relative. History is filled with a multiplicity of contingent elements related to time, place, and circumstance. The beliefs and practices of churches are frequently infiltrated with the ethos of some particular secular Gestalt. Hence, for any church to claim that its tradition exclusively embraces the universal truth and divine will simply lacks cogency to the modern historical mentality. The humanity of the church is all too obvious when we look at its theologies and its practices. To claim divine authority for some single strand of these humanly created patterns of thought strikes the contemporary mind as arrogant. This does not mean that no norms apply which have universal validity. It does imply that truth is complex, that history is the story of particular efforts to embrace universal truth with partial success, and that some values can be given priority only at the risk of obscuring others. This respect for particularity and diversity which mark all historical phenomena with relativity would appear to be at work in the minds of modern theologians, thus undermining confidence in dogmatic claims to universal truth. This creates an atmosphere in which adherents to one view of the church can recognize the legitimacy and the limits of their own outlooks in ways that open them up to the complementary but likewise partial truths that other perspectives have to offer.

A part of the historical consciousness is the recognition that all metaphysical systems and empirical interpretations of nature and life are historically relative. The rise of modern science and of new philosophies has taught the church that no one set of conceptual models and symbols can be identified with God's own preferred language. Catholic scholar Kenan Osborne points out, for example, that twentieth-century physics raised fundamental questions for theology about the meaning of substance as it was used in the doctrine of transubstantiation. Moreover, the rise of phenomen-ology led theologians to see that more important than what a thing is in itself (substantially) may be the meanings something has in particular human contexts. This resulted in new ways of thinking about the eucharist which focused on how a sign or symbol may take on new meanings when set within some particular human situation. Hence, some Catholics began to speak of transignification instead of transubstantiation as a way of interpreting what happens to the bread and wine in the celebration of the eucharist.65 The recognition that more than one philosophical scheme may illuminate theological truths frees one from dogmatic insistence on some privileged metaphysics.

3. The ecumenical movement itself arose out of the quest for unity and has in turn furthered the breakdown of ancient walls of separation and controversy. A new Spirit has been present in the 20th century growing out of a deepening sense of the scandal of disunity among churches who profess one faith, one Lord, one baptism, one saving act in Jesus Christ which is said to break down dividing walls of hostility (Ephes. 2:13-16).

Historical perspective lends support to the hope that ancient quarrels need not forever fragment the people of God. When churches yearning for unity began to confront each other with a desire to seek agreement and not to defend established positions and refute the error of the other, new doors were opened. The result has been that beneath forms of expression has been found a unity of faith. Even conflicting positions have been seen to be complementary and not mutually exclusive. Dogmatism and arrogance have been replaced by openness and humility. Each genuinely seeks to learn from the other. Deep differences persist still, but the degree of consensus that has been achieved is remarkable given past conflicts. The previous points made about modern methods of studying and understanding Scripture and history have supported and contributed to the sense of modesty about the truth possessed by a particular tradition. What the future holds no one can say for sure, but all the evidence indicates that the momentum toward unity is irreversible, though countertrends may halt progress indefinitely. A commitment to this goal will itself contribute toward its attainment.

The recognition of the growing secularization of society in the modern world has itself been an impetus to the quest for unity. To a disbelieving world the spectacle of churches squabbling among themselves about which of them has the supreme approval of God only contributes to a sense of their irrelevance to the real problems of life and human progress. How can churches preach the good news of reconciliation to a divided world when they themselves cannot sit in a common fellowship around the Lord's Table -- the supposed sign of communion with Christ and each other?

Hence, in addition to the internally motivated quest to bring about an answer to the prayer of Jesus for his followers "that they may all be one" (John 17:21), the other great challenge of the church is its ministry of service to the world. While there is value in the fellowship of unity and love within the body of Christ itself, many would argue that an equally or more compelling reason for the church to get its own act together is for the sake of its witness to the Gospel and its work for justice everywhere. The Lima statement of 1982 notes that as the churches grow toward unity, "they are asking how their understandings of baptism, eucharist, and ministry relate to their mission in and for the renewal of human community as they seek to promote justice, peace, and reconciliation."[66] A continuing question facing the churches will be to determine how to divide its energies between the internal quest for unity of fellowship and faith and the external ministry of proclamation and of loving service to a world in desperate need of hope and justice. The fundamental barrier to the success of the church in both areas will be the stubborn persistence of pride, narrowness of vision, and idolatrous devotion to self-interest which have always branded the church as a thoroughly human as well as a divinely-established community.

IV. The Church in Twentieth Century Theology

The discussion of modern thought so far in this chapter has examined the thinking of individual theologians largely as representatives of a particular church body. While it is the case that ecclesiology, more than any other doctrine, does reflect denominational membership, it is also true that doctrines of the church express the total Gestalt of a theologian's perspective. Hence, it will be useful to conclude this chapter with a brief survey of three thinkers who represent schools of thought, although their membership in a particular church body is not irrelevant to their point of view.

A. LIBERALISM -- WALTER RAUSCHENBUSCH: Liberalism flourished in America from about 1890 to about 1930. It stressed the immanence of God, a confidence in human possibilities, and hope for moral and social progress on earth as the ideals of Jesus become embodied in all aspects of human life. As the chief exponent of the social gospel tradition, Rauschenbusch exhibited the common liberal tendency to subordinate the church to the Kingdom of God. The church exists for the sake of the Kingdom, not for itself. The community of Christian believers is the social factor in the process of salvation. It is a superpersonal power for the redemption of society, engaging in battle with the superpersonal powers of evil and injustice. Rauschenbusch thought that the church had many resources to offer as an organized body of committed people with a long tradition, possessing Scriptures, hymns, trained moral and aesthetic feelings, a disciplined membership with strong morale, etc. He urged the churches to commit these powerful tools to the service of social righteousness in the spirit of Jesus. The Christian community needs to put aside ancient quarrels that have no contemporary practical relevance and join forces with each other and other agencies in the battle against social evils. But to do so the church must move out of its spiritual isolation and join other justice-making influences in the quest for a better world. And the church must free itself from bondage to the dominating evil forces of the age and dedicate itself to the task of organizing humanity according to the will of God. The church, then, exists as a social agent dedicated to the coming of the Kingdom of God on earth.[67]

B. NEO-ORTHODOXY -- REINHOLD NIEBUHR: Three decades later after two world wars and the collapse of confidence in steady forward progress, Niebuhr's thought about the church reflected a theology centered around the transcendence of God, the radical sinfulness of humanity, salvation by grace, the moral ambiguity of history, and a final redemption beyond history. In this context the church is viewed as a community of contrite sinners who have experienced the mercy of God. As hopeful believers, Christians face the future and the vicissitudes of life with courage, being persuaded that history stands under the sovereign rule of a loving God. Ideally, the church is a community of forgiven sinners whose gratitude toward God leads to a renewal of life and to a responsible existence in quest of justice for all. Actually, the church faces two opposite dangers: arrogant over-confidence in its own virtue and achievement, on the one hand, and pessimism about life both inside and outside the church that leads to passivity and otherworldliness, on the other hand. The church is not the Kingdom of God but the community where the Kingdom impinges most forcefully on the lives of believers, shattering their pride and pretensions and transforming them into grateful recipients of grace who reach out to their neighbors in humility and love. The church looks beyond history for the realization of its ultimate goal, but it seeks to achieve partial and tentative victories of justice and harmony amid all the tragedies and moral ambiguities within history. The church lives by its sacraments which symbolize a life of grace lived between memory and hope. In baptism and the Lord's Supper, believers participate in and express a love revealed in Christ but which they never possess within themselves as a secure achievement.[68]

C. THEOLOGY OF HOPE -- JÜRGEN MOLTMANN: Eschatological theology shifted the neo-orthodox dialectic which moved between time and eternity and between sinful humanity saved by grace and a graceful, Sovereign God to a dialectic which moved between the sin-dominated, suffering present and a liberated, joyful, righteous future. From the future God will act to consummate the Kingdom of God on earth. The promise of God to save the world is proleptically embodied in the resurrection of Christ -- a sign and first fruit of the redemption that is to come. Within this framework Moltmann sees the church as the community of hope. Its total life is lived within the horizon of eschatological expectation. Its existence is grounded in the promise of God to bring to pass a perfected future in which sin and evil are no more. Believers are baptized into the past of Christ's death and at the same time designated for citizenship in a future Kingdom that is being brought by the risen Christ. At the Lord's table, Christians are not in possession of the sacred presence of God but wait in expectant confidence in communion with the coming Christ. In the present, experience and hope contradict each other. Sin and suffering still reign, but the

Church lives joyfully by faith in the Word which promises a redemption to come. The church's mission is two-fold: to proclaim the good news of God's coming reign and to expend itself in loving service to humanity. The goal of church mission can be described both as reconciliation with God (II Cor. 5:18ff.) and also as <u>shalom</u> in the Old Testament sense -- peace, justice, and liberation from all dehumanizing oppressions that rob life of its joy and fullfillment. The transformation of the whole of life in all its dimensions is the aim of the service rendered to the world in militant action based on the hope of a total redemption that is to come. Hope leads not to passive waiting but to active works of love.[69]

Even this brief exposition will indicate how doctrines of the church are organically related to the total outlook of a given theologian. We have seen three distinctly different conceptions of what the church ideally is. For Rauschenbusch, the liberal, the church is an organized body of persons morally renewed and energized by the inspiration of the personality and teachings of the historical Jesus. It exists as an instrument, along with other institutions of good will and high ideals, as an agent of the gradual coming of the Kingdom on earth. For Niebuhr, the neo-orthodox thinker, the church is a community of forgiven sinners living by the grace of God amidst moral tragedy and social evils, whose hope is that in the end the love revealed in Christ will be triumphant beyond but not in history. Meanwhile, gratitude for the mercy of God leads to a renewal of life and to responsible efforts at achieving partial, tentative structures of justice in the midst of continuing moral ambiguity, conflict, and struggles for power. Moltmann, the eschatological theologian, sees the church as a community of hope based on confidence in the promise of God revealed in Christ to redeem the future. Like the neo-orthodox, he sees every present as dominated by sin, injustice, and oppression, thus contradicting hope, which is based not on worldly evidence but faith in the revealed promises of God. Yet present evil leads not to despair, passivity, and other-worldly hope but to militant action to transform the whole of life in accordance with the vision of the future which hope generates.

Like Rauschenbusch, but unlike Niebuhr, Moltmann expects the Kingdom to come as the goal of earthly history. But like Niebuhr, and unlike Rauschenbusch, he sees the eschatological end as coming by the power and grace of God and not as a cooperative work of God and humanity. Yet all three see the church as an activist community which seeks not only to bind up the wounds of individuals but also to transform the institutions of society in the direction of liberation and justice. All three see the church not as identical with the more inclusive reality of the Kingdom but as having its existence through and in the context of the Kingdom and as the point at which the Kingdom becomes most visible and manifest.

As it confesses in the celebration of the Lord's Supper, the church lives between memory and hope. The meal is eaten in remembrance of the saving deed of Christ and in anticipation of the final victory yet to come (I Cor. 11:23-26). The church lives between the initiation of the Kingdom in the message and ministry of Jesus and its final consummation at the end of the age.

The next chapter will deal with the Christian understanding of history and the consummation of the creative purpose of God. It will set forth the hope that is given with faith.

CHAPTER VI
HISTORY, HOPE AND THE KINGDOM OF GOD

I. The Centrality of History

It can be argued that the distinctive contribution of the Bible to religion has been its understanding of history. In the faith of Israel history is the pattern of events created over time by the interaction of God and humanity as free, purposive agents. While human beings can provisionally accept or reject the destiny intended for them by the divine will, it is clear that in the end the sovereignty of God will be established. Moreover, meaning, harmony, and fulfillment result when persons attune their lives to God, while confusion, conflict, and misery follow when the divine intention is ignored in the selfish quest for power, glory, and special advantage. Moral (good and evil, justice and injustice) and religious (faith and distrust) categories, then, are central to this understanding of human events. Within some such framework as this, history is a realm of meaning and purpose, of divine and human encounter, fundamentally directed by a Sovereign Will which in the end will be triumphant over all evil. This implies that the historical process is directional, morally-grounded, and goal-directed, so that time is fundamental to its reality and meaning. In this sense, history may be said to be the central category of Biblical religion. God, humanity, Christ, and creation are understood in terms of an Ultimate Good Will whose purpose is to create a cosmos and a people and to bring them at last to a destiny of perfected justice and everlasting joy. This outlook is the special contribution of Israel to the world.

The idea that history is a linear process composed of a series of unique, unrepeatable events impregnated with meaning and undergirded by purpose is basic to Western civilization. The conception of the human story as divinely-directed toward a perfected end entered into the stream of European philosophy through the influence of Augustine in the 5th century A.D. Since that time the belief that history has meaning, direction, and purpose has fundamentally informed the culture of the West, even when the supernatural and otherworldly dimensions of Biblical religion have been abandoned. At no point has modern secular thought been more deeply permeated with Biblical motifs than this, even when atheism has replaced faith in God. Hence, the theme of the Kingdom of God is fundamental to the ideology of the whole of Western civilization as well as to the tradition of the church.

Moreover, a world-view in which history is the central organizing principle is associated with a whole configuration of themes which taken together constitute a distinctive outlook on the meaning and destiny of human existence. History is not just a single category but is the focus of a total Gestalt, a unified pattern of understanding which stands in sharp contrast to its polar alternative. A typology can be constructed which exhibits the inner logic and meaning of two different ways of viewing reality, human existence, and salvation. Following is an outline of how the major features of each might be conceived as ideal types. The column on the left, generally speaking, includes Judaism, Christianity, and Islam. The right-hand listing points to tendencies found in some elements of Greek thought, as well as in various forms of Hinduism and Buddhism.[1]

1. Time or history is the central category and predominates over space and nature.

1. Space or nature is the central category and predominates over time and history.

2. Time is linear, having a beginning, a direction, and an end.

2. Time is circular, repeating itself endlessly through recurring cycles.

3. The finite world (creation) is essentially good though corruptible and is redeemable.

3. The temporal world is of no ultimate value and is relatively unreal.

4. Salvation is the fulfillment of this finite life, beginning in time and history though consummated beyond. It includes body and soul and preserves the identity of individuals.

4. Salvation is escape or release from finitude, involving a union with the One or All in which individuality and particularity are dissolved in an undifferentiated unity.

5. Ultimate reality is a Sovereign Personal Being conceived of in terms of moral energy or will (theism).

5. Ultimate reality is an undifferentiated Totality or Unite which assumes the ultimate identity of everything that is (pantheism).

With this general background in mind, we can examine in more detail the specific motifs about history and its fulfillment which developed in the Bible and in the interpretive tradition of the church.

II. Biblical Conceptions

The Bible is a future-oriented book. It is a document of hope and promise. The central message of the Bible is that God has created a cosmos and a people and that it is the divine intention to bring both at last to a perfected existence. The Sovereign One who brought the world into being "in the beginning" (Gen. 1) will bring it in the end to a glorious consummation in "a new heaven and a new earth" (Rev. 21). While the cosmic framework of creation and redemption is fundamental to the Biblical witness, its vision is focused on human history. The Bible is more than anything else the story of the calling, judging, and redeeming of a royal people with whom God enters into an everlasting covenant. For the Christian community the Old Covenant with Israel mediated through Moses has been fulfilled in the New Covenant with the church (the New Israel) mediated through Jesus in his role as the Christ. Both Israel and the church look back to the covenant-making events within the context of creation (Gen. 1:1; John 1:1). In these revelatory-redemptive occasions the faith of the community is grounded. But both Israel and the church look ahead in hope to an Endtime consummation based on the promise of God to perfect the creation. The drama that begins with the calling of the world into being and ends in the New Jerusalem "coming down out of heaven from God" (Rev. 21:2 RSV) provides the context within which the meaning and destiny of human existence is understood. The people of God are required to be loyal to the covenant by loving their Maker and each other in a response of gratitude and joy for the gift and promise of the new age to come. Human life occurs in the presence of a God who wills the ultimate fulfillment of all things.

If creation and consummation define the ultimate horizon -- the beginning and the end -- of the Biblical story, clearly human history is in the foreground and center. Moreover, the story of humanity is presented as the history of salvation. With this understanding in mind, it can be argued that the central theme of the Bible is the Kingdom of God.[2] The human story is unintelligible except in the context of the divine story -- the drama in which God is the central Actor and whose theme is the working of the Sovereign Purpose by which history is directed creatively and redemptively toward an End willed from the beginning. The promise of a good future in which hope is grounded takes many forms over the centuries, but from Genesis to Revelation one motif shines through: THE WILL OF GOD IS TO MAKE HEAVEN REAL. If Jesus as the Christ is the theological center of the Bible, his person and work can be understood only as they are framed by the larger unifying theme of the Kingdom of God.

A. THE KINGDOM OF GOD. This idea is based on a social analogy taken from the Israelite monarchy. It refers basically to the sovereign reign of God over all things, especially the history in which the people of God move forward toward their intended destiny. It represents a combination of two traditions.[3] (1) The roots of the symbol of the Kingdom of God are to be found in the ancient Near Eastern myth of the kingship of God, taken over by the Israelites most immediately from the Canaanites. The idea itself was widespread in that part of the world. The basic motif is that a god (assigned various names differing with the region) had brought the world into being by slaying a primeval monster. Moreover, the deity annually renews the fertility of the earth and stands guard over the people. Remnants of this myth can be found in the so-called enthronement Psalms -- 47, 93, 97, 98, and 99. (2) This myth was combined with a recital of the mighty acts of God in choosing, delivering, convenanting with, and promising a good future to Israel. Summary recitals of the history of salvation can be found in Deut. 26:5b-10, 6:20-24; Josh. 24:2b-13.

The Bible speaks of the Kingdom of God under three aspects: (1) It is an eternal fact. God as Creator is the supreme authority in the universe for evermore (Gen. 1; Dan. 4:3; Ps. 84:3). (2) It has a present manifestation. God's rule here and now is real but imperfect, due to the rebellion and disobedience of humanity. (3) It will have a perfected consummation in the future. The exact phrase "Kingdom of God" never appears in the Old Testament, though related and even equivalent ideas do (I Chron. 28:5, 29:11; Ps. 22:28, 45:6, 103:19, 145:12; Dan. 2:44). The idea of God as Ruler and Supreme Sovereign over all things is, of course, pervasive throughout the Bible.[4]

The coming of the Kingdom of God was the central theme of the preaching of Jesus (Mk. 1:14-15). The idea was familiar to his hearers and needed no definition.

The astounding claim was that the expected new age was beginning to irrupt into history. His own message and ministry were signs that the promised day was arriving. A new era was dawning, and this becomes the primary fact about history and human life. Hence, what matters above all else is the urgency of making an appropriate response to reality of the coming Kingdom that was already breaking in. Three themes highlightedJesus, proclamation of the Kingdom.[5] (1) It was a threat in that the present world order is under judgment and will soon brought to an end (Mk. 13). Moreover, those who are unprepared for the coming Day are in great danger (Luke 12:1-13; Matt. 8:12, 11:23-24, 24:1-25:46). (2) It was a promise of redemption to the poor, the out-casts, and the righteous (Matt. 5:1-11, 25:31-46). The "little flock" to whom God would give the Kingdom (Luke 12:32) would be full of surprises and reversals of present status (Luke 6:20-26). It was for the poor not the rich (Luke 6:20; Mk. 10:23). Tax collectors and sinners would enter before the Pharisees (Matt. 21:31). Not the Jews alone but folks from everywhere would come (Matt. 8:11-12). (3) Those who would avoid the threat and receive the promise must meet the demand and live in accordance with the righteousness of the Kingdom (Matt. 5-7). Supreme among the requirements are repentance, faith, and obedience to God's will (Mk. 1:14-15; Luke 6:27-46). Above all, the requirement is single-minded love of God and love of neighbor (Mk. 12:28-34; Luke 10:25-37). The Kingdom is of such great value that it demands and justifies surrender of all else in order to enter it (Matt. 6:33; Mk. 9:47; Luke 9:62; Matt. 13:44-45).

The Kingdom is both a present reality (Luke 4:16-21, 7:18-23, 10:18, 23, 11:20, 17:20-21) and a future event (Matt. 24; Mk. 13; Luke 11:2, 22:14-18). Many of the parables combine the present and the future aspects (Mk. 4:26-32; Matt. 13:24-30; Luke 13:18-21). While Jesus denied that he knew the exact day of the Kingdom's final consummation (Mk. 13:32), evidently he expected it to come within the lifetime of some of his hearers (Mk. 8:38-9:1, 13:30, 14:62; Matt. 10:23; Luke 17:7-8). Moreover, the Kingdom is both a public, historical, objective reality and an individual, spiritual, subjective reality.[6] It is a society, a corporate reality, a community and a realm to be established by God's own direct action in history (Matt. 8:11, 13:31-32, 24-30, 36-43, 47-50; Luke 11:2, 13:28-29). It is also a matter of radical inwardness in terms of attitudes, aims, and styles of life here and now (Mk. 10:14-15, 29-30; Matt. 5:1-16, 28, 33-48, 6:6, 19-24, 11:28-29). In this latter sense the Kingdom can be gained or entered by individual motivation, choice, and action (Matt. 25:31-46; Luke 14:16-24).

Given the prominence of the Kingdom of God in the teachings of Jesus, its comparatively rare usage in the rest of the New Testament is surprising. However, outside the synoptic Gospels the relative focus is on the saving work of God in Jesus as the Christ rather than on the Kingdom itself. However, the idea is essentially the same, and the interdependence and intimate connection between Christ and the Kingdom are everywhere in evidence. The new age has dawned in the appearance of Jesus as the Messiah and will shortly be consummated. This is the Good News taught nearly everywhere. The cross and the resurrection are the decisive events in an impending victory over sin and death which dominate the old age that is passing away (I Cor. 1:17-2:8; Rom. 5:6-21; Gal. 4:3-9; Ephes. 1:3-2:10). The Gospel of John, however, speaks not so much of the Kingdom of God but of life or eternal life. Salvation so understood is a present possession, a quality of existence here and now which comes from being united to Christ through faith (John 3:3-5, 16: 5-24).

B. BIBLICAL VIEWS OF HOPE. From the beginning the covenant of God with Israel had a future reference. The promise of God may conveniently be considered under two aspects: hope for the community and for the individual.

1. Corporate Hope. In the very beginning the promise of God to Abraham was that his descendants would be a great nation and be a blessing to the world (Gen. 12:1-3). The making of the covenant at the time of the Exodus was the decisive event by which Israel became the special people of God with a special destiny. The later faith of Israel took two major forms with respect to the good future: the prophetic and the apocalyptic.

a. The Prophetic Hope. The classical prophets who appeared from about 750 BC to 540 BC looked forward to a perfected future on earth characterized by righteousness, peace, and prosperity (Is. 9:1-7, 11:1-9; Joel 2:24-29; Micah 4:1-4; Is. 66:12-14, 22-23). Beyond the terrible judgment of the Day of Yahweh which Israel must suffer for violating the covenant (Amos 5:18-20), a remnant will enjoy the blessings of a new age (Hos. 2:19-20; Is. 4:2-4, 10:20-22, 37:30-32). A messianic King of the house of David will rule with justice (Is.

9:6-7, 11:1-5), and a new covenant will be written on the hearts of all (Jer. 31:31-34). Though clearly on earth and presumably in Palestine, the new age will take place in a transformed nature and history free from sin, conflict, poverty, injustice, or any of the usual human afflictions.

b. The Apocalyptic Hope. This-worldly expectations tended to disappear after the Babylonian Exile (587-538 BC). They were gradually replaced by the hope of a supernatural intervention that would soon, suddenly, and miraculously overthrow the evil powers and establish a new heaven and a new earth. The persistent oppression of Israel for centuries by a series of foreign powers led to a deepening sense of historical evil and a loss of hope for a this-worldly deliverance. Under the influence of Persian religion, Israel came to believe that evil was not simply the product of tyrannical nations but the work of supernatural powers, demonic hosts headed by Satan. A strong dualism arose which sharply contrasted this age of sin, death, and innocent suffering with the age to come in which good would at last be triumphant forever. God would put evil down once and for all by a mighty victory. The Book of Daniel (2nd century BC) is the classic expression of the apocalyptic outlook in the Old Testament. Jesus and the writings of the New Testament generally assume an apocalyptic eschatology, although the Book of Revelation is the purest and most thoroughgoing example of it.

2. Individual Hope. Generally speaking, in the Old Testament the hope of individuals was bound up with the destiny of Israel as a nation. Individualism does emerge at points, both with respect to this life (Jer.

31:29-30; Ezek. 18) and the life to come. A study of the Bible reveals a long period of development with respect to what happens beyond the grave. Throughout most of the Old Testament period the common belief was that at death all go to sheol, a large underground cavern (Gen. 37:35; Job 7:9; Ezek. 32:17-32; Num. 16:31-33; Job 26:16). There the "shades" of the departed continue to live in a weak, shadowy form. Generally, existence in sheol is dreaded (Job 7:9-10, 10:22; Ps. 22:15, 49:19, 94:17, 95:17, 138:12). Long life is valued as postponing this fate. Another view -- perhaps an older, more popular one -- is that sheol is a realm of freedom, equality, superior knowledge, and greater power (I Sam. 28; Job. 3:11-19, 31:17; Ezek. 32:17; Is. 14:9-11). All these ideas are common to that time and place and have no particular connection with the worship of Yahweh, the God of Moses and the prophets.

Two developments in the Old Testament point to a conception different from the gloomy prospect of sheol. (1) In the post-exilic period there grew up the idea of a relationship with a loving God which is so intimate and precious that God will not permit even death to break it. Several of the Psalms seem to express the idea that God will deliver the faithful from sheol (16, 17, 18, 49, 73, and 139). In these cases the reference may be simply to prolonged and good life on earth (Ps. 23), but others do seem to refer to redemption from death itself. Job 19:25-29 may also imply this. (2) In the latest period of the Old Testament the idea of the resurrection of the dead was introduced. Only two passages clearly teach this (Is. 26:19, Dan. 12:2). The logic seems to be that at the end of history, the righteous who died before the consummation will be raised to enjoy their reward, while the wicked will receive their punishment. This concern that everyone get at the end what they deserve, which they may not have received in this life, reflects the rise of individualism.

The New Testament assumes the resurrection of the dead and a final judgment which will separate the righteous from the wicked. Hades is the New Testament equivalent of sheol. Logically, it became the place where the dead awaited resurrection, though sometimes an immediate experience of one's ultimate destiny is assumed (Matt. 11:23, 16:18; Luke 16:19-31). Gehenna is the place where the wicked will be punished forever or annihilated (Matt. 18:8-9, 24:41, 46; Rev. 14:10, 19:20, 20:10; Rom. 2:509; II Thess. 1:9). The righteous will enjoy everlasting bliss, generally defined as life in the new age (Rom. 8:18-25; I Cor. 15: Rev. 20-22; Luke 16:19-31; Matt. 5:12). The general pattern is that at the Parousia (the return of Christ) the dead will be raised, a last judgment will occur, and a final separation of the righteous and the wicked will take place (Matt. 25:31-46; I Cor. 15:20-28, 35-58; II Thess. 1:5-2:15; II Peter 2:4-3:13: Rev. 19-22). While the general scheme of things is clear, no completely consistent scheme of ideas can be derived from the Bible regarding last things. A variety of notions can be found, and it is futile to try to harmonize them all in detail, either factually or logically.[7]

III. Views of Hope in Christian History

A. CLASSICAL THEMES. The non-occurrence of the Parousia called for some adjustments in theology. It was necessary to come to terms with the fact that world history continued, contrary to the dominant New Testament expectation. Attention was necessarily focused on the church, life in the world, and a reconsideration of the Endtime events due to their indefinite postponement. Yet all of this involved no more than a shift in the already/not yet dialectic that pervaded New Testament thought. In the early centuries the main line of tradition repeated the familiar pattern of events -- the catastrophic end of history at the return of Christ, a final judgment, and the separation of the righteous and the wicked into their respective everlasting destinies. In the middle of the 2nd century the Montanists revived the idea of an imminent Parousia framed in apocalyptic terms, but the general trend was in the direction of relaxing this expectation. Ideas of an earthly millennium (Rev. 20:1-10) were prominent but not universal. Orthodox thinkers were careful to affirm the resurrection of the body in opposition to Gnostic and neo-Platonic claims that the body was evil. They typically did this by combining the Platonic notion of the immortality of the soul with the Aristotelian idea of the psychomatic unity of body and soul. But how could the same body be raised, given the fact that corpses rotted into dust, were devoured by fish or animals, or were burned? In reply many simply appealed to the omnipotence of God as a guarantee that the same body could be reconstituted. Some, however, followed Origen in saying that the form (eidos) constituted the identity of the body not the particular material elements which composed it at some given time.

Origen's views are distinctive enough to warrant brief attention. He foresaw a provisional division among souls at death where an intermediate stage ensued which served as a period of probation and preparation for a definitive separation at the last judgment. He spiritualized the Parousia, seeing it not as a localized event but a universal manifestation of the divinity and authority of Christ by which all people everywhere come to see themselves as they really are; hence, they are judged. The punishment of the wicked is likewise deliteralized. The fires of hell are symbols of an interior anguish at being separated from God. Moreover, Origen spoke of an eventual restoration of all things (apocatastasis), following I Cor. 15:24-28. A vast cosmic evolution will carry the universe through a series of cycles until at last all things will be perfectly good as they were in the beginning. Given the reality of free will and the goodness of God, Origen believed that all rational creatures would finally be won over to righteousness by persuasion, instruction, and discipline. Hell is temporary, and even the Devil will in the end be saved. His theory of ultimate universal salvation was condemned in the sixth century.

It was the theology of history set forth by Augustine and his more orthodox eschatology that was to mark subsequent Christian thought. In THE CITY OF GOD he set forth a comprehensive account of the human drama which begins at the creation, proceeds through the fall of humanity to subsequent events of world history and ends with the separation of saints and sinners to be followed by everlasting blessedness for the former and unending torment for the latter. History is the story of two cities that have been formed by two loves. The earthly city is ruled by love of self and contempt of God and the heavenly city is defined by love of God in preference to self. From the time of Cain and Abel these two societies have been commingled and inter-twined. Hence, life in this world is ambiguous. The state is a devilish instrument full of tyranny, compulsion, and injustice. At the same time it is a means by which God restrains evildoers and brings order to human affairs. Likewise, the other city is marked by a similar ambiguity. The church is at once the presence and reality of the heavenly Kingdom and a mixed body containing both saints and sinners. In the latter sense the church and the Kingdom are not identical. The millennium (a symbol of an indefinite future) is not another stage yet to come. It is taking place now through the rule of Christ in the church. Change and development occur in history but no continuing progress. Augustine did not envision a transformation of society and of human institutions by which the good would eventually overcome evil. Rather the two cities will exist side by side until the end.

At the appointed time Christ will return, and all the dead will be raised to be judged, each having the identical body that was buried but now made incorruptible. The saints will have perfect bodies, all ugliness and deformity having been overcome. Children will have the bodies of adults. The wicked will experience the anguish of remorse and separation from God, but the fire is real and everlasting. Various degrees of punishment will be meted out, with that of unbaptized children being "the most mild of all." The righteous will experience their highest good, which consists in knowing, loving, and praising God in a perpetual Sabbath. Heaven will involve different degrees of honor and reward based on merit, but no jealousy will be found. The saints will exercise free will but now completely liberated from the desire or ability to sin. Never ending joy in perfect harmony free from all earthly ills will be the destiny of the elect in the presence of the Holy Trinity.[8]

The next significant development in Christian thought with regard to history and eschatology occurred in Joachim of Floris (d. 1202). Here the idea of an actual transformation of the structures of worldly history comes into prominence. This note was not altogether absent in Augustine, although he basically saw the two cities intermingled until the end. Moving through time "both alike enjoy temporal good things, or are afflicted with temporal evils, but "with diverse faith, diverse hope, and diverse love" (XVIII, 54). Yet there are positive advances in knowledge, technology, and the arts. Moreover, the church is a powerful force for good, and even religious understanding may advance. But none of this adds up to a hope in a steady improvement of life on earth. No doctrine of evolutionary progress or revolutionary transformation is present. Rather the tension and conflict between the two cities continues until Christ returns to overcome Satan and the powers of evil.

Even less of a dynamic element can be found in Thomas Aquinas. He sees an identity between the church and the Kingdom. The eschatological events lie ahead, of course, but they are important mainly as other-worldly expectation. Attention is centered on God as Pure Being and on the vision and contemplation of the divine perfection, not on the Lord of History who rules and directs events toward a goal. The focus is hierarchical, vertical, static, and mystical. The meaning of life has been realized, established, and institutionalized in the church which imparts salvation through the sacraments. Given such an understanding, it follows that an expectation of a transformed future, whether historically achieved or apocalyptically enacted, will not have a vital place. The church is the Kingdom here and now. It has life-giving sacraments and a leader who rules with the authority of Christ. The church, not history, is the primary sphere of God's redemptive activity. Hence, little or no sense of new worldly possibilities that alter life's meaning can be found in his thought, much less any sense of a radical transformation of history and its institutions.

With Joachim a quite new perspective emerges. He saw three ages in history. The age of the Father ran from Adam to John the Baptist and Jesus. This was the period of law, of slavery, and of marriage. The age of the Son would run from Christ to 1260 AD. This was the period of law and grace mixed, of filial service, and of the clergy. The age of the Spirit would begin in 1260 A.D. It was to be the period of love, liberty, and the monks. Here was the idea of a radical transformation of history itself, a progressive movement in which new realities, involving society and politics as well as the church and religion, break into human life and remake it. Each period is appropriate for a time and prepares the way for the next age that succeeds it. Each age, in fact, overlaps its successor. This combination of ideas was to be the basis of many a revolutionary, utopian movement in the modern world. History moves toward a progressive culmination. The root of the idea of progress is here, along with views of historical hope to be found in liberal and liberation theologies. Sectarian movements in Protestantism, socialism and Marxism, Enlightenment philosophers, American utopians, and all who have looked forward to a new age to come on this earth have been dependent on the revolutionary ferment which Joachim set loose in European thought, whether they knew his name or not.

Martin Luther represented a return to the idea of otherworldly eschatology. He believed himself to be living in the last days before the return of Christ. He made such a sharp separation between the kingdoms of this world and the Kingdom of God that the idea of a dynamic transformation of history was lost. The Kingdom is present in the inner life and in interpersonal relationships in the reality of faith and of loving deeds. World history, however, remains unredeemed and is governed by force, law, tyranny, conflict, and injustice. God's sovereignty is real but remains hidden. God raises up empires and then foes to punish them for their wrongdoing. The divine will is worked out through many human instruments. Ultimately, righteousness will reign when Christ returns. But he foresaw no possibility that human institutions could be fundamentally transformed or that the course of history itself -- the movement of world events -- would or could be redirected toward justice and harmony.

The hope for transforming society finds solid rootage in John Calvin. Calvinism is famous for its moral activism, from the experiment in theocracy in Geneva to efforts to transform the whole of life in its political, economic, and social forms. Calvin shared with Luther the idea of the radical sinfulness of humanity and of the inscrutability of the divine will which ruled, despite outward appearances, in all events. But instead of despairing of a sinful world, the Calvinist credo was to go out and conquer it in obedience to God for the glory of God. God is an active, willing, creating, redeeming Sovereign who works in and through the human will to remake all of life in accordance with the divine ideal. Yet the fact of God's transcendence forbids the identification of any historical achievement with the Kingdom, and there is no hope that progress on earth will ever lead to the fullness of the Kingdom. One works for good in obedience to God, not out of hope for earthly attainment. Sin deeply persists in all of life, despite the transforming power of God and the saints in the marketplace, in the halls of government, and in other human institutions.

The idea that history itself can be transformed was taken much further by some of the sectarian Protestants. Some groups, such as the Mennonites, simply tried to live out their radical righteousness, including pacifism, while they waited for God to bring in the Kingdom at the appointed time. Their holiness of life was a sign of the approaching end, but they had little confidence that love would be triumphant in history as a whole. Other groups hoped for social perfection on earth. These radicals were of two types: (1) the "soft utopians" or "suffering sects" and (2) the "hard utopians" or "fighting sects." The first group are represented by the Quakers who hoped that suffering love and non-violence would gradually win its way in history and lead to the perfection of society. The second group were social revolutionaries who were willing to engage the enemy as God's agents to bring in the new age. Some of the Continental Anabaptists of the 16th century as well as the Cromwellian sects of 17th century England, such as the fifth Monarchy Men, the Diggers, and the Levellers, took this position. They believed themselves to embody and champion an ideal society for which they were willing to fight. These sects tended to believe that the oppression from which they suffered was the final form of historical evil and that its overcoming constituted the ultimate crisis which would mark the beginning of a period of perfection in history. Frequently coming from the poorest classes, the height of their future hope matched the depth of their present misery as they worked and waited for the reign of perfect love (Quakers), perfect liberty (Levellers), or perfect equality (Diggers) in history itself.[9]

This section can be brought to a close with a brief examination of the conceptions of life after death which could be found among the scholastic theologians in the period immediately following the Reformation. The schemes found in both Catholic and Protestant manuals of theology were similar. At the time of death, the soul undergoes an immediate but preliminary judgment, while the body perishes in the grave. Catholics believed in purgatory, an intermediate state for those baptized souls who had died with unforgiven venial sin or who needed to suffer more for sins whose guilt had been removed. Protestants rejected this idea as unscriptural. At the return of Christ a last judgment will be held. The dead will be resurrected with their original bodies but now transformed and made fit for an everlasting destiny. Those who are alive at the time will not die, but their bodies will simply be remade to be like those whose bodies are resurrected. The final judgment will confirm the preliminary verdict. The saved will enter a period of everlasting joy in the presence of God, while the wicked will be punished forever. Some, however, taught that the unsaved would simply be annihilated. The physical universe would be transformed or burned up. In any case a new heaven and earth would become real. Catholics believed in a kind of in-between state called limbo where the souls of unbaptized infants and the Old Testament saints would reside. Protestants rejected this idea as having no Biblical foundation. Neither Catholic nor Protestant orthodoxy held out any hope that eventually all would be saved. Heaven and heaven are final and forever.

B. SUMMARY AND ANTICIPATION. It may be useful before examining ideas of history and hope in modern theology to offer an analysis of the themes introduced in traditional Christian thought. Three perennial motifs may be lifted out.[10] All of them are found in Augustine in varying degrees. However, taken individually they may be seen with greater clarity in others who stressed one or the other as central. (1) The first theme identifies the church with the Kingdom (Aquinas). The focus and locus of God's saving work are found in the Christian community, which may or may not have consequences for the life of humanity in transforming society or remaking history. (2) The second notion is the apocalyptic expectation that history will be redeemed only at the end by God's supernatural intervention (Luther). Christian existence is centered in the church or in the individual believer who must live in the world in accordance with the righteousness of the Kingdom but who does not expect a reshaping of social institutions or the reforming of earthly history either by evolution or revolution. (3) The third idea looks to the transformation of society itself and even to a perfected social order on earth as the culmination of history (Joachim, sectarian Protestantism). The saving acts of God are to be found not only in the church or in the lives of individuals but also in the remaking of the institutions of society and the ideals by which economic and political life are actually governed in the world. These three motifs may, of course, be combined in various ways. All can be found to some degree and in some form in nearly every Christian thinker, but each point of view tends to have a particular focus. The same ideas, singly or in combination, will reappear in modern theology, although frequently in quite different frames of reference. No theme occupies that subject of eschatology in recent centuries more than the question of the extent to which history is fulfilled in history or beyond history. To these developments we now turn.

C. THE CHALLENGE OF MODERN THOUGHT. In every chapter it has been pointed out that modernity presented the Christian world with fundamental challenges resulting in a reformulation of doctrine. In no area is this more true than with respect to ideas of history and hope. In fact, changed conceptions of history itself have frequently been at the root of the reconceptualization of other beliefs. Frequent mention has been made throughout these pages of the historical consciousness that has so dominated modern culture in the West. This refers to a configuration of emphases which adds up to the conviction that history is the peculiar locus and focus of human existence. In contrast to nature, which is the realm of law, necessity, and regularity, history is the arena of freedom, contingency, and novelty. It is the product and consequence of human creativity which constructs realms of meaning, morality, culture, and religion, as well as technological innovations which overlay the givens of natural and biological existence. Modern science seemed to present a physical world of neutral events devoid of freedom and purpose. Hence, a dualism arose between the sphere of cosmic fact and the arena of personal purpose, i.e., between nature and history. In this sense, history is the specifically human world.

It is not easy in a brief survey to describe accurately the new ideas about history which arose during the Renaissance and the Enlightenment to flower in the 19th century. Variety and conflicting counter currents are plentiful and will inevitably be lost in oversimplified generalizations. Nevertheless, a combination of four motifs will suggest the skeleton of the emerging orientation which was both a challenge and an opportunity for theology to offer reconstructed versions of Biblical religion.

1. Autonomy. Humanity became the subject and agent of history, the originator of novelty. In fully secularized versions, humanity became the sole creator of meaning and direction.

2. Dynamism. This means not only that things change but also that the very structures of society evolve or are radically transformed by human action. Greek philosophers and medieval theologians knew that

changes take place. But this referred primarily to the coming into being and passing away of individual beings (plants, animals, people) and of human societies which have essentially permanent forms. The modern conception rejected the notion of static patterns and replaced it with the belief that the genuinely new (novel form) comes into being and undergoes development and mutation into still further forms of social and historical life. In the 19th century Charles Darwin added the idea that the forms of biological life also change, so that new species as well as new individual organisms come into being. Hence, evolution became the clue to understanding both the emergence of novel forms of both natural (biological) and social (economic, political, cultural) existence over periods of time.

3. <u>Relativity</u>. This notion is closely related to and follows from the fact of social dynamism. Every humanly originated form of thought and culture has a certain fittingness for its time and place. Given the radical understanding of novelty and change in the modern world, it follows that each historical epoch and every facet of life within that period is relative to the surrounding circumstances and hence is not universally or permanently valid. Hardly anything has been more characteristic of recent centuries than the recognition that every aspect of social life is historically conditioned and culturally relative. Patterns of thought and forms of social organization come into being and have their day to be replaced with other ideologies and institutions that are likewise epoch-specific in terms of appropriateness and validity.

4. <u>Developmentalism</u>. This facet of modern understanding means that history is going somewhere.

Despite the coming and going of particular and relative forms of natural and social existence, there is a pattern of growth and advance in the process of change. History in this sense has both a direction and a goal. This frequently involves the notion that certain stages are passed through on the way toward some final point. The most important conviction here is that not only the new and different come into being but also that the movement is forward and upward toward the better and even in the direction of the perfect. This amounts to the idea of progress, which is the centerpiece of the faith of modern Western culture. Progress, whether through evolution or revolution, is the key to the interpretation of history which has most challenged theology in the last three centuries.

The central theme of the Enlightenment was that all people could in some future time enjoy a kind of happiness on this earth which had hitherto been reserved for the life beyond and then only for the saints.[11] This represents, of course, a secularizing of the Biblical hope of the Kingdom of God.[12] But the new age has been brought down from heaven to this world and is to be reached through human effort, though perhaps in cooperation with some divine plan. In the 18th century the key ideas were reason and nature. There is an order in nature which reason can discover and by living in accordance with it humanity can overcome the error and superstition of the past and move toward rational morality, prosperity, and general happiness. Just as Sir Isaac Newton had discovered the laws of nature by which a rational God governed the physical universe, so Adam Smith discovered a law in the social world whereby the pursuit of economic self-interest would be guided by an "invisible hand" toward a general harmony and the wealth of nations. In France Condorcet argued for inevitable progress based on his confidence in reason to guide human destiny.

While conflicting ideas and counter currents are plentiful, a great deal that is characteristic of the Enlightenment mentality can be derived from a combination of the principle of social nominalism and the law of social harmony.[13] Social nominalism refers to the view that only individuals are real, while society emerges by contract and interaction among individuals. Social harmony refers to the order which emerges when individuals follow their own inclinations and interests. (1) When individuals seek their own economic self-interest an "invisible hand" will produce an unintended orderliness and prosperity (Adam Smith). (2) Set individuals free to govern themselves, and a harmonious political order will emerge which coordinates self-interest with the common good. (3) Let individuals interpret the Bible under the guidance of the Spirit, and religious truth will come to light. (4) Let individual men and women choose their own marriage partners after "falling in love," and stable marriages and family life will result. While this way of putting it is too neat and idealistic, nevertheless one may find here the basis for four characteristic institutions of the modern world: capitalism, democracy, Protestantism, and romantic marriage. What is important in this connection is the underlying faith in the rationality of things by which individual self-interest is at least tolerably coordinated with the common good by the operation of some apparent law of harmony which is ingredient in the universe itself. This confidence in rationality, harmony, and progress broke down, of course, in the 20th century.

In the 19th century various thinkers saw progress as a law of nature, reality, or God working itself out in the cosmos and in human history through various stages of development. August Comte saw three great periods in the life of humankind, each representing an advance: the mythical (theological), the metaphysical (philosophical or rational), and the positivist (scientific). Hegel saw nature and history as the dialectical evolution of Spirit by which each age or phase generated first its opposite and then an inclusive and progressive integration (thesis/antithesis/synthesis). Karl Marx turned the Hegelian dialectic on its head and argued for a materialist conception of history which led from primitive communism through a succession of class conflicts toward capitalism, its dissolution, and finally to the emergence of a socialist, harmonious, classless society. In 1859 Charles Darwin presented evidence for the origin of new species over time through the mechanisms of the struggle for survival, random mutations, and natural selection. Herbert Spencer universalized evolution into a law of progress rooted in nature which carried society and history toward perfection and happiness. Many and varied were the interpretations of progress, of its basis, and of the end toward which it moved, but the idea itself became an article of faith. Modern thinkers "of all shades of opinion agreed in the belief that historical development is a redemptive process."[14] Not least among the grounds for hope was the confidence that science and technology could point the way toward both material and moral improvement.[15]

D.   HISTORY AND HOPE IN MODERN THEOLOGY. The new historical consciousness stands in sharp contrast to conceptions of providence and history in classical theology. Since by definition modern theology is, in part, the attempt to incorporate major elements of the historical consciousness into its interpretation of the Gospel, it follows that it too will be at odds with orthodoxy in certain basic ways. (1) Acceptance of the fact of human autonomy appears to put limits on the sovereignty of God. Moreover, the modern vision also assumes that a whole host of finite factors -- geography, climate, social facts of the past and present, etc. -- enter into the determination of the course of history. Orthodoxy has assumed that God completely determined history through the secondary causes of nature and human will. Finally, modern culture assumes an order of physical law which governs all finite beings, including persons. The attempt to interpret the rule of God in nature and history given this cluster of themes -- human creativity, finite factors which shape events, and the reality of unalterable causality -- has posed formidable challenges to theology in recent centuries. (2) Acceptance of the principle of dynamism, which assumes that the forms of natural and social life evolve and change, conflicts with orthodox notions of their relative permanence. Theologians of the past had taught that all the varieties of plant and animal life had been created at the beginning, each to reproduce "after its kind" (Gen. 1-2) from then until now. The same holds for the human species as well, which was a unique and special creation. Moreover, institutions and social practices were thought to be of limited variety and relatively static, if not eternal. (3) The idea of historical relativity does not fit well with the older view that thereisa natural law rooted in the divine will which provides universal eternal norms for the fixed forms of society and its institutions. (4) Developmentalism, which assumes autonomy, dynamism, and relativity, had little place in the main lines of Christian orthodoxy. Change there was, and even some advance, but not the steady and continuous evolution and revolution through various stages which modernity has taken for granted.

Obviously the streams of thought flowing from Joachim of Floris and sectarian Protestantism -- and to a lesser extent the dynamic thought of Calvinism -- provide exceptions to some of the generalizations just made about the main line of orthodoxy. However, it remained for modern theologies under the influence of the new historical consciousness to make more decisive breaks with traditional Christian thought. These theologies in all their many varieties have accepted the motifs of autonomy, dynamism, and relativity. The developmental principle has also been appropriated, but sharp division has occurred over whether this involves or necessarily implies progress.[16]

1. Liberalism. Liberal theology arose in the 19th century to reinterpret the Gospel in the light of modern thought, including the new historical consciousness. However, these thinkers incorporated the emerging cultural views of history into a theological framework which assumed the reality of an immanent God working in and through natural, social, and historical processes to bring about a gradual realization of the Kingdom of God

on earth. These progressivist tendencies are present in leading exponents of Continental liberalism such as Freidrich Schleiermacher, Albrecht Ritschl, and Adolf Harnack. Some of the most extravagant statements of the doctrine of progress can be found in American liberals during the last half of the 19th century. Lyman Abbott used the theory of natural evolution as a basis for asserting that gradual advance was the sure law of historical development as well.[17] Henry Drummond maintained that Christianity and evolution were identical -- God's way of creation working through love to perfect humankind.[18] Newell Dwight Hillis, a Brooklyn pastor, taught that practically everything was becoming better and better, laws more just, rulers more humane, music sweeter, homes happier, the heart more gentle -- all marching triumphantly behind Christ toward perfection.[19]

More cautious hopes were expressed by American Protestants during the early 20th century, particularly after World War I. Harry Emerson Fosdick was justified in protesting that he challenged the notion of inevitable progress a decade before neo-orthodoxy appeared in the United States.[20] Walter Rauschenbusch made the Kingdom of God the central theme of his theology, claiming to recover from the teachings of Jesus what had long been lost in theology with its emphasis on the church. He defined the Kingdom as "humanity organized according to the will of God." Progress toward that goal could be and had been made. In 1912 he declared that major areas of social life had been essentially "Christianized." The church, the state, education, and the family had made such advances that they were now suitable organs through which the Spirit of Christ could operate. The major institution still under the domination of Mammon and selfishness instead of the law of love was the economic order. The outbreak of World War I was a blow to his optimism. He warned that selfish vested interests would resort even to totalitarianism and violence to protect special privilege. Every child comes into the world a kicking, screaming egotist and has to learn how to love. Sinful corporate powers would always resist the new order of unselfishness and service to others. Social perfection is not possible on earth. The Kingdom of God is always coming but never fully arrives.[21] Shailer Mathews, writing in 1916, could still hope that the spirit of Jesus would win its way in the world so that war would be outlawed, democracy would flourish, and brotherhood would reign.[22]

Liberal theologians rejected a literal interpretation of Biblical apocalypticism. The second coming of Christ, the resurrection of the same bodies that were buried, and the final judgment were not regarded as real events to occur at some future time. Belief in the everlasting punishment of the wicked was abandoned as too cruel to be attributed to the God revealed by Jesus. Immortality was generally affirmed. Harry Emerson Fosdick said that he believed in "the persistence of personality" beyond death. God would not create so precious a reality as human personality and allow it to perish, he reasoned. Walter Rauschenbusch, like many liberals, spoke of the life beyond in terms of continuing growth and development for all -- the good and the bad alike. In the end no one would remain unredeemed. Hence, the Kingdom of God is fulfilled beyond history, although it stands incontinuity with progressive tendencies in this life. In short, liberalism rejected the dualism which orthodoxy has posited between the saved and the lost, the present age andthe coming age, and the two-fold destiny of human beings in an everlasting heaven and hell.23

2. <u>Neo-orthodoxy</u>. Neo-orthodoxy arose to restate essential elements of Biblical faith and classical theology (especially Augustine and the Protestant Reformers) that liberalism had abandoned or obscured. Two reasons account for the reassertion of classical themes. (1) Johannes Weiss and Albert Schweitzer had convinced the scholarly world that Jesus had an apocalyptic view of the Kingdom of God, contrary to what the liberals had asserted.24 The dualism of discontinuity between the old age that was passing and the new age that God would soon, suddenly and miraculously bring about had to be taken into account by any theology that claimed to be Biblical. (2) The castastrophes of the 20th century -- world wars, Hitler, the holocaust, widespread economic disaster, and nuclear bombs, etc. -- undermined the idea of smooth, sure historical progress. Two theological motifs were of special importance in the reinterpretation of history that follows: the reassertion of the sovereignty and transcendence of God and the radical sinfulness of humanity.

Both liberalism and neo-orthodoxy are distinctly "modern" as compared to the classical theologies of Augustine, Aquinas, Luther, and Calvin. The neo-orthodox theologians, as well as those in the liberal camp, accepted the principles of autonomy, dynamism, and relativism which has characterized the historical consciousness of recent centuries. With some fundamental qualifications they also agreed with the principle of developmentalism. Neo-orthodox thinkers frequently made distinctions among the areas in which cumulative advances took place and those in which it did not. They, of course, recognized that scientific knowledge and technology were in many ways progressive -- in overcoming disease, for example. They doubted that later necessarily meant better in literature, art, morality, and religion. Economic and material advances for millions of people could not be denied. It was the idea of moral progress that was most sharply subjected to criticism. All agreed that no certain, consistent, or necessary progress could be discerned or hoped for. History is most certainly not evolving gradually and surely toward the Kingdom of God on earth. The more extreme among them, Karl Lowith, for example, argued that the course of world events gives no discernible clues to divine activity and provides no empirical evidence of progress whatsoever.[25] Yet others argued that to give up entirely the hope of secular history by divine and human action would be as contrary to Biblical teachings.

Neo-orthodoxy burst upon the European scene with the publication in 1918 of Karl Barth's ROMERBRIEF (Commentary on Romans). During World War I Barth was a pastor in Switzerland. He remarked that with a little imagination he could hear the guns booming in the north -- the symbol of the dissolution of the hopes of Western civilization. In the thundering words of this new prophet, secular world history seems to be an arena void of the immanent presence of God and of any movement toward the eschatological goal. The process of world events seems, in fact, to be meaningless, directionless, purposeless. If he had a system, said Barth, it consisted in the recognition of the "infinite qualitative distinction between time and eternity" (Kierkegaard).[26] God was the Wholly Other, invisible to humanity except at the one point at which the Word Incarnate lit up the darkness of the finite, sinful world. Christ was a sheer vertical intrusion into history. He touched the human sphere as a tangent touches a circle, that is, without touching it. The eschatological Kingdom is not "ahead," not present in history, but totally "above." It is encountered in a thundering Word of judgment -- the divine NO which stands over against all human strivings and efforts at goodness -- which accompanies the forgiving Word of grace -- the divine YES which justifies unworthy sinners who have no merit at all. Barth later modified this purely vertical conception of God's encounter with humanity in a given moment directly from above and made room for a present rule of the Sovereign Will in all events. The result is a view much like Augustine's conception of the City of God, commingled and interacting with the earthly city, but not leading to any progressive reign of love in human affairs. The center of attention is the salvation of the covenant community -- the church -- within the world, not on a transformation of the processes of world events in the direction of the immanent realization of the Kingdom of God on earth.[27]

Reinhold Niebuhr also attacked the modern idea of progress but did not disavow it as completely as some versions of Continental neo-orthodoxy did. Clearly Niebuhr exhibits the historical consciousness in so far as the motifs of autonomy, dynamism, relativity, and development express it. Human freedom is the capacity to rise above any given structures of nature, history, or even the self to create new realms of meaning and to give history a dynamic quality in which growth in many areas can be discerned. Arguing that "no fixed limits can be set for the expansion of human capacities,"[28] he found growth taking place in science and technology, culture, human rational powers, and in religion, while our basic rootedness in nature, which makes us finite and mortal, remains. Modern culture was not wrong in seeing development in all these areas but did tend to exaggerate it. More importantly, a fundamental error was made in identifying the increase of freedom with increasing virtue, i.e., in concluding that growth and development in the extension of human powers meant certain and continuing progress. In short, moderns forgot about or neglected the reality of sin -- the misuse of freedom for selfish ends arising out of insecurity, anxiety, and pride. Hence, the dynamic but not the progressive interpretations of history in recent centuries have been vindicated.

Niebuhr proposed a synthesis of "Reformation and Renaissance."[29] Developments in history present new opportunities and obligations to realize possibilities of good in history. But each new level brings corresponding hazards of destructiveness. The perils rise with the promises. Moreover, no historic achievements in the short-run or long run offer any possibility of overcoming the contradictions, limitations, and ambiguities of existence. History is not its own redeemer. Progress does and may occur in certain areas and eras. Limited fulfillment and gains are possible and real, but humanity is ever tempted to claim finality and ultimate validity for some provisional meaning, trend, or group with tragic consequences. The parable of the wheat and the tares gives us the clue (Matt.

13:24-30). Good and evil grow together intertwined and inseparable, awaiting the harvest at the end of the season. Likewise, history requires a final judgment and a final fulfillment beyond history.

The eschatological symbols of the End are essential to the understanding of history, although they must be taken "seriously but not literally."[30] Three in particular are noteworthy. (1) The second coming of Jesus means that history cannot finally defy its own norm (love) and that in the end the sovereignty of God will at last unify all things in a vindication of goodness. (2) The last judgment symbolizes the truth (a) that history will be judged, not by the contrast between the finite and the infinite, but in terms of its ideal possibilities, (b) that distinctions of good and evil in history are evaluated and not dissolved in eternity, and (c) that history requires a judgment and completion at the "end," since no final redemption occurs within the historical process itself. (3) The resurrection of the body teaches us that eternity fulfills and does not negate the richness and variety of temporal and bodily achievements on earth. However, such fulfillment is an act of grace which is consummated beyond this life. Consummation is a loving fellowship among persons and with God in the unity of body and spirit (wholeness) not an absorption into the divine, like a drop of water falling into the ocean. Niebuhr urged a decent restraint in talking about the details of the future life, suggesting that we should not speculate about the "furniture of heaven or the temperature of hell."[31] But he also said that such caution should not obscure the validity of the hope by which we are sustained. He does not venture an opinion on whether some will be finally excluded from heaven or whether ultimately all will be saved, except for the suggestion that it is prudent to approach the End with a "fear of judgment."[32]

A similar reticence in asserting dogmatic claims about last things can be found in other thinkers of the period. The emphasis of Karl Barth on the sovereignty of God's love combined with the notion that there is only one election revealed in Christ -- and that to grace and salvation -- seems to imply a doctrine of universal restoration. However, he denied that this was a necessary implication.[33] Emil Brunner and Gustaf Aulén were content to rest in the unresolved tension between God's love and will to overcome sin, on the one hand, and the fact of divine holiness and judgment, on theother hand. Hence, neither an ultimate two-fold destiny (heaven and hell) nor the idea of universal salvation can be held as a matter of belief.[34] Brunner accused Barth of undercutting the reality of human freedom by a divine decision that is made objectively for humanity by God from the other side.[35] Nels Ferré, however, who was perhaps more neo-liberal than neo-orthodox, believed that in the end, however remote, all would be saved. His hope rested in the power of divine love finally to persuade the free will of all people into an acceptance of their true nature and destiny, namely, that they were made for agape-fellowship with each other and with God. Hence, hell as judgment for the wicked is real but temporary because of the ultimate sovereignty of love over all resistance.[36]

3. <u>Current</u> <u>Trends</u>. During the last quarter century the theological winds have shifted once more.

This brief review of Christian conceptions of history and hope will conclude with a look at two contemporary points of view.

a) Eschatological and Liberation Theologies. A variety of perspectives in Europe, the United States, and Latin America have appeared in which the central theme is the hope for a transformed and liberated history brought about by God's action from the future.[37] They go under a number of names -- theology of hope, eschatological theology, liberation theology, political theology, and futurist theology. Prominent figures are Jürgen Moltmann, Wolfhart Pannenberg, Johannes Metz, Gustavo Gutiérrez, Rubem Alves, and others. Some overlapping with themes of feminist and black theology is also in evidence, although these perspectives have their own distinctive centers and aims. It is impossible to be fair to the richness, variety, and individuality represented by such a diverse group of thinkers. However, the focus will be on distinctive motifs widely shared which set this general orientation apart from preceding theologies.

A frequent critical thrust of these thinkers is the focus on faith as an inward, subjective reality in the lives of individuals or in the church by which life is sustained in a godless world -- a note characteristic of many existentialist and neo-orthodox theologies of the preceding generation. Moltmann, for example, levels such an attack on Karl Barth and Rudolf Bultmann.[38] Positively these thinkers claim to be recovering a genuinely Biblical eschatology which hopes for a good and perfected future on earth. The central theme is that redemption is social, historical, public, and this-worldly. The coming age is not primarily a matter of blessedness beyond this life. Neither is salvation the rescue of individuals one by one from the world or in the world while secular history remains in bondage. Nor is it primarily a matter in which only believers in the context of the church participate. Rather the coming age includes the transformation of the political, economic, social, and cultural spheres of earthly history. The basic dialectic in these theologies is not between time and eternity or between the immanent and the transcendent God but between the sin and death dominated present and the redeemed future which is to come and is always coming. Present and future, experience and hope, stand in contradiction to each other. The confidence of the believer in a sanctified social order lies in the reliability of the promise of God to remake all things.

The new age will not evolve gradually out of the present as the ideals of Jesus become triumphant in human hearts and social institutions, as the liberals thought. It will, however, as the liberals taught, involve the perfection of society and history on earth, contrary to the social realism of the neo-orthodox. Social redemption comes by God's action from ahead, from the future which is the primary locus of the being and activity of the God of hope. The liberation of history will not emerge out of the actualities and possibilities of the empirical present but appears as the radically new based on God's promise and power to establish the Kingdom. Hence, the resurrection of Christ is the epitome and proleptic embodiment of what is to come. The new creation, it appears, will come about ex nihilo, just as the initial creation did. Yet the future that is expected is not some once and for all ending of history but a continuing power that comes from ahead and beyond to liberate the present from its bondage to sin, injustice, and misery. Eschatological theologies speak of "the moving horizon of the future"[39] which goes forward, just as the "pillar of cloud" and the "pillar of fire" went before the Israelites to lead them through the wilderness (Ex. 13:21-22).

Eschatology, then, is not about the sequence of events that will occur after this life and history are over. Rather it affects every moment of existence here and now. The believer lives in tension between the "no more" of the old age and the "not yet" of the new age. The Kingdom is present as hope and as liberating power, but since sin, misery, injustice, and death still hold the world in bondage, the fullness of the Kingdom is still ahead. The rule of God can not be banished to a future world unconnected with our present history on earth, but neither can it be identified with existing conditions here and now. The faithful live in anticipation based on the resurrection of Christ from the dead, which is the first fruits of the End that is to be. Existence in faith and hope issues in works of love.

It is at this point that Christian hope in life after death becomes relevant to the present life. Heaven is not the prospect of a good time which enables us to endure while we wait passively for the end to come. Scorn is heaped upon this understanding of eschatology. Hope for the good future is not morphine to dull our senses against the pain of the present. Rather hope is an energizing power which enables

Christians to be totally committed to the remaking of life here and not after the pattern of the new age that is expected. Says Moltmann, the believer is "expendable," i.e., can surrender and give all without reservation or restraint to works of love and reconciliation without fear of what the enemy can do, since even death is no longer a threat. "Faith can expend itself in the pain of love, it can make itself `into a thing' and assume the form of a servant, because it is upheld by the assurance of hope in the resurrection of the dead."[40] Black theologian James Cone likewise says, "If we really believe that death is not the last word, then we can fight, risking death" in the battle for freedom.[41]

Generally speaking, the foregoing has been more descriptive of the Continental versions of eschatological theology, especially of Moltmann's views, than of the Latin American theologians of liberation. Among them variety is present also, but a few references will help to clarify both the issues involved and the complexity of the wide-ranging perspective that is being surveyed. One point has to do with the relative roles of God and humanity in establishing the future Kingdom. While Moltmann urges that hope will expend itself in proclaiming the Gospel and in the service of humanity, he is clear that this human action is not the cause of the new world that is coming. One serves out of gratitude and obedience and in the light of faith's expectation, but the eschatological Kingdom is God's work which "we can only await in active hope."[42] In this respect Moltmann sounds more like Calvin than like Rauschenbusch. Some of the Latin Americans are more willing to speak of the causal effectiveness of the human role, without, however, denying the reality and centrality of divine action. They speak variously of our "freedom to construct the Kingdom" (Juan Luis Segundo),[43] and of the realization of freedom as a "joint enterprise" of God and humanity (Rubem Alves).[44]

A closely related issue is that Moltmann maintains more of a dualism between world history and the eschatological Kingdom than do some of the Latins. Gutierrez writes that "salvation is an intrahistorical reality"[45] and that the "history of salvation is the very heart of human history."[46] Hence, a utopian element enters with respect to what is actually expected in the general course of this worldly history. Liberation from economic and political bondage is "the growth of the Kingdom."[47] Yet the Kingdom is not identified with the sanctification of the social order as such. Liberation theology has been accused of a reductionism in which salvation is identified with intraworldly societal goals. Gutiérrez, however, distinguishes three inter-related levels of freedom: (1) liberation from every form of historical oppression -- economic, political, and social, (2) liberation which leads to a new humanity in which persons and groups are free agents who create and manage their own futures, and (3) liberation from sin, which is the root of all forms of oppression. Salvation itself is defined as communion with God and with each other.[48]

In summary, it must be said that eschatological and liberation theologians are not always clear or in agreement with each other about "when," "where," and "how" the Kingdom will come in its fullness. They are certain that Biblical faith requires that we live by the hope that it will come ultimately as the culmination of this worldly history and that its certainty rests on the promise and power of God. Meanwhile, any immediate future is likely to be ambiguous and imperfect. However, only radical hope in the ultimate and perfect transformation of all of life in its bodily and social as well as its spiritual dimensions is adequate. Without utopian visions of the absolute ideal, reforms are likely to be timid and shallow, failing to go to the root of social evil. A revolutionary faith, hope, and love are required which work for and expect that the perfect will come if not soon then ultimately. As Gutierrez says, "it is a matter of partial fulfillments through liberating historical events, which are in turn new promises marking the road towards total fulfillment."[49] As Jesus said about the coming of the Son of Man, no one knows the day or the hour when that perfect Kingdom will finally appear, but we live in hope that it will in God's own time and way.[50]

Some of the most fruitful debates about the Christian understanding of history today engage representatives of Niebuhrian realism and exponents of eschatological theology with its tendency toward utopianism. Langdon Gilkey, for example, admits to having been much influenced by futurist and liberation theologies but argues against some of them on several grounds.[51] (1) They lack a proper doctrine of providence and hence have an insufficient place for the present rule of God. The sharp contrast between a present Godless world and a future in which the Reign of God will be full and complete is overdrawn. (2) They tend to see liberation and self-determination as the meaning of salvation, without acknowledging that freedom can be used sinfully by the newly liberated as well as by old oppressors. The fundamental contrast is between grace and sin, not between the liberated and the unliberated or between oppressed and oppressors. (3) Political action must deal with possibilities latent in present actuality and historical fact. Eschatological theologies tend to expect the radically new by divine and human action ex nihilo. The present and even hidden work of God in preparing the groundwork in the structures and processes of present-day reality is neglected. (4) Far from solving the theodicy problem, as some of them claim, they heighten it. If God is the master of every future that is to come, then God must have been sovereign over every past "future" and therefore responsible for not redeeming the present which was "future" to yesterday. W.R. Jones, himself a humanocentric black theologian, poses this question for black theology in IS GOD A WHITE RACIST?[52] If God is the liberator of the poor and oppressed, the sovereign Lord who acts to free those who are in bondage, why have blacks been oppressed for so long? Why are they still not free?

b) Process Theologies. Many of the influential process thinkers on the scene today have been much influenced by Reinhold Niebuhr and so combine a realism about history and the future with the cosmological vision of Alfred North Whitehead. Increasingly process theologians have engaged in conversation with theologies of liberation and are being influenced by them while offering critical assessments.[53] Perhaps the key theme in process theologies is that progress is potential in process but not necessary or certain. The beginning point is the reality of the present as it has developed out of the past. The future is open within limits determined by the present. God is active in every historical event and movement luring human agents into new and better realizations of justice and enjoyment. God plays this role by offering for each historical occasion a range of relevant possibilities for actualization, one among which is best. Best here means that organization of the total situation most productive of complex and intense harmonies which yield the most experientially satisfying outcomes. God works in history to maximize enjoyment by the increase of rich, deep, and complex feelings that satisfy and fulfill. The norm of justice for process theology is frequently said to be self-realization in community. This refers to a situation of giving and receiving by members of a society in ways that are appropriate to each and which tend to promote mutual fulfillment. However, the achievement of justice, joy, fulfillment, and harmony in society depends on the extent to which human beings respond appropriately by attuning themselves to God's aims for them individually and for the whole community. Hence, the future is the joint outcome of divine persuasion and human response. Process theologians call people to the principle and process of creative trans-formation under the guidance of norms revealed in the Logos made flesh in the person of Jesus of Nazareth. Progress is thus possible to the extent that humanity responds positively to the lure of persuasive love which leads toward the coming of the Kingdom of God on earth. The degree, type, and actuality of progress are empir-ical matters and are not determined in advance. The future is open, always pregnant with new possibilities of justice and joy but also fraught with peril and destruction when humanity rejects the leading of God's aims.

The main line of process theology today follows Whitehead in denying that history is moving toward some foreordained outcome guaranteed by divine action. While there is purpose <u>in</u> history, there is not one determinate purpose <u>for</u> history. The simultaneous realization of the sum total of all positive values is not possible even for God. All realization is finite, i.e., represents the actualization of some particular ensemble of values. Not all ideals are compatible with each other. Moreover, every type and level of achievement open up new possibilities in a never ending sequence of creative advance. Even if this earth comes to an end or if this cosmic epoch passes, other worlds and other paths of achievement may follow everlastingly. The only ultimate or final consummation is in the moment by moment organization in God's experience of all emerging facts and values into the best possible harmony in the light of what they could be in some perfected system, taking "tender care that nothing be lost."[54] By intuitively participating in the divine life in which ones own puny existence is caught up in transcendent purposes and harmonies and values which will persist and grow everlastingly, we can have the gift of peace and tranquility in the midst of the sorrows and ambiguities of life. Such is the experience of the Kingdom of heaven here and now.[55]

Process thinkers are generally cautious about life after death for the individual. The position is typically stated in terms of a contrast between objective versus subjective immortality. Whitehead argued that all achieved values are preserved everlastingly in the mind and memory of God (objective immortality), while individual entities perish. In the case of human beings, however, he left the door open to the possibility of affirming on special religious and experiential grounds that the soul might survive death (subjective immortality). Objective immortality is affirmed as a matter of course by process thinkers. It is argued, in agreement with Whitehead, that the ultimate evil is "perpetual perishing," the fading and vanishing of all particular finite experiences and values.[56] However, if all that is good and positive is caught up into God's imaginative vision of some perfected harmony and preserved forever, the great evil of "perpetual perishing" loses its destructive threat. Some affirm objective immortality as sufficient. Schubert Ogden leaves the question of subjective immortality as an open question about which he has no affirmative word as yet.[57] David Griffin sees it as an optional belief.[58] Neither thinks that the survival of the individual beyond the grave is essential to Christian faith or hope. John Cobb agrees that on philosophical (Whiteheadian) grounds, life beyond death can only be affirmed as a possibility.[59] However, as a Christian he ventures to believe that God may continue in the beyond to offer new possibilities of achievement, reached perhaps through suffering and pain, as is the case now. Apart from such confidence life can be declared good, but "only with such a hope can we share in the affirmation that it is very good."[60]

Clearly process theologians have modified ideas of divine omnipotence and sovereignty which have dominated Christianthought over the centuries. This comes out plainly when it is asserted in dealing with theodicy that God cannot unilaterally bring about any desired state of affairs.[61] This conclusion follows once it is granted that God's power is primarily persuasive, that human freedom and creativity are real, and that events in nature have some autonomy which includes both causal and self-determinative features. The consummation in traditional thought depends on the coercive assertion of divine power on persons and events to conform them at last to the divine will. Process thinkers reject this orthodox view. The reality of massive historical injustice, misery, and absurd natural evils leads some to affirm a suffering, struggling God whose intentionality is pure love but whose power is limited. Cross and resurrection become symbols of the fact that history is the story of suffering and triumph, of defeat and victory, of sin and the overcoming of sin, of evil and the rebirth of good out of death and destruction. History is an adventure full of peril and of promise undergirded by a Creative Power and Purpose whose character is defined by boundless love and whose steady aim is to fulfill the potentialities of the creation. The historical future is open, and the ultimate future is shrouded in mystery beyond knowing, except that the God of the past and present will also be the God of the future as well.[62]

IV. Summary and Analysis of Continuing Issues

Diversity of content and change of content from one generation to another are characteristic features of 19th and 20th century theologies, but not of them alone. This is the story of eschatology from the time of Abraham in the early Biblical period to the present.

Are there any constants? A positive answer can be given along two lines. (1) PATTERN OF THOUGHT. It has already been noted that Christian thinking revolves around three major motifs: the close association and/or identification of the church with the reign of God on earth, the hope of heaven beyond, and the transformation of earthly life and secular history. These motifs can, of course, be interpreted, modified, and combined in various ways, with emphasis put in quite different places. Modern theology in its own ways incorporates the same three emphases with respect to history and hope that were found in the classical theologians. Protestant thinkers, of course, do not typically identify the Kingdom on earth with the church. However, for them as well the church is a special focus of the reign of God, at least in the sense of being that community which has grasped the true meaning of life and history and which to some extent manifests styles of living appropriate to the Kingdom.

Modern theology has given up the notion of a sudden, supernatural intervention by which history will be literally ended. Rather such symbols as the second coming, the last judgment, and the resurrection of the body have been dismissed as crude and primitive or reinterpreted in symbolic terms. However, the idea that history will be fulfilled beyond this life and this earth is a prominent feature of most theologies in the 19th and 20th centuries. Liberalism tended to see immortality and the social hope beyond history in continuity with earthly life, i.e., in terms of continuing growth toward perfection on a higher plane. Neo-orthodoxy retained more of the dualism characteristic of apocalypticism in seeing a sharp contrast between the moral ambiguities of history and the perfected order of life beyond history. Eschatological and liberation theologies are more complex. They agree with liberals that the promised future involves the perfection of worldly history and secular society. Yet they also agree with the neo-orthodox in viewing every present as sin-dominated and full of oppression. The resurrection of the body and life everlasting remain for nearly all theologies as the ultimate referent of Christian hope.

The transformation of history is central in the "social gospel" liberalism of Walter Rauschenbusch, in the "social realism" of Reinhold Niebuhr, and in the hope for worldly liberation found in contemporary eschatological theologies. It is true, of course, that some neo-orthodox theologies (Karl Löwith, Rudolf Bultmann, and early Karl Barth, e.g.) in the wake of the massive historical evils of the 20th century not only gave up the theory of progress but abandoned any significant hope for a redemption of the structures of secular society. Taking a more balanced view, Reinhold Niebuhr saw the perils growing equally with the promises of history and hence rejected the modern version of progress. Yet he asserted that "indeterminate possibilities of good" came with every future, though sin might corrupt them all.

(2) PROCESS OF THOUGHT. In every generation, including the history of Israel which produced the Bible, the content of hope has arisen out of a dialectical engagement of the logic of faith and the logic of experience. By the logic of faith is meant those beliefs about the future and ultimate matters which are current in the community and in the individual

at a given time. These ideas have changed from age to age, as this survey has noted. In the Bible itself different expectations arose as the faith of Israel developed over the centuries. The same process has continued, with a special reworking of the tradition in modern times. By the logic of experience is meant the interpretation of what is happening and of what is needed and possible in a particular situation. Hope must be relevant to experience. Experience produces a set of yearnings and desired resolutions which con-tradict the oppressiveness of the present. Specific hopes and doctrines of hope are created by the interac-tion of faith and experience. The logic of faith leads to a horizon of hopeful possibilities generated by the faith of the community. The logic of experience creates the felt needs and dreams which hope must address. This dialectical engagement occurs in every generation and in every theologian. Hence, doctrinal systems must be judged in part by the effectiveness with which authentic notes of the universal Gospel are made pertinent to the particular context in which they arise and to which they speak.

Liberal theologies united the Biblical hope for the coming of the Kingdom of God on earth with the belief in social progress which reigned in the 19th century. Faith and experiences seemed mutually confirmed in this rendering of historical expectation. The 20th century brought changes in both theological interpretation and global context. A rediscovery of Biblical realism about humanity and the centrality of the apocalyptic framework of New Testament thought contributed to revised estimates of what was possible and likely in history, given the reality of Hitler and the Bomb as symbols of the depths of human evil. Classical themes about history, the sinfulness of humanity, the moral ambiguity of history, and the relevance of apocalypticism to life here and now were introduced in connection with a new appreciation of Augustine, Luther, and Calvin. Contemporary liberation theologies in their several varieties arise out of the experience of oppression and create a horizon of expectation in which emancipation from every form of social and spiritual bondage becomes the central element of Christian hope. Basic to these perspectives is the claim that the divine promise of a good future to the downtrodden is the key to unlocking the Biblical view of life and history. The result is a "theology from below" or from "the underside of history" which is critical of established theologies as ideologies of the ruling class which are complacent in the face of the oppression of those who are experientially and often visibly hidden from the privileged. The experiential base of liberation thought in the suffering of the outcasts provides the setting in which the logic of faith and the logic of experience are once again seen as mutually supporting grounds of Christian hope.

Underlying both the pattern of thought and the process of thought is something fundamental to both -- a basic life-stance of hope. Hope in Christian thought has a double grounding. One source is the conception of God as Purposive Good Will. The aim of God is to create and perfect a cosmos and a people. Hence, creation is goal-oriented. The other source is the freedom and creativity of humanity. Human beings are capable of envisioning and actualizing possibility. We can become or achieve what now we only potentially are. Possibility, however, is ambiguous. There are possibilities of fulfillment and possibilities of destruction, of salvation and damnation. Heaven and hell are symbols of the ultimate and absolute polarities toward which and between which we move. This is why our finite existence is experienced as anxiety. We can imagine possibilities of good that we cannot with certainty attain. We can imagine possibilities of evil that we cannot with certainty avoid. The anxiety of uncertainty can be converted into the confidence of salvation, or it can be converted into the dread of damnation. Actual life is ambiguous, a mixture of fulfillment and frustration. It is in this context that the idea and possibility of an ultimate, complete, and final fulfillment arises. In this framework hope arises as confidence in the goodness and power of a Sovereign Will whose aim is to bring history at last to an End in which the potentialities of the creature and of creation are brought to complete fulfillment.

Hope always hopes for fulfillment, though the form and content may vary with circumstances and possibilities as determined by the interaction of faith with experience. Fulfillment may take three forms. (1) The first can be described as the transcendence of the immediate and the actual. The world and life remain for the time being what they factually are, but they are spiritually transcended. a) There is the fulfillment of the self-transcending moment. By this is meant a transient and occasional rising above the structures of actuality in which the joy of loving union with God and with all creation is experienced in a moment of mystical ecstasy. The ordinary world does not cease to be, and we must return from "the mountain top experience" to the reality of brute, stubborn fact. But for the occasion

the world is overcome. b) Believers can experience
blessedness in the midst of suffering. This is a more
continuous and steady transcendence of actuality which
provides a victory in the midst of "peril, famine, and
sword" (Rom. 8:31-19, 5:1-5; Matt. 5:1-11).

(2) The second type can be described as the
fulfillment of growth, development, and achievement in
individual and communal life. a) This may refer to the
fulfillment of given potential. An individual acorn may
become an oak tree. A baby may grow up to become a
healthy, fully functioning, adult. In given situations
justice may be done, love may be experienced, and
happiness may become real. b) Novel forms of
fulfillment may be created. There appears to be an
upward, forward thrust in nature and history which
brings the new, the different, and sometimes the better
into being. Emergent evolution over billions of years
has produced species of life on earth never seen before.
New structures of justice may be created in novel social
arrangements. Tyranny and oppression may be replaced
with democracy and equality. These achievements are
partial, ambiguous, always subject to corruption, but
nevertheless real. Life can be transformed. Its
potentialities can be fulfilled to an indeterminate
degree. But failure also is real. Moreover, in the end
we all die. Hence, hope always reaches for a final and
complete triumph beyond the present realm of earth and
human history.

(3) The third form may be described as the
fulfillment of transcendent perfection. Beyond the
occasional and the transient, beyond the spiritual
triumph over actual conditions here and now, and beyond

the partial, ambiguous achievements and transformations
of life in historical fulfillment -- beyond all this is
the hope of ultimate, final, and complete redemption.
The new heaven and the new earth await in which there is
no more pain, no more dying, no more injustice, no more
seeing though a glass darkly (Rev. 21-22). This is the
consummated Kingdom of God in the mysterious beyond in
which a union of all with all and with God is
experienced in unrestrained, unambiguous joy. The final
hope is that ultimately all enemies will be put down,
and God will reign absolutely and for evermore (I Cor.
15:24-28).

Part of the task of Christian theology is
discernment, i.e., a sensitivity to the form of Christian fulfillment that is fitting in given situations.
Sometimes the positive potentialities of life can be
actualized. Often they cannot. At times the actualities of life and history can be transformed in the
direction of the new and the better, but frequently only
spiritually transcended. The ordinary believer and the
theologian have the task of discerning when and where
hope is to hope for what. But the constant in Christian
thought and experience is hope itself.

This chapter concludes the survey of the major
topics of Christian doctrine. The concluding chapter
will take a look at the present state and future
prospects of the theological enterprise.

CHAPTER VII
THE PRESENT AND FUTURE OF THEOLOGY

Where does the theological enterprise stand now? What are the trends and future prospects of Christian thinking? This concluding chapter will offer a glimpse at today and some hunches about tomorrow. As attention is shifted from the present to the future, the tone will become less descriptive and more subjective, conjectural, and controversial.

I. The Recent Past and Present

By mid-century two major responses to the challenge of the modern world had appeared -- liberalism and neo-orthodoxy. Liberalism had attempted to reconstruct the Christian message in order to come to terms with the new mentality that had arisen in the West since the Reformation. Neo-orthodoxy shifted the attention away from the situation toward the recovery of essential elements in the message that liberalism had obscured. However, it was the new appreciation of the authority of Scripture and of themes prominent in Augustine, Luther, and Calvin that were thought to be most relevant to a culture whose foundations had been shaken by the catastrophes of the 20th century. In the 1950's Walter Marshall Horton could set forth the consensus that had been reached in a broad-based ecumenical theology with neo-orthodox accents.[1] The first thing to be said about the present situation in theology is that no such consensus exists in the leading intellectual centers of American Protest-

antism today. Neither are there any giants with the
commanding stature of Karl Barth, Emil Brunner, Rudolf
Bultmann, William Temple, and the Niebuhr brothers --
Reinhold and H. Richard.

In describing the recent past and present of
American theology, it will be helpful to speak first of
internal developments and then of influences from
overseas. In this country since about 1960 a shift has
occurred away from neo-orthodoxy. A major characteristic of the last quarter of a century has been the stress
upon experience and the cultural situation as the
starting point of theological reflection. This can be
spelled out by noting a difference between those perspectives which begin with some aspect of experience or
human experience in general, on the one hand, and those
that start with the experience of a particular group, on
the other hand.

1. Secular Theology: The hottest thing in
American theology in the 1960's was secular theology.
This grew out of renewed efforts to come to terms with
the scientific, pragmatic, secularized consciousness
that had made belief in God problematic for many people.
Dietrich Bonhoeffer wrote from prison before he was
martyred by the Nazis for attempting to kill Hitler that
people have "learned to cope with all questions of
importance without recourse to God."[2] His phrases were
heard everywhere -- "worldly Christianity," "non-
religious interpretation of the Bible," "God moved to
the edges of life," "living before God without God," and
so on. THE SECULAR CITY by Harvey Cox[3] and HONEST TO
GOD by John Robinson[4] popularized the themes of secular
Christianity. With respect to the doctrine of God,

which had come to the center of attention, two responses can be noted. The moderate view was represented by John Cobb,[5] Schubert Ogden,[6] Langdon Gilkey,[7] and others who tried to show that belief in a revised conception of God was an intelligent option for modern people. The radical view was represented by a small minority who proclaimed "the death of God." William Hamilton, Paul van Buren, and Thomas Altizer got considerable attention for a few years by arguing that Christianity must be reinterpreted without God for a "world come of age."[8]

2. Dionysian theology: In the latter part of the decade some theologians exulted in the need for festivity, joy, and celebration. The body was appreciated as a locus of the sacred and a channel of divine grace. Theologies of play appeared. The quest for ecstasy was extolled. Dancing, feasting, fantasy and riotous letting go were encouraged as the path to an expanded consciousness. Grace is carnal, perhaps Jesus was a harlequin, and theology must be visceral. Dionysus is not the enemy of Yahweh, said Harvey Cox[9] and Sam Keen.[10]

3. Ecological theology: The threats of population growth, the exhaustion of resources, and environmental pollution evoked a call for a new theology of nature. The over emphasis on history in much theology was criticized. An ethics of frugality was advocated. Many theologians were troubled by Lynn White's thesis that Christianity was in part responsible for the ecological crisis by robbing nature of spirit, so that the non-human world could become an object of manipulation and exploitation.[11] The response was an attempt to develop a theology of nature and of life that was Biblical and that led toward ecological sanity.[12]

4. Black Theology: The civil rights movement led by Martin Luther King, Jr. and others in the 1950's and 1960's was the occasion of considerable gains for black people in this country. Toward the middle 1960's appeals were heard in the black power movement for blacks to assume more autonomy, to become less dependent on white leadership, and to become more militant. In theology this took the form of a call for theology done by and for blacks and directed toward their full emancipation from all white oppression in every form. James Cone maintained that black theology was necessary because no white theologian had ever made black suffering the starting point for theological reflection.[13] The early stages of the movement included a debate as to whether liberation should be the primary theme for the moment (Cone) or whether liberation from oppression and reconciliation with whites should be stressed together (Deotis Roberts).[14]

5. Feminist Theology: Along with the civil rights movement focused on racial minorities, the women's movement emerged dedicated to the achievement of full equality between the sexes. Feminist theologians began to expose the patriarchal bias in the Bible, in Christian theology through the centuries, and in the church. A thoroughgoing reconstruction was called for in language, thought, and practice which would wipe out every vestige of sexism in church and society. A debate early ensued among feminists as to whether the tradition could be salvaged by the discovery of a usable past in Scripture and tradition that was equalitarian or whether

theology and church are so thoroughly corrupted by male bias as to be beyond recovery. Rosemary Radford Ruether became the leader of the moderates who wanted to be both feminists and Christians,[15] while Mary Daly in time led a minority into exodus from church and Biblical faith.[16]

Two other theological movements also point to human experience as a starting point for theology. However, the emphasis in both cases is not so much an aspect of experience or the experience of a particular group but common human experience in its more universal aspects. These distinctions are real but relative.

6. Revisionist Theology: David Tracy has given the name revisionist theologies to a number of outlooks on the contemporary scene which share some common methodological assumptions. Apart from their methodological unity, they differ considerably among themselves. They begin with common human exeriences (anxiety, death, the quest for meaning, the search for scientific knowledge, or the affirmation of moral values, etc.) and seek to discover clues to the ultimate questions, including God. These conclusions are then related to truth claims which arise in Christian experience as interpreted by the Bible and tradition.[17]

7. Process Theology: Theologies influenced by the philosophy of Alfred North Whitehead are both a major subtype of revisionism and an independent way of doing theology. Process thinkers quote approvingly the dictum of Whitehead that the sole justification of any thought whatsoever is immediate experience. On "this" basis a metaphysical vision is elaborated which sees reality as an organic process of life-events lured toward complex

harmonies by a Persuasive Purpose which is the source of
both order and novelty in all things. This philosophical world-view is then united with Christian understandings of God, humanity, Christ, history, and
eschatology.[18]

No survey of present-day American Protestantism
would be complete without mention of a wide variety of
conservative theologies, especially the more recent
forms of evangelical thought. Evangelicals may now in
fact constitute the mainline Protestant establishment in
the United States. These movements are so diversified
in doctrine, mood, attitude, aim, and social-ethical
outlook that any brief description will be incomplete if
not misleading.[19] Moreover, each decade or so on this
side of the spectrum is different, as is the case also
with non-conservative thought. The focus here will be
on the 70's and 80's. For purposes of this brief examination, three forms of conservative thought will be
outlined in full recognition that an adequate presentation would require much more careful delineation of the
subgroups within the larger whole. The three types
described here in general terms constitute the right,
the broad center, and the newly emerging left among
conservative theologies.

8. Fundamentalist Theology: This group itself is
internally diverse with many overlappings of outlook and
attitude. a. On the far right are several groups of
militant separatists who still carry on the old battles
against modernist theology, evolutionary science, higher
criticism, and the like, based on a verbally inspired
Bible, dictated by God and thus free from all error of
any kind. They typically employ a strict list of

doctrinal "fundamentals" to identify the true believers.[20]

b. Nearby are the new right fundamentalists with a reactionary public agenda represented by Jerry Falwell and some of the TV evangelists. Also insisting on an infallible Bible, this movement has grown in protest against what are regarded as ungodly trends in American life. Secular humanism in the schools, pornography, legalized abortion, sexual promiscuity, divorce, homosexuality, left-leaning politics soft on Communism, etc. are undermining the moral foundations of the nation. Right=wing theology and right=wing politics unite in this many-sided resurgence of Protestant conservatism.[21]

9. <u>Main-Line</u> <u>Evangelical</u> <u>Theology</u>. In the 1940's and 1950's a group of conservatives emerged who were impatient with the separatism, militant bad temper, and intellectual obscurantism of the fundamentalists. They were also critical of their lack of attention to social ethics and of their narrow and superficial views of personal morality. The Christian life is more than avoiding the vices of smoking, drinking, dancing, card-playing, theatre-going, and the like. And it is more than being upright, honest, and fair in one to one relationships, i.e., more than obedience to a set of conservative cultural mores. The new conservatives called themselves evangelicals and were eager to differentiate their views from those of the fundamentalists. They are more moderate in tone and outlook, more intent on defining their terms and grounding their thought in sound scholarship and precise thinking. Nevertheless, Biblical inerrancy when properly understood is still central to their understanding of authority. Early

theological leaders were Carl F.H. Henry, Bernard Ramm, and E.J. Carnell.[22] Henry has recently set forth a scholarly form of Protestant orthodoxy in learned conversation with leading intellectual currents of the age.[23] Some theologians in this group are cautiously and critically open to moderate forms of historical criticism and to guarded theistic interpretations of biological evolution. Carnell was further from the fundamentalists than Henry, and Ramm today is perhaps better listed with the left wing than with the center. The magazine CHRISTIANITY TODAY and evangelist Billy Graham, along with Henry, are representative of main-stream evangelicalism at the present.

10. The New Evangelical Theology: The term "new" has been applied to both the center and to the left wing of evangelicalism. The aim here is to describe what Richard Quebedeaux has called "the young" or "worldly evangelicals," an emerging group who are often in conflict with the center and thoroughly in opposition to the far right fundamentalists.[24] Just as what are now the main-line evangelicals broke with the fundamentalists on the right in the 1940's, so in the 1970's and 1980's a new movement has developed on the left that in its far reaches begins to make touch with neo-orthodox and post-neo-orthodox tendencies in the liberal wing of American Protestantism. Young, upwardly mobile, highly educated evangelicals have moved into the mainstream of American life. They have become more intellectual, sophisticated, and thus receptive to more "liberal" social attitudes and interests. This may include tendencies toward sexual permissiveness and tolerance if not acceptance of homosexuality. Theologically, they display an openness toscience, biblical

criticism, and modifications in the notion of Biblical infallibility. A doctrine of "limited inerrancy" is taught at Fuller Theological Seminary, which means that the Bible is infallible on matters of doctrine and ethics but not necessarily in all areas of historical or scientific fact. Paul Jewett has even taught that the Apostle Paul was wrong on some things relating to women.[25]

Virginia Ramey Mollenkott and others havedeveloped a biblical feminism which recognizes that some of the sexist passages in the New Testament are culturally bound and not universally normative.[26]

The new evangelical left shatters the usual associations of Protestant orthodoxy with conservative politics. Approaching theology and ethics with a high view of Biblical authority, "worldly evangelicals" are often found on the more liberal or radical side of many social issues, especially those having to do with peace, poverty, American foreign policy, women's liberation, the environment, rights of racial and sexual minorities, and so on. Especially in the social-ethical wing of the movement, many of the theological concerns overlap or coincide with those prominent in black, feminist, and third world theologies of liberation. SOJOURNERS, a monthly magazine, illustrates the ecumenical attraction of this Bible-centered approach to life and thought, evangelical in theology but radical in life-styles and political orientation.

It is clear that currents of thought flowing in American theology during the last quarter of a century are, in part, religious expressions of one or another of the various movements and moods within the general culture. The new mood of optimism that temporarily accompanied John F. Kennedy into the presidency, the civil rights movement, the counter-culture movement, the black power movement, the environmental movement, the women's movement and the general secular mood all found adherents and theorists in the church as well as in society. No one theological expression has achieved the dominance and wide following attained by liberalism and neo-orthodoxy in earlier decades of the century. Instead, what we find is a variety of probes and projects exploring many themes, some of which attracted brief attention among scattered audiences. Black and feminist theologies, however, are prominent though not dominant and are still in the midst of their creative phase. Likewise, revisionist and process theologies are widespread and influential. The latter two continue to work with the issues that gave rise to secular theologies twenty-five years ago. These concerns in one form or another, of course, define the central question of the last two hundred years -- the compatibility of Christianty with the modern mind. Meanwhile, the left-wing evangelicals have also responded positively to some of the same cultural influences, while the new reaction-ionaries among fundamentalists and some moderate evangelicals have protested against these same social currents and made alliance with conservative political movements centered around the rise of Ronald Reagan.

Theological reflection does not take place simply within national boundaries. American theology has been influenced during its entire history by modes of thought from Europe. That continues to be the case, but developments in other places are playing a greater role than before. Two movements from outside the United States have been of special significance in recent years -- eschatological theology and liberation theology.

11. Eschatological Theology: The key thinkers here are Wolfhart Pannenberg[27] and Jürgen Moltmann.[28] Both make eschatology the key to theology as a whole. All concepts and symbols are reinterpreted in the light of God's promise to perfect history at the End. Human beings are understood in terms of their openness to the future as creative beings with unfulfilled potential. The resurrection of Jesus is the proleptic disclosure of what is to be -- the first-fruit of the coming fullness of the Kingdom. The Gospel is the proclamation of the promise of God to perfect the world, accompanied by a call to faith by which life is lived by hope and joyful anticipation. God is ahead not above or behind us. The God who is coming acts from the future to redeem everything at last. Theology speaks of God historically and of history eschatologically, since it is only at the End that the meaning of the past and present is known.

12. Liberation Theology: While feminist and black theologies arising in this country give their own specific accents to the idea of the Gospel as freedom from bondage, developments in Latin America especially, and to a lesser extent Africa and Asia, have reinforced and enriched this motif. Third world theologies, however, focus on poverty and economic domination associated with class rather than sex or race. Liberation theologies of all sorts arise out of and speak to some situation of oppression and interpret the good news as release into the liberty of the children of

God. Liberation becomes the key to the reinterpretation of all Christian symbols and concepts. The Almighty Creator is the God of the oppressed: Christ is the Word and Deed of God's liberating action. History is seen from the bottom as the wretched of the earth view it. The Exodus from Egypt becomes the paradigm of God's saving action, which is always partial to the poor, the outcasts, and the down-trodden. The Gospel is primarily for those who have been left out and comes as a promise of liberation by which the weak, the despised, and the rejected are set free to inherit the blessedness of the coming Kingdom.[29]

It is important to note that eschatological and liberation theologies frequently annunciate similar themes and thus in those respects are mutually reinforcing. Moltmann in particular has influenced Latin American as well as North American theologians. The themes of hope and liberation, indeed, have become the leaven in the loaf of a wide variety of contemporary theologies. Catholics and Protestants, liberals and evangelicals, process thinkers and revisionists, who otherwise may differ widely, all speak appreciatively of eschatological and liberation motifs, even though they may have reservations about the theologies based centrally upon them. Liberation themes focused on the women and the poor, on issues of justice for racial minorities and cultural outcasts, and on global problems of poverty, peace, and political oppression frequently unite ecumenical groupings made up of evangelical and liberal Protestants as well as liberal Catholics. This loose coalition stands in opposition to political and culture status quo or reationary Christians who may also be either Protestant or Catholic in ecclesiastical identification and either liberal, conservative, or fundamentalist in theological outlook.[30]

In summary, the last quarter of a century has seen an astonishing variety of outlooks and moods, ranging all the way from right-wing fundamentalists who see the Bible as an error-free source of doctrine to the radical or death of God theologians who proclaim the end of theism. Somebody can be found representing nearly every point on the continuum between these extreme polarities.

II The Present and Near Future

Another way to come to an understanding of the present situation and probable future of theology is to recognize that forty years ago most of the creative thinking was being done in the leading intellectual centers in Europe and the United States and then imported around the world. While it would not have been thought about that way in those days, the most prominent thinkers in Protestantism were white males with Northern European backgrounds. Today that situation is very different as a result of globalization, indigenization, and contextualization. Women and blacks in this country plus third world thinkers from around the globe are making major contributions to Christian thinking, along with white males from Europe and America. The central factor in all of this is that many groups and nationalities which previously had more or less received passively the work of the establishment theologians now insist that theological thinking must be contextual. It must proceed from the situation of some particular group in a self-conscious way. Theology has always been written from a given context, but the unspoken assumption generally was that some context could be taken as normative for the rest. Nineteenth century thinkers made us conscious of the fact that dominant cultural and intellectual motifs molded theological thought in every epoch and location. Liberation theologies have made us more conscious than we were that nationality, race, sex, and class also relativize theology. Western, European, and American modes of thinking exhibited by established intellectual and cultural groups are not normative for all Christians, especially those whose socio-historical situations differ from the dominating ones. In particular, liberation theologies have maintained that the most important differences in theology may not be those between Protestants and Catholics or between liberals and conservatives but those between points of view favorable to the ruling classes and theologies that speak for the oppressed.

A. TRENDS AND CONCERNS. Against this background three areas of concern can be enumerated which enter into the shaping of the present and emerging future of theology.

1. Liberation Theology: The single most important theme in theology today on a world-wide scale is liberation. That motif will likely continue to be influential for an indefinite future.[31] Asian, African, and Latin American theologians are increasingly being read by Americans and are contributing to the rich mix already present as blacks and women add their own interpretations of liberation. It may not be too much to suggest that in the long run the most lasting and

beneficial result of liberation thinking will be the demand for equality of consideration. No particular perspective can be universally normative. No group, race, class, or sex has a privileged standing before God or unique insight into the Gospel. Only when all are heard and contrasting perspectives both limit and enrich each other is the fullest grasp of the total truth likely to emerge.

Theologies developed around the central theme of liberation from the point of view of the poor, the weak, and the oppressed will make a permanent and powerful contribution to the ongoing theological enterprise. But in due time the limits of this outlook will also come more to the forefront. Liberation alone cannot contain the whole truth of God for the world. The contrast between the oppressed and the oppressors does not take into account all human realities and relationships. There are significant areas of life that may involve human beings as non-oppressed non-oppressors though, of course, not always. Husbands and wives, parents and children, brothers and sisters, pastors and parishioners, Democrats and Republicans, pro-choice and pro-life proponents, the USA and the USSR, the President and the Congress, employers and employees -- all these and many more pairings could be listed where liberation may not be the best key to justice and fulfillment of life. In any estranged relationship among more or less equals -- whether the parties be individuals, groups, races, or nations -- reconciliation, for example, may be the more pertinent theme.

Moreover, the stress in liberation theologies on the meaning of the Gospel for certain specified groups

-- whether black, female, poor, and so on -- may obscure the commonalities which all human beings share and to which the Gospel speaks. Sin, sickness, tragedy, anxiety, accident, pain, suffering, and death suggest but do not exhaust the perils from which all need deliverance. There is a relative distinction between the particularities of somebody's experience and the universalities of everybody's experience which may define the focal point of a given theology. But the interaction between both perspectives is needed to correct and enrich the other. Liberation theologies by stressing the former may neglect the latter. To put it differently, God is not only the Liberator of the oppressed but the Creator of the whole world and the Redeemer of every phase of life. The problems of bioethics, ecology, technology, and of freedom of expression in the artistic and cultural arena, for example, may include dimensions which relate to the oppression of some by others, but the dominance/subordination elements do not exhaust these social realities. If liberation theologies do not finally speak of the whole Gospel of God for all people in the whole of life, then other correcting and complementary theologies must.

2. <u>Christianity</u> <u>and</u> <u>other</u> <u>Religions</u>: Today in many quarters an attempt is being made to remain loyal to Christ and yet accept other world faiths, especially Buddhism, on an equal basis. The dominant notes in the most creative work being done today in this area are indicated by the terms dialectical engagement, complementarity, and pluralism. The first term implies that if Christian norms are used to judge other religions, then Christianity must subject itself to an equally

searching judgment by Buddhist standards. Complementarity refers to a pattern in which one truth is seen as
completing and being completed by another. An analogy
must be the complementarity of the right and left hemis-
pheres of the brain. Eastern and Western religions are
seen not as opposites but as apposites. They have a
mutual fittingness in which one requires the other for
its completion. Pluralism recognizes that the Infinite
Other may be experienced in many different, culturally
relative ways. The future is likely to produce an
unpredictable degree of convergence in thought and
practice in a context of mutual respect.

In a previous generation Paul Tillich established a
polarity of logical types which allowed him to view the
dialectical relationship between Christianity and
Buddhism. All religions arise out of the experience of
the holy in some person, event, or thing. But this
primordial encounter takes two directions: the mystical
and the ethical. The former is the pattern taken by
Indian-born religions, while the latter is the way of
Israel. Likewise, the aim of existence takes a
dialectical form in the two religions: "in Christianity
the telos of every<u>one</u> and everything united in the
Kingdom of God; in Buddhism the telos of every<u>thing</u> and
everyone fulfilled in Nirvana."32

On the current scene Peter Berger follows a similar
pattern of ideal types. He contrasts two forms of
religious experience. In the first the divine is
confronted as a personal revealer and redeemer. This is
characteristic of the religions of Western Asia --
Judaism, Christianity, and Islam. In the second the
divine is experienced as the deepest ground of interior

consciousness. This is characteristic of Eastern Asian religions -- Hinduism and Buddhism. God confronted from beyond the self or ultimacy experienced at the depths of mystical consciousness -- these are the two poles. Berger asks whether it is possible that both may be valid and whether each experience might be a prelude or a stepping stone toward the complementary way of experiencing ultimacy.[33]

A different option can be found in the thought of John Cobb. Here the fullness of religious truth is seen, not as lying in the past in one of the many historic traditions nor in a complementary joining of dialectical opposites in the present, but as still to be discovered in the future. This possibility views the world religions as stages along the way to some final and ultimate wholeness of truth which may differ markedly from any historic tradition in its present stage of development. The way forward toward this goal is through a process of creative mutual transformation whereby now separate traditions may contribute something toward a fuller truth which may be different from anything we presently know. Cobb is a process theologian who believes that the convergence of Buddhism and Christianity toward a higher and more comprehensive truth can be especially fruitful if the philosophy of Alfred North Whitehead is used as a guide. The Whiteheadian vision denies the truth of substance philosophies and provides a view of the self and the world in event-processive terms which may be congenial with Buddhist conceptions.[34]

Finally, the views of John Hick may be brought within this general orientation. He urges a Copernican revolution whereby Christianity and/or Jesus are no longer in the center of the religious universe but God. Within this framework the world religions may be seen as different but valid human responses to one Transcendent Reality in which different perceptions of the divine reflect a variety of cultural and historical factors. Let us move, he urges, toward a global theology in the context of a world ecumenism in which the historic religions will view each other as cooperating Christian denominations in Britain now see each other, i.e., as representing different but overlapping perspectives on one transcending truth and reality. Hick does not anticipate one world religion with an agreed upon theology. He frankly accepts religious pluralism on a global scale, though it would not be unreasonable to expect some convergence on common themes amidst continuing differences of belief and practice.[35]

As productive as these conversations may be of new insights, it is not at all certain that they can provide a resolution of an old dilemma. Christ brought a particular message to the world containing some claims about God, life, and human destiny. Presumably these convictions cannot be transformed, synthesized, or abandoned for new beliefs beyond a certain point without violating the integrity of the original revelation to which the New Testament gives authoritative witness. While the gain may be a new and even deeper truth, can it be possessed without relinquishing loyalty to Christ? Unless there is some identifiable commonality underlying Christianity and Buddhism, the possibilities for reconciliation and synthesis would seem to be limited. Even the theme of complementarity carries with it the admission that not all the truth about ultimate matters is given in Christ -- a concession which pluralism clearly implies. It is the old dilemma, the old tension, between particularity and universality. If some particular claims of the Gospel are true, then those which assert the contrary are not. But if there is one ultimate reality, surely there must be one truth which prevails universally. Yet to claim that truth for Christ is once again to run the risk of the old imperalism and absolutism. If there is a universal truth beyond Jesus and the Buddha, then Christianity seems but a step along the way toward higher things. But that is certainly not what most Christians have believed or possibly can believe without relativising Christ, who then could hardly be called the very Word of God, Agent of creation, God made flesh.

3. Theology in a Planetary Society: A final factor shaping the future of theology is the continuing problem of coming to terms with the modern world. For three hundred years theology has wrestled with new ways of understanding nature, history, and human existence growing out of science, the historical consciousness, and a wide range of modern philosophical outlooks. Every previous chapter in this book has spelled out both the challenge and the response in considerable detail. While it cannot be said that all the problems raised by modern consciousness have been resolved, the sting has been taken out of them by two centuries of creative theological reflection. Moreover, the confidence that once attended a rising secularism has been chastened by the course of history as well as by the recognition that the modern mind is another stage in the human quest, itself relative to time and place, not the possessor of the final truth about all things. Science, the ring

leader in it all, no longer seems to require either the death of freedom, God, and immortality or a dualism by which values are humanly created and subjectively introduced into a world of neutral facts. Nevertheless, from the perspective of modern theology, the old orthodoxy is as dead as the old science. Moreover, relating the claims of faith to the findings of science and to contemporary cultural views of reality and values is a necessary part of any credible and relevant theology in the years to come as well as in the centuries past.

However, new challenges from the present and future may be equally or even more formidable. A few paragraphs cannot delineate the threats and promises with which theology must now deal. Suffice it to say that it may lie in part at the very point at which a previous era located its hope, namely, science and technology. Simply consider as evidence the threats of nuclear destruction and ecological disaster plus the potential threats that may lie in all the other strange and wonderful powers the scientific-technological giant may put in the hands of moral midgets. Beyond that are the perennial problems of the struggle for power among competing groups and the domination of the weak by the powerful, whether in the local church or at the global level involving the nation-states. These issues of survival, justice, peace, and of finding a meaningful, satisfying existence are set within the growing reality of a planetary society in which all the peoples of the earth are caught up in an interdependent if not converging destiny. Given these challenges, theologians might well be excused for expressing a preference for dealing with the old issues raised by science and historical criticism rather than to face the monster perils that lie ahead. Yet the promises of the future are equally astounding if, if the conditions for their realization can be met and folly avoided.[36]

The world is undergoing a major transition toward a planetary society while we approach the biological limits of the earth in terms of population, production of life's necessities, and pollution. This transition also takes place while the superpowers do not know how to live together without threatening to engulf the world in a nuclear holocaust. Some mad tyrant of a small and desperate nation may in time threaten nuclear blackmail or deliberately try to provoke war between the larger powers. Conventional wars, revolutions, terrorism, and civil strife continue to frustrate the yearning for peace. The masses of the wretched of the earth still wait for prosperity and justice. Spaceship Earth has become the potent symbol of this vulnerable planet in its quest for a just, sustainable, and good future for all. Humanity faces a set of problems that are unprecedented in number, magnitude, and importance for the future of life on this globe. No theology of the next quarter of a century can be adequate which does not center upon or at least take into account the global convulsions through which the human race is passing as the most inclusive context in which the creating, judging, and redeeming activity of God is manifesting itself.

The future will require a closer union between theology and ethics. While the intellectual challenge is still fundamental, the basic issues may be those posed by a science-based technology. The conversation partner in this case will be not only philosophy but also the scientific-technological disciplines and the social sciences plus ecology. The world is being organized as a diverse but interdependent economic-political unity based on scientific technologies. The organizing paradigm for a credible and relevant theology/ethics may not be metaphysics or history but biopolitics[37] or ecological-political economics -- a union of disciplines concerned with survival, justice, prosperity, and meaningful living in a planetary setting.

The eschatological theologies prominent today (Pannenberg, Moltmann, e.g.) need to be balanced by creation centered theologies which inquire into the purpose of God embodied in the cosmos and in the evolution of life. Biology and ecology as well as economics, sociology, and politics can contribute to this enterprise. Cosmic as well as historical questions are combined in this effort. A theological perspective capable of rising to this challenge could be based on the process philosophy of Alfred North Whitehead.[38]

In the long run liberation theologies concerned about the poor and the oppressed will need to connect their themes to careful biopolitical or ecological analysis as well as to social inquiries. For third world settings Marxism may be a necessary but not a sufficient resource. Moreover, theologians concerned with emancipating the masses of the poor in underdeveloped countries might do well to give attention to the potential virtues of democratically controlled market economies in generating wealth in an equalitarian context liberated from the dominating tyranny of aristocratic elites. Moreover, while much poverty is the result of injustice and oppression, not all is. Hence, attention must be given to those positive factors which generate prosperity, as well as to those which lead to democratic polities and cultures. Theologies of justice are called for which are more complex, sophisticated, comprehensive, and precise than those based on a simple oppressor-oppressed framework.

B. REFLECTIONS AND CONJECTURES: This survey of the present and future of theology can be concluded with three comments, the first more descriptive and the last two more speculative. 1. Theology in responding to the challenge of the future will continue to deal with some very old problems in new contexts. The methodological issues raised in the first chapter will all rise up again as always. Struggling to state the Christian message for new settings will involve bringing together the universal norm given in Christ with a situational norm arising in culture. In this effort theological programs will run the risk of losing the message by aiming at relevance and of being irrelevant out of concern to preserve the abiding Gospel. It is the old dilemma all over again. Moreover, theology will wrestle once again with the related problem of uniting particularity with universality. This particularity may relate to the aim to speak to a particular group of Christians within the church (the poor, blacks, women, homosexuals, e.g.). Or it may have to do with the specific truth claims of the Christian Gospel in relation to the universal religious needs of the human race in encounter with other historic faiths such as Buddhism. In carrying out these enterprises theology will create a great deal of variety within the unity of the Christian message centered on one Lord, one faith, one baptism.

2.   The ferment generated by the three factors enumerated above -- liberation themes, the conversation with other world religions, and the economic, ecological, political challenges of a planetary society -- will produce forms of theology different from anything the past has seen. We may expect to see in the early 21st century types of theological expression that are as different from the classical Protestantism of the 16th century as those theologies were different from the medieval theologies associated with Anselm and Aquinas. Protestant thought for the last four centuries has been organized around an intellectual Gestalt created by the Protestant Reformers.   Even the liberals who wanted to reconstruct theology in the 19th and 20th centuries did so around the agenda created by Luther and Calvin. Given the new ecumenical settings and the new global challenges of theology, we should not expect that situation to continue indefinitely into the future.   When Karl Barth appeared on the scene at the end of World War I, his Word of God theology was hailed as the beginning of a new age of theological reflection.   For a few decades it was, but in the long run Barth may be seen as representing the end of an old era, not the beginning of a new one.   It should be remembered that the sun is most beautiful just before it sets.

Yet in this country at least, it may be that as non-conservative theologies move on in ecumenical fashion away from Reformation and neo-Reformation theologies (Barthianism, e.g.), the left-wing evangelicals may take them up again in a new setting.   It has already been noted that some of the younger evangelicals are already close to neo-orthodoxy. Barth has become the hero of many, along with Emil Brunner and Reinhold Niebuhr. Outside the United States and Europe, similar unions may take place between evangelical modes of thought implanted by 19th century and 20th century missionaries and modern liberation and/or neo-orthodox theologies. Roman Catholic and Eastern Orthodoxy traditions have their own peculiar pasts and futures. The line between the interests, methods, and themes of Protestant and Catholic theologians may become more blurred. Too much pressure from Rome to resist the march into the ecumenical future of shared global concerns could generate realignments beyond our capacity to imagine at this point. When all these and other elements are added to the mix, as they will be in real life, the future of theology is indeed unpredictable.

3. Despite what has been said about the impossibility of knowing what the form and content of future theologies may turn out to be, one particular element in the shape of things to come may be guessed. We may expect a multiplicity of particular theologies differing much from one another but sharing a common global, ecumenical consciousness. The particularity may be defined in terms of region, culture, group, aim, theme, or audience. African and Asian theologians are already producing theologies expressing the Christian Gospel against the background of the traditional religions and world-views of their own cultures. Feminist theologians will continue to reconstruct theologies freed from partriarchal bias at least until their concerns have become part of the agenda of all. Black theologians will continue to take racism as an organizing principle of a liberating Gospel. White

males may more immediately be able to address directly the ecological-technological-nuclear issues as the center of their concern. Latin American theologians will try to discover the meaning of liberation in a culture that is numerically Christian but in which poverty and autocracy are still too much the rule rather than the exception. Native American theologians, the growing minority concerned with freeing homosexuals from the oppression of past sexual norms and ideologies, and many other groups will work at theological norms and themes relevant to specific interests. Theologians whose concerns are with doctrinal and systematic theology will also be asking what conceptions of God, Christ, Spirit, humanity, and eschatology erected on which philosophical and hermeneutical foundations are appropriate for a planetary society.

Feminist theologies will be faced with some choices. Beyond the critical work of condemning one-sided theologies which exalt males and denigrate females, what is the constructive contribution that can be made by feminists? Beyond the demand for equality in thought and practice in church and society, what else is there to say? This raises a fundamental and as yet unsolved question. Are there psychological, cognitive, experiential, or even ontological correlates of the reproductive functions that distinguish men and women? Are there dimensions of sexuality relevant to doctrines of God and humanity which are identifiable, verifiable, and non-culturally produced? Do men and women think differently, experience differently, know reality differently, function differently as teachers and ministers? And are these differences rooted in biology and not socialization and cultural influences from the past? Is there any truth at all in the notion that "anatomy is destiny"? Can contemporary scientific disciplines help answer these questions in an objective way? Can a study of history and of those religions and cultures that have featured a Goddess or Goddesses contribute anything? Are women theologians and feminist theologians the same? To what extent will theology done by women devote itself to "feminist" concerns and to what extent will they work at the global/ecumenical/ ecological problems that face everyone, including the basic questions of systematic theology that are not sex related (assuming there are any!)? What can men contribute to the common task of finding equalitarian ways of thinking and acting? What does Gen. 1:26-27 imply for the reality of God and for the structure of human personhood? Is it enough to give equal place to feminine and masculine images and to neutralize or equalize pronoun references? Or is there something fundamentally and ontologically masculine about the concept of God in the Bible that is deeper than pronouns and gender related metaphors? Is God conceived of as Transcendent Self, the Sovereign Lord of History, and defined in terms of Purposive Will masculine in some intelligible sense? We do not yet know the full and adequate answers to these questions.

Black theology will face a set of equally challenging questions. Will black suffering continue to be the focal point around which theological concerns are organized? Will such theology, then, be written for and by blacks, others learning from it as they may? Or will "black" become symbolic of all groups in so far as they suffer unjustly -- women, the poor, homosexuals, Native Americans, and the poverty-stricken world-wide? If the latter, will black theologians make central these wider concerns and unite their efforts with other liberation theologians? What forms might such alliances with other liberation theologies take? Or if "black" is retained in the primary sense of a racial designation, will further efforts be made to link theological affirmations to African religions and philosophies, aspects of which are present in black religion in this country? Will attempts be made to locate and develop the connections between the world view of process philosophy and the cosmic outlook of African religions and philosophies? What will be the aim and the norm of such an enterprise? How will global/ecological/ecumenical concerns be factored into whatever forms of black theology persist or develop? What implications for systematic theology might result from any and all of these efforts, relating both to method and content, both to motifs and modes of organizing thought?

White males, likewise, have issues before them. What shall be their distinctive tasks in the years ahead? Should they concentrate on the more traditional questions of systematic theology that may not be in the center of concern for liberation theologies? Should they focus on questions that relate to persons in their roles as non-oppressed non-oppressors? Is their special function to work on questions of justice that involve conflicts between values rather than between groups, although different groups may be involved, as for example in the tension between "affirmative action" and "reverse discrimination"? Should they work on issues related to the universalities of everybody's experience rather than on those which involve the particularities of somebody's experience? Is it their specific responsibility to tackle directly and immediately the ecological/global concerns on the horizon and those which arise out of the impact of science and technology of human life, e.g., the possible long term impact of the use of robots and computers on employment, as well as the whole range of bioethical and biopolitical questions? And how can they both respond and contribute to the issues being raised by feminist and black theologies? How can they be open to them non-defensively and receive them as prophetic critiques of white male theologies and yet be responsibly critical of possible excesses or doubtful claims when they appear in liberation thought? (It should be noted for the record that one can be a white male and still be poor, oppressed, or among the outcasts in some roles at least.)

These questions are in part speculative, and they may not all be the right ones. Moreover, most of them are already being investigated. They are intended to be provocative and exploratory, not definitive. New directions may emerge which have not yet entered the minds of anyone. Assuming that these questions are plausible, they serve to illustrate the point that there are particular agendas which specific groups will need to work on in the future. At the same time the best of them will be done in the context of an acute ecumenical and global consciousness. Local agendas will be worked on surrounded by an awareness of the larger, even world-wide, currents of thought in the church and society. Specialized theological concerns directed to a specific audience will be integrated with a global-ecumenical consciousness aware of the perils and promises which are increasingly shared by enlarging networks of people.

All theologies, no matter how particular in aim, need to take into account the planetary implications of possible nuclear and/or ecological disaster as the common lot of all. The biblical principle that we are members one of another has a new and global reference in which the neighbor is not simply next door but a continent away. Can it be otherwise when the whole earth is becoming one economic marketplace organized by multinational corporations whose incomes exceed the budgets of most nations, when missiles on one continent can destroy cities in another, when communication satellites carry messages around the world at the speed of light, when the burning of fossil fuels plus the addition of other toxic substances to the atmosphere could eventually alter the global climate, when nuclear war could bring on a "nuclear winter" involving equally devasting world-wide consequences, and when global interdependence is growing in all sorts of other ways? Whether the countertrends suggested by the revival of Islamic fundamentalism in some parts of the world is _the_ or _a_ wave of the future or just the last gasp of resistance to the triumph of modernity, no one knows for sure. And it may be both/and instead of either/or.

When theologies are both agenda/audience-specific and globally/ecumenically-conscious, the results are unpredictable. In this situation is it possible for a new Schleiermacher of a new Barth -- names which conjure up a whole epoch in theology -- to emerge? Systematic theologies with that much influence may be difficult to write. More likely is a situation in which creative thought proceeds from many persons in many places with none achieving the status of the epoch-making giant or dogmatician for the world. Yet, to argue from the global/ ecumenical side of the equation rather than the audience/ agenda specific side, some gifted someone might, to use Barth's familiar metaphor, reach out for a rope to hold on to only to ring the church bell and awaken the whole town. What can be said with more confidence is that the best theologies will be both self-consciously particularized but informed by an awareness of planetary perils, promises, possibilities, and necessities involving the whole Gospel for the whole world. Ideally, each will learn from all, and all will learn from each in a church that is becoming, perhaps for the first time, truly one and universal, if not yet holy or fully apostolic. In that emerging world, there will continue to be a strand of thought which can be identified as the non-conservative academic tradition in American Protestant thought, but it too will be transformed by the enrichment of global/ecumenical perspectives as it seeks to be responsible to God and to the church in a planetary society.

NOTES
Chapter I

[1]A useful discussion of the theological task can be found in Theodore Jennings, Jr., INTRODUCTION TO THEOLOGY (Philadelphia: Fortress Press, 1976).

[2]Emil Brunner, THE CHRISTIAN DOCTRINE OF GOD (Philadelphia: Westminster Press, 1950), pp. 6-13.

[3]See Millar Burrows, AN OUTLINE OF BIBLICAL THEOLOGY (Philadelphia: Westminster Press, 1946), pp. 8-53; A COMPANION TO THE BIBLE, ed. by J. J. Allmen (New York: Oxford University Press, 1958), articles on "Revelation" and "Scripture."

[4]See Robert Grant, A SHORT HISTORY OF THE INTERPRETATION OF THE BIBLE (New York: The Macmillan Co., 1963); J. N. D Kelly, EARLY CHRISTIAN DOCTRINES (New York: Harper & Brothers, 1960), pp. 29-79; Jaroslav Pelikan, THE EMERGENCE OF THE CATHOLIC TRADITION (100-600) (Chicago: University of Chicago Press, 1971), pp. 332-357; Paul Tillich, A HISTORY OF CHRISTIAN THOUGHT (New York: Simon and Schuster, 1968), pp. 24-39, 111-115, 183-198, 242-245, 274-283; A COMPEND OF LUTHER'S THEOLOGY, ed. by Hugh T. Kerr, Jr. (Philadelphia: Westminster Press, 1943), pp. 3-20; John Calvin, INSTITUTES OF THE CHRISTIAN RELIGION, I, iii-x; Justo Gonzáles, A HISTORY OF CHRISTIAN THOUGHT (Nashville: Abingdon Press, 1975), III, 35-48, 124-127, 238-241.

[5]See Kenneth Cauthen, THE IMPACT OF AMERICAN RELIGIOUS LIBERALISM (Washington: University Press of America, 1983), pp. 3-25.

[6]See Carl F. Henry (ed.), BASIC CHRISTIAN DOCTRINES (New York: Holt, Rinehart and Winston, 1962), esp. pp. 14-20, 297-302, for a brief discussion and references to other works.

[7]See Kenneth Cauthen, THE IMPACT OF AMERICAN RELIGIOUS LIBERALISM. The book contains a chapter on Fosdick.

[8]Ibid, pp. 228-255. See also Langdon Gilkey, NAMING THE WHIRLWIND (Indianapolis: Bobbs-Merrill, Inc., 1970), pp. 73-106, for a discussion of both liberalism and neo-orthodoxy in relation to each other.

[9]See John Cobb and David Griffin, PROCESS THEOLOGY (Philadelphia: Westminster Press, 1976).

[10] See Robert McAfee Brown, THEOLOGY IN A NEW KEY (Philadelphia: Westminister Press, 1978). For an introduction to third world liberation themes, see Sergio Torres and Virginia Fabella (eds.), THE EMERGENT GOSPEL (Maryknoll: Orbis Books, 1978). For black theology, see James Cone and Gayraud Wilmore, BLACK THEOLOGY: A DOCUMENTARY HISTORY, 1966-1979 (Maryknoll: Orbis Books, 1980). For feminist theology, see Rosemary Radford Ruether, SEXISM AND GOD-TALK (Boston: Beacon Press, 1983), and Mary Daly, BEYOND GOD THE FATHER (Boston: Beacon Press, 1973).

[11] David Tracy, BLESSED RAGE FOR ORDER (New York: The Seabury Press, 1975), esp. pp. 32-63.

[12] For an excellent discussion of these issues in modern theology, especially liberalism and neo-orthodoxy, see John Baillie, THE IDEA OF REVELATION IN RECENT THOUGHT (New York: Columbia University Press, 1956). For a contemporary evangelical (conservative) view, see Bernard Ramm, SPECIAL REVELATION AND THE WORD OF GOD (Grand Rapids: William B. Eerdmans Publishing Co., 1961).

[13] See Hans Frei, "Niebuhr's Theological Background," FAITH AND ETHICS, ed. by Paul Ramsey (New York: Harper & Brothers, 1957), pp. 9-64. I am much indebted to this essay. On faith and history, see esp. pp. 21-32, 53-64.

[14] For brief discussions of these issues and an introduction to the vast literature on the subject, see Kenneth Cauthen, SCIENCE, SECULARIZATION AND GOD (Nashville: Abingdon Press, 1969), esp. pp. 13-31; and Kenneth Cauthen, THE IMPACT OF AMERICAN RELIGIOUS LIBERALISM, pp. 3-25.

[15] See Hans Frei, "Niebuhr's Theological Background," pp. 32-53.

[16] Friedrich Schleiermacher, THE CHRISTIAN FAITH (New York: Harper Torchbook, 1963), I, 12-18.

[17] See H. Richard Niebuhr, THE MEANING OF REVELATION (New York: The Macmillan Co., 1946), pp. 23-48.

[18] Douglas Clyde Macintosh, THEOLOGY AS AN EMPIRICAL SCIENCE (New York: The Macmillan Co., 1919). For a chapter on Macintosh, see Cauthen, THE IMPACT OF AMERICAN RELIGIOUS LIBERALISM, pp. 169-187.

[19] See Hans Frei, "Niebuhr's Theological Background," pp. 49-50. Barth's crucial book in this connection is ANSELM: FIDES QUAERENS INTELLECTUM (Richmond: John Knox Press, 1960).

[20]Langdon Gilkey, NAMING THE WHIRLWIND, pp. 305-413.

[21]See John Cobb, A CHRISTIAN NATURAL THEOLOGY (Philadelphia: Westminster Press, 1965).

[22]See Letty Russell, HUMAN LIBERATION IN A FEMINIST PERSPECTIVE (Philadelphia: Westminster Press, 1974); Majorie Suchocki, GOD, CHURCH, CHRIST (New York: The Crossroad Publishing Co., 1982); and Sheila Collins, A DIFFERENT HEAVEN AND EARTH (Valley Forge: Judson Press, 1974).

[23]James Cone, A BLACK THEOLOGY OF LIBERATION (Philadelphia: J. B. Lippincott, 1970), pp. 79-80.

[24]John Baillie, THE IDEA OF REVELATION IN RECENT THOUGHT, pp. 3-18.

[25]See Cauthen, THE IMPACT OF AMERICAN RELIGIOUS LIBERALISM, pp. 26-30. For W. A. Brown, see pp. 41-49; for the personalists, see pp. 108-115.

[26]Ibid, pp. 228-255.

[27]Langdon Gilkey, NAMING THE WHIRLWIND, pp. 305-470.

[28]For Barth's voluminous detailing of his views, see CHURCH DOGMATICS (Edinburgh: T and T Clark, 1936, 1956), I, 1 and 2; and II, 1.

[29]For the famous debate between Barth and Brunner on natural theology or the "point of contact," see NATURAL THEOLOGY, ed. by John Baillie (London: Centenary Press, 1946). For Brunner's major work on this subject, see REVELATION AND REASON (Philadelphia: Westminster Press, 1946).

[30]H. Richard Niebuhr, THE MEANING OF REVELATION, pp. 175-191.

[31]Langdon Gilkey, NAMING THE WHIRLWIND, pp. 31-145, esp. pp. 73-106.

[32]See Kenneth Cauthen, SCIENCE, SECULARIZATION AND GOD, pp. 13-48.

[33]Paul Tillich, SYSTEMATIC THEOLOGY (Chicago: University of Chicago Press, 1951), I, 3-8.

[34]Henry Nelson Wieman, THE SOURCE OF HUMAN GOOD (Carbondale: Southern Illinois University Press, 1946), p. 268.

[35]See James Cone, A BLACK THEOLOGY OF LIBERATION, pp. 74-80.

[36]On the norm of theology, cf. Tillich, SYSTEMATIC THEOLOGY, I, 47-59; Brunner, THE CHRISTIAN DOCTRINE OF GOD, pp. 43-49; Langdon Gilkey, MESSAGE AND EXISTENCE (New York: Seabury Press, 1979), pp. 36-37; Gordon Kaufman, SYSTEMATIC THEOLOGY (New York: Charles Scribner's Sons, 1968), pp. 75-80; and Harold DeWolf, A THEOLOGY OF THE LIVING CHURCH (New York: Harper & Brothers, 1953), pp. 23-45.

[37]See Kenneth Cauthen, THE IMPACT OF AMERICAN RELIGIOUS LIBERALISM, pp. 154-159.

[38]See Harry Emerson Fosdick, THE LIVING OF THESE DAYS (New York: Harper & Brothers, 1956), pp. 237-238.

[39]For an account of the Chicago school of theology which in some expressions moved into naturalism and humanism, see Harvey Arnold, NEAR THE EDGE OF BATTLE (Chicago: The Divinity School Association, 1966). For Ames, see pp. 53-58, or see Edward Scribner Ames, RELIGION (New York: H. Holt and Co., 1929).

[40]See Walter Rauschenbusch, A THEOLOGY FOR THE SOCIAL GOSPEL (New York: The Macmillan Co., 1917; reprinted, Nashville: Abingdon Press, no date).

[41]For the modernistic liberals, see Kenneth Cauthen, THE IMPACT OF AMERICAN RELIGIOUS LIBERALISM, pp. 29-30, 145-206. For the death of God theologies, see Langdon Gilkey, NAMING THE WHIRLWIND, pp. 107-145; also, Thomas Ogletree, THE DEATH OF GOD CONTROVERSY (Nashville: Abingdon Press, 1966).

[42]Rudolf Bultman, "New Testament and Mythology," in KERYGMA AND MYTH, ed. by Hans Werner Bartsch (New York: Harper Torchbook, 1961), pp. 1-44.

[43]Karl Barth, THE HUMANITY OF GOD (Richmond: John Knox Press, 1960), pp. 37-65.

[44]See Hans Frei, "Niebuhr's Theological Background," pp. 27-29, and Alasdair Heron, A CENTURY OF PROTESTANT THOUGHT (Philadelphia: Westminster Press, 1980), pp. 57-60.

[45]See Kenneth Cauthen, THE IMPACT OF AMERICAN RELIGIOUS LIBERALISM, pp. 150-152.

[46]See David Griffin and Thomas Altizer (eds.), JOHN COBB'S THEOLOGY IN PROCESS (Philadelphia: Westminster Press, 1977), pp. 21-23, 165-170.

[47]The famous and very influential book by Adolf Harnack published in Germany in 1900 was WHAT IS CHRISTIANITY? (New York: Harper Torchbook, 1957).

[48]George Tyrell, CHRISTIANITY AT THE CROSS-ROADS (London: Longmans, Green and Co., 1910), p. 44. My thanks to Kenneth Smith, Robert Page, and Larry Greenfield for helping me track down this loosely floating "well image." A reference is made in John Dillenberger and Claude Welch, PROTESTANT CHRISTIANITY (New York: Charles Scribner's Sons, 1954), p. 221, without naming the author. Alasdair Heron attributes the remark to Tyrell but not as directed specifically to Harnack. See A CENTURY OF PROTESTANT THEOLOGY, pp. 53-54. Neither cites an original source.

[49]The phrase "center and vicinity of the New Testament" is simply to indicate that the boundaries of the canon are fluid and not fixed or absolute.

[50]Karl Barth, CHURCH DOGMATICS, I, 1, 1-97.

[51]Paul Tillich, SYSTEMATIC THEOLOGY, I, 3-8.

[52]Langdon Gilkey, MESSAGE AND EXISTENCE, pp. 7-19.

[53]H. Richard Niebuhr, CHRIST AND CULTURE (New York: Harper & Brothers, 1951).

[54]John Calvin, INSTITUTES OF THE CHRISTIAN RELIGION, I, i, 1-3.

[55]Cf. Langdon Gilkey, MESSAGE AND EXISTENCE, pp. 23-38, for a discussion of faith and belief which touches on many of these issues.

NOTES
Chapter II

[1]Alfred North Whitehead, SCIENCE AND THE MODERN WORLD (New York: The Macmillan Co., 1925), chapter 11.

[2]Stephen Ely, THE RELIGIOUS AVAILABILITY OF WHITEHEAD'S GOD (Madison: University of Wisconsin Press, 1942).

[3]Cf. Paul Tillich, SYSTEMATIC THEOLOGY (Chicago: University of Chicago Press, 1951), I, 18-28.

[4]Dietrich Bonhoeffer, PRISONER FOR GOD (New York: The Macmillan Co., 1957), pp. 146-147.

[5]See Kenneth Cauthen, SCIENCE, SECULARIZATION AND GOD (Nashville: Abingdon Press, 1969).

[6]For brief but excellent discussions of the emergence of the modern mentialty, see Langdon Gilkey, NAMING THE WHIRLWIND (Indianapolis: Bobbs-Merrill, 1969), pp. 3-145, and Langdon Gilkey, REAPING THE WHIRLWIND (New York: The Seabury Press, 1976), pp. 70-114, 188-208.

[7]Henri de Lubac, THE DRAMA OF ATHEIST HUMANISM (New York: Sheed & Ward, 1950), p. v.

[8]For a description of this kind of thinking, see Harvey Cox, THE SECULAR CITY (New York: The Macmillan Co., 1965).

[9]A classic statement of this point of view is found in John Dewey, A COMMON FAITH (New Haven: Yale University Press, 1934).

[10]For an account of this movement, see Frederick Ferré, LANGUAGE, LOGIC AND GOD (New York: Harper & Row, 1961).

[11]Key figures here are Albert Camus and Jean-Paul Sartre.

[12]See Peter Berger, THE HERETICAL IMPERATIVE (Garden City: Doubleday, 1979), See also, Huston Smith, FORGOTTEN TRUTH (New York: Harper & Row, 1976), and BEYOND THE POST-MODERN MIND (New York: Crossroad Publishing Co., 1982).

[13]See Charles Hartshorne and William L. Reese, PHILOSOPHERS SPEAK OF GOD (Chicago: University of Chicago Press, 1953), pp. 416-437.

[14]See Justo Gonzáles, HISTORY OF CHRISTIAN THOUGHT (Nashville: Abingdon Press, 1971), II, 257-269.

[15]Paul Tillich, SYSTEMATIC THEOLOGY, I, 235-252, 271-274.

[16]For brief discussions of these issues and the whole question of God-language, see Roger Schmidt, EXPLORING RELIGION (Belmont: Wadsworth, Inc., 1980), pp. 83-100, 123-147.

[17]Rudolf Bultmann, "New Testament and Mythology," KERYGMA AND MYTH, ed. by Hans Werner Bartsch (New York: Harper Torchbook, 1961), pp. 1-44; see also his JESUS CHRIST AND MYTHOLOGY (New York: Charles Scribner's Sons, 1958).

[18]Reinhold Niebuhr, THE NATURE AND DESTINY OF MAN, one volume ed. (New York: Charles Scribner's Sons, 1949), II, 289.

[19]For a recent discussion of these issues, see Schubert Ogden, THE POINT OF CHRISTOLOGY (New York: Harper & Row, 1982), pp. 131-147.

[20]See the articles on "God" and "Holy" in A COMPANION TO THE BIBLE, ed. by J. J. Von Allmen (Oxford: Oxford University Press, 1958), and in THE INTERPRETER'S DICTIONARY OF THE BIBLE (Nashville: Abingdon Press, 1962), Vol. II. See also Millar Burrows, AN OUTLINE OF BIBLICAL THEOLOGY (Philadelphia: Westminster Press, 1946), pp. 54-82.

[21]See J. N. D. Kelly, EARLY CHRISTIAN DOCTRINES (New York: Harper & Brothers, 1960), pp. 83-108, 252-279, 310-343; Jaroslav Pelikan, THE EMERGENCE OF THE CATHOLIC TRADITION (100-600) (Chicago: The University of Chicago Press, 1971), pp. 132-140, 172-276.

[22]Etienne Gilson, THE SPIRIT OF MEDIEVAL PHILOSOPHY (New York: Charles Scribner's Sons, 1940), pp. 42-63.

[23]See Paul Tillich, A HISTORY OF CHRISTIAN THOUGHT (New York: Simon and Schuster, 1968), pp. 247-249, 262-270.

[24]See Kenneth Cauthen, THE IMPACT OF AMERICAN RELIGIOUS

LIBERALISM (Washington: University Press of America, 1983), pp. 3-25, and note 6 above.

[25]Langdon Gilkey, NAMING THE WHIRLWIND, pp. 31-78. See also, Cauthen, THE IMPACT OF AMERICAN RELIGIOUS LIBERALISM, section on God in Chapters 3-10.

[26]Gilkey, NAMING THE WHIRLWIND, pp. 78-106.

[27]Wolfhart Pannenberg, THEOLOGY AND THE KINGDOM OF GOD (Philadelphia: Westminster Press, 1969); Jurgen Moltmann, THEOLOGY OF HOPE (New York: Harper & Row, 1967).

[28]Gustavo Gutiérrez, A THEOLOGY OF LIBERATION (Maryknoll: Orbis Books, 1972); Hugo Assmann, THEOLOGY FOR A NOMAD CHURCH (Maryknoll: Orbis Books, 1976).

[29]James Cone, A BLACK THEOLOGY OF LIBERATION (Philadelphia: J. B. Lippincott, 1970); Deotis Roberts, LIBERATION AND RECONCILIATION (Philadelphia: Westminster Press, 1971).

[30]W. R. Jones, IS GOD A WHITE RACIST (Garden City: Doubleday, 1973).

[31]Rosemary Ruether, SEXISM AND GOD-TALK (Boston: Beacon Press, 1983); Phyllis Trible, GOD AND THE RHETORIC OF SEXUALITY (Philadelphia: Fortress Press, 1978).

[32]John Cobb, A CHRISTIAN NATURAL THEOLOGY (Philadelphia: Westminster Press, 1965); Schubert Ogden, THE REALITY OF GOD (New York: Harper & Row, 1966).

[33]Two classic studies of the human experience of the Holy are Rudolf Otto, THE IDEA OF THE HOLY (London: Oxford University Press, 1923), and Mircia Eliade, THE SACRED AND THE PROFANE (New York: Harper Torchbook, 1961).

[34]Paul Tillich, SYSTEMATIC THEOLOGY, I, 215-218; Gustaf Aulén, THE FAITH OF THE CHRISTIAN CHURCH (Philadelphia: Muhlenberg Press, 1948), pp. 120-124.

[35]Emil Brunner, THE CHRISTIAN DOCTRINE OF GOD (Philadelphia: Westminster Press, 1950), pp. 157-174.

[36]Anselm, PROSLOGIUM, VI AND VII. Quoted in John Cobb and David Griffin, PROCESS THEOLOGY (Philadelphia: Westminster Press, 1950) pp. 157-174.

[37]John Calvin, INSTITUTES OF THE CHRISTIAN RELIGION, I, xvii, 13.

[38]Quoted in J. K. Mozley, THE IMPASSIBILITY OF GOD (Cambridge: Cambridge University Press, 1926), p. 120.

[39]Mozley, THE IMPASSIBILITY OF GOD.

[40]Cf. Langdon Gilkey, "God," in CHRISTIAN THEOLOGY, ed. by Peter C. Hodgson and Robert H. King (Philadelphia: Fortress Press, 1982), p. 79.

[41]Paul Tillich, SYSTEMATIC THEOLOGY, I, 235-252, 271-274.

[42]See Gilkey, "God," pp. 76-80. See also, Brunner, THE CHRISTIAN DOCTRINE OF GOD, pp. 248-255, 266-271.

[43]See Hartshorne and Reese, PHILOSOPHERS SPEAK OF GOD, pp. 1-25, 499-514, and Hartshorne, THE DIVINE RELATIVITY (New Haven: Yale University Press, 1948).

[44]Paul Tillich, SYSTEMATIC THEOLOGY, I, 241-249.

[45]Emil Brunner, THE CHRISTIAN DOCTRINE OF GOD, (Nashville: Abingdon Press, 1930), pp. 285-324.

[46]A. C. Knudson, THE DOCTRINE OF GOD (Nashville: Abingdon Press, 1930), pp. 285-324.

[47]See John Cobb, A CHRISTIAN NATURAL THEOLOGY (Philadelphia: Westminster Press, 1965), p. 188. See also Hartshorne and Reese, PHILOSOPHERS SPEAK OF GOD, pp. 1-25, 499-514.

[48]H. Richard Niebuhr, RADICAL MONOTHEISM AND WESTERN CULTURE (New York: Harper & Row, 1960), pp. 11-48.

[49]Henry Nelson Wieman, THE SOURCE OF HUMAN GOOD (Chicago: University of Chicago Press, 1946).

[50]Shailer Mathews, THE GROWTH OF THE IDEA OF GOD (New York: The Macmillan Co., 1931).

[51]A. C. Knudson, THE DOCTRINE OF GOD, p. 334.

[52]Nels Ferré, THE CHRISTIAN UNDERSTANDING OF GOD (New York: Harper & Brothers, 1951), pp. 114-118; Paul Tillich, SYSTEMATIC THEOLOGY, I, 283-284.

[53]Gordon Kaufman, SYSTEMATIC THEOLOGY (New York: Charles Scribner's Sons, 1968), p. 154; and James Cone, A BLACK THEOLOGY OF LIBERATION, pp. 125-138.

[54]Letty Russell, HUMAN LIBERATION IN A FEMINIST PERSPECTIVE (Philadelphia: Westminster Press, 1974), pp. 100-103; Joan Chamberlain Engels, THE FEMININE DIMENSION OF THE DIVINE (Philadelphia: Westminster Press, 1979), pp. 139-153.

[55]Claude Welch, IN THIS NAME (New York: Charles Scribner's Sons, 1952), pp. 3-48.

[56]Karl Barth, CHURCH DOGMATICS (Edinburgh: T & T Clark, 1936), I, 1. See Welch, IN THIS NAME, pp. 161-213.

[57]J. S. Whale, CHRISTIAN DOCTRINE (Cambridge: Cambridge University Press, 1950), pp. 112-120. See Welch, IN THIS NAME, pp. 125-133.

[58]C. C. Richardson, THE DOCTRINE OF THE TRINITY (Nashville: Abingdon Press, 1958).

[59]Consult any standard history of Christian doctrine. Two worthy of note area: J. N. D. Kelly, EARLY CHRISTIAN DOCTRINES (New York: Harper & Row, 1960), pp. 223-279, and Jaroslav Pelikan, THE EMERGENCE OF CATHOLIC TRADITION (Chicago: University of Chicago Press, 1971), pp. 172-225.

[60]On both these points see Welch, IN THIS NAME, pp. 293-302.

[61]Leonard Hodgson, THE DOCTRINE OF THE TRINITY (New York: Charles Scribner's Sons, 1944).

[62]For a good discussion of the meaning of creation in both its classical and contemporary interpretations, see Langdon Gilkey, MAKER OF HEAVEN AND EARTH (New York: Doubleday, 1959).

[63]Gilkey, MAKER OF HEAVEN AND EARTH, pp. 106-207.

[64]In addition to Gilkey on these points (notes 62, 63), see Emil Brunner, THE CHRISTIAN DOCTRINE OF CREATION AND REDEMPTION (Philadelphia: Westminster Press, 1952), pp. 3-45.

[65]The Old Testament has more to say on providence than the New Testament. See Gerhard von Rad, OLD TESTAMENT THEOLOGY (New York: Harper & Row, 1962), I, 152, 426-427. See also, Millar Burrows, AN OUTLINE OF BIBLICAL THEOLOGY (Philadelphia: Westminster Press, 1946), pp. 130-132.

[66]See Gilkey, "God," and Julian Hartt, "Creation and Providence," in CHRISTIAN THEOLOGY, Hodgson and King (eds.), pp. 62-82, 115-136. For more extended discussions, see Gilkey, REAPING THE WHIRLWIND, pp. 159-187; and David Griffin, GOD, POWER AND EVIL (Philadelphia: Westminster Press, 1976), chapters 6-15.

[67]See Griffin, GOD, POWER AND EVIL, pp. 80-82.

[68]Cf. Gilkey, REAPING THE WHIRLWIND, pp. 167-168, 395, note 36.

[69]Karl Barth uses this analogy approvingly. See CHURCH DOGMATICS (Edinburgh: T & T Clark, 1960), III, 3, 133-134.

[70]James Ross, PHILOSOPHICAL THEOLOGY (Indianapolis: Bobbs-Merrill, 1969), p. 258. Cf. Griffin, GOD, POWER AND EVIL, chapter 14.

[71]Hulrich Zwingli, DIE PROVIDENTIA.

[72]John Calvin, INSTITUTES, III, xxiii, 3, 6, 13.

[73]Calvin, INSTITUTES, I, xvii, 5; I, xviii; 1, 2, 4; III, xxiii, 8, 9, 10.

[74]Calvin, INSTITUTES, III, xxiv, 17; I, xvii, 2-5; I, xviii, 1-4; and III, xx, 43. Actually, Calvin explains, there is only one will in God as such; it just appears to us that there are two. See I, xviii, 3.

[75]Calvin, INSTITUTES, III, xxiv, 17.

[76]Calvin, INSTITUTES, III, xxiii, 7.

[77]See Griffin, GOD, POWER AND EVIL, p. 107.

[78]Martin Luther, ON THE BONDAGE OF THE WILL.

[79]Augustine, CONFESSIONS, VII, 11; CITY OF GOD, XI, 22, 24-27. See Gilkey, REAPING THE WHIRLWIND, pp. 165-168.

[80]See Gilkey, pp. 383-384, footnote 35.

[81]See Gilkey, REAPING THE WHIRLWIND, p. 169.

[82]See Griffin, GOD, POWER AND EVIL, chapter 7, for a discussion, and for citations of original sources. See also Gonzáles, HISTORY OF CHRISTIAN THOUGHT, II, 258-279.

[83]Henry Bettenson, DOCUMENTS OF THE CHRISTIAN CHURCH (New York: Oxford University Press, 1947), p. 347. Yet a neo-orthodox theologian like Brunner can reassert the inpenetrable mystery, possibly saved from a like contradiction only by the concession that God's self-limitation makes room for a more genuine freedom. See THE CHRISTIAN DOCTRINE OF CREATION AND REDEMPTION, pp. 170-175.

[84]See Gilkey, "God," p. 70.

[85]Cauthen, SCIENCE, SECULARIZATION AND GOD, pp. 13-31.

[86]Kenneth Cauthen, THE IMPACT OF AMERICAN RELIGIOUS LIBERALISM (Washington: University Press of America, 1983), pp. 3-25.

[87]Gilkey, REAPING THE WHIRLWIND, pp. 188-208.

[88]Cauthen, THE IMPACT OF AMERICAN RELIGIOUS LIBERALISM, esp. pp. 209-213, for a summary of the whole movement documented throughout the book. See also Gilkey, REAPING THE WHIRLWIND, pp. 210-216.

[89]Cauthen, THE IMPACT OF AMERICAN RELIGIOUS LIBERALISM, pp. 228-255. See also, Gilkey, REAPING THE WHIRLWIND, pp. 216-226.

[90]Reinhold Niebuhr, FAITH AND HISTORY (New York: Charles Scribner's Sons, 1949).

[91]See Gilkey, REAPING THE WHIRLWIND, pp. 226-238.

[92]Tillich, SYSTEMATIC THEOLOGY, I, 263-267.

[93]Bultmann, JESUS CHRIST AND MYTHOLOGY, pp. 60-85.

[94]Cobb and Griffin, PROCESS THEOLOGY, pp. 63-79.

[95]Tillich, SYSTEMATIC THEOLOGY, I, 271-274.

[96]Hartshorne, THE DIVINE RELATIVITY.

[97]Barth, CHURCH DOGMATICS, II, 2.

[98]This is the thesis of Griffin, GOD, POWER AND EVIL. See also Cobb and Griffin, PROCESS THEOLOGY, p. 69.

[99]Cf. Langdon Gilkey, MESSAGE AND EXISTENCE (New York: The Seabury Press, 1979), p. 89.

[100]Griffin develops the technical argument for this conclusion throughout GOD, POWER AND EVIL, but see especially his chapter on Aquinas, pp. 72-95.

[101]See Griffin, GOD, POWER AND EVIL, pp. 31-37, and Gilkey, REAPING THE WHIRLWIND, p. 417, note 17, for a listing of passages which cannot easily be reconciled, thus giving a Biblical basis for those theologians who affirm both divine sovereignty and human freedom as true in ways we cannot understand.

[102]Ignorance is an appeal widely made, but see, e.g., Brunner, THE CHRISTIAN DOCTRINE OF CREATION AND REDEMPTION, pp. 175-185.

[103]Practically everybody makes this appeal.

[104]See John Hick, EVIL AND THE GOD OF LOVE (New York: Harper & Row, 1966). See also, Gordon Kaufman, GOD THE PROBLEM (Cambridge: Harvard University Press, 1972), pp. 171-200.

[105]See Nels Ferré, EVIL AND THE CHRISTIAN FAITH (New York: Harper & Brothers, 1947).

[106]See Tillich, SYSTEMATIC THEOLOGY, I, 269-270. See also Gilkey, MAKER OF HEAVEN AND EARTH, pp. 178-207. See also Cobb and Griffin, PROCESS THEOLOGY, pp. 69-75.

[107]E. G. Brightman, THE PROBLEM OF GOD (New York: Abingdon Press, 1930). For another version of the limited God thesis, see Cauthen, SCIENCE, SECULARIZATION AND GOD, pp. 164-181. See Stephen David (ed.), ENCOUNTERING EVIL (Atlanta: John Knox Press, 1981), in which various options are explored. John Hich and Davis qualify the existence of genuine evil. John Roth and Frederick Sontag question the perfect goodness of God. David Griffin puts limits on omnipotence. Their views are more complex than this, but the element named is

present, however qualified it may finally be.

[108]See Griffin, GOD, POWER AND EVIL, pp. 251-310.

[109]Cauthen, SCIENCE, SECULARIZATION AND GOD, pp. 90-130.

[110]Alfred North Whitehead, SCIENCE AND THE MODERN WORLD, and MODES OF THOUGHT (New York: The Macmillan Co., 1938).

[111]Brunner, THE CHRISTIAN DOCTRINE OF CREATION AND REDEMPTION, pp. 186-192.

[112]Bultmann, "New Testament and Mythology," and JESUS CHRIST AND MYTHOLOGY.

[113]Henry Stob, "Miracles," BASIC CHRISTIAN DOCTRINES, ed. by Carl F. Henry (New York: Holt, Rinehart and Winston, 1962), pp. 82-88. See also, C.S. Lewis, MIRACLES (New York: The Macmillan Co., 1947).

[114]Dale Moody, THE WORD OF TRUTH (Grand Rapids: Wm. B. Eerdmans Publishing Co., 1981), pp. 161-165.

[115]Gordon Kaufman, SYSTEMATIC THEOLOGY, pp. 305-308; GOD THE PROBLEM, pp. 180-184; John Macquarrie, PRINCIPLES OF CHRISTIAN THEOLOGY, 2nd ed. (New York: Charles Scribner's Sons, 1977), pp. 247-253.

[116]Douglas Clyde Macintosh, THE REASONABLENESS OF CHRISTIANITY (New York: Charles Scribner's Sons, 1925), p. 98.

[117]Tillich, SYSTEMATIC THEOLOGY, I, 111-118, 266-267.

[118]A.C. Knudson, THE DOCTRINE OF GOD, pp. 139-145; Harold DeWolf, A THEOLOGY OF THE LIVING CHURCH (New York: Harper & Brothers, 1953), pp. 126-127.

[119]Karl Barth, CHURCH DOGMATICS (New York: Charles Scribner's Sons, 1956), I, 2, 172-202; III, 2, 439-455; IV, 1, 341.

[120]Brunner, THE CHRISTIAN DOCTRINE OF CREATION AND REDEMPTION, pp. 160-170, 328-329, 250-256, 263-378. See also THE MEDIATOR (Philadelphia: Westminster Press, 1947), p. 308, note 1.

[121]For a discussion of the influence of Kant on the concept of nature in 19th and 20th century Protestant theology, see Richard R. Niebuhr, RESURRECTION AND HISTORICAL REASON (New York: Charles Scribner's Sons, 1957), esp. pp. 72-89.

[122]F. D. Schleiermacher, ON RELIGION: SPEECHES TO ITS CULTURED DESPISERS (New York: Harper Torchbook, 1958), p. 6.

[123]Tillich, SYSTEMATIC THEOLOGY, I, 115-118.

[124]Moody, THE WORD OF TRUTH, pp. 151-161; DeWolf, A THEOLOGY OF THE LIVING CHURCH, pp. 355-363.

[125]Tillich, SYSTEMATIC THEOLOGY, I, 267; Kaufman, SYSTEMATIC THEOLOGY, pp. 511-515; Macquarrie, PRINCIPLES OF CHRISTIAN THEOLOGY, pp. 493-497.

[126]Roger Hazleton, GOD'S WAY WITH MAN (Nashville: Abingdon Press, 1956), pp. 181-202; Barth, CHURCH DOGMATICS, III, 3, 267-288.

[127]For a good summary of the Christian consensus on providence, prayer, and miracle, along with a treatment of issues in dispute, see Walter Marshall Horton, CHRISTIAN THEOLOGY: AN ECUMENICAL APPROACH, 2nd ed. (New York: Harper & Brothers, 1958), pp. 111-139.

NOTES
Chapter III

[1]H. Wheeler Robinson, INSPIRATION AND REVELATION IN THE
OLD TESTAMENT (Oxford: The Clarendon Press, 1946), p.
70.

[2]For more detailed discussions of Biblical
anthropology, consult the articles on flesh, body,
soul, spirit, etc. in THE INTERPRETER'S DICTIONARY OF
THE BIBLE, 4 vols. (Nashville: Abingdon Press, 1962),
and A COMPANION TO THE BIBLE, ed. by J. J. von Allmen
(New York: Oxford University Press, 1958).   See also
Millar Burrows, AN OUTLINE OF BIBLICAL THEOLOGY
(Philadelphia: Westminster Press, 1946), Chapter VI,
and Hans Walter Wolff, ANTHROPOLOGY OF THE OLD
TESTAMENT (Philadelphia: Fortress Press, 1974).

[3]See J. N. D. Kelly, EARLY CHRISTIAN DOCTRINES, 2nd ed.
(New York: Harper & Row, 1960), Chapters VII and XIII.

[4]D. R. G. Owens, BODY AND SOUL (Philadelphia:
Westminster Press, 1956).

[5]Calvin, INSTITUTES, I, xv, 2; II, xiv, 1.

[6]Ibid., I, xv, 6.

[7]Ibid., I, xv, 1-8.

[8]On Augustine, Aquinas, Luther, and Calvin, see Justo
González, A HISTORY OF CHRISTIAN THOUGHT, 3 vols.
(Nashville: Abingdon Press, 1970-1975).   Cf. Reinhold
Niebuhr, THE NATURE AND DESTINY OF MAN (New York:
Charles Scribner's Sons, 1949), I, 150-177.

[9]Soren Kierkegaard, CONCLUDING UNSCIENTIFIC POSTSCRIPT
(Princeton: Princeton University Press, 1944), pp.
169-244.

[10]Reinhold Niebuhr, THE SELF AND THE DRAMAS OF HISTORY
(New York: Charles Scribner's Sons, 1955).

[11]Albrecht Ritschl, THE CHRISTIAN DOCTRINE OF
JUSTIFICATION AND RECONCILIATION (Edinburgh: T & T
Clark, 1900), p. 199.

[12]For a discussion of the cultural background of modern views of humanity, see Langdon Gilkey, REAPING THE WHIRLWIND (New York: The Seabury Press, 1976), pp. 188-208. For liberal views of humanity, see Kenneth Cauthen, THE IMPACT OF AMERICAN RELIGIOUS LIBERALISM (Washington: University Press of America, 1983).

[13]For Paul Tillich, see SYSTEMATIC THEOLOGY (Chicago: University of Chicago Press, 1957), II, 19-96; for Reinhold Niebuhr, see THE NATURE AND DESTINY OF MAN, I, 1-77.

[14]B. F. Skinner, BEYOND FREEDOM AND DIGNITY (New York: Bantam Books, 1971).

[15]E. O. Wilson, SOCIOBIOLOGY (Cambridge: The Belknap Press, 1975).

[16]David Tracy, BLESSED RAGE FOR ORDER (New York: Seabury Press, 1975), p. 47.

[17]Paul Tillich, "The Theological Significance of Existentialism and Psychoanalysis," THEOLOGY OF CULTURE (New York: Oxford University Press, 1959), pp. 112-126.

[18]See Marianne Micks, OUR SEARCH FOR IDENTITY: HUMANITY IN THE IMAGE OF GOD (Philadelphia: Fortress Press, 1982).

[19]See the article on "Sin," in THE INTERPRETER'S DICTIONARY OF THE BIBLE, Vol. 4; and Burrows, AN OUTLINE OF BIBLICAL THEOLOGY, pp. 165-172.

[20]See Kelly, EARLY CHRISTIAN DOCTRINES, pp. 163-188, 344-357.

[21]Ibid., pp. 357-374.

[22]Calvin, INSTITUTES, II, i, 8.

[23]On Luther and Calvin, see Gonzáles, A HISTORY OF CHRISTIAN THOUGHT, III, 48-50, 127-135. Cf. Niebuhr, THE NATURE AND DESTINY OF MAN, I, 186-188, 228-233, 245-251, and Paul Tillich, A HISTORY OF CHRISTIAN DOCTRINE (New York: Simon and Schuster, 1967), pp. 192-198, 245-247, 262-270.

[24]For the view of sin in liberal theology, see the relevant sections in Cauthen, THE IMPACT OF AMERICAN RELIGIOUS LIBERALISM, esp. pp. 52-53, 76-80, 97-99, 118-

120, 135-137, 159-160, 181-183.

[25]Friedrich Schleiermacher, THE CHRISTIAN FAITH, par. 71, part 2.

[26]Reinhold Niebuhr, THE NATURE AND DESTINY OF MAN, I, 150-300.

[27]Dennis McCann, CHRISTIAN REALISM AND LIBERATION THEOLOGY (Maryknoll: Orbis Books, 1981).

[28]"The Human Situation: A Feminine View," in WOMANSPIRIT RISING, ed. by Carol R. Christ and Judith Plaskow (New York: Harper & Row, 1979), and Judith Plaskow, SEX, SIN AND GRACE (Washington: University Press of America, 1980).

[29]See the articles on forgiveness, salvation, reconciliation, justification, regeneration, repentance, and sanctification in THE INTERPRETER'S DICTIONARY OF THE BIBLE, See also, Burrows, AN OUTLINE OF BIBLICAL THEOLOGY, pp. 165-187, 220-240.

[30]Calvin, INSTITUTES, III, i-xxiv.

[31]For the understanding of salvation in the early church, Augustine, the medieval church, and the Reformers, see the works already cited by Kelly, Gonzáles, and Tillich. See also Jaroslav Pelikan, THE CHRISTIAN TRADITION: A HISTORY OF THE DEVELOPMENT OF DOCTRINE (Chicago: The University of Chicago Press, 1971), Vol. I; (1978), Vol. III; (1984), Vol. IV.

[32]Gonzáles, A HISTORY OF CHRISTIAN THOUGHT, III, 215-225. Cf. Tillich, A HISTORY OF CHRISTIAN THOUGHT, pp. 226-237, 212-215.

[33]On Arminianism and Wesley, see Gonzáles, A HISTORY OF CHRISTIAN THOUGHT, III, 254-262, 279-287. The five points of the TULIP theology are Total depravity, Unconditional predestination, Limited atonement, Irresistible grace, and Perserverance of the saints. These themes were set forth at the synod of Dort (1618-1619) in opposition to the Remonstrance (1610), which had elaborated Arminian views.

[34]For the view of salvation in liberalism, see the relevant sections in each of the thinkers discussed in Cauthen, THE IMPACT OF AMERICAN RELIGION LIBERALISM.

[35]See Gilkey, REAPING THE WHIRLWIND, pp. 216-226. "God works in history only inwardly through his word of judgment and of grace in creating inner repentance, faith, decision and obedience; he does not work `outwardly' at all directing nature and social history to the fulfillment of their own intrinsic goal or goals." pp. 222-223.

[36]Emphases vary across the neo-orthodox spectrum. In his systematic theology, Brunner offers a balanced view of justification, regeneration, and sanctification resembling the position of Calvin in which there is a place for growth in holiness and love. See THE CHRISTIAN DOCTRINE OF CHURCH, FAITH AND CONSUMMATION (Philadelphia: Westminster Press, 1962), pp. 191-211, 269-305.

[37]Reinhold Niebuhr speaks of a "hidden Christ" who operates in history converting those who do not know the historical Christ. Presumably the "hidden Christ" is also at work in those who are acquainted with the Gospel but have made no explicit confession of faith. See THE NATURE AND DESTINY OF MAN, II, 108-110, and especially footnote 6.

[38]See THE NATURE AND DESTINY OF MAN, II, 68-126.

[39]Ibid., p. 125.

[40]Daniel Day williams, GOD'S GRACE AND MAN'S HOPE (New York: Harper & Brothers, 1949).

[41]See Robert McAfee Brown, THEOLOGY IN A NEW KEY (Philadelphia: Westminster Press, 1978), and Gilkey, REAPING THE WHIRLWIND, pp. 226-238.

[42]Gilkey, REAPING THE WHIRLWIND, p. 409.

[43]Paul Tillich, SYSTEMATIC THEOLOGY, II, 44.

[44]Williams, GOD'S GRACE AND MAN'S HOPE, p. 36. Robert Calhoun, "Review of THE NATURE AND DESTINY OF MAN," Vol. 1," THE JOURNAL OF RELIGION (October 1941), pp. 473-480.

[45]Reinhold Niebuhr, THE NATURE AND DESTINY OF MAN, II, 127-212.

[46]John Hick, EVIL AND THE GOD OF LOVE (New York: Harper & Row, 1966).

[47]Teilhard de Chardin, THE PHENOMENON OF MAN (New York: Harper Torchbook, 1961); Gordon Kaufman, GOD THE PROBLEM (Cambridge: Harvard University Press, 1972), chapter 8; and John Cobb and David Griffin, PROCESS THEOLOGY (Philadelphia: Westminster Press, 1976), pp. 63-75. Cf. Robert R. Williams, "Sin and Evil," CHRISTIAN THEOLOGY, ed. by Peter C. Hodgson and Robert H. King (Philadelphia: Fortress Press, 1982), pp. 190-193. Williams maintains that the Irenaean model is "dominant among contemporary theologians." p. 195.

NOTES
Chapter IV

[1]Donald Baillie, GOD WAS IN CHRIST (New York: Charles Scribner's Sons, 1948), pp. 79-84.

[2]For further discussion of New Testament Christology, see Rudolf Bultmann, THEOLOGY OF THE NEW TESTAMENT (New York: Charles Scribner's Sons, 1951), I, 42-53, 121-133; (1955), II, 155-202; THE INTERPRETER'S DICTIONARY OF THE BIBLE, 4 vols. (Nashville: Abingdon Press, 1962), articles on "Jesus" and "Christ"; Millar Burrows, AN OUTLINE OF BIBLICAL THEOLOGY (Philadelphia: Westminster Press, 1946), pp. 83-112; Oscar Cullman, THE CHRISTOLOGY OF THE NEW TESTAMENT (London: SCM Press, 1964); Reginald Fuller, THE FOUNDATIONS OF NEW TESTAMENT CHRISTOLOGY (New York: Charles Scribner's Sons, 1965).

[3]For more detailed discussion of these controversies regarding the person of Christ from the New Testament period through the 17th century, see Jaroslav Pelikan, THE CHRISTIAN TRADITION (Chicago: University of Chicago Press, 1971), I, 12, 24, 172-210, 226-277; (1984), IV, 187-203, 350-362; J. N. D. Kelly, EARLY CHRISTIAN DOCTRINES (New York: Harper & Row, 1960), pp. 138-162, 280-343; Justo L. Gonzáles, A HISTORY OF CHRISTIAN THOUGHT, 3 vols. (Nashville: Abingdon Press, 1970-1975), I, 344-392; II, 74-89, 94-96; Aloys Grillmeier, CHRIST IN CHRISTIAN TRADITION (Atlanta: John Knox Press, 1975), Vol. I.

[4]For a brief account of developments in modern philosophy and theology relevant to Christology, see Kenneth Cauthen, THE IMPACT OF AMERICAN RELIGIOUS LIBERALISM (Washington: University Press of America, 1983), pp. 3-25, 228-225. For a more technical discussion, see Hans Frei, "Niebuhr's Theological Background," FAITH AND ETHICS, ed. by Paul Ramsey (New York: Harper & Brothers, 1957), pp. 16-64. See also Alasdair Heron, A CENTURY OF PROTESTANT THEOLOGY (Philadelphia: Westminster Press, 1980), pp. 1-21.

[5]Walter Rauschenbusch, A THEOLOGY FOR THE SOCIAL GOSPEL (New York: The Macmillan Co., 1917), p. 151.

[6]Albrecht Ritschl, JUSTIFICATION AND RECONCILIATION (Edinburgh: T & T Clark, III, 203-214, 285-484.

[7]This was the title of Albert Schweitzer's famous book which recounted the history of the writing of the many lives of Jesus in the 19th century (1906).

[8]Friedrich Schleiermacher, THE CHRISTIAN FAITH, par. 94.

[9]See Cauthen, THE IMPACT OF AMERICAN RELIGIOUS LIBERALISM, pp. 55-57.

[10]James Robinson, THE NEW QUEST OF THE HISTORICAL JESUS (London: SCM Press, 1959), pp. 26-47.

[11]Ibid.

[12]Baillie, GOD WAS IN CHRIST, pp. 11-20.

[13]For further discussion of neo-orthodox tendencies in Christology, see Cauthen, THE IMPACT OF AMERICAN RELIGIOUS LIBERALISM, pp. 228-255; Baillie, GOD WAS IN CHRIST, pp. 9-105; and Daniel Day Williams, WHAT PRESENT-DAY THEOLOGIANS ARE THINKING (New York: Harper & Brothers, 1959), pp. 120-148.

[14]Reinhold Niebuhr, THE NATURE AND DESTINY OF MAN (New York: Charles Scribner's Sons, 1949), II, 35.

[15]Ibid., p. 68.

[16]Reinhold Niebuhr, AN INTERPRETATION OF CHRISTIAN ETHICS (New York: Harper & Brothers, 1935), pp. 103-135.

[17]Niebuhr, THE NATURE AND DESTINY OF MAN, II, 81.

[18]Paul Tillich, SYSTEMATIC THEOLOGY (Chicago: University of Chicago Press, 1957), II, 117.

[19]Ibid., p. 148.

[20]Ibid.

[21]Robinson, A NEW QUEST OF THE HISTORICAL JESUS.

[22]David Griffin, A PROCESS CHRISTOLOGY (Philadelphia: Westminister Press, 1973), pp. 195-246.

[23]John Cobb, CHRIST IN A PLURALISTIC AGE (Philadelphia: Westminster Press, 1975), pp. 62-81.

[24]Schubert Ogden, THE POINT OF CHRISTOLOGY (San Francisco: Harper & Row, 1982).

[25]James Cone, A BLACK THEOLOGY OF LIBERATION (Philadelphia: J. P. Lippincott, 1970), pp. 197-227.

[26]Majorie Suchocki, GOD, CHRIST, CHURCH (New York: Crossroad Publishing Co., 1982), pp. 93-121.

[27]Gustavo Gutiérrez, A THEOLOGY OF LIBERATION (Maryknoll: Orbis Books, 1973), pp. 149-187.

[28]Isabel Carter Heyward, THE REDEMPTION OF GOD (Washington: University Press of America, 1982), pp. 25-71; Jon Sobrino, CHRISTOLOGY AT THE CROSSROADS (Maryknoll: Orbis Books, 1978); Rosemary Radford Ruether, SEXISM AND GOD-TALK (Boston: Beacon Press, 1983), pp. 116-138.

[29]Denis P. McCann, CHRISTIAN REALISM AND LIBERATION THEOLOGY (Maryknoll: Orbis Books, 1981), p. 184.

[30]Wolfhart Pannenberg, JESUS -- GOD AND MAN (Philadelphia: The Westminster Press, 1968), pp. 281-397.

[31]Baillie, GOD WAS IN CHRIST, pp. 106-132.

[32]John Knox, THE HUMANITY AND DIVINITY OF CHRIST (Cambridge: Cambridge University Press, 1967), pp. 93-116.

[33]For more detailed discussions of New Testament views of the work of Christ, see the article THE INTERPRETER' DICTIONARY OF THE BIBLE, on "Atonement" (Nashville: Abingdon Press, 1962), Vol. I; Rudolf Bultmann, THEOLOGY OF THE NEW TESTAMENT I, 42-53, 164-183, 288-314; II, 155-202; Millar Burrows, AN OUTLINE OF BIBLICAL THEOLOGY, pp. 220-227; Vincent Taylor, THE ATONEMENT IN THE NEW TESTAMENT TEACHING (London: The Epworth Press, 1940).

[34]Gustaf Aulén, CHRISTUS VICTOR (New YOrk: The Macmillan Co., 1961).

[35]Kelly, EARLY CHRISTIAN DOCTRINES, pp. 375-377.

[36]For detailed treatments of the doctrine of atonement during the first 1000 years of Christian history, see

Kelly, EARLY CHRISTIAN DOCTRINES pp. 163-188, 375-400; Aulén, CHRISTUS VICTOR, pp. 1-84; Robert S. Franks, THE WORK OF CHRIST (New York: Thomas Nelson and Sons, 1962), pp. 3-125.

[37]See Aulén, CHRISTUS VICTOR, pp. 84-92; and Franks, THE WORK OF CHRIST, pp. 126-142.

[38]Franks, THE WORK OF CHRIST, pp. 279-351.

[39]THE INSTITUTES OF THE CHRISTIAN RELIGION, II, xv-xvii.

[40]Aulén, CHRISTUS VICTOR, pp. 101-122.

[41]Karl Barth, CHURCH DOGMATICS (Edinburgh: T & T Clark, 1956), IV, 1, 3-642, esp. 157-357; Emil Brunner, THE MEDIATOR (Philadelphia: Westminster Press, 1948), pp. 435-535.

[42]Quoted by Franks, THE WORK OF CHRIST, p. 145.

[43]For a discussion of Abelard's views, see Frank, THE WORK OF CHRIST, pp. 142-149; and Aulén, CHRISTUS VICTOR, pp. 95-96.

[44]Friedrich Schleiermacher, THE CHRISTIAN FAITH, pars. 100-105.

[45]Albrecht Ritschl, JUSTIFICATION AND RECONCILIATION, II, 285-484.

[46]A. C. Knudson, THE DOCTRINE OF REDEMPTION (Nashville: Abingdon Press, 1930), pp. 369-387.

[47]For brief discussions of the views of eight American liberal theologians, see Cauthen, THE IMPACT OF AMERICAN RELIGIOUS LIBERALISM, pp. 55-58, 80-82, 104-106, 122-125, 138-141, 162-166, 183-185, 202-203.

[48]Niebuhr, THE NATURE AND DESTINY OF MAN, II, 56.

[49]Ibid., I, 142-148; II, 46, 54-61.

[50]Tillich, SYSTEMATIC THEOLOGY, II, 168-176.

[51]Baillie, GOD WAS IN CHRIST, pp. 157-202.

[52]Jürgen Moltmann, THE CRUCIFIED GOD (San Francisco: Harper & Row, 1974), pp. 160-290.

[53]Rauschenbusch, A THEOLOGY FOR THE SOCIAL GOSPEL, Chapter VIII.

[54]For an affirmative answer to this question, see John Cobb, BEYOND DIALOGUE (Philadelphia: Fortress Press, 1982).

NOTES
Chapter V

[1]For further detail see Rudolf Bultmann, THEOLOGY OF THE NEW TESTAMENT (New York: Charles Scribner's Sons, 1951), I, 153-164, 330-340; Millar Burrows, AN OUTLINE OF BIBLICAL THEOLOGY (Philadelphia: Westminster Press, 1946), pp. 74-78; and the article on "Holy Spirit," in A COMPANION TO THE BIBLE, ed. by J.J. Von Allmen (New York: Oxford University Press, 1958).

[2]Forfurther details see Bultmann, THEOLOGY OF THE NEW TESTAMENT, I, 37-42, 53-62, 92-121, 133-152, 306-314; (1955), II, 95-118; the article on "Church," and "Church Life," THE INTERPRETER'S DICTIONARY OF THE BIBLE (Nashville: Abingdon Press, 1962), Vol. 1; Burrows, AN OUTLINE OF BIBLICAL THEOLOGY, pp. 146-153, 238-240, 254-276; A COMPANION TO THE BIBLE, articles dealing with church, ministry and the sacraments; and Paul Minear, IMAGES OF THE CHURCH IN THE NEW TESTAMENT (Philadelphia: Westminster Press, 1960).

[3]Walter Marshall Horton, CHRISTIAN THEOLOGY: AN ECUMENICAL APPROACH (New York: Harper & Brothers, 1958), pp. 202-243.

[4]J. Robert Nelson, THE REALM OF REDEMPTION (London: The Epworth Press, 1951), pp. 3-19.

[5]Ibid., pp. 19-36.

[6]Ibid., pp. 37-66.

[7]Leslie Newbigin, THE HOUSEHOLD OF FAITH (New York: Friendship Press, 1954), pp. 24-122.

[8]Nelson, THE REALM OF REDEMPTION, pp. 95-100.

[9]John Calvin, INSTITUTES OF THE CHRISTIAN RELIGION, IV, i, 7.

[10]Nelson, THE REALM OF REDEMPTION, pp. 161-167.

[11]Ibid, pp. 211-234; Paul Tillich, A HISTORY OF CHRISTIAN THOUGHT (New York: Simon and Schuster, 1968), pp. 121-122.

[12]Quoted in Nelson, THE REALM OF REDEMPTION, p. 220.

[13]Kenneth Cauthen, THE IMPACT OF AMERICAN RELIGIOUS LIBERALISM (Washington: University Press of America, 1983), pp. 84-107.

[14]Horton, CHRISTIAN THEOLOGY, pp. 218-243.

[15]Ibid, pp. 221-222.

[16]The polarity and continuum, plus much of the discussion of various views of church, ministry, and sacraments are based on my article "The Ministry and the Sacraments," ENCOUNTER (Summer, 1957), pp. 341-352.

[17]For further analysis and description of these basic ideas of the church, see Horton, CHRISTIAN THEOLOGY, pp. 230-243. Cf. Angus Dun, PROSPECTING FOR A UNITED CHURCH (New York: Harper & Brothers, 1948), and Newbigin, THE HOUSEHOLD OF GOD.

[18]T. W. Manson, THE CHURCH'S MINISTRY (London: Hodder and Stoughton, 1948), p. 181.

[19]K. E. Kirk (ed.), THE APOSTOLIC MINISTRY (London: Hodder and Stoughton, 1946).

[20]Charles Gore, THE CHURCH AND THE MINISTRY (New York: Longmans, Green & Co., 1919), p. 392.

[21]T. W. Manson, THE CHURCH'S MINISTRY, p. 54.

[22]Stephen C. Neil (ed.), THE MINISTRY OF THE CHURCH (London: The Canterbury Press, 1947).

[23]Gustaf Aulén, THE UNIVERSAL CHURCH IN GOD'S DESIGN (New York: World Council of Churches, 1948), pp. 23-28.

[24]Daniel T. Jenkins, THE NATURE OF CATHOLICITY (London: Faber & Faber, 1947).

[25]H. W. Robinson, THE LIFE AND FAITH OF THE BAPTISTS (London: The Carey Kingsgate Press, 1946), p. 104.

[26]Ibid, p. 102.

[27]Leonard Hodgson, Unpublished Seminar Notes, Oxford, 1949. Quoted by Nelson, THE REALM OF REDEMPTION, p. 157.

[28] See Daniel Day Williams, WHAT PRESENT-DAY THEOLOGIANS ARE THINKING (New York: Harper & Brothers, 1952), p. 144.

[29] F.W. Dillistone, THE STRUCTURE OF THE DIVINE SOCIETY (London: Lutterworth Press, 1951).

[30] Dun, PROSPECTING FOR A UNITED CHURCH, p. 52. Quoted in Horton, CHRISTIAN THEOLOGY, p. 232.

[31] Roderic Dunkerly (ed.), THE MINISTRY AND THE SACRAMENTS (New York: The Macmillan Co., 1937), pp. 206-207.

[32] Jenkins, THE NATURE OF CATHOLICITY, p. 96.

[33] Gustaf Aulén, THE FAITH OF THE CHRISTIAN CHURCH (Philadelphia: The Muhlenberg Press, 1948), p. 390.

[34] Dunkerly (ed.), THE MINISTRY AND THE SACRAMENTS, p. 237.

[35] Robinson, THE LIFE AND FAITH OF THE BAPTISTS, pp. 77, 97-101.

[36] For a discussion of the sacraments in more detail, see Nelson, THE REALM OF REDEMPTION, pp. 120-141.

[37] Justo Gonzáles, A HISTORY OF CHRISTIAN DOCTRINE (Nashville: Abingdon Press, 1975), III, 57.

[38] Aulén, THE FAITH OF THE CHRISTIAN CHURCH, p. 381.

[39] John Whale, CHRISTIAN DOCTRINE (New York: Cambridge University Press, 1941), p. 164.

[40] Aulén, THE FAITH OF THE CHRISTIAN CHURCH, p. 385.

[41] P.T. Forsyth, THE CHURCH AND THE SACRAMENTS (London: Independent Press, 1941), p. 211.

[42] Dunkerly (ed.), THE MINISTRY AND THE SACRAMENTS, p. 224.

[43] Robinson, THE LIFE AND FAITH OF THE BAPTISTS, p. 73.

[44] Ibid.

[45] Karl Barth, THE TEACHING OF THE CHURCH REGARDING BAPTISM (London: SCM Press, 1948), p. 40.

[46]David A. Scott, "The Eucharist: An Anglican Perspective," THE EUCHARIST IN ECUMENICAL DIALOGUE, ed. by Leonard Swidler (New York: Paulist Press, 1976), p. 38.

[47]Gonzáles, A HISTORY OF CHRISTIAN THOUGHT, III, 149-156.

[48]Ibid, pp. 73-77.

[49]Arthur B. Crabtree, "The Eucharist in Baptist Life and Thought," THE EUCHARIST IN ECUMENICAL DIALOGUE, pp. 106-113.

[50]Ross Mackenzie, "Reformed and Roman Catholic Understanding of the Eucharist." Ibid., pp. 70-76.

[51]J. Robert Nelson, "Methodist Eucharist Usage," Ibid., pp. 88-95.

[52]LUTHERANS AND CATHOLICS IN DIALOGUE (Washington: USA National Committee of the Lutheran World Federation, 1967), III, 188-198; THE FINAL REPORT (Cincinnati: Forward Movement Publications, 1982), pp. 12-25. THE FINAL REPORT is a Statement of the Anglican-Roman Catholic International Commission.

[53]Christopher Kiesling, "Roman Catholic and Reformed Understanding of the Eucharist," THE EUCHARIST IN ECUMENICAL DIALOGUE, pp. 76-84. See Leonard Swidler's summary of how things stand today between Roman Catholics and a wide variety of other churches regarding the eucharist. Ibid., pp. 141-154.

[54]Maximos Aghiorgoussis, "The Holy Eucharist in Ecumenical Dialogue: an Orthodox View." Ibid., pp. 14-21, 30-31.

[55]George A. Lindbeck, "A Lutheran View of Intercommunion with Roman Catholics," Ibid., pp. 52-58, 65-67. See also, LUTHERANS AND CATHOLICS IN DIALOGUE, Vols. III (1967), and IV (1970).

[56]Ibid., IV, 22, 31-32.

[57]THE FINAL REPORT, pp. 86-87.

[58]Ibid., p. 88.

[59]Ibid., p. 45.

[60]Leonard Swidler, "The Eucharist in Ecumenical Perspective," THE EUCHARIST IN ECUMENICAL DIALOGUE, p. 152.

[61]BAPTISM, EUCHARIST AND MINISTRY (Geneva: WORLD COUNCIL OF CHURCHES, 1982), Faith and Order Paper No. 111. For a discussion of the issues surrounding this document, see ECUMENICAL PERSPECTIVES ON BAPTISM, EUCHARIST AND MINISTRY, ed. by Max Thurian (Geneva: World Council of Churches, 1983), Faith and Order paper No. 116.

[62]TOWARDS AN ECUMENICAL CONSENSUS ON BAPTISM, THE EUCHARIST AND THE MINISTRY (Geneva: World Council of Churches, 1977), pp. 17-19.

[63]Ibid., p. 18.

[64]Swidler (ed.), THE EUCHARIST IN ECUMENICAL DIALOGUE, pp. 28-31.

[65]Kenan B. Osborne, "Contemporary Understandings of the Eucharist." Ibid., pp. 2-11.

[66]BAPTISM, EUCHARIST AND MINISTRY (Faith and Order Paper No. 111), pp. vii-ix.

[67]Walter Rauschenbusch, A THEOLOGY FOR THE SOCIAL GOSPEL, 1917 (Nashville: Abingdon Press, no date), Chapters XII and XVII.

[68]Reinhold Niebuhr, FAITH AND HISTORY (New York: Charles Scribner's Sons, 1949), pp. 235-243.

[69]Jürgen Moltmann, THEOLOGY OF HOPE (New York: Harper & Row, 1967), pp. 216-224, 325-328.

NOTES
Chapter VI

[1]See Paul Tillich, THE PROTESTANT ERA (Chicago:
University of Chicago Press, 1948), pp. 16-31; and A.
Th. van Leeuwen, CHRISTIANITY IN WORLD HISTORY (New
York: Charles Scribner's Sons, 1964), who makes a
distinction between ontocratic and theocentric patterns
of thought similar to the one I have made here.

[2]John Bright, THE KINGDOM OF GOD (Nashville: Abingdon
Press, 1953).

[3]Norman Perrin, JESUS AND THE LANGUAGE OF THE KINGDOM
(Philadelphia: Fortress Press, 1976), pp. 16-32.

[4]THE INTERPRETER'S BIBLE (New York: Abingdon-Cokesbury
Press, 1951), VII, 145-154; THE INTERPRETER'S
DICTIONARY OF THE BIBLE (Nashville: Abingdon Press,
1962), Vol. 3, article on "Kingdom."

[5]Martin Dibelius, JESUS (Philadelphia: Westminster
Press, 1949), pp. 64-88. See also Perrin, JESUS AND THE
LANGUAGE OF THE KINGDOM.

[6]Cf. Langdon Gilkey, MESSAGE AND EXISTENCE (New York:
Seabury Press, 1981), pp. 166-171. See also Rudolf
Bultmann, THEOLOGY OF THE NEW TESTAMENT (New York:
Charles Scribner's Sons, 1951), I, 3-32.

[7]In addition to relevant articles in THE INTERPRETER'S
DICTIONARY OF THE BIBLE, see Millar Burrows, AN OUTLINE
OF BIBLICAL THEOLOGY (Philadelphia: Westminster Press,
1946), pp. 188-219.

[8]For views held in the early centuries of the church;,
see J.N.D. Kelly, EARLY CHRISTIAN DOCTRINES (New Y ork:
Harper & Row, 1960), pp. 459-489; and Jaroslav Pelikan,
The Emergence Of The Catholic Tradition (100-600), Vol.
I of THE CHRISTIAN TRADITION (Chicago: University of
Chicago Press, 1971), pp. 123-141.

[9]For interpretations of Augustine, Aquinas, Joachim,
Luther, Calvin, and the sectarian Protestants, see
Roger Shinn, CHRISTIANITY AND THE PROBLEM OF HISTORY
(New York: Charles Scribner's Sons, 1953); Reinhold
Niebuhr, THE NATURE AND DESTINY OF MAN (New York:
Charles Scriner's Sons, 1949), II, 144-180; FAITH AND

HISTORY (New York: Charles Scribner's Sons, 1949), pp. 196-213; and Paul Tillich, A HISTORY OF CHRISTIAN THOUGHT (New York: Simon and Schuster, 1968), pp. 121-122, 131-133, 175-180, 192-198, 227-275.

[10] I am indebted to Roger Shinn for this analysis. See CHRISTIANITY AND THE PROBLEM OF HISTORY, pp. 52-97.

[11] Crane Brinton, IDEAS AND MEN (New York: Prentice-Hall, Inc., 1950), p. 369.

[12] Carl Becker, THE HEAVENLY CITY OF THE EIGHTEENTH CENTURY PHILOSOPHERS (New Haven: Yale University Press, 1932).

[13] Cf. Paul Tillich, A HISTORY OF CHRISTIAN THOUGHT, pp. 320-366.

[14] Reinhold Niebuhr, FAITH AND HISTORY, pp. 1-2.

[15] For an interpretation of the historical consciousness and the idea of progress, see Shinn, CHRISTIANITY AND THE PROBLEM OF HISTORY, pp. 101-272 Niebuhr, FAITH AND HISTORY, pp. 1-101; and Langdon Gilkey, REAPING THE WHIRLWIND (New York: Seabury Press, 1981), pp. 188-208.

[16] For an interpretation of ideas of history and hope in modern theology, see Gilkey, REAPING THE WHIRLWIND, pp. 209-238.

[17] Lyman Abbott, THE THEOLOGY OF AN EVOLUTIONIST (Boston: Houghton, Mifflin, 1898).

[18] Henry Drummond, THE ASCENT OF MAN (New York: Pott, 1894).

[19] See Harry Emerson Fosdick, THE LIVING OF THESE DAYS (New York: Harper & Brothers, 1956), pp. 237-238.

[20] Ibid., pp. 237-247.

[21] See Kenneth Cauthen, THE IMPACT OF AMERICAN RELIGIOUS LIBERALISM (Washington: University Press of America, 1983), pp. 84-107.

[22] Ibid., pp. 161-162.

[23] See relevant sections dealing with the thought of eight American liberals in Cauthen, THE IMPACT OF AMERICAN RELIGIOUS LIBERALISM.

[24]Johannes Weiss, JESUS' PROCLAMATION OF THE KINGDOM OF GOD, 1892 (Philadelphia: Fortress Press, 1971); Albert Schweitzer, THE QUEST OF THE HISTORICAL JESUS, 1906 (London: A & C Black, 1954).

[25]Karl Löwith, MEANING IN HISTORY (Chicago: University of Chicago Press, 1949).

[26]Karl Barth, THE EPISTLE TO THE ROMANS (New York: Oxford University Press, 1933), p. 10.

[27]For a useful discussion of Barth's view of providence and history, see Gilkey, REAPING THE WHIRLWIND, pp. 216-220. For neo-orthodoxy generally, see Shinn, CHRISTIANITY AND THE PROBLEM OF HISTORY, pp. 187-223.

[28]Niebuhr, FAITH AND HISTORY, p. 71.

[29]Niebuhr, THE NATURE AND DESTINY OF MAN, II, 204-212.

[30]Ibid., II, 289.

[31]Ibid., p. 294.

[32]Ibid.

[33]Karl Barth, CHURCH DOGMATICS (Edinburgh: T & T Clark, 1957), II, 2, 3-506.

[34]Emil Brunner, THE CHRISTIAN DOCTRINE OF CHURCH, FAITH AND CONSUMMATION (Philadelphia: Westminster Press, 1962), pp. 415-424; Gustaf Aulén, THE FAITH OF THE CHRISTIAN CHURCH (Philadelphia: The Muhlenberg Press, 1948), pp. 169-180.

[35]Emil Brunner, THE CHRISTIAN DOCTRINE OF GOD (Philadelphia: Westminster Press, 1950), pp. 346-353.

[36]Nels Ferré, THE CHRISTIAN UNDERSTANDING OF GOD (New York: Harper & Brothers, 1951) pp. 217-249.

[37]For a brief discussion and evaluation, see Gilkey, REAPING THE WHIRLWIND, pp. 236-239. See also John Cobb, PROCESS THEOLOGY AS POLITICAL THEOLOGY (Philadelphia: Westminster Press, 1982), for discussions of Metz, Pannenberg, Moltmann, and others.

[38]Jürgen Moltmann, THEOLOGY OF HOPE (New York: Harper & Row, 1967), pp. 45-69.

[39]Ibid., pp. 106-112.

[40]Ibid., p. 338. See also, pp. 15-36.

[41]James Cone, A THEOLOGY OF BLACK LIBERATION (Philadelphia: J. B. Lippincott, 1970), p. 248.

[42]Moltmann, THEOLOGY OF HOPE, p. 16.

[43]Juan Luis Segundo, THE LIBERATION OF THEOLOGY (Maryknoll: Orbis Books, 1976), p. 150.

[44]Rubem Alves, A THEOLOGY OF HUMAN HOPE (St. Meinrad: Abbey Press, 1974), p. 144.

[45]Gustavo Gutiérrez, A THEOLOGY OF LIBERATION (Maryknoll: Orbis Books, 1973), p. 173.

[46]Gutiérrez, A THEOLOGY OF LIBERATION, p. 152. See also pp. 153-168.

[47]Ibid., p. 177.

[48]Ibid., pp. 36-37, 176-178.

[49]Ibid., p. 167.

[50]For a good discussion in more detail of these issues, see Delwin Brown, TO SET AT LIBERTY (Maryknoll: Orbis Books, 1981), pp. 108-133.

[51]Gilkey, REAPING THE WHIRLWIND, pp. 233-239. See also, Dennis McCann, CHRISTIAN REALISM AND LIBERATION THEOLOGY (Maryknoll: Orbis Books, 1981).

[52]W. R. Jones, IS GOD A WHITE RACIST? (Garden City: Doubleday & Co., 1973).

[53]John Cobb, PROCESS THEOLOGY AS POLITICAL THEOLOGY; Delwin Brown, TO SET AT LIBERTY; and Schubert Ogden, FAITH AND FREEDOM: TOWARD A THEOLOGY OF LIBERATION (Nashville: Abingdon Press, 1979). Daniel Day Williams stated a process theology of hope in a previous generation in conversation with liberalism and neo-orthodoxy in GOD'S GRACE AND MAN'S HOPE (New York: Harper & Brothers, 1949).

[54]Alfred North Whitehead, PROCESS AND REALITY (New York: The Macmillan Co., 1929), p. 525.

[55]Process theologies of history may be found in John Cobb and David Griffin, PROCESS THEOLOGY: AN INTRODUCTORY EXPOSITION (Philadelphia: The Westminster Press, 1976), pp. 111-127; Lewis Ford, "Divine Persuasion and the Triumph of Good," PROCESS PHILOSOPHY AND CHRISTIAN THOUGHT, ed. by Delwin Brown, et. al. (Indianapolis: Bobbs-Merrill, 1971), pp. 287-304, as well as in the works mentioned in note 5.

[56]Whitehead, PROCESS AND REALITY, p. 517.

[57]Schubert Ogden, THE REALITY OF GOD (New York: Harper & Row, 1966), pp. 206-230.

[58]David Griffin, GOD, POWER AND EVIL (Philadelphia: Westminster Press, 1976), pp. 311-313.

[59]John Cobb, A CHRISTIAN NATURAL THEOLOGY (Philadelphia: Westminster Press, 1965), pp. 63-70.

[60]John Cobb, GOD AND THE WORLD (Philadelphia: Westminster Press, 1969), pp. 102, 42-102.

[61]Griffin, GOD, POWER AND EVIL, pp. 251-310.

[62]Kenneth Cauthen, SCIENCE, SECULARIZATION AND GOD (Nashville: Abingdon Press, 1969), pp. 159-229.

NOTES
Chapter VII

[1]Walter Marshall Horton, CHRISTIAN THEOLOGY: AN ECUMENICAL APPROACH (New York: Harper & Brothers, 1955, 1958.

[2]Dietrich Bonhoeffer, LETTERS AND PAPERS FROM PRISON (New York: Macmillan Paperback, 1953), p. 195.

[3]Harvey Cox, THE SECULAR CITY (New York: The Macmillan Co., 1963).

[4]John Robinson, HONEST TO GOD (Philadelphia: Westminster Press, 1963).

[5]John Cobb, Jr., A CHRISTIAN NATURAL THEOLOGY (Philadelphia: Westminster Press, 1965).

[6]Schubert Ogden, THE REALITY OF GOD (New York: Harper & Row, 1966).

[7]Langdon Gilkey, NAMING THE WHIRLWIND (Indianapolis: Bobbs-Merrill, 1969).

[8]See Thomas Ogletree, THE DEATH OF GOD CONTROVERSY (Nashville: Abingdon Press, 1966).

[9]Harvey Cox THE FEAST OF FOOLS (Cambridge: Harvard University Press, 1969).

[10]Sam Keen, TO A DANCING GOD (New York: Harper & Row, 1970).

[11]Lynn White, Jr., "The Historical Roots of our Ecologic Crisis," SCIENCE (March 10, 1967).

[12]See Kenneth Cauthen, CHRISTIAN BIOPOLITICS (Nashville: Abingdon Press, 1970).

[13]James Cone, A BLACK THEOLOGY OF LIBERATION (Philadelphia: J. B. Lippincott, 1970).

[14]Deotis Roberts, LIBERATION AND RECONCILIATION (Philadelphia: Westminster Press, 1971).

[15]Rosemary Radford Ruether, LIBERATION THEOLOGY (New York: Paulist Press, 1972), and NEW WOMAN/NEW EARTH

(New York: Seabury Press, 1975).

16Mary Daly, BEYOND GOD THE FATHER (Boston: Beacon
Press, 1973). For a recent example of her post-
Christian phase, see PURE LUST (Boston: Beacon Press,
1984).

17David Tracy, BLESSED RAGE FOR ORDER (New York: The
Seabury Press, 1975).

18Delwin Brown, et. al. (eds.) PROCESS PHILOSOPHY AND
CHRISTIAN THOUGHT (Indianapolis: Bobbs-Merrill, 1971).

19See David F. Wells and John D. Woodbridge (eds.), THE
EVANGELICALS (Grand Rapids: Baker Book House, 1977).

20See George W. Dollar, A HISTORY OF FUNDAMENTALISM IN
AMERICA (Greenville, S.C.: Bob Jones University, 1973),
and Louis Gasper, THE FUNDAMENTALIST MOVEMENT (The
Hague: Mouton, 1963).

21See Jerry Falwell (ed.), THE FUNDAMENTALIST OPTION:
THE RESURGENCE OF CONSERVATIVE CHRISTIANITY (Garden
City: Doubleday, 1981). For a critical analysis, see
Gabriel Fackre, THE RELIGIOUS RIGHT AND CHRISTIAN FAITH
(Grand Rapids: Wm. Eerdmans, 1982).

22See Millard Erickson, THE NEW EVANGELICAL THEOLOGY
(Old Tappan, N.J.: Flemming H. Revell, 1968), and Donald
Bloesch, THE EVANGELICAL RENAISSANCE (Grand Rapids: Wm.
Eerdmans, 1973).

23Carl F. H. Henry, GOD, REVELATION AND AUTHORITY, 6
vols. (Waco: Word Books, 1976-83).

24Richard Quebedeaux, THE YOUNG EVANGELICALS (New York:
Harper & Row, 1974), and THE WORLDLY EVANGELICALS (New
York: Harper & Row, 1978).

25Paul K. Jewett, MAN AS MALE AND FEMALE (Grand Rapids:
Wm. Eerdmans, 1975).

26Virginia Ramey Mollencott, WOMEN, MEN AND THE BIBLE
(Nashville: Abingdon Press, 1977), and THE DIVINE
FEMININE (New York: Crossroad, 1983). See also Letha
Scanzoni and Nancy Hardesty, ALL WE'RE MEANT TO BE
(Waco: Word Books, 1974).

27Wolfhart Pannenberg, THEOLOGY AND THE KINDGDOM OF GOD
(Philadelphia: Westminster Press, 1969), and BASIC

QUESTIONS IN THEOLOGY, 2 vols. (Philadephia: Westminster Press, 1970-71).

[28]Jürgen Moltmann, THEOLOGY OF HOPE (New York: Harper & Row, 1967).

[29]See Robert McAfee Brown, THEOLOGY IN A NEW KEY (Philadelphia: Westminster Press, 1978). The best known early book from Latin America was Gustavo Gutiérrez, A THEOLOGY OF LIBERATION (Maryknoll: Orbis Books, 1973).

[30]For a recent survey of American theology, see Deane William Ferm, CONTEMPORARY AMERICAN THEOLOGIES (New York: Seabury, 1981).

[31]See Theo Witvliet, A PLACE IN THE SUN: LIBERATION THEOLOGY IN THE THIRD WORLD (Maryknoll: Orbis Books, 1985). See also the latest catalogue from Orbis Books for an astonishing variety of books and authors from Asia, Africa, and Latin America.

[32]Paul Tillich, CHRISTIANITY AND THE ENCOUNTER OF THE WORLD RELIGIONS (New York: Columbia University Press, 1963), p. 64.

[33]Peter Berger, THE HERETICAL IMPERATIVE (Garden City: Doubleday, 1979), pp. 157-189.

[34]John Cobb, BEYOND DIALOGUE (Philadelphia: Fortress Press, 1982).

[35]John Hick, GOD AND THE UNIVERSE OF FAITHS (New York: The Macmillan Co., 1973).

[36]Dieter T. Hessel (ed.), FOR CREATIONS'S SAKE (Philadelphia: The Geneva Press, 1985). See also, Gordon Kaufman, THEOLOGY FOR A NUCLEAR AGE (Philadelphia: Westminster Press, 1985).

[37]See Kenneth Cauthen, CHRISTIAN BIOPOLITICS.

[38]Kenneth Cauthen, "Process Theology and Eco-Justice," Hessel (ed.), FOR CREATION'S SAKE, pp. 82-93.

INDEX OF SUBJECTS

TORONTO STUDIES IN THEOLOGY

mellen

The Scholarly Career

After publishing one's Ph.D. thesis as a book or several articles, what are the next steps in the development of a scholarly career?

In Europe, it is recognized that there are scholarly tasks equivalent to "second" and "third" doctorates: the *Habilitation*, the *Doctorat d'Etat*, and the *Festschrift*. Drawing upon this European experience, we can chart how a scholarly career is developed by noting the characteristic tasks and genres at the later stages of life.

The Habilitation Stage
(the 10-15 years following the Ph.D.)

In this period, scholarly research consists primarily of projects involving translation or methodology; with editing texts; with essays seeking to define the parameters of one's discipline; with bibliographic and *status quaestionis* projects which clarify the problematics of frontier issues in scholarship; with the writing of at least one full length monograph within one's Ph.D. area of expertise, but on a different subject from the dissertation.

The Doctorat d'Etat Stage
(the 10-15 years following the *Habilitation*)

In this period, scholarly research consists increasingly with the widening of one's expertise by bridging into new disciplines; with autobiographical reflection whereby a scholar seeks to maintain the inward continuity of his thought while articulating his intellectual change as he moves into mid-life; with original reflection aimed at solving institutional or political problems; and, most importantly, with the mapping out a "life project" which is to be executed through the writing of several related volumes--and then writing these volumes one after the other.

The Magister Stage
(the 10-15 years following the *Doctorat d'Etat*)

This stage consists in responding to those who evaluate and use one's work (e.g. through a *Festschrift*); with utilizing one's wisdom to explore and write essays on a wide range of intellectual interests which may be distant from one's disciplinary specializations; with the writing of personal history or meditations on the meaning of scholarly life; with the completion or compilation for publication of earlier unpublished writings.

The **Mellen Center for Career Development** seeks to assist scholars through its research, its seminars, and its counseling programs. For free brochure, *Developing the Scholarly Career*, write MCCD, 315 Center Street, Lewiston, New York, 14092. (716)-754-8566.

Edwin Mellen

Out of Print?

A frequent complaint of authors is that publishers let their books go out of print. The problem is especially acute for scholarly books because the review process often takes so long that it is not uncommon for a book to be out of print even before all its reviews appear.

Some authors are unaware that there is a continuing cost for a publisher to keep a book in print: the cost of warehousing, the cost of cataloging, and the manufacturing cost of the inventory (now that depreciation tax laws have been changed). Once sales of a book drop below a certain level, publishers can no longer recover these fixed costs and so they let it go out of print.

At the heart of the problem is the fact that most publishers concentrate promotion on their new titles and do not advertise their previously published books. Since these "back list" titles are not constantly advertised, their sales drop off to the point where a publisher cannot afford to keep them in print.

The solution is for a publisher not to have a back list, but constantly to keep presenting all its titles to potential readers. The Edwin Mellen Press does this by publishing its books as numbered volumes in continuing series--so that every earlier volume in a series is readvertised in conjunction with every new title published.

Of course, the method of publishing books in scholarly monograph series is not our invention. It is, rather, the basic form of German scholarship--which we gladly acknowledge and imitate. So we urge you to seek a publisher for your next book who guarantees to keep it in print. We hope you will consider us. Here are some of the series which we presently sustain:

Studies

in

**the History of Philosophy
German Thought and History
Asian Thought and Religion
Spanish History and Culture
the History and Interpretation
of Music
Art and Religious Interpretation**

**Toronto Studies in Theology
Translation of Classic Texts**